LONG-SUFFERING LOVE

Eugen J. Pentiuc

LONG-SUFFERING LOVE

A COMMENTARY ON HOSEA
WITH PATRISTIC ANNOTATIONS

HOLY CROSS ORTHODOX PRESS
Brookline, Massachusetts

Reprinted 2005
© Copyright 2002 Holy Cross Orthodox Press
Published by Holy Cross Orthodox Press
50 Goddard Avenue
Brookline, Massachusetts 02445

All rights reserved. No part of this publication may be reproduced, stored in a retrieval system, or transmitted in any form or by any means—electronic, mechanical, photocopy, recording, or any other—without the prior written permission of the publisher. The only exception is brief quotations in printed reviews.

ISBN 1-885652-58-5

LIBRARY OF CONGRESS CATALOGING-IN-PUBLICATION DATA
Pentiuc, Eugen J., 1955–
Long-suffering love: a commentary on Hosea with patristic annotations/ Eugen J. Pentiuc.
   p. cm.
Includes bibliographical references.
ISBN 1-885652-58-5 (paper)
1. Bible. O.T. Hosea—Commentaries. I. Title.
BS1565.53.P46 2002
224'.6077—dc21
                                                    2002023290

*This work is dedicated to my wife, Flora,
and to our children, Daniel and Cristina*

CONTENTS

Abbreviations ix
Acknowledgments xv

INTRODUCTION

I. Historical Background: The Assyrian Expansion and the Last Years of Israel — 1
II. The Eighth-Century Prophets: Yaweh's Heralds at the Crossroads of History — 4
III. Hosea: The Man and the Prophet — 9
IV. The Book of the Prophet Hosea — 12
    1. *Structure and Literary Composition* — 12
    2. *Language and Style* — 13
    3. *Text and Versions* — 17
    4. *Authenticity, Integrity, and Canonicity of the Book* — 19
    5. *Conjugal Drama of Hosea: Preliminaries* — 23

COMMENTARY

The Book's Title (1:1) — 43

I. Hosea's Conjugal Drama and Yahweh-Israel's Covenant: From a Latent Crisis to an Obvious Breakup (1-3)

1. Hosea's Marriage and Children (1:2-9) — 47
2. Restoration after Judgment (2:1/1:10-2:3/1) — 59
3. The Last Warnings before Separation (2:4/2-15/13) — 63
4. A Date in the Wilderness (2:16/14-25/23) — 71
5. Love and Abstinence (3:1-5) — 83

II. Israel Between Punishment and Forgiveness (4-11)

1. Yahweh's Dispute with Israel (4:1-3)	129
2. God's Dispute with the Priests, Prophets, and People (4:4-19)	132
3. Leaders and People on a Wrong Path (5:1-7)	152
4. Ephraim and Judah in Conflict (5:8-15)	162
5. Repentance, Revival, and Yahweh's Response (6:1-6)	173
6. Turmoil in Israel (6:7-7:2)	186
7. Political Instability (7:3-7)	195
8. Failed International Politics (7:8-16)	199
9. Ephraim's Unfaithfulness (8:1-14)	207
10. On Exile and Prophecy (9:1-9)	221
11. Baal-peor and Gilgal (9:10-17)	232
12. Israel without Cult or King (10:1-8)	240
13. Gibeah and Beth-arbel (10:9-15)	249
14. God's Tenderness (11:1-11)	257

III. The Last Sayings (12-14)

1. Ephraim and Jacob (12:1/11:12-12:15/14)	345
2. The Destruction (13:1-14:1/13:16)	360
3. Love's Triumph (14:2/1-9/8)	374
4. Epilogue (14:10/9)	383

Selected Bibliography	399

ABBREVIATIONS

α'	Aquila
AB	Anchor Bible
Acts	Acts
AJSL	*American Journal of Semitic Languages And Literature*
Am	Amos
ANET	*Ancient Near Eastern Texts Relating to the Old Testament,* Edited by J. B. Pritchard. 3rd ed. Princeton, 1969
ARW	*Archiv für Religionswissenschaft*
ATD	Das Alte Testament Deutsch
BASOR	*Bulletin of the American Schools of Oriental Research*
BBB	Bonner biblische Beiträge
BDB	Brown, F., S. R. Driver, and C. A. Briggs. *A Hebrew and English Lexicon of the Old Testament.* Oxford, 1907
BHS	*Biblia Hebraica Stuttgartensia.* Edited by K. Elliger and W. Rudolph. Stuttgart, 1983
Bibl	*Biblica*
BN	*Biblische Notizen*
BWANT	Beiträge zur Wissenschaft vom Alten und Neuen Testament
BZ	*Biblische Zeitschrift*
BZAW	Beihefte zur Zeitschrift für die alttestamentliche Wissenschaft

CBQ	*Catholic Biblical Quarterly*
CCSL	Corpus Christianorum: Series latina. Turnhout, 1953–
1-2 Chr	1-2 Chronicles
Col	Colossians
1-2 Cor	1-2 Corinthians
CSEL	Corpus scriptorum ecclesiasticorum latinorum, Vienne
Dan	Daniel
Deut	Deuteronomy
Eccl	Ecclesiastes
Eph	Ephesians
Esth	Esther
EvTh	*Evangelische Theologie*
Exod	Exodus
Ezek	Ezekiel
Ezra	Ezra
f(f).	and the following one(s)
FRLANT	Forschungen zur Religion und Literatur des Alten und Neuen Testaments
Gal	Galatians
GCS	Die griechischen christlichen Schriftsteller der ersten drei Jahrhunderte. Leipzig-Berlin
Gen	Genesis
GK	*Gesenius' Hebrew Grammar.* Edited by E. Kautzsch and translated and revised by A. E. Cowley. 2nd ed. Oxford, 1910
Hab	Habakkuk
Hag	Haggai
Heb	Hebrews
Hos	Hosea
HUCA	*Hebrew Union College Annual*
ICC	International Critical Commentary
Is	Isaiah

Jas	James
JB	Jerusalem Bible
JBL	*Journal of Biblical Literature*
Jer	Jeremiah
Jn	John
1-2-3 Jn	1-2-3 John
JNES	*Journal of Near Eastern Studies*
Job	Job
Joel	Joel
Josh	Joshua
JSOT	*Journal for the Study of the Old Testament*
JSOTSup	Journal for the Study of the Old Testament: Supplement Series
JTS	*Journal of Theological Studies*
Judg	Judges
KAT	Kommentar zum Alten Testament
KBL	Koehler, L., and W. Baumgartner, *The Hebrew and Aramaic Lexicon of the Old Testament*. Translated and edited by M. E. J. Richardson. Leiden, 1994–2000
1-2 Kgs	1-2 Kings
KSchr	Alt, A, *Kleine Schriften zur Geschichte des Volkes Israel*. 3 vols. München, 1959, 1959, 1963
Lam	Lamentations
Lev	Leviticus
Lk	Luke
LXX	Septuagint
1-2 Macc	1-2 Maccabees
Mal	Malachi
Mic	Micah
Mk	Mark
ms(s).	manuscript(s)
MT	Masoretic Text
Mt	Matthew

n	note
Neh	Nehemiah
NRTh	*La nouvelle revue théologique*
Num	Numbers
OL	Old Latin
OTL	Old Testament Library
1-2 Pet	1-2 Peter
PG	Patrologia graeca [= Patrologiae cursus completus: Series graeca]. Edited by J.-P. Migne. 162 vols. Paris, 1857–1886
Phil	Philippians
PJ	*Palästina-Jahrbuch*
PL	Patrologia latina [= Patrologiae cursus completus: Series latina]. Edited by J.-P. Migne. 217 vols. Paris, 1844–1864
Prov	Proverbs
Ps	Psalms
Q	Qumran texts
RB	*Revue biblique*
Rev	Revelation
RevSR	*Revue des sciences religieuses*
RHPhR	*Revue d'histoire et de philosophie religieuses*
RHR	*Revue de l'histoire des religions*
Rom	Romans
Ruth	Ruth
σ′	Symmachus
S	Syriac (Peshitta)
1-2 Sam	1-2 Samuel
SAT	Die Schriften des Alten Testaments in Auswahl übersetzt und erklärt. Edited by H. Gunkel
SC	Sources chrétiennes. Paris: Cerf, 1943–
SEÅ	*Svensk exegetisk årsbok*
Sem	*Semitica*

Song	Song of Songs
θ'	Theodotion
Tg	Targum
Tarbiz	*Tarbiz*
TDOT	*Theological Dictionary of the Old Testament*. Edited by G. J. Botterweck and H. Ringgren. Translated by J. T. Willis, G. W. Bromiley, and D. E. Green. 14 vols. Grand Rapids, 1974–
1-2 Thess	1-2 Thessalonians
ThLZ	*Theologische Literaturzeitung*
ThStKr	*Theologische Studien und Kritiken*
1-2 Tim	1-2 Timothy
Tob	Tobit
UT	*Ugaritic Textbook*. C. H. Gordon. AnOr 38. Rome, 1965
v(v).	verse(s)
V	Vulgate
VT	*Vetus Testamentum*
VTSup	Vetus Testamentum Supplements
ZAW	*Zeitschrift für die alttestamentliche Wissenschaft*
ZDPV	*Zeitschrift des deutschen Palästina-Vereins*
Zech	Zechariah
Zeph	Zephaniah
ZThK	*Zeitschrift für Theologie und Kirche*

ACKNOWLEDGMENTS

First, I would like to thank His Eminence Metropolitan Methodios of Boston for his support without which this work could not have been published, as well as the Greek Orthodox Metropolis of Boston for their generous financial gift in honor of the twentieth anniversary (2004) of His Eminence's consecration to the episcopate.

Words of gratitude are due to Rev. Nicholas C. Triantafilou, President of Hellenic College and Holy Cross Greek Orthodox School of Theology for his assistance in my teaching and scholarly endeavors.

I wish to express my appreciation to Rev. Dr. Constantine Newman for double checking my Greek patristic translations, and Dr. Stephen Ott for verifying my Latin patristic renditions. Both improved the quality of my work through their pertinent comments and suggestions. Due to these combined efforts, the patristic annotations are being made available in English for the first time.

I am grateful as well to my teaching assistant Anya Rozonoer and Misha Kruk for help with font conversion and other computer-related issues.

Lastly, I wish to thank my wife, Flora, whose love and hard work for the well being of our family facilitated the completion of this commentary.

INTRODUCTION

I. Historical Background:
The Assyrian Expansion and the Last Years of Israel

Given the historical dimension of the Old Testament prophecy,[1] in general, and Hosea's frequent references to concrete events,[2] in particular, an overview of the period in which this man of God prophesied is a prerequisite for better understanding of his message.

From the title[3] and the content of his writing we learn that Hosea was ministering as a prophet within the borders of the Northern Kingdom (Israel), in the second half of the eighth-century B.C.

Below are listed the most important moments of that troubled period in the history of Israel which coincided with the imperial expansion of Assyria.

745 B.C.: Tiglath-pileser III (745-727 B.C.), the founder of the Neo-Assyrian empire[4] turned into reality the dream of his predecessors, who for almost one hundred years had tried to subdue the lands beyond the Euphrates.[5] These western lands were wanted both for their rich natural resources and for their corridor-like position leading to Mediterranean, Egypt, and southern Asia Minor.

Unlike his predecessors who were content with collecting tribute from the native princes, Tiglath-pileser III inaugurated a new policy by transforming the conquered territories into provinces of the Assyrian empire. In case of a rebellion, deportation of the disturbers rather than military intervention came to be preferred.[6]

743 B.C.: In northern Israel, the death of king Jeroboam II (784-743 B.C.) ushered in a period of anarchy. Three of the five kings who succeeded him in a span of ten years usurped the throne by violence (2 Kgs 15:8-28).

740 B.C.: Tiglath-pileser III conquered northern Syria.

738 B.C.: Among the tribute-paying princes from Syria and Palestine the Tiglath-pileser's inscription mentions I'nil of Hamath, Rezon (*Ra-ḫi-a-nu*; cf. Rezin in 2 Kgs 15:37) of Damascus (*Ša-imērišu*), Hiram (*Ḥi-ru-um-mu*) of Tyre, Sibittibiʾli of Byblos, and Menahem of Samaria (*Me-ni-ḫi-im-me* ᵘʳᵘ*Sa-me-ri-na-a-a*).[7]

With respect to king Menahem (743-737 B.C.) of Israel, 2 Kgs 15:19 makes the point that he willingly paid a heavy tribute to "king Pul of Assyria"[8] in order to fortify his shaky throne. Menahem's son, Pekahiah, succeeded him for two years (2 Kgs 15:22f.).

736 B.C.: Pekah son of Remaliah, an Israelite officer, ascended to the throne of Samaria (2 Kgs 15:25 // Hos 6:7f.) by murdering the king Pekahiah, and adopting his throne name.[9]

734 B.C.: Tiglath-pileser III conducted a victorious campaign in Philistia, occupying Gaza and other coastal cities.[10] Then, going as far as the River of Egypt (today *Wâdī el-ʿArîš*; Josh 15:4), he established a military base meant to cut off any future links between Syria-Palestine and Egypt.[11]

Interestingly, the Old Testament is quite silent regarding this campaign, but its silence is justifiable since Tiglath-pileser III's advance into the coastal region had no direct effect on the Northern Kingdom.

733 B.C.: The king of Israel, Pekah, soon joined Rezin of Damascus in his bid against Assyria. The war waged by this coalition is known in history as the "Syro-Ephraimite war." After an unsuccessful attempt to involve Ahaz, king of Judah, in their plot against the Assyrian colossus, the

Introduction

two conspirators Pekah and Rezin invaded the Southern Kingdom seeking to depose Ahaz and replace him with a certain "ben Tabeel" (2 Kgs 15:37; 16:5; Is 7:6).[12]

Instead of listening to Isaiah's warning (Is 7:4f.) to place his trust in God and not to be afraid of the two invaders,[13] Ahaz made repeated appeals to Tiglath-pileser III, sending him gifts from the Temple's treasury, in exchange for his throne's security (2 Kgs 16:7-8).[14]

Tiglath-pileser III intervened immediately and put an end to the "Syro-Ephraimite" coalition by first attacking Israel. According to 2 Kgs 15:29, Galilee and Gilead fell into the hands of the Assyrians. In one of his inscriptions, the Assyrian king speaks with great pride about his victory over "all the cities" of Israel except for Samaria and the mountainous region of Ephraim.[15] Many of these cities were destroyed[16] and the leading class was deported. A new elite was brought in from other provinces of the empire.

The conquered territory was divided into three provinces: a) "Megiddo"— including Galilee and the plain of Jezreel; b) "Dor"—covering the coastal plain south of Carmel up to present Tel Aviv; and c) "Gilead"—comprising the Transjordanian region.[17]

732 B.C.: Damascus shared the same fate as Israel.[18]

Since she went out unwisely on the chess-board of the great powers, refusing prophetic counsel, Judah lost her independence. Yet, in exchange for a heavy tribute the Southern Kingdom avoided Assyrian occupation.[19]

In the same year, 732 B.C., Pekah was assassinated by a certain "Hoshea ben Elah" (732-724 B.C.) who took the throne as the last king of Samaria (2 Kgs 15:30). One of Tiglath-pileser III's inscriptions is slightly different in describing this event, by insisting on the role of the Assyrian king in Hoshea's accession to power.[20]

The Assyrian sources mention no other campaign led by Tiglath-pileser III. Probably, the "great king" (Hos

5:13)²¹ became content with the results of his former military actions. The entire Syria-Palestine region was under the Assyrian dominance either as provinces or as vassal states. The latter category included, besides Judah, the small states of Ammon, Moab and Edom.²²

727 B.C.: Tiglath-pileser III was succeeded by his son Shalmaneser V (727-722 B.C.). During the latter king's reign, Hoshea of Samaria sought help from Egypt against Assyria. The ruler "So, king of Egypt" mentioned in 2 Kgs 17:4 was apparently king Tefnakhte (730-720 B.C.) of the 24th Dynasty who reigned in Sais,²³ in the Delta.

724 B.C.: Hoshea's refusal to pay tribute led Shalmaneser V to take action. The Assyrians occupied the land and besieged the fortified city of Samaria which held out for almost three years. Hoshea, who probably met with the invader in a last bid for peace, was taken prisoner (2 Kgs 17:4-6).

722-721 B.C.: The city was probably captured in the fall of the year 722/721 B.C., shortly before Sargon II (721-705 B.C.) succeeded to the throne of Assyria.²⁴ Thousands²⁵ of Israelites were deported to other provinces of the Assyrian empire whereas people from Babylon, Cuthah, Avva, Hamath,²⁶ and Sepharvaim were brought in to replace the exiles.²⁷

II. The Eighth-Century Prophets: Yaweh's Heralds at the Crossroads of History

From the very outset, one needs a clarification concerning the attribute "writing" which is usually attached to the eighth-century prophets Amos, Hosea, Micah, and Isaiah. This title could be considered inappropriate, for there is no evidence in these prophets' books that they had ever put in writing the divine message. Conversely, the fact that the so-called "primitive" prophets had left no writings does not necessarily mean that they had never written. One can only assume that the eighth-century prophets, as did their predecessors, "spoke out" what they have received from God. But unlike the "primitive" prophets such as Nathan, Elijah, and Elisha, the eighth-century prophets came to be known to us through their own writings. Obviously, these literary products bear the mark of a long and intricate process which started during these prophets' public activity (Jer 36:2, 32). Still, if one takes into account their influence on the later representatives of the Old Testament prophecy whose origins go back to days of Moses (cf. Deut 18:18), the term "classical prophets" seems to be more fitting.

What was the engine that set in motion the tedious process of writing down the prophetic sayings for the first time? Apparently the threat of the Assyrian empire in the eighth century was so great that it led to a rapid concentration and preservation of the prophetic material concerning Israel's religious-moral status among the nations. There were but a few decades before the fall of the Northern Kingdom, and the divine word transmitted by the prophets had to be preserved in a written form for the later generations as both a witness and a warning. Thus the emphasis fell in those days on what the prophet "said," rather than what he "did" as had been the case in the past.[28] Given the complexity of that period, the prophetic word acquired a paradigmatic value. Outliving the gloomy present, it opens up to future events, trying to answer the fundamental questions of the human person in his restless quest for truth, order and beauty. Moreover, the appearance of the first Assyrian oracular compilations, even though quite different from the Old Testament prophecies, had probably provided a certain impetus to the emergence of the first prophetic collections in Israel.[29]

The main characteristics of the eighth-century prophecy will be briefly discussed under three aspects: (1) the dialogue between the prophet and the religious tradition; (2) the relationship between history and divine Revelation; and (3) the interaction of the moral-social-religious factors at the societal level. It should be noted that though found in a certain degree in all prophets, these characteristics occur with more persistence and clarity in the eighth-century prophets.

(1) The eighth-century prophets did not begin to proclaim the word of God on their own initiative or at the demand of a social group (institution), but rather as a result of a divine call (vocation).[30] Although "called" by God to take his word to a disobedient people, the Old Testament prophets are not to be considered isolated personalities or "revolutionaries"[31] about to break with the living stream of the religious tradition. Nor were they simple "interpreters"[32] of the historical events seen through the prism of the tradition. In order to avoid these extreme views one should take into account both the charismatic personality of the prophet and the aura of the religious tradition.[33] Rooted in the solid ground of the tradition, the eighth-century prophets left the marks of their own personalities in the way they spread and explained God's word. It was the word of God that functioned as a bridge during the passionate dialogue between these men of the Spirit and the religious tradition of their people.[34]

(2) In the eighth century the international situation made its first great impact on Israel's national history. Israel was, more than ever before, confronted with foreign nations and unexpected events. Questions concerning its place and role within the concert of other nations had to be answered, and more than ever the divine Revelation was the authoritative word. History and divine Revelation got closer and closer to one another as intertwined realities.[35]

God had revealed his glory within Israel since its birth as a nation during the wondrous deliverance from Egyptian slavery. Since king David's reign, the culture of Israel had become gradually more profane, Yahweh's role was relegated to the Sinai covenant, while Israel took destiny in her own hands. To this secular view of history, quite silent with respect to God's active presence, the eighth-century prophets opposed an original picture in which history became a stage for the revealing Godhead. This occupied the center of the prophetic message in the trouble-filled eighth century.

A certain "relativization" of the basic concepts of election and covenant marked this period.[36] It was a time of self-confidence but also of harsh iconoclasm. Popular beliefs, which in the past seemed untouchable, became the target of serious criticism. It was the great contribution of the eighth-century prophets to cast away the illusions of their contemporaries for whom Yahweh was always present in the midst of his people regardless of its moral conduct (see Am 5:14; Hos 8:2; Is 28:15; Mic 2:6). Thus, in Am 9:7, Yahweh's people are mentioned beside the Syrians and Philistines, two possible beneficiaries of the title of "chosen people" which Israel was initially granted.

These inspired men launched an eleventh-hour warning for Israel to change her conduct. But she still believed in a great intervention of God in her favor, based on the fundamental fact of election at Sinai. According to these prophets, however, the people's very election may well point to its imminent perdition (Am 3:2). Once more Yahweh would show up on the stage of history, but to punish rather than to save his people.[37] In this concrete historical context, obviously with a universalistic dimension, the notion of foreign people—"instrument of the divine wrath"—was for the first time crafted. Thus, Assyria is seen not only as a foreign enemy, but also as an instrument of God's wrath (Is 7:18; 10:5-19). Nevertheless, beyond this gloomy perspective, salvation was still an option.[38] Yahweh was believed to be still willing to forgive completely the sins of his people and to create the appropriate conditions for making a new covenant with Israel (Is 43:25; Hos 14:4; cf. the "new covenant" in Jer 31:31-34). By focusing on God's forgiving love for Israel despite her sinful past, the classical prophets should be considered the forerunners of the New Testament Gospel.

(3) In the view of the eighth-century prophets, human history is guided by God according to certain moral principles.[39] For these men of the Spirit, religious, moral, and social factors are tightly interrelated. Thus, while condemning idolatry they were also critical of pagan influences on moral life (Hos 2:10/8; 4:17-18; 8:1; Mic 6:6-8; Is 1:11-17, 21; 2:6). They reclaimed the moral dimension for Israelite worship which was heavily marked at that time by syncretism and formalism (Hos 6:6; 9:4; Is 58:3-9; Am 5:21-24; Mic 6:6-8).

There is also a close relationship between moral and social factors which the classical prophets would underscore in their writings. The eighth-century Israelite society experienced significant changes in its very fabric. The unprecedented growth of a few large holdings sped up the process of the impoverishing of most of the population. The merit of the classical prophets lies in the fact that they went to the root of the social injustices, that is, moral evil. The social ideal outlined by these men could be reached by a return to the simple but honest life of the ancestors. Under such harsh circumstances, the luxury and opulence of the great proprietors would represent true obstacles in reaching that ideal (Am 2:6; 4:1; 5:7; Hos 4:2, 18; 6:9; 10:4; Is 1:17, 23; 3:16; Mic 2:2, 8).

Should one define in a few words the place and the role of the classical prophets within the larger framework of the divine revelation of the Old Testament as well as their contribution to human thinking, one may want to quote the well-known biblical scholar Cazelles who wrote, "By its philosophers, Athens served the reason, Rome served the justice, and by its prophets Jerusalem served the moral conscience."[40] The classical prophets belonged to the "axial age"[41] of human history as bold advocates of the moral conscience vis-à-vis the dark forces trying to depersonalize it.

III. Hosea: The Man and the Prophet

In the particular case of Hosea,[42] the man identifies perfectly with the prophet. Marked by a unique conjugal experience, his life was a passionate message. Unfortunately, the book gives no details with respect to the place[43] or date of birth, or to the age when he began his ministry (cf. Jer 1:6). One knows nothing about his former occupation (cf. Am 7:14). One does know a few aspects relating to his personal life, namely, those details about his conjugal drama. In any event, the prophet's father, Beeri, was probably a man of substance in the Israelite society of the late eighth century B.C., since his name was listed in the book's title.[44]

Three children, a girl and two boys, are born as the result of Hosea's marriage to Gomer, the daughter of Diblaim (Hos 1:3).[45] Important for reconstructing the chronological frame of these births is Hos 1:8 which mentions that the third child was conceived after Gomer weaned her daughter. This means that between the second and the third birth a period of almost three years has been elapsed.[46] Even though not explicitly said, it seems that Gomer, leaving her husband suddenly, commits the great sin of adultery (Hos 3:1). At Yahweh's express command, the prophet welcomes back his unfaithful wife and a period of abstinence ushers the renewed relationship of love between Hosea and Gomer.

With respect to Hosea's ministry, a few assumptions may be projected. The divine call was probably addressed at the end of Jeroboam II's reign (784-743 B.C.) or in the years following the king's death (cf. Hos 5:11-13; 7:7; 8:4, 10; 13:10, 11). Some of Hosea's prophetic words presuppose the Syro-Ephraimite war of 733 B.C. (cf. 5:8-6:6), while others allude to Israel's oscillating alliances between Assyria and Egypt, which marked the post-war period (7:8-16; 9:3, 6; 8:8-10). A few passages can be explained only by reference to the last years of king Hoshea (cf. 7:3-7; 8:1-3; 10:3, 5, 8; 12:1f.; 13:1f.). All these details and many others found in the book of Hosea are consonant with the political landscape of the last decades of the eighth century B.C.

If Hosea's first prophecy regarding the end of Jehu's dynasty (1:4) was indeed fulfilled in 743 B.C. by the assassination of king Zachariah, then the beginnings of his ministry should be placed before this date, at least five years earlier, when the prophet's children were born. Provided that Hos 13:10, 16 relates to the imprisonment of king Hoshea, the last north-Israelite monarch, and the siege of Samaria, one may conclude that the end of Hosea's ministry occurred in 724/3 B.C. There is no indication at all supporting the assumption that Hosea might have continued his ministry after the fall of Samaria (722/1 B.C.), which, based on Hos 14:1, still belongs to a future time. Thus, one can suppose that Hosea ministered as a prophet between 748-724 B.C.[47]

Although the writing is quite silent regarding the place of Hosea's ministry, most of the interpreters think that the prophet was originally from the Northern Kingdom.[48] Julian of Eclanum[49] takes a step further, when he opines that after the fall of Samaria (721 B.C.) Hosea continued his ministry in Judah. Interestingly enough, Jerusalem is never mentioned in the book, although the prophet speaks quite often about several localities in the territories of Benjamin and Ephraim, such as the city of Samaria (7:1; 8:5ff; 10:5, 7; 14:1),[50] the sanctuaries in Bethel (4:15; 5:8; 10:5; 12:5) and Gilgal (4:15; 9:15; 12:12),[51] the Valley of Achor (2:17/15),[52] Adam at Jordan (6:7),[53] Gibeah and Ramah (5:8),[54] Gilead in Transjordan (6:8; 12:12).[55] Moreover, Hosea calls the king of Israel "our king" (7:5). One might add though that, despite no mention of Jerusalem, Judah is sometimes presented besides Israel waiting for God's punishment (5:12, 13; 6:11).[56]

With respect to the prophet's former occupation and the spiritual milieu in which he lived, some authors,[57] taking into account Hosea's taste for images found in surrounding nature, regarded him as a farmer called by Yahweh to carry his word. Yet, one should not forget his familiarity with the religious traditions of Israel.[58] Although Hosea makes frequent references to the former prophets and praises them (cf. 6:4-6; 9:7-9; 12:8-11, 13-15), there is no clear evidence that he was a member of a prophetic group or guild.[59] Apparently, Hosea had listened to Amos while the latter was speaking in Bethel, hence the spiritual and, to a certain degree, literal kinship between these two prophets.[60] According to Wolff,[61] 4:6; 6:6; 8:12 would indicate a close relationship between Hosea and the Levitic circles which had facilitated for him a better understanding of people's traditions. Indeed, some of Hosea's prophecies were originally addressed to the cultic personnel (e.g., 9:10-10:8; 11:1-11; 14:2-9), but this does not mean that Hosea was in direct contact with such circles or that his message was considerably influenced by them.

One may assume with the vast majority of the interpreters that most of Hosea's public prophecies were probably delivered in the capital city of Samaria (5:1-7; 7:7, 16; 8:1-14; 10:9-15), Bethel and Gilgal (4:4-19; 12:1-15; 13:1-14:1).

After 733 B.C. when some of Hosea's sayings were fulfilled, the people's hostility against the prophet forced him to withdraw from the public arena (9:7-9; 11:5, 7; 12:1). In such circumstances, Hosea kept on preaching his prophecies within the circle of his disciples, where he would taste the same bitterness Yahweh experienced vis-à-vis his unfaithful people (8:1; 14:1).[62]

The book is also silent with respect to the prophet's end. The assessment of St. Epiphanius of Cyprus[63] that Hosea died peacefully, and that he was buried in his native region, does not necessarily imply that the prophet did not witness the fall of Samaria.

IV. The Book of the Prophet Hosea

1. Structure and Literary Composition

Commonly, the biblical scholars divide Hosea's book into two unequal parts or sections: chapters 1-3 and chapters 4-14.[64] Although differing in theme and form, these sections are not to be considered two different writings coming from two different authors (so Ginsberg, Kauffmann). The present commentary follows a tripartite division: 1-3; 4-11; 12-14 (so Jacob). Each of these three sections ends in an optimistic note (3:5; 11:11; 14:8).

According to some scholars,[65] though the first three chapters (1-3) exude a sort of unity due probably to a redaction process carried out in Jerusalem a few decades after Hosea's death, the remaining chapters (4-14) are literary fragments dating from different periods and fused together into a composite block.

The second section (4-11) opens with the phrase

שִׁמְעוּ דְבַר־יְהוָה "Listen to the word of the Lord" (4:1a) and ends with an expression frequently found in the prophetic writings נְאֻם־יְהוָה "The word of the Lord" (11:11b). This section is made of several "kerygmatic units,"[66] prophetic sayings delivered by Hosea on various occasions. According to some authors,[67] the second section has four cycles of "kerygmatic units" grouped around two major themes: divine judgment and final salvation. The first cycle (4:9. 11-14, 15-19; 5:1-7) deals with the cultic aspects; the second cycle (5:8-10; 5:11-7:7; 7:8-16; 8:1-7; 8:8-10) examines the social life; the third cycle (8:11-13; 9:1-9) goes back to the cultic sphere; and the fourth cycle (9:10-17; 10:1-8; 10:9-15; 11:1-11) shows a special interest in the history of Israel. There is agreement among the interpreters that, though dating from different periods, these "kerygmatic units" follow the chronological order in which they were delivered. A strong argument for this point is the present position of chapters 5 and 6, both dating from the period of the Syro-Ephramaite war.

The third section (12-14) consists of three prophetic cycles which, in fact, resume, with more examples, the major themes found in the second section. Some of these sayings were delivered in front of a public audience (12:8ff; 13:9ff.), others within the inner circle of Hosea's disciples (14:2-9), but all date from the last years of the Northern Kingdom.[68]

2. Language and Style

The language of Hosea reflects a profound religiosity and an extraordinary intimacy between Yahweh and his messenger throughout the entire prophetic discourse.

There are two basic forms[69] by which Hosea transmitted the inspired word of God, namely the "divine speech" - *Gottesrede* (1:4f., 6, 9.; 2:4-25; 4:4-9; 5:1-3; 5:8-7:16; 8:1-12) and "prophetic speech" – *Prophetenrede* (3:5; 4:1-3; 5:4-7; 7:10; 8:13, 14; 9:1-9; 10:1-8; 12:3-7, 13-15). There is also a quite interesting case when these two forms are found side by side, in other words when God appears both in the first and the third person within the same pericope (cf. 4:10-15; 8:11-13; 12:1-15). This unusual situation reflects an intimate relationship between Yahweh and his prophet.

According to Wolff,[70] most of Hosea's sayings (especially in chapters 4-8) have their setting (*Sitz im Leben*) in those legal disputes (*Rechtsauseinandersetzung*; or the *rîb*-pattern,[71] from Hebrew ריב "to contend") which in ancient Israel were held in front of the elders at the city gates (4:1-3; 5:1-7; 12:1-14:1) or in the neighborhood of various sanctuaries (2:4-17; 4:4-19; 9:1-9). But Wolff's over-estimation of the legal *Sitz im Leben* with respect to Hosea's sayings can hardly apply to the chapters 9-13 and 2:4-25 which are clear examples of prophetic meditations. As Macintosh[72] rightly noticed, the Israelite prophets were able to communicate without necessarily resorting to the literal clichés, such as the *rîb*-pattern.

Some of Hosea's sayings show a strong cultic influence, e.g., from the stereotyped formulae preceding the proclamation of the divine law (12:10; 13:4)[73] up to the lamentations replete with the believer's hopes that his prayer will be heard by God (6:1-3; 8:1-3; 14:5-9).[74]

At first sight, Hosea's book presents itself as a collection of both narrative and oracular units. The first section (1-3) contains narrative material, while the second and third sections (4-14), along with the chapter 2, consist of oracular material. This division into oracular and narrative material may be found in the books by Hosea's contemporaries Isaiah and Amos.

With respect to the literary genres, based on the frequency of the "prose particles" (i.e., את, the accusative marker, אֲשֶׁר, the relative pronoun, and הַ, the definite article) found in the Masoretic Text, Andersen and Freedman[75] notice that in the standard prose the frequency of the "prose particles" is 15% or higher of all words. When these particles are under 5% of all words one may speak of poetry.

	No. of words	No. of prose particles	Percentage
Section I	556	61	11%
Sections II and III	1824	54	3%
Total	2380	115	4.8%

As one can see in the chart above, prose dominates section I (11% prose particles) compared to the sections II and III where poetry is prevalent (3% prose particles). Taken as a whole, Hosea's book with a total of 2380 words (4.8% prose particles) is closer to poetry than to prose. One may add nevertheless that the poetry of the prophetic writings of the eighth century B.C. differs from the poetry of the Pentateuch or Psalms. Moreover, prophetic prose has a certain rhythm and relies on stylistic features characteristic of poetry. This kind of prose so different from that found in Deuteronomy is conventionally designated as prose-poetry or elevated prose (Andersen and Freedman). Typical to the pre-exilic prophetic literature is a genuine synthesis of prose and poetry which differs in degree from one author to another. For instance, in Isaiah and Micah classical poetry is better represented than in Amos and Hosea. With respect to Hosea, his writing stands at the crossroads between poetry and elevated prose.

Among the lyrical means, repetition is used on a high scale from the simple forms like assonance (vowel repetition) and alliteration (consonant repetition), e.g., צָרַר רוּחַ (4:19); חֶסֶד חָפַצְתִּי (6:6); בֹּעֵר ... בֹּקֶר (7:6); הֲפוּכָה ... עֻגָה (7:8); גָּלָה ... (10:5); יָגִילוּ, to the more elaborate *parallelismum membrorum*, the backbone of Hebrew poetry.⁷⁶ Noteworthy is Hosea's predilection for the synonymous parallelism (more than 80 times), compared to the synthetic (about 40 times) and antithetic (a few times) parallelisms.

The poetry of this book is marked by several lexical peculiarities such as archaisms and rare words (e.g., וְהַקְשִׁיבוּ...הַאֲזִינוּ in 5:1), figurative usage of common terms (e.g., כשל "to stumble" in 4:5; 5:5; 14:2, 10), and original expressions created by the author (e.g., יִשְׂאוּ נַפְשׁוֹ in 4:8).

The book's language is lively, abundant in similes (4:16; 5:12. 14; 7:4, 6f.; 9:10; 11:4, 10f.) and metaphors (e.g., 5:1f.; 7:8; 8:9; 10:1, 11; 11:1), often very bold and hardly translatable. Hosea's style is dynamic, sometimes nervous and enigmatic. The sudden transition from a verbal aspect to another within the same strophe represents another characteristic of the prophet's style.

The book contains a considerable number of *hapax legomena* (31) and about 20 words found three times and fewer in the entire Old Testament. Given these peculiarities,⁷⁷ Hosea's language may be considered a sample of the north-Israelite dialect.⁷⁸ Below are listed some of the dialectical features: transitive verbs used as intransitive, e.g., פרד (10:2), חלק (7:9), זרק (5:6), חלץ (4:14); nouns with a gender different from the one given by the dictionaries, e.g., וְשָׁדַיִם (9:14), גֶּפֶן (10:1), מִזְבְּחוֹת זְבָחוֹת — as plural of זֶבַח is a *hapax legomenon*; common nouns with a new meaning, e.g., יַיִן and תִּירוֹשׁ (4:11) in Hosea's book are not synonyms but two terms designating two phases in wine industry; in the north-Israelite dialect שֵׂיבָה was probably synonymous with זְקֵנִים "old people" (7:9), and אֶתְנָה (2:14) a dialectal variant of the more common term אֶתְנַן "gift, present" (9:1).

Among the syntactic peculiarities one may mention:

the use of asyndetons (4:18; 5:3; 9:6) and particle עַתָּה "now" in a sequel of verses (4:16; 5:7; 7:2; 8:8, 13), the choice for the negative בְּלִי instead of בַּל used with verbal forms (7:8; 8:7; 9:16).

According to E. Jacob,[79] the book contains a number of Aramaisms, but only three forms are certain, i.e., יִגְהֶה (5:13), תִּרְגַּלְתִּי (11:3), תַּלְאֻבוֹת (13:5).

3. Text and Versions

The Hebrew text of Hosea's book is one of the more corrupt in the entire Old Testament, comparable only to that of Job.[80] This fact was recognized very early, as evidenced by several obscure expressions that may be found already in LXX, e.g., כְּשָׁמְעָ / ἐν τῇ ἀκοῇ (7:12), לֹא עָל / εἰς οὐδὲν (7:16).

Among the versions used to restore the original text, the Septuagint holds a place of priority.[81] The Septuagint is sometimes very free in rendering the Hebrew text, e.g., καὶ πάντα ὅσα μοι καθήκει "and all my necessaries" for שִׁקּוּיָי "and my drink" (2:7/5), καὶ ἀπέστειλεν πρέσβεις "and he sent ambassadors" for וַיִּשְׁלַח "and he sent" (5:13). The Greek version is, at times, a word-for-word translation of the Hebrew,[82] e.g., ἐν τῷ τόπῳ οὗ "in the place where" for בִּמְקוֹם אֲשֶׁר "instead of" (2:1/1:10), οὐ μὴ προσθήσω "I will not add" for לֹא אוֹסִיף "I will no longer ..." (1:6; cf. 9:1; 13:2). This situation may be explained by the lack of the "matres lectionis" in the Hebrew text or the LXX tendency toward paraphrasing the Hebrew terms and idioms whose translation into Greek seems difficult. There is also a possibility that the Hebrew text used by the LXX might have occasionally differed from the MT.[83] The additions of the LXX with respect to MT refer primarily to those prophetic sayings trying to explicate historically the covenant between

Yahweh and Israel, the cult of Baal (2:10/8), the creation (2:14/12), the imminent Assyrian deportation (8:13). On the other hand, the omissions of the LXX with respect to MT are few and of no great semantic value. One might add, nevertheless, that the LXX shows a certain tendency toward actualization and generalization of the prophetic discourse.[84] In a nutshell, even though the LXX is some times at odds with the MT, there is no clear indication that the *Vorlage* of the LXX differed substantially from the received Hebrew text (i.e., MT).

The other versions play a lesser role in the attempt to restore the original text. In his commentary on Hosea, Macintosh[85] lists the ancient versions of Hosea and their role in restoring the original text. After a detailed presentation of the LXX, the author mentions the Old Latin version or *Vetus Latina*, a translation of the LXX done in the second-third centuries A.D. Its importance is owing to the fact that this version antedates the recensions of the LXX in the third-fourth centuries.

With respect to the minor Greek versions, Macintosh points out that, though Aquila (ca. A.D. 130) shows a certain literalness in rendering the Hebrew, Symmachus (second century A.D.) is interested in a better Greek translation of the original text, and Theodotion (second century A.D.) may be qualified as a revision of the LXX. In a study dedicated to the Twelve, J. Ziegler[86] presents the main differences of the minor Greek versions with respect to the LXX text of Hosea. (Many of these readings were transmitted in Syriac, i.e., in the Syro-Hexapla.) His conclusion is that the *Vorlage* of these versions did not differ substantially from the MT.

The Peshitta,[87] the Syriac translation made within a Jewish community in the middle of the first century A.D., had seemingly a similar *Vorlage* to the MT, differing sometimes in vocalization and word-division from the latter.

The Targum of Jonathan,[88] whose origin goes back to the end of the first century A.D., offers a free rendering, sometimes a paraphrase, of the text of Hosea. Profound prophetic actions (1:2; 3:1) are replaced by theological conclusions. In its relentless attempt to erase any anthropomorphisms, the Targum resorts at times to explanatory words such as, *Memra* "word" of God as his agent, *Shekinah* "dwelling" as a symbol of divine presence in the midst of Israel. At any rate, its *Vorlage* is very close to the MT.

The Vulgate or the *Hebraica veritas*, made by Jerome in Bethlehem between A.D. 390 and A.D. 405, is an important witness to the Hebrew text since it ante-dates the final vocalization of the latter. The Vulgate usually follows the Hebrew text but sometimes it is influenced by the LXX and Symmachus. Of great importance not only from a theological point a view but also for textual matters is Jerome's commentary on Hosea, where he cites the LXX version and, occasionally, the minor Greek versions. Both the Vulgate and Jerome's commentary presuppose a *Vorlage* very similar to the MT.

Our reluctance for textual emendations alongside this commentary relies primarily on the fact that Hosea's vocabulary is dialectical and its treatment as Standard Biblical Hebrew led to various readings proposed by the ancient versions.[89]

4. Authenticity, Integrity, and Canonicity of the Book

The authenticity and integrity of the book were for the first time questioned at the end of the nineteenth century when Scholz,[90] separating himself from the traditional view, refers to some late "interpolations" (e.g., 8:14) dictated probably by the use of the book within the Judaean synagogue. A few years later, W. R. Harper[91] lists a number of "secondary" fragments. For the sake of clarity, the texts whose authenticity was contested will be presented into three groups.

(a) According to the representatives of the liberal school, all references to Judah (e.g., 1:7; 5:10, 12, 13, 14; 6:4, 11; 8:14; 10:11; 12:1) are redactional.[92] Gelin[93] follows a more moderate path when he suggests that, due to a Judaean reading of the book, "Ephraim/Israel" was substituted with "Judah" (e.g., 8:14; 10:11; 12:3). The weak point of such views is that, besides a fragile argumentation, they reduce the Old Testament literature in general and the Hosean writing especially to an artificial schematism. According to the traditional view, Hosea, although originally from the Northern Kingdom, behaved as a true prophet who, called and sent by Yahweh, communicated his word to the entire people regardless the geo-political boundaries.[94]

(b) The authenticity of the eschatological and messianic passages (e.g., 2:1/1:10-2:3/1, 16/14-25/23; 3:1-5; 5:15-6:3, 5; 11:8-11; 12:10/9-11/10; 14:2/1-9/8) fell under a similar criticism since these hope-giving passages can be read to contradict Hosea's sayings concerning the imminence of the divine judgment (cf. 13:9, 14). As B. Kutal[95] well remarked in his commentary, those passages pointing to the future fate of Israel are part of the very structure of Hosea's book, and they assume at a certain degree the dramatic situation of the present. Moreover, H. Gressmann[96] points to the thematic and literary unity between these passages and the rest of the book. One might add that, no matter how paradoxical appearing at first sight, the fusion between the prophetic sayings announcing judgment and those promising final salvation represents a key feature of the Old Testament prophecy. The hope for a better future bursts out even from the most gloomy prophetic passage.[97]

(c) The book's final verse (14:10/9) has often been considered a literary unit by itself, a product of the wisdom literature, and by consequence redactional.[98] Again, the traditional view has its merit by underscoring the Hosean origin of the book's conclusion. Hosea himself might have written this final verse as a caveat for his readers lest they underestimate the realistic character of his prophetic actions (i.e., his marriage to a "woman of prostitution" as a metaphor for Yahweh's relationship to Israel in the second half of the eighth century B. C.).

In conclusion, we may mention Macintosh's[99] pertinent observation that rather than looking for a variety of forms and then identifying them with different sayings delivered at separate times and compiled by a later redactor, it would be much easier, and, one may add, much closer to reality, to recognize the unity of the book and a single author, the prophet Hosea, who makes use of different forms and motifs. Far from denying any redactional work of Hosea's words, Macintosh questions the validity of those studies that overestimate form critical analysis.

The canonicity of Hosea's book was never contested. Below are listed the important moments of the "external history" (Harare) of this book.

(a) Since its appearance, Hosea's book has been considered a God-inspired writing. The strong proof is the influence exerted by Hosea on other Old Testament books and especially on Jeremiah (Jer 2:2; 3:6-13; 6:1; 31:31-34; Ezek 16; 23).

(b) In the second century B.C. book of Ecclesiasticus (49:10), Jesus ben Sirach refers to a book or collection comprising the Twelve Prophets (… τῶν δώδεκα προφητῶν), and surely Hosea was one of these prophets.

(c) The place of priority held by Hosea among the Twelve was probably determined by the phrase of Hos 1:2 תְּחִלַּת דִּבֶּר־יְהוָה בְּהוֹשֵׁעַ "the beginning of Yahweh's speaking through Hosea," an indication to the eighth-century prophets and by extension to the Twelve Minor Prophets.

With respect to the order of the prophetic books within the Twelve, the ancient versions follow the MT (Hosea, Joel, Amos, Obadiah, Jonah and Micah) except for the LXX (Hosea, Amos, Micah, Joel, Obadiah and Jonah). Macintosh[100] notices, while the MT order is based on the chronological principle (the six prophets mentioned above are considered to have lived in the second half of the eighth century B.C.; Nahum, Habakkuk and Zephaniah in the second half of the seventh century B.C.; and Haggai, Zechariah and Malachi in the sixth and fifth centuries B.C.), the LXX order relies on a different principle, namely the length of the books.

In the Jewish (*B. Megillah*) and Christian (Jerome: *unum librum esse duodecim prophetarum*; Melito, Athanasius, Epiphanius: τὸ Δωδεκα-προφητόν) canons, the collection of the Twelve was considered as one book. The title the Twelve is found in *Numbers Rabba* (Aramaic: תרי עסר), whereas "the Minor Prophets," a common name today, is attested in Augustine.[101]

(d) The manuscript fragments discovered at Qumran show that Hosea's book enjoyed a great deal of esteem among the Essenes.[102]

(e) Philo of Alexandria[103] quotes from Hos 14:8/7, 10/9, and Flavius Josephus[104] mentions Isaiah and "the others, which were twelve in number" (i.e., the Twelve Minor Prophets).

(f) In the New Testament, the Lord and his Apostles quote often from Hosea's book, e.g., Rom 9:25f. (Hos 2:25/23); Mt 9:13 (6:6); Lk 23:30; Rev 6:16 (10:8; 12:7/6); Mt 2:15 (11:1); 1 Cor 15:55 (13:4).

5. *Conjugal Drama of Hosea: Preliminaries*

The conjugal drama of Hosea has always been a topic of endless scholarly discussions, without reaching thus far any concrete agreement.[105]

According to the structuralists,[106] the first section of Hosea's book (1-3) may be divided into two parts: chapters 1-2 (A) and chapter 3 (B). In the part A (chapter 1), Hosea, at Yahweh's command, marries Gomer, a "wife of whoredom." The three children resulting from this marriage receive symbolic names (Jezreel, Lo-Ruhamah, Lo-Ammi), pointing to the imminence of Yahweh's judgment. The chapter 2, which concludes the part A, is a prophetic explanation of the chapter 1. Here, the personal drama of Hosea becomes a powerful metaphor describing the relationship between Yahweh and Israel marked by impasse. Part B, consisting only of chapter 3, presents Hosea about to marry an "adulteress," again at Yahweh's command.

From the outset we are facing two basic questions: (1) Was Hosea's marriage to a "wife of whoredom" (chapter 1) a real, historical act, a vision, or a simple literary fiction? (2) What is the relation between the two parts (A and B), or more exactly between a "wife of whoredom" (chapter 1) and an "adulteress" (chapter 3)?

(1) With respect to the first question, below are briefly listed the main interpretations of the biblical exegesis, past and present.

a) The allegoric interpretation tries to reconcile Yahweh's command to Hosea (1:2; 3:1) with the moral law of the Old Testament, which condemns prostitution and adultery altogether (Lev 19:29; 20:10; 21:14; Exod 20:14; Deut 5:18), suggesting that Hosea's marriage to a "wife of whoredom" was not a real act but rather an allegory[107] or a prophetic vision.[108]

The presence of the concrete details which do not fit into the schematism of the allegoric creations (e.g., the position of Lo-Ruhama, a girl, between two boys, and the weaning of Lo-Ruhama), can be considered a strong argument supporting the historicity of this episode. Moreover, Hosea did not point to a possible allegoric or visionary character of his action (cf. Jer 25:15f.; Zech 11). At any rate, the allegoric interpretation does not solve the moral dilemma. Recent studies in psychology show that even in a dream state the human person cannot completely escape the moral constraints.[109]

b) The historical interpretation today has two directions. According to the proponents of the first direction,[110] the conjugal drama of Hosea represents the starting point of the prophetic ministry. Hosea married Gomer, a decent woman, who later became a "wife of whoredom." The very moment Hosea realized who she was, he evicted her, and just at that time the prophetic call occurred. Now, the prophet sees in his own conjugal drama a reflection of the drama between Yahweh and Israel unfolded within the historical realm. Eventually, at Yahweh's command, Hosea receives back his unfaithful wife (3:1f.). This interpretation faces nevertheless a series of difficulties. For instance, while the "wife of whoredom" fits into a "retrospective" interpretation, the symbolic names of the children do not. On the contrary, those names testify to a prophetic ministry begun prior to the dramatic end of the marriage. In addition, the first divine command (1:2) suggests that Hosea was already a prophet before his marriage with Gomer. Thus, the prophetic call obviously preceded the onset of Hosea's conjugal life.

The second direction of the historical interpretation, seemingly much closer to the historical truth,[111] sets the conjugal act itself in the center of the prophetic ministry. Thus, the conjugal drama becomes a precious complement of God's word to Israel. Here are the main arguments supporting such an interpretation.

(a) The Hebrew idiom לקח לוֹ אִשָּׁה "to take a woman to himself" (cf. 1:2) has a concrete meaning, "to marry."[112]

(b) The fact that "Gomer" is found in other biblical passages, (e.g., "the table of nations," Gen 10:2; cf. 1 Chr 1:5) testifies to this name's historicity.[113]

(c) The choice for the idiom אֵשֶׁת זְנוּנִים "wife of whoredom"[114] instead of the more common word זוֹנָה "harlot," represents a concrete detail supporting a historical interpretation of Hosea's marriage.

Needless to say, Hosea's actions are loaded with a profound symbolism, but this is not enough to label them as allegoric or visionary.[115] As a conclusion, we can ascertain that Hosea's marriage to Gomer, a "wife of whoredom," was a real, historical event. The apparent discord between Yahweh's command and the prophet's actions, on the one hand, and the moral law of the Old Testament, on the other hand, can be, if not completely resolved, at least explained to a certain degree. We know that Hosea prophesied in a critical period in Israel's history. Yahweh's appeal to repentance and reconciliation had to be the last warning before the great national tragedy of the year 722/1 B.C. There was no time to waste. That is why, in order to make clear his will, Yahweh chooses not only the prophet's voice but also his own life that becomes a living message for a senseless people. In the exceptional period in which he lived, the prophet will obey in all humility to God's command, while tasting in his own being Yahweh's bitterness over the people's apostasy.[116]

(2) The second question raised by chapters 1-3 refers to the relation between A and B. At the first sight, B seems a doublet of A. The narrative starts off again with a divine command, this time pertaining to Hosea's marriage to an "adulteress" (3:1), followed again by the prophet's

unconditional obedience. In addition, the prophet had to pay a redeeming price to take back his wife (3:2). We are also told about a period of "abstinence" imposed on the "adulteress" (3:3). Part B ends as Part A with a prophetic meditation on Israel's imminent fate.

With respect to the relation between A and B, here are some scholarly opinions.

a) Part B is a simple repetition of Part A made by a late redactor, and by consequence the episode narrated in B is just a literary creation. Thus, there is only one marriage, that narrated in A.[117]

b) Initially, A and B were a single narrative unit written as an autobiography, whence a later editor of Hosea's book separated the actual biographic fragment (A).[118]

c) A and B are authentic fragments but each part deals with a separate topic. Thus, the "adulteress" (B) is not the same with the "wife of whoredom" (A).[119]

d) A and B narrate the same episode: Hosea's marriage to a prostitute.[120] Thus, the adverb עוֹד "again" must be taken along with the verbal form וַיֹּאמֶר "and he said," as in Exod 4:6. Perhaps, this adverb was inserted later by a redactor of Hosea's book trying to create an idea of time sequence.[121]

According to most interpreters,[122] A and B are authentic passages, and the actions narrated by the author have a historical basis. The two parts view the prophet's conjugal drama in two different moments in time. Thus, A refers to Hosea's marriage with Gomer, a "wife of whoredom" who gave birth to three children. Later, though the text is not quite clear,[123] Gomer leaves her husband, committing the sin of adultery. From this point on, the story is told by Part B which labels Gomer an "adulteress" (3:1). Here are some arguments supporting this view.

The presence of concrete details constitute, as in the first part, proof that this fragment narrates a historical episode. For instance, the intricate way in which the redemption price is described (3:2)[124] is not compatible with an allegory built in most cases on simplicity and schematism. This argument raises still another question: What is the goal of each part? As one can notice, A focuses more on the symbolic names of Hosea's children, whereas B underscores the need for a period of "abstinence" following the act of reconciliation. If A mentions only in passing and within a context of judgment the future union of the two kingdoms (2:1/1:10-2:3/1), B shows that the union would be possible only after Israel's sincere return to God and to the legitimate Davidic dynasty (3:5).

The two parts date from different periods within the long ministry of Hosea.[125] Part A originated probably in the last years of the reign of Jeroboam II (784-743 B.C.), hence the similarity between the situation described here and that found in the book of Amos. The prophecies are centered on the divine judgment, and the symbolic names of Hosea's children point to the imminence of God's punishments concerning Israel.

Part B dates from the end of Hosea's prophetic ministry, more exactly the eve of the fall of Samaria (ca. 724 B.C.). The accent falls now on words of consolation and hope for a better future. The final restoration requires a preliminary moral revision translated into a state of "abstinence."

Here is a chronological synopsis of the actions related in A and B.

A (748 B.C.—): 1. Hosea's marriage to Gomer (1:2);
2. the birth of the three children and their symbolic names (1:3-9);

B (—724 B.C.): 3. receipt of the adulterous wife (3:1-2);
4. a period of "abstinence" (3:3-4);
5. the final restoration (3:5).

Notes

[1] According to the classic passage from Deut 18:18-22, which underscores the Mosaic origin of the Old Testament prophecy, the distinguishing characteristic of the true prophet is the fulfillment of his predictions regarding specific events. Thus the true prophet is at the same time a messenger of God and a witness to a continuous and passionate dialogue between the Creator and the human person in a concrete historical setting. On the phenomenon of prophecy in ancient Israel, the reader is directed to J. Blenkinsopp, *A History of Prophecy in Israel* (Louisville, Kentucky: Westminster JKP, 1996).

[2] As H. W. Wolff (*Hosea. A Commentary on the Book of the Prophet Hosea* [translated by G. Stansell; edited by P. D. Hanson; Hermeneia; Philadelphia: Fortress, 1989], xxi) observes, no other prophet uses the adverb "now" more than Hosea (4:16; 5:3, 7; 7:2; 8:8, 10, 13; 10:2, 3; cf. 13:13). This shows a certain preoccupation with the present, concrete time.

[3] See the commentary on 1:1.

[4] The Neo-Assyrian empire (934-610 B.C.) is usually divided into two periods. In the second period (745-610 B.C.), Assyria expanded over a large area from the Arab-Persian Gulf to Commagene in Turkey. See A. Kuhrt, *The Ancient Near East* (2 vols.; Routledge History of the Ancient World; London & New York: Routledge, 1995), 2:473.

[5] One of these attempts was the campaign of Shalmanesers III in Syria (841 B.C.). See A. L. Oppenheim, *ANET*, 280.

[6] See J. Bright, *A History of Israel* (3rd ed.; 3rd impression; London: SCM Press, 1984), 271.

[7] A. L. Oppenheim, *ANET*, 283.

[8] The Bible calls Tiglath-pileser III "Pul," the name used by the Assyrian king after he took the Babylonian throne in 729 B.C. See J. Bright, *A History of Israel*, 270.

⁹ Isaiah (7:4f.; 8:5) calls him simply *ben Remaliah* "son of Remaliah." See J. Bright, *A History of Israel*, 271 n. 5.

¹⁰ A fragmentary annalistic text (year unknown) shows how Hanno, the king of Gaza, saved his life by fleeing to Egypt: "As to Hanno of Gaza (*Ḫa-a-a-nu-ú-nu* ᵘʳᵘ*Ḫa-az-za-at-a-a*) who fled before my army and ran away to Egypt, [I conquered] the town of Gaza, ... his personal property, his images ... [and I placed (?)] (the images of) my [... gods] and my royal image in his own place ... and declared (them) to be (thenceforward) the gods of their country. I imposed upon th[em tribute]." Cf. A. L. Oppenheim, *ANET*, 283.

¹¹ J. Bright, *A History of Israel*, 274. See also A. Alt, "Tiglath-pilesers III erster Feldzug nach Palästina," *KSchr*, 2:150-62.

¹² According to W. F. Albright, *BASOR* 140 (1955) 34f., *ben Tabeel* would have been a son of Uzziah or Jotham by an Aramaean princess.

¹³ According to 2 Chr 28:17f., the Edomites, who then were subject to Judah, joined the forces of Rezin and Pekah, attacking Ahaz from the east. Moreover, the Philistines made forays in Negeb and Shephelah. See J. Bright, *A History of Israel*, 274.

¹⁴ In J. Bright's view (*A History of Israel*, 274 n. 12), Ahaz's appeal preceded the 734 B.C. campaign in Philistia.

¹⁵ "In my former campaigns I had considered all the cities [which ... as ...] and I had carried away as booty and ... the town of Samaria only I did le[ave/except ...] their king [... like a] fog/snow-storm ... districts of the town [...]bara, 635 prisoners of the town ... of the town Hinatuna, 650 prisoners of the town Qana[... of the town . .]atbiti, 650 prisoners of the town Ir[... all these] people together with their possessions [I brought away ...] the town Aruma, the town Marum [... (as to) Mitinti from] Ashkelon (who) had [violated] the oath sworn to me [and had revolted], (when) he learned about the [defeat inflicted upon] Rezon he [perished] in in[sanity]." Cf. A. L. Oppenheim, *ANET*, 283.

[16] Among those sharing such a fate was the city of Megiddo. Megiddo III was then rebuilt as a provincial capital. In this city was found the palace of the Assyrian governor. Cf. J. Bright, *A History of Israel*, 274 n. 14.

[17] See A. Alt, "Das System der assyrischen Provinzen auf dem Boden der Reiches Israel," *KSchr*, 2:188-205; 209-212.

[18] One of Tiglath-pileser III's inscriptions offers the following description: "I laid siege to and conquered the town of Hadara, the inherited property of Rezon of Damascus (*Ša-imēriŠu*), [the place where] he was born. I brought away as prisoners 800 (of its) inhabitants with their possessions, ... their large (and) small cattle. 750 prisoners from Kurussa [... prisoners] from Irma, 550 prisoners from Metuna I brought (also) away. 592 towns ... of the 16 districts of the country of Damascus (*Ša-imēriŠu*) I destroyed (making them look) like hills of (ruined cities over which) the flood (had swept)." Cf. A. L. Oppenheim, *ANET*, 283.

[19] Ahaz of Judah appears among the tribute-paying princes, under a slightly different name "Jehoahaz" (a long form which is not found in the Bible): "[I received] the tribute of ... Jehoahaz (*Ia-ú-ḫa-zi*) of Judah (*Ia-ú-da-a-a*)...." Cf. A. L. Oppenheim, *ANET*, 282.

[20] "Israel (lit.: "Omri-Land" *Bît Ḫumrya*) ... all its inhabitants (and) their possessions I led to Assyria. They overthrew their king Pekah (*Pa-qa-ḫa*) and I placed Hoshea (*A-ú-si-ʾ*) as king over them. I received from them 10 talents of gold, 1,000 (?) talents of silver as their [tri]bute and brought them to Assyria." Cf. A. L. Oppenheim, *ANET*, 284.

[21] See the commentary on 5:13.

[22] Edom is listed among tribute-paying states in one of Tiglath-pileser III's inscriptions, "Kaush-malaku of Edom (*Ú-du-mu-a-a*)." Cf. A. L. Oppenheim, *ANET*, 282.

[23] *So* (*sôʾ*) is the Hebrew spelling of the Egyptian word *s'w* for "Sais" (= Akkadian *Sa-a-a*). Thus 2 Kgs 17:4 should have originally said "to So, to the king of Egypt." Cf. J. Bright, *A*

History of Israel, 275 and n. 17.

²⁴ The book 2 Kgs (17:5-6) is right when it mentions that Shalmaneser V captured Samaria, even though Sargon's inscriptions boastfully state in the first person: "I besieged and conquered Samaria (*Sa-me-ri-na*)." Cf. A. L. Oppenheim, *ANET,* 284. See J. Bright, *A History of Israel,* 275.

²⁵ According to an inscription of Sargon II, 27,290 Israelites were exiled. Cf. A. L. Oppenheim, *ANET,* 284-85.

²⁶ The mention of "Hamath," which fell in 720 B.C., is quite important because it implies a gradual colonization of Samaria. See S. Herrmann, *A History of Israel in Old Testament's Times* (Translated by J. Browden; Philadelphia, 1975), 251.

²⁷ One of Sargon's inscriptions reads: "[The town (Samaria) I] re[built] better than (it was) before and [settled] therein people from countries which [I] myself [had con]quered. I placed an officer of mine as governor over them and imposed upon them tribute as (is customary) for Assyrian citizens." Cf. A. L. Oppenheim, *ANET,* 284.

²⁸ See, e.g., the "Elijah Cycle" in 1 Kgs 17:1–2 Kgs 1:18, where the "deeds" of the prophet occupy a good portion of the narrative collection.

²⁹ For a more detailed discussion of the main factors that caused the shift from "oral" to "written" within the Israelite prophecy, see J. Blenkinsopp, *Prophecy in Israel,* 66, 73-74. Unlike the past when the sayings were addressed to a specific individual (e.g., a ruler), starting with the "classical" prophets the message was directed to a larger audience. This fact may be explained by the new international situation, the threat of Assyria which faced the nation as a whole. The emphasis on the role of the prophet will occur once again after the two kingdoms were engulfed by the great empires. This feature appears in Jeremiah, the Servant of Yahweh in Deutero-Isaiah, and the Deuteronomic portrait of Moses.

³⁰ F. I. Andersen and D. N. Freedmnan, *Hosea. A New*

Translation with Introduction and Commentary (AB 24; New York: Doubleday, 1980), 41-42.

[31] So J. Wellhausen, *Prolegomena zur Geschichte Israels* (Berlin, 1883), 398ff.

[32] So G. Fohrer, "Tradition und Interpretation im Alten Testament," *ZAW* 73 (1961): 24-30.

[33] According to W. Brueggemann (*Theology of the Old Testament. Testimony, Dispute, Advocacy* [Minneapolis: Fortress, 1997], 624), placing the accent on either of these elements depends on the mood of one's culture. Thus, in the nineteenth century the personality occupied a place of priority whereas in the twentieth century, following von Rad, a greater emphasis was placed on the collective aspects of faith.

[34] Among the eighth-century prophets, only Isaiah (Is 6) describes the divine "call" by which he was commissioned to proclaim God's word. The goal of this call narrative, as in the case of other calls (Moses: Exod 3:1-4:7; Gideon: Judges 6:11-24; Jeremiah: 1:4-10), is to suggest that God takes the initiative. Nonetheless, the stylized form of the "call" narratives mirrors a traditional, institutionalized form of faith. See W. Brueggemann, *Theology of the Old Testament*, 630.

[35] G. Pidoux ("Le Dieu qui vient. Espérance d'Israël," *Cahiers Théologiques* 17 [1947]: 12ff.) observes that history turns into Revelation as soon as God makes his appearance on the historical scene.

[36] A. S. Kapelrud, *The Prophets in the Shelter of Elyon*—G. W. Ahlström, JSOTSup 31 (1984), 175-83.

[37] Amos (5:2) announces people's perdition. Those who live now in Yahweh's land will be soon exiled (2:9; 7:11, 17). For Hosea (1:9), the covenant is considerably altered, and Isaiah (28:21) underscores the fact that Yahweh himself is marching in front of the nations in order to punish his people. In the same vein, Micah (3:12) announces the imminent ruin of Jerusalem. On this topic, see J. A. Soggin, "Der prophetische Gedanke über den heiligen Krieg, als Gericht

über Israel," *VT* 10 (1960): 79-83.

[38] The classical prophets sought to underline the healing character of the divine punishment. Thus an announcement of national destruction is an appeal to repentance (Hos 2:9/7), hence the purifying function of God's judgment (Is 1:21-26). See J. Lindblom, *Prophecy in Ancient Israel* (2nd ed.; Philadelphia: Fortress, 1963), 360ff.

[39] W. Eichrodt, *Theologie des Alten Testaments* (5th ed.; 2 vols.; Stuttgart, 1957), 1:241.

[40] H. Cazelles, *Introduction critique à l'Ancien Testament* (*Introduction à la Bible*, vol. 2; ed. H. Cazelles; Paris: Cerf, 1973), 331-61.

[41] According to K. Jaspers (*The Axial Age of Human History. Identity and Anxiety: Survival in Mass Society* [Glencoe, 1960], 597), the "axial age" coincides with the first millennium B.C. See also J. Blenkinsopp, *Prophecy in Israel*, 49 and n. 13.

[42] E. Day's view ("Is the Book of Hosea Exilic?," *AJSL* 26 [1909]: 108) that Hosea is just a legendary prophet for the simple fact that his name is not mentioned by 2 Kings cannot be accepted. According to C. Begg (*The Nonmention of Amos, Hosea and Micah in the Deuteronomistic History* [BN 32 (1986)]: 46-48), the explanation of this fact lies in Hosea's attitude toward Jehu (Hos 1:4), so different from that found in 2 Kgs 9-10.

[43] Various interpreters of Hosea from the second part of the nineteenth century and the beginning of the twentieth century refer to an old tradition mentioned by Epiphanius of Cyprus (*De vitis prophetarum*, PG 43, 415) that sets the prophet's birth in the city of Belemoth (Βελεμωθ) in the territory of the tribe of Issachar. See P. Haupt, "Hosea's Erring Spouse," *JBL* 34 (1915): 41-53.

[44] Cf. B. M. Vellas, ΩΣΗΕ. ΕΙΣΑΓΩΓΗ-ΜΕΤΑΦΡΑΣΙΣ ΕΚ ΤΟΥ ΕΒΡΑΙΚΟΥ-ΚΕΙΜΕΝΟΝ ΤΩΝ Ο '-ΣΧΟΛΙΑ (5 vols.; ΕΡΜΗΝΕΙΑ ΠΑΛΛΙΑΣ ΔΙΑΘΗΚΗΣ; Athens, 1947-50), 8. See the commentary on 1:1.

⁴⁵ See the commentary on 1:3.
⁴⁶ See the commentary on 1:8.
⁴⁷ See the commentary on 1:1. With respect to the length of Hosea's ministry, the rabbinic tradition differs from case to case. Thus *Piska* 33:9 observes: "For ninety years, The Most Holy One, blessed be He, has spoken to Israel by Hosea, but they have not returned." In addition, *Pesahim* 87a describes Hosea as an "elder" at the beginning of his ministry. Modern interpreters' views on the chronological frame of Hosea's ministry include: Harper (743-734 B.C.), Kutal, Mauchline (750-734 B.C.), Vellas, Offenheimer, Macintosh (750-725 B.C.), Tadmor (743-739 B.C.), and Wolff (752-724 B.C.).

⁴⁸ According to N. H. Tur-Sinai ([3] הלשון והספר vols.; Jerusalem, 1948-55], 304ff.), Hosea was originally from the Southern Kingdom, but he delivered his prophetic words to Israel so that they may return to "David, their king." Among his arguments: (a) the title (1:1) of the book mentions four kings from Judah and only one from Israel; (b) the prophet's kind words on Judah and Davidic dynasty (3:5; 4:15; 12:1); and (c) the normative value of the rabbinic assessment "the prophet who does not mention anything about his city, that prophet is from Jerusalem" (cf. R. Johanan, לאיכה רבתי 24:1, apud Y. Kyl, ספר הושע [Jerusalem: Mosad Harav Kook, 1973]).

⁴⁹ *Commentarius in Oseam*, PL 21, 963A: "After the people of Samaria migrated to the Assyrian territories, Saint Hosea, while being in Judah, was contemplating the time famous in miracles of king Hezekiah, under whom he exercised the prophetic mission."

⁵⁰ See the commentary on 8:5.
⁵¹ See the commentary on 4:15.
⁵² See the commentary on 2:17/15.
⁵³ See the commentary on 6:7.
⁵⁴ See the commentary on 5:8.

⁵⁵ See the commentary on 6:8.

⁵⁶ See the commentary on 10:11.

⁵⁷ Thus E. Sellin, *Das Zwölfprophetenbuch. Hosea* (3rd ed.; 2 vols.; KAT 12; Leipzig 1930), 1:6; Vellas, ΩΣΗΕ, 9.

⁵⁸ See A. Weiser and K. Elliger, *Das Buch der Zwölf Kleinen Propheten* (2 vols.; ATD 24-25; Göttingen, 1967), 1:13.

⁵⁹ See O. Eissfeldt, *Eileitung in das Alte Testament* (3rd ed.; Tübingen, 1964), 519. On the other hand, A. H. J. Gunneweg (*Mündliche und schriftliche Tradition der vorexilischen Prophetenbücher als Problem der neueren Prophetenforshung* [FRLANT 73; Göttingen, 1959], 101f.) considers Hosea a "cultic" prophet who was in service of an Israelite sanctuary. But Hosea's harsh critique of the cultic syncretism so widely spread in the Northern Kingdom does not strongly support Gunneweg's view.

⁶⁰ Compare Hos 4:15 with Am 4:4, and Hos 13:4 with Am 3:1, 2.

⁶¹ "Hoseas geistige Heimat," *ThLZ* 81 (1956): 83-94. Wolff's arguments were found unconvincing by, among others, R. Rendtorff ("Erwägungen zur Frühgeschichte des Prophetentums in Israel," *ZThK* 59 [1962]: 149ff.) and W. Rudolph (*Hosea* [KAT 13.1; Gütersloh: Gerd Mohn, 1966], 23). In our judgment, 1 Kgs 12:31 considered by Wolff a solid argument, aside from presenting some textual difficulties, does not refer categorically to an expulsion of the Levites, but rather to a gradual introduction of non-Levitic elements within the north-Israelite cult.

⁶² Cf. H. W. Wolff, *Hosea*, xxiii.

⁶³ *De vitis prophetarum*, PG 43, 415. According to an old tradition, Hosea died in Babylon, but his remains were brought to Tsephat in Galilee. Another tradition places the tomb of Hosea as far away as Tripolis in Phoenicia. See, for details, A. Scholz, *Commentar zum Buche des Propheten Hoseas* (Würzburg, 1882), xxv-xxvi.

⁶⁴ This division follows the principle of content: the first

part (section) more or less narrative, and the second part (section) made mostly of prophetic sayings. The editors of the JB divide this book into three parts: 1-3; 4:1-14:1; 14:2-10, underlining the shift in tone within the prophetic section (chapters 4-14). Other interpreters, for instance Wolff, focus rather on the individual units regarded in their literary succession.

[65] H. S. Nyberg, *Studien zum Hoseabuche. Zugleich ein Beitrag zur Klärung des Problems der alttestamentlichen Textkritik* (Uppsala Universitets Årsskrift; Uppsala: Almqvist & Wiksells, 1935), 17; E. M. Good, "The Composition of Hosea," *SEÅ* 31 (1966): 21-63.

[66] The expression was coined by Wolff (*Hosea*, xxv). On careful reading, one may notice that the book of Hosea is replete with short prophetic units, often loosely linked to each other. Jerome (*Praefatio in XII prophetas*, PL 28, 1015) was the first interpreter to observe this feature when he wrote: "Hosea is brief in speech, as if his book was made of independent sayings."

[67] See M. J. Buss, *The Prophetic Word of Hosea, a Morphological Study* (BZAW 111; Berlin, 1969), 31-32.

[68] Probably from the year 724 B.C. when king Hoshea ben Elah was imprisoned. See "Introduction. I. Historical Background: The Assyrian Expansion and the Last Years of Israel."

[69] With respect to the forms of the prophetic discourse, in general, see J. H. Hayes, ed., *Old Testament Form Criticism* (Trinity University Monograph Series in Religion 2; San Antonio: Trinity University Press, 1974) and, in the case of Hosea, see Buss' monograph and R. E. Clements, "Understanding the Book of Hosea," *Review and Expositor* 72 (1975): 405-423.

[70] *Hosea*, xxiii, and Wolff's commentary (passim).

[71] See J. Harvey, "Le 'rîb-Pattern,' réquisitoire prophétique sur la rupture de l'alliance," *Bibl* 43 (1962): 172-96.

⁷² *A Critical and Exegetical Commentary on Hosea*, lxii.
⁷³ See the commentary on 12:10/9.
⁷⁴ See the commentary on 6:1-3.
⁷⁵ *Hosea*, 60-66. See also D. N. Freedman, "Pottery, Poetry, and Prophecy," *JBL* 96 (1977): 5-26.
⁷⁶ On parallelism, see W. G. E. Watson, *Classical Hebrew Poetry. A Guide to its Techniques* (2nd ed.; reprint; *JSOT* 26; Sheffield, 1995), 114-159.
⁷⁷ According to H. S. Nyberg ("Das textkritische Problem des Alten Testaments am Hoseabuch demonstriert," *ZAW* 52 [1934]: 241-54), the peculiarities belong to the lexical-grammatical register rather than to vocalism which is due to the Masoretes' intervention.
⁷⁸ W. Rudolph, "Eigentümlichkeiten der Sprache Hoseas," *Studia Biblica et Semitica* (1960): 313. See also A. Szabø, "Textual Problems in Amos and Hosea," *VT* 25 (1975): 500-524.
⁷⁹ "Osée," in E. Jacob, C.-A. Keller, S. Amsler, *Osée, Joël, Abdias, Amos* (Commentaire de l'Ancien Testament 11a; Neuchatel: Delachaux et Niestlé, 1965), 12. See also the commentaries on 5:13; 11:3 and 13:5.
⁸⁰ Among those who tried to reconstruct the original form, one may cite H. S. Nyberg, *ZAW* 52 (1934): 241-54; D. Barthélemy, "Redécouverte d'un chaînon manquant de l'histoire de la Septante," *RB* 60 (1953): 18-29; idem, *Les devanciers d'Aquila. Première publication intégrale du texte des fragments du Dodekaprophéton*, VTSup 10 (1963).
⁸¹ On the differences between LXX and MT, see L. Treitel, *Die alexandrinischen Uebersetzung des Buches Hosea* (Karlsruhe, 1887), passim; G. H. Patterson, *The Septuagint Text of Hosea compared with the Massoretic Text*, (New Haven: Tuttle, Morehouse & Taylor, 1891); H.-D. Neef, "Der Septuaginta-Text und der Massoreten-Text des Hoseabuches im Vergleich," *Bibl* 67 (1986): 195-220. Compared with the LXX of Samuel, the Greek version of Hosea is of less importance in

emending the MT. Cf. A. A. Macintosh, *Hosea,* lxxvii.

[82] This is an indication that the LXX was confronted with the same Hebrew text which reached us. Cf. A. A. Macintosh, *Hosea,* lxxvii.

[83] Note the following examples of disagreement between the LXX and the MT: σύνεσιν αὐτῆς "her understanding" for תִּקְוָה "hope" (2:17/15), ἡρέτισε Χαναναίους "he has chosen the Canaanites" for סָר סָבְאָם "they drink to excess" (4:18), τοῦ χρίειν "to anoint" for מִמַּשָּׂא "under burden" (8:10).

[84] See H.-D. Neef, *Bibl* 67 (1986): 220.

[85] *Hosea,* lxxiv-lxxxiii.

[86] *Duodecim prophetae* (Septuaginta, Vetus Testamentum Graecum 13; Göttingen, 1963), 345ff.

[87] Cf. A. Gelston, ed., *The Old Testament in Syriac According to the Peshitta Version* (Leiden: Brill, 1980).

[88] Cf. A. Sperber, ed., *The Bible in Aramaic Based on Old Manuscripts and Printed Texts* (vol. 3: *The Latter Prophets According to Targum Jonathan;* 2nd impression; Leiden: Brill, 1992).

[89] A. A. Macintosh (*Hosea,* lxxv), who resorts to a few emendations, points to the subjective character of such emendations, hence the reluctance on the part of the contemporary scholars to posit an alteration of the Hebrew text.

[90] *Commentar zum Buche des Propheten Hoseas,* xxviiiff.

[91] *Amos and Hosea* (ICC; Edinburgh: T & T Clark, 1905), clixf.

[92] There are still some differences among scholars with respect to this topic. For instance, in Harper's view (*Hosea,* clx), Hos 4:15 and 5:5, though referring to Judah, were written by Hosea himself. On the other hand, B. S. Childs (*Introduction to the Old Testament as Scripture* [5th ed.; Philadelphia: Fortress, 1979], 379) considers 5:10, 14 as part of Hosean preaching.

⁹³ *Osée*, 934.

⁹⁴ J. Mauchline (*The Book of Hosea. Introduction and Exegesis* [*The Interpreter's Bible*, vol. 6; eds. G. A. Buttrick et al.; Nashville: Abingdon, 1956], 564), defending the Hosean authorship of Hos 8:14, brings the following argument: if this passage was composed in the south how should we explain the prophet's negative attitude toward Judah?

⁹⁵ *Liber Prophetae Hoseae. E textu originali latine et metrice versus, explanatus, notis criticis et philologicis illustratus* (*Commentarii in Prophetas Minores* 1; Olomucii, 1929), 30-32.

⁹⁶ *Die älteste Geschichtsschreibung und Prophetie Israels. Von Samuel bis Amos und Hosea* (SAT 2.1; 2nd ed.; Göttingen, 1921), 365. Gressmann argues that the sayings centered on the judgment theme and those focusing on reconciliation are complementary.

⁹⁷ For instance, Jeremiah, on the very eve of the great national tragedy of the year 586 B.C., tries to encourage his contemporaries, promising them a new covenant with Yahweh (Jer 31:31-34). See A. Lods, *Histoire de la littérature hebraïque et juive, depuis des origines jusqu'à la ruine de l'état juif (135 après J. Chr.)* (Paris: Payot, 1950), 249.

⁹⁸ B. S. Childs (*Introduction to the Old Testament*, 382-83) shows that, although many of the Old Testament prophetic sayings are influenced by wisdom literature (e.g., Amos, Isaiah), the influence occurs not on the redactional level but rather on the primary proclamation. With respect to Hos 14:10, this wisdom saying functions in a "redactional role," labeling Hosea's sayings as wisdom.

⁹⁹ *Hosea*, 142.

¹⁰⁰ *Hosea*, lii.

¹⁰¹ *De civitate Dei*, 18, 29. See A. A. Macintosh, *Hosea*, liii.

¹⁰² It is surprising, though, that Hosea's book does not appear in either of these lists: "The Scroll of the Twelve" (Murabbat, ca. A.D. 135): Joel, Amos, Obadiah, Jonah, Micah, Nahum, Habakkuk, Zephaniah, Haggai; or the "Greek

Scroll of the Twelve Prophets": Jonah, Micah, Naum, Habakkuk, Zephaniah, Zechariah. Cf. G. -W. Nebe, "Eine neue Hosea-Handschrift aus Höhle 4 von Qumran," *ZAW* 91 (1979): 292.

[103] *On the Change of Names*, 24, 139.

[104] *The Antiquities of the Jews*, 10, 2, 2.

[105] An historical overview of the interpretations occasioned by Hos 1 and 3 may be found in S. Bitter, *Die Ehe des Propheten Hosea. Eine auslegungsgeschichtliche Untersuchung* (Göttinger Theologische Arbeiten 3; Göttingen: Vandenhoeck & Ruprecht, 1975).

[106] See, among others, W. Vogels, "'Osée-Gomer' car et comme 'Yahweh-Israël.' Os 1-3," *NRTh* 103 (1981): 711-727; idem, "Diachronic and Synchronic Studies of Hosea 1-3," *BZ*, NF 28 (1984): 94-98; B. Renaud, "Osée 1-3: analyse diachronique et lecture synchronique. Problèmes de méthode," *RevSR* 57 (1983): 249-60.

[107] Among the patristic writers embracing such an allegoric interpretation one may mention Origen, Didim the Blind, Cyril of Alexandria (oscillating like Jerome between a historical and allegoric meaning), Isidore of Sevilla. Within the sphere of the Jewish interpretation, the Targum of Jonathan offers an allegoric paraphrase: איזיל אתנבי נבואה על יתבי קרתא טעיתא "Go (and) speak a prophecy against the inhabitants of the idolatrous city," representing the starting point for a series of allegoric interpreters such as Japhet ben Ali Halevy, Shlomo ben Isaac, Josesph ben Kara. Among the modern interpreters, one may mention von Hoonacker, Regnier, Hirschfeld, Kaufmann ("a dramatic prophetic allegory"), Humbert, North.

[108] The father of the "visionary" interpretation was ibn Ezra (twelfth century), who, based on Num 12:6, asserted that all the prophetic actions occurred during a nocturnal vision. Following in his foot's steps are other authors from the Middle Ages such as, Maimonides, David Kimchi, Jo-

seph ben Kaspi, Isaac Abrabanel, Shlomo ben Melek, Samuel Almosmino. A similar interpretation is found in Calvin. Today, the "visionary" interpretation is not so popular (Ridderbos).

[109] See C. H. Gordis, "Hosea's Marriage and Message: A New Approach," *HUCA* 25 (1954): 11.

[110] Among others: Ephrem Syrus, Eusebius, Basil the Great, Theodore of Mopsuestia, Ambrosius of Milan, Theodoret of Cyrus, Theodor bar Konay, Jacob of Sarug, Abu'l Farag, Theophylact of Bulgaria. Among the modern interpreters: Nowack, Marti, Smith, Robinson, Schmidt, Mauchline. Some of the proponents of the historical interpretation such as Irenaeus and Augustine tried to diminish the "contrast" between the divine command and the moral law of the Old Testament by offering a typological interpretation. These authors insist on the theological significance of the prophetic action without negating its historicity. Thus Hosea's marriage to a prostitute is a "type" or prefiguration of the conversion of the idolatrous people to Christ. Cf. Augustine, *De Doctrina Christiana*, CSEL 80, 91. An echo of this typological interpretation may be found in P. Pezron, *Essay d'un commentaire literal et historique sur les prophètes* (Paris, 1693).

[111] See J. L. Mays, *Hosea* (OTL; Philadelphia: Westminster, 1969), 23f.

[112] See the commentary on 1:2.

[113] H. H. Rowley, "The Marriage of Hosea," *Bulletin of the John Rylands Library* 39 (1956): 200-233.

[114] See the commentary on 1:2.

[115] P. Humbert, "Les trois premiers chapitres d'Osée," *RHR* 77 (1918): 158.

[116] Mauchline, *Hosea*, 562f.

[117] Thus, P. Humbert, *RHR* 77 (1918): 170; idem, "Osée le prophète bédouin," *RHPhR* 1 (1921): 100; P. Haupt, *JBL* 34 (1915): 42; L. W. Batten, "Hosea's Message and Marriage,"

JBL 48 (1929): 271f.

[118] Cf. K. Budde, "Der Abschnitt Hosea 1-3 und seine grundlegende-religionsgeschichtliche Bedeutung," *ThStKr* 96 (1925): 7.

[119] Cf. C. H. Toy, "Note on Hosea 1-3," *JBL* 32 (1913): 75-79.

[120] Cf. R. Kittel, *Geschichte des Volkes Israel* (2nd ed.; Stuttgart, 1925), 348f.; Lindblom, *Hosea literarische untersucht* (Acta Academiae Aboensis. Humaniora 5; Âbo: Âbo Akademie, 1927), 41.

[121] A. D. Tushingham, "A Reconsideration of Hosea, Chapters 1-3," *JNES* 12 (1953): 156f.

[122] See H. H. Rowley, *Bulletin of the John Rylands Library* 39 (1956): 200-233.

[123] See the commentary on 2:2/1:11.

[124] See the commentary on 3:2.

[125] See H. W. Robinson, *The Hebrew Prophets. Studies in Hosea and Ezekiel* (London, 1948), 16f.

COMMENTARY

The Book's Title (1:1)

1:1 The word[1] of Yahweh that occurred to Hosea,[2] son of Beeri, in the days of Uzziah, Jotham, Ahaz, Hezekiah, kings of Judah, and in the days of Jeroboam, son of Joash, king of Israel.
The introductory formula דְּבַר־יְהוָה אֲשֶׁר הָיָה אֶל "The word of Yahweh that occurred to" is found, with minor variations, in the titles of other prophetic books (Ezek 1:3; Joel 1:1; Jon 1:1; Mic 1:1; Zeph 1:1; Hag 1:1; Zech 1:1; Mal 1:1).

The construct phrase דְּבַר־יְהוָה "the word of Yahweh" refers to the entire prophetic message, including besides Yahweh's word concerning Israel and Judah, the divine command given to Hosea, and the prophet's personal life as a response.

Hosea's name, הוֹשֵׁעַ,[3] which appears also in its longer form, הוֹשַׁעְיָה (Jer 42:1; 43:2), means "he helped, saved" (perfect Hiphil of ישׁע),[4] and expresses the joy occasioned by the birth of a child or other happy event, viewed as a result of God's saving intervention.[5]

According to the book's title, Hosea was the son of Beeri, בְּאֵרִי,[6] which might be related to the ancient Beeroth[7] on the Ephraimite border (today *el-bire*, two miles southwest of Bethel). But, as the derivation of a personal name from a place-name seems unlikely, the name Beeri should be considered as Hosea's own name, an expression of joy at the birth of a child, meaning "My Spring!" or "O Spring!" with reference to the continuity of a clan.[8]

Interestingly, the author dedicates more space to the historical background than to his own biography. He lists five kings, four from Judah (Uzziah, 787-756 B.C.; Jotham, 756-741 B.C.; Ahaz, 741-725 B.C.; Hezekiah, 725-697 B.C.)[9] and only one from Israel (Jeroboam II, 784-743 B.C.). The discrepancy in number may be explained by Hosea's view on monarchy: the legitimate Judah contrasted with the corrupted Israel.[10] Based on this list, as well as on the content of the book, we may assume that Hosea was active as a prophet of Yahweh between 748-724 B.C.[11]

What is the theological significance of this title? First, the word of God is not a subjective state of mind but, as one of the ancient interpreters, Theodore of Mopsuestia,[12] puts it, a dynamic event (γιγνομένην), a divine energy (τῇ ἐνεργείᾳ ... τῇ θείᾳ), "happening" or "occurring" to (MT: הָיָה; LXX: ἐγενήθη) rather than being possessed or induced by the prophet.

Second, though its origin is beyond this physical world, the "word of God" has nothing to do with the mythical realm. On the contrary, the transcendental word comes down to a concrete human being, Hosea son of Beeri, a man among men, living in a society with kings and subjects, at a certain moment in time. In his commentary on Hosea, Theophylact of Bulgaria[13] shows that by approaching Hosea, the word of God began a "soft" but "disciplining" dialogue with men: "But the word came (γίνεται) to (πρὸς) Hosea as a teacher of God, softly speaking to the disobedient and making them return through what he says and does.... And the Word (ὁ Λόγος) comes to those who are heading for salvation, and by disciplining the irrational part of the soul (τὸ ἄλογον τῆς ψυχῆς) he prevails over them."

Third, by its willingness to accommodate itself to the level of human understanding, in a concrete historical setting, the word of God occurring to Hosea might be seen as a type of and a step toward the great coming of the Logos, that is the Incarnation (Jn 1:14: ὁ λόγος σὰρξ ἐγένετο "the Word became flesh").

Notes

[1] Tg: ... פתגם נבואה מן קדם יוי דהוה עם "The word of prophecy from the Lord that was with... ."

[2] MT: הוֹשֵׁעַ; LXX: Ὡσῆε; V: Osee.

[3] This name is borne in the Old Testament by four persons (Num 13:8; 2 Kgs 15:30; Neh 10:24; 1 Chr 27:20). Outside the Bible, it is found in one of the fifth century B.C. papyri from Elephantine, e.g., "Hosea the son of Yatom." Cf. M. Ginsberg, *ANET*, 492.

[4] The attestation of the longer form is a strong argument against Koehler's suggestion that Hosea's name would derive from יוֹשִׁיעַ and יְהוֹ (KBL, 228). Moreover, during the period of the monarchy the usual way of forming proper names was using a perfect followed by a noun (most of the time omitted), e.g., "Nathan" (נָתַן) "He (Yahweh) gave."

[5] M. Noth, *Die israelitischen Personennamen im Rahmen der gemeinsemitischen Namengebung* (BWANT 3.10; Stuttgart, 1928), 175f.

[6] The name appears one more time in the Old Testament (Gen 26:34). It is also found in one of the El Amarna tablets: "Bieri, the ruler of Hashabu" (EA 174:3; cf. *The Amarna Letters*. Edited and Translated by W. L. Moran (Baltimore & London: The Johns Hopkins University Press, 1992), 260.

[7] Cf. K. von Rabenau, "Beeroth," *Biblisch-historisches Handwörterbuch* 1 (eds. B. Reiche and L. Rost; Göttingen, 1964-66), 210f.

[8] Cf. H. W. Wolff, *Hosea*, 5. Jerome (*In Osee prophetam*, PL 25, 820) translates "well": "Thus, that 'savior' (i.e., Hosea) is the son of Beeri, that is 'my well.'"

[9] The years of each king's reign are taken from A. Jepsen,

Untersuchungen zur israelitisch-jüdischen Chronologie (BZAW 88; Berlin, 1964), 42.

[10] On the contrary, some scholars (e.g., Wolff, Macintosh) see in this discrepancy the proof that the title was inserted into Hosea's book by a Judaean redactor.

[11] For details, see "Hosea: The Man and the Prophet."

[12] *Commentarius in Oseam prophetam*, PG 66, 125.

[13] Theophylactus of Bulgaria, *Commentarius in Oseam*, PG 126, 576 B.

I. HOSEA'S CONJUGAL DRAMA AND YAHWEH-ISRAEL'S COVENANT: FROM A LATENT CRISIS TO AN OBVIOUS BREAKUP (1-3)

1. Hosea's Marriage and Children (1:2-9)

2. The beginning of the word[1] of Yahweh through[2] Hosea. Yahweh said to Hosea: "Go, take for yourself a wife of whoredom, and (have) children of whoredom, for the land commits great whoredom far away from Yahweh." 3. Then he went and took Gomer, the daughter of Diblaim. She conceived and bore him[3] a son. 4. And Yahweh said to him:[4] "Call his name Jezreel![5] For in a little while I will punish the house of Jehu[6] for the blood of Jezreel, and I will put an end to the kingdom of the house of Israel. 5. And on that day I will break the bow of Israel in the valley of Jezreel." 6. And she conceived again and gave birth to a daughter. Then he[7] said to him: "Call her name 'Lo-Ruhamah.'[8] For I will no longer show compassion towards the house of Israel; on the contrary, I will withdraw it from them.[9] 7. But I will show compassion towards the house of Judah[10] and I will save them by Yahweh their God. I will not save them by bow or sword or weapons of war, by horses or horsemen." 8. After she weaned Lo-Ruhamah, she conceived[11] and gave birth to a son. 9. And he said: "Call his name 'Lo-Ammi' for you are not my people, and I, I am not for you."

The passage 1:2-9, marked by symmetry and unity, contains the first four divine commands given to Hosea at the beginning of his public ministry. The first command refers to Hosea's marriage to Gomer (v. 2), whereas the following three commands concern the children's symbolic names (vv. 4, 6, 9).[12]

The accent falls primarily on God's severe judgment toward Israel (king, land, people). Each baleful name of the three children carries along a threat, each time harsher in scope and intensity.

Since the prophet appears here in the third person, vis-à-vis the autobiographic chapter 3, most modern interpreters[13] believe that 1:2-9 was written by one of Hosea's disciples. Nevertheless, there is no need to resort to such a hypothesis. The third person account of the beginning of Hosea's ministry may be explained as an expression of the emphatic style used by the prophet writing under God's inspiration.

"The beginning of the word" (v. 2) refers to the beginning of Hosea's ministry that coincided with his marriage.[14] The prophet is portrayed as an instrument "through"[15] whom God speaks to his people. Speaking of the choice of "in" (*in*) in his translation of the Hebrew Bible into Latin (the Vulgate), Jerome[16] makes an interesting point on the deeper meaning of this preposition: "It is one thing for the Lord to speak in (*in*) Hosea; it is another thing for him to speak to (*ad*) Hosea. 'In' Hosea does not mean 'to' Hosea himself but 'through' (*per*) Hosea 'to' (*ad*) others." On the other hand, Cyril of Alexandria,[17] based on the LXX reading ἐν "in," interprets God's speaking "in" Hosea in terms of inspiration: "For God begins to reveal the mysteries in (ἐν) the prophet, according to what was clearly said through another prophet somewhere, 'I shall stand on my watch tower, and I shall climb on a rock so that I may see what the Lord God will speak in me' [Hab 2:1]. For the God of all reveals the knowledge of the future things to the saints by pouring (ἐνιεὶς) it into their mind (εἰς νοῦν)."

The first of the four commands given to Hosea by Yahweh refers to his marriage. To express the conjugal act, the Hebrew language uses the idiom לקח לוֹ אִשָּׁה "to take to himself a wife" (cf. Gen 4:19; 24:3). Hosea is ordered to marry אֵשֶׁת זְנוּנִים "a wife of whoredom"[18] which probably should be understood as a woman inclined or given to prostitution.[19] This realistic interpretation may be found in most of the ancient and modern interpreters.[20] At the other end of the semantic spectrum there is the metaphorical interpretation which sees in Hosea's wife a "worshiper of Baal."[21] For the proponents of the metaphorical interpretation, the accent does not fall on the wife's moral profile but rather on her faithlessness toward Yahweh. She was one of the numerous Israelites who rebelled against God by importing Canaanite elements into their monotheistic religion or at the worst by embracing other beliefs. Between the realistic and metaphorical interpretations lies Wolff's view labeled by its author a "metaphorical-ritual explanation."[22] According to Wolff, Hosea's wife was a young Israelite woman who before marriage was involved in the Canaanite rites of initiation prescribed for the future brides and intended to assure their fertility.

The weakness of both interpretations, metaphorical and metaphorical-ritual, is that they diminish the strength of the metaphor by erasing the differences between the two levels of comparison (i.e., the inter-human and divine-human levels). Both levels are dominated by religious relationships either between Yahweh and Israel or between Israel and the Canaanite deities. By giving the faithlessness of Hosea's wife a religious coloration, these interpretations ignore the very nature of a metaphor which implies two objects or actions, at the same time different and analogous. On the contrary, the realistic interpretation keeps distinct the two levels by considering the wife's faithlessness a moral matter. Thus, the inter-human level represented by the conjugal union between Hosea and his given-to-prostitution wife becomes a type or symbol for the divine-human level defined by the covenant between Yahweh and his faithless people.

As for Hosea's marriage to a woman given to prostitution, the ancient interpreters focus more on the prophet's moral qualities than on his wife's promiscuous inclinations. Thus, Cyril of Alexandria[23] points to Hosea's willingness to fulfill God's command, "When Hosea heard that he must join a shameless and promiscuous woman leading an accursed life, he did not give up; he did not hesitate; he did not prayed to be dismissed; but, as it is fitting in most shameless cases, and without delay, he quickly seized (her) as if he was overwhelmed by the desire for (that) woman." Interestingly, when mentioning Gomer, Cyril resorts to a typological interpretation, "Gomer is the type of a seduced soul that has chosen to spend (its) life in a shameful and indecent way, while the prophet fulfils the icon of the one who is from above, from heaven, that is, of God the Word (coming) from the Father, who, having joined spiritually (νοητῶς) our souls, implants (ἐνίησι) (in them) the seeds of the virtuous life."

As an attempt to alleviate the contrast between the prophet and a "wife of whoredom," Irenaeus[24] draws one's attention to the beneficial result of such an odd association: "From these people God will build the Church, which will be made holy through the union with the Son of God as this woman was made holy by her union with the prophet: Paul says that the unbelieving wife is made holy by her believing husband (1 Cor 7:14)." Similarly, Jerome[25] praises the prophet for converting his wife to a life of honor: "As we follow the story, meanwhile we should not blame the prophet, if he converted a prostitute to virtue, but we should rather praise him because he turned a bad woman into a good one.... Hence, we understand that it was not the prophet who lost virtue by joining with a prostitute, but rather the latter gained virtue that she never had before."

וְיַלְדֵי זְנוּנִים "And children of whoredom" relies on the former imperative "take" which refers also to a "wife of whoredom." Is this due to a sort of narrative "economy" or does it mirror the author's intention to set mother (Israel of the past) and children (the Israelites of the eighth century B.C.), although separated in time, on the same level of faithlessness?[26] At any rate, this abbreviated way of speaking, with one verb used for two objects, should not lead one to the conclusion that these children were born before the marriage, and thus are not Hosea's.[27] The qualification "of whoredom" is given to Hosea's children because they are also children of a "wife of whoredom," meaning that they are not necessarily inclined or given to prostitution like their mother.[28] Probably, the position of this phrase near to that defining Hosea's wife as well as the absence of a verb are meant to underscore this transfer of qualification from mother to children.

"For the land commits great whoredom far away from Yahweh" is an explanation (כִּי "for") of Yahweh's command to Hosea to marry a "wife of whoredom" and have with her "children of whoredom." "The land" (הָאָרֶץ) refers to the people of Israel,[29] the nation, rather than to the soil. The clause "commits great whoredom" is a tentative translation of the *constructio praegnans*[30] (זָנֹה תִזְנֶה), gravitating around the same root as זְנוּנִים "whoredom," i.e., זנה "to commit whoredom," which in a religious context designates the sin of idolatry (cf. Lev 17:7; Num 14:33; 15:39; Deut 31:16; Judg 2:17; 1 Chr 5:25). In addition, the phrase "far away from Yahweh" (מֵאַחֲרֵי יְהוָה)[31] emphasizes the idea that any act of idolatry or religious syncretism is an act of apostasy from Yahweh. Thus, while going after other deities, the Israelites abandon Yahweh, they distance themselves from him. Cyril of Alexandria[32] explains: "She (Israel) committed whoredom behind (ἀπὸ ὄπισθεν) the Lord, having not kept on following (him). For she became an apostate (ἀποστάτης) and a profane being, and having dedicated herself to the worship of the idols, she hurt the Lord."

Yahweh commands Hosea to marry a "wife of whoredom" (v. 2), but the choice for "Gomer, the daughter of Diblaim," matching the description, lies with the prophet himself (v. 3). By doing so, God wants Hosea, his partner of dialogue, to act freely and to share with him within the history of salvation.

The name "Gomer" (גֹּמֶר),[33] (as a man's name in Gen 10:2f.; cf. 1 Chr 1:5f.; Ezek 38:6),[34] is the abbreviated form of the name גְּמַרְיָהוּ (Jer 36:10-12, 25; cf. 29:3), from the root גמר "to finish, to accomplish." In its longer form, the name means "Yahweh accomplished (the birth of a child)." We should mention here Jerome's[35] allegorical interpretation of Hosea's wife based on her name, "complete in promiscuity and a perfect daughter of voluptuousness."

With respect to the name of Gomer's father, "Diblaim" (דִּבְלָיִם), this hardly looks like a personal name. The dual ending ‑ַיִם, attested as early as the time of the LXX (Δεβηλαίμ), is more appropriate with place-names than personal names (e.g., מִצְרַיִם "Egypt").[36] The same cloud of uncertainty hovers over the etymology and meaning of this proper name. Jerome[37] took it as a dual number of the noun דְּבֵלָה "fig" (BDB, 179a: "lump of pressed figs, pressed [fig-]cake"), hence the interpretation, a very cheap (two figs worth!) prostitute.[38] Note, nevertheless, that the dual of this noun is not attested elsewhere. Macintosh[39] relates this name to the Ammonite form *dblks*, consisting of *ks*, perhaps a variant of the Edomite/north Arabian god's name *Qōs*, and the common noun *dbl* "prince" (cf. Hebrew *zebul*, Ugaritic *zbl* in *zbl ym* "Prince Sea"). But, the Hebrew reflex of the Proto Semitic **d̠*, present in the root from which this noun derives, i.e., **d̠-b-l*, is not *d*, but rather *z*, as in *zebul*. Thus, Hebrew "Diblaim" cannot be connected with Ammonite *dblks*.

The presence of the personal pronoun לוֹ "to him" underscores the Hosean paternity of the three children who are about to be mentioned along with God's threats against Israel.

Hosea's marriage to Gomer is followed by the birth and naming of the first child (v. 4).[40] The name "Jezreel" (יִזְרְעֶאל "May God sow!") was uncommon as a personal name in biblical times; it appears only twice in the entire Old Testament, here and in 1 Chr 4:3. But as a toponym, "Jezreel" had a deep resonance in the hearts of Hosea's listeners. It refers to both the town and the valley of the same name located between the highlands of Galilee and Samaria, northwest of Mount Gilboa.[41]

"Jezreel" in the first part of v. 4 designates the town of the same name[42] (today the Arab village of *Zerʿin*). God's judgment connected with the first child's name concerns "the house of Jehu," that is, Jehu's dynasty. To what does "the blood of Jezreel" (דְּמֵי יִזְרְעֶאל)[43] for which the dynasty of Jehu is held accountable refer? At the onset, any reference to the execution of Naboth (1 Kgs 21) should be excluded since the Omride dynasty (i.e., Ahab and his wife Jezebel) rather than Jehu's was guilty of that crime.[44] In order to answer this question a few glimpses into the history of the north-Israelite monarchy might be quite useful.

In 876 B.C., after an uproar between various factions occasioned by king Zimri's suicide, Omri, a general of the army, accedes to the throne of Israel, founding one of the more important dynasties in the history of the northern state (1 Kgs 16:23-28).[45] Though socio-economically and militarily the Omride dynasty succeeded in reviving some of the past fame, nevertheless religiously there was a time of regression marked by an open apostasy from Yahweh. Through a political marriage with king Ahab, Omri's son, the Phoenician princess Jezebel came to Samaria with a whole religious agenda: to introduce massively and to support zealously Baalism. In this setting dominated by religious syncretism and moral decadence, the prophet Elisha, the champion of the true Yahwism, played an important role in the demise of the Omride dynasty and the rise of Jehu (2 Kgs 9-10).

It was in 843 B.C. when by a *coup d'état* the general Jehu seized the throne. While Jehoram, the last member of the Omride dynasty, was recuperating from his wounds in Jezreel, one of the "sons of the prophets" was dispatched by Elisha to Ramoth-Gilead to anoint Jehu king over Israel. Emboldened by this great prophet's support, Jehu kills Jehoram of Israel and Ahaziah of Judah, and has the queen mother Jezebel thrown from a window. Israel is cast into a bath of blood. Actual and potential enemies were exterminated at Jehu's command. Eventually, Jehu reached the capital, massacred the worshipers of Baal, and destroyed their temple, posing himself as a defender of Yahwism. In Jehu's own words the bloody purge just accomplished was out of "zeal for Yahweh" (2 Kgs 10:16). Further, the author of 2 Kgs 10:30 assessing Jehu's actions against the Omride dynasty concluded that they were according to the will of Yahweh.

How could we resolve the obvious contrast between these favorable views found in 2 Kgs and Hosea's oracle on God's judgment of "the house of Jehu"? The answer is to be found nowhere but in 2 Kgs. Evaluating Jehu's life and reign, the author of 2 Kgs 10:31 makes a pertinent observation: "But Jehu was not careful to follow the law of the Lord the God of Israel with all his heart; he did not turn from the sins of Jeroboam, which he caused Israel to commit." Although for a while Jehu was the instrument of God's judgment concerning the Omride dynasty, he himself fell into "the sins of Jeroboam," that is, idolatry. Thus, from an instrument of judgment at God's disposal Jehu becomes, in Hosea's inspired view, an object of the same judgment. This interpretation is supported by the basic meaning of the root פקד "to visit," which in a context of judgment like that of 1:4 may be rendered "to punish."[46] As the Judge of all, Yahweh is free in choosing times "to visit" or to check his rational creatures' moral behavior. At the time when Jehu killed the last representative of the Omride dynasty, Yahweh was "visiting" the sin of the latter, but a few years later, the same God came to "visit" Jehu's reign. This king's violent actions against Omri's house as well as his own idolatrous inclinations, already remarked by the book of 2 Kgs, are now "visited" or checked by Yahweh through the prism of his eternal law. Even though Jehu's contemporaries regarded him as a defender of Yahwism, now he and his dynasty are found guilty of "the blood of Jezreel," which refers to both murder and idolatry.

God's judgment concerns not only the dynasty of Jehu, but also "the kingdom of the house of Israel" (מַמְלְכוּת בֵּית יִשְׂרָאֵל), which in Hosea's book designates the north-Israelite monarchy.

According to this prophecy, the punishment of Jehu's dynasty as well as the end of the north-Israelite monarchy had to occur "in a little while" (עוֹד מְעַט; cf. Exod 17:4; Ps 37:10). The first threat was indeed fulfilled in 743 B.C. by the assassination of king Zechariah, the last representative of Jehu's dynasty, at Ibleam, not far from Jezreel (2 Kgs

15:8-13; cf. 10:30).⁴⁷ As for the second punishment, the end of the monarchy, this took some time, getting through the crisis of Syro-Ephraimite war (733 B.C.), and culminating with the imprisonment of the last king Hoshea and the fall of Samaria (722/1 B.C.).

Here, as in the case of Maher-shalal-hash-baz, Isaiah's son (Is 8:3), the word of God comes to dwell in Hosea's son Jezreel, as a living sign up to its fulfillment. This temporary "dwelling" in a flesh-and-bone human being was viewed as a type of the Incarnation of the Logos by Cyril of Alexandria⁴⁸ and Jerome.⁴⁹ Having translated "Jezreel" with "the seed of God" (σπορὰ Θεοῦ), Cyril goes on: "For from her [i.e., "the synagogue of the Judaeans"] was born the first-born (πρωτότοκον), namely, Christ, who truly is the seed of God. For the Son is born from the Father, although he became flesh." On the other hand, Jerome remarks that "Jezreel" is "a type of the seed of God (*seminis Dei*) and the revenge of his blood refers to the Passion of the Lord."

This threat refers to the "bow of Israel" (קֶשֶׁת יִשְׂרָאֵל) which is to be broken "on that day" (בַּיּוֹם הַהוּא)⁵⁰ in the "valley of Jezreel" (עֵמֶק יִזְרְעֶאל)⁵¹ (v. 5).

As the bow in the Old Testament (Gen 49:24; Job 29:20; Jer 49:35; Hab 3:9; Zech 9:10) and the ancient Near Eastern literature⁵² was a symbol of power,⁵³ we may conclude that the whole military might in which Israel put her trust is now threatened with annihilation. Hosea follows a sort of gradation in launching these threats from particular (Jehu's dynasty) to general (the north-Israelite monarchy and the nation as a whole).

Is the prophetic saying in v. 5 a *vaticinium ex eventu*,⁵⁴ a prophetic statement centered on a well known battlefield such as the valley of Jezreel,⁵⁵ or an actual prophecy alluding to a future event? Given the hypothetical status of the first two views, we would like to stay with the traditional interpretation which, relying on the authority of the Scripture, considers v. 5 a piece of authentic prophecy.

To what events in the history of Israel does this prophecy refer? Probably, it alludes to the events of 733 B.C. when, during the Syro-Ephraimite war, the Assyrian king Tiglath-pileser III occupied a large territory of the north-Israelite state, including the fertile valley of Jezreel (2 Kgs 15:29).[56]

For Cyril of Alexandria,[57] this prophecy refers literally to the victory of Hazael of Damascus (842-806 B.C.) over Israel, and spiritually it points to Christ's resurrection: "Having been laid in the tomb, he [i.e., Christ] rose again, turning their insidious schemes into nothing, and breaking the bow, he is no longer subject to suffering."

Verses 6 and 7 describe the birth of the second child of Hosea, a girl who is to be named לֹא רֻחָמָה "Lo-Ruhamah" ("Without-Compassion").[58] Two prophetic sayings, one for Israel, another for Judah, are made public with this occasion.

Modern scholars argue for the non-Hosean authorship of v. 7 based on the simple fact that Judah is mentioned by name in a context of salvation.[59] Since the assumption of these scholars that Hosea could concern himself only with Israel is not a strong argument, we should hold the traditional view by considering this verse a part of Hosea's book.

If in the case of Jezreel, the doom oracle is to be fulfilled עוֹד מְעַט "in a little while" (v. 4), with respect to Hosea's daughter it does come with no delay. The prophet declares that Yahweh will no longer show compassion toward the Northern Kingdom. The realization of the prophetic saying coincides in time with the birth of Hosea's daughter.

A gradation regarding the threats, similar to that found

in vv. 4-5, may be discerned in v. 6. The final part of this verse emphasizes the idea of abandonment by making clear that Yahweh not only does not show compassion to them anymore but worse, he is now also withdrawing his compassion from Israel. This harsh statement refers perhaps to the events following the end of Jehu's dynasty (743-740 B.C.), a period marked in the history of Israel by anarchy and palace revolts.[60]

By contrast, Yahweh will show compassion towards Judah, the Southern Kingdom, delivering it by himself (בַּיהוָה "by Yahweh") rather than by military might.

This miraculous victory without weapons and casualties, prophesied in v. 7, occurred in 701 B.C., when the troops of the Assyrian king Sennacherib, while besieging Jerusalem, unexpectedly left the battle field and returned home (cf. 2 Kgs 19:32-34; Is 29:5ff.; 30:27ff.).[61]

For Theophylact of Bulgaria,[62] Judah's deliverance by God represents a type of the salvation by the faith of Christ: "They (i.e., the Christians) are not saved by Greek wisdom, neither by arguments, nor by convincing words of human wisdom, from which quarrel, discussions, and controversies come out; but rather by the faith of Christ which is our peace."

Even though the mention of "weaning" in Hosea's narrative (v. 8), so marked by economy, looks quite surprising, nevertheless it aids reconstruction of the chronological framework. Since in ancient times a child was nursed almost three years,[63] one may conclude that the prophecy connected to the third child of Hosea refers to the events following the year 737/6 B.C., provided that the previous prophecy related to Lo-Ruhamah was fulfilled in the period 743-740 B.C.[64]

With the birth and naming of the third child, לֹא עַמִּי "Lo-Ammi" ("Not-My-People") (v. 9), not only a dynasty or even the northern monarchy, but rather the people of

Israel, as a religious entity, are called to judgment. Yahweh issues the most severe threat: Israel will no longer be his people. The community of faith born in the years following the exodus under the guidance of Moses (ca. 1250 B.C.) reached its end in the year 737/6 B.C. when Pekah became king of Israel.[65] His reign may be considered the beginning of the end, since the territorial amputation done in 733 B.C. was only the prelude of the fall of Samaria in 722/1 B.C.

The verbal form אֶהְיֶה in "And I am not for you" (וְאָנֹכִי לֹא־אֶהְיֶה לָכֶם)[66] was interpreted by Wolff[67] as a predicate noun replacing the tetragrammaton Yahweh (cf. Exod 3:14), hence his translation "And I—I-Am-Not-There for you." Since the book of Hosea lacks references to such an important event, the revelation of the divine name, one should consider this clause as another example of narrative economy, so characteristic to Hosea. *BHS* supplies even a predicate noun, אֱלֹהֵיכֶם, hence the rendition "And I am not your God."[68]

2. Restoration after Judgment (2:1/1:10-2:3/1)

2:1/1:10. The number of the sons of Israel shall be[69] **as the sand of the sea which cannot be measured**[70] **or counted. And instead**[71] **of saying to them: "You are not my people," it will be said to them "You are sons of the living God." 2:2/1:11. The sons of Judah and the sons of Israel shall be gathered together, and they shall appoint for themselves one head**[72] **and shall come up out of the land.**[73] **For great is the day of Jezreel. 2:3/2. Say to your brothers,**[74] **"Ammi," and to your sisters, "Ruhamah."**

The consecutive perfects, encountered in the Hebrew text of 2:1-3, underscore the oracular character of this passage which deals with a future time coined "the day of Jezreel" (יוֹם יִזְרְעֶאל),[75] when Israel will experience a turning point in her fate. If in 1:1-9 the births and names of Hosea's three children are connected to prophecies of doom concerning Israel (king, monarchy, and people), in 2:1-3 the same children are bearers of good news. The shining future is marked by an increase in number of the "sons of Israel." The comparison with "sand of the sea" (כְּחוֹל הַיָּם) echoes God's promise to the patriarchs (Gen 22:17; cf. 15:5). To understand better the significance of such a promise against the background of the second half of the eighth century B.C., one may mention that according to 2 Kgs 15:19-20 only 60,000 wealthy men used to live in Israel during the reign of Menahem (ca. 738 B.C.), and after the fall of Samaria in 721 B.C., the Assyrian king Sargon II[76] deported 27,290 men from the capital of the Northern Kingdom.[77] As one can see, this prophecy was not fulfilled during the second half of the eighth century B.C., but it seemingly belongs to a remote future.

The name "Lo-Ammi" (לֹא־עַמִּי) "Not-My-People," as a part of a doom prophecy heralding the end of the covenant (1:9) is now changed into "sons of the living God" (בְּנֵי אֵל־חָי) which stands in sharp contrast with the "children of whoredom" (יַלְדֵי זְנוּנִים) or the idolatrous Israelites (1:2). Thus, Yahweh is about to announce a new, revived relationship with his people. A similar expression is found in Deut 14:1, again in a covenantal context, "You are sons of Yahweh your God." The title "living God" (אֵל־חָי)[78] in the Hosean passage, like the tetragrammaton in the Deuteronomy text already cited, is meant to emphasize the active presence of Yahweh in the history of Israel vis-à-vis the vanity and inefficiency of the Canaanite idols.

The "day of Jezreel" is also defined by national unity, for the Israelites and the Judaeans shall be gathered together, and they shall appoint one leader. This prophetic saying was probably issued in the years following the

Syro-Ephraimite war in 733 B.C., during which the two Israelite kingdoms were in a state of enmity. But now Yahweh announces a day of reconciliation and unity between Israel and Judah. The word used here, "head" (ראש), instead of the more common term מֶלֶךְ "king" mirrors Hosea's negative view of the representatives of the northern monarchy in contrast with the Davidic dynasty of Judah, the only legitimate one.[79] By choosing such an archaic designation for leader (i.e., "head"; cf. Num 14:4; Judg 11:8), Hosea intends to paint Israel's future with colors of the pre-monarchical age, the ideal period of Yahweh-Israel relationship (cf. 2:16-25).

United under one leader, Israel and Judah will experience a new "exodus," provided that this is the meaning of וְעָלוּ מִן־הָאָרֶץ "And they shall come up out of the land."[80] Macintosh[81] enumerates three types of solutions with respect to this *crux interpretum*: (1) the Jewish interpretation (cf. Targum, Peshitta, Kimchi) suggests that this clause points to an exodus from the land (of captivity); (2) a series of interpretations are based on the comparison with Exod 1:10; e.g., Lambert argues that both texts should be rendered "and they will gain ascendancy over the land"; for Holaday, ארץ in both texts designates the underworld (cf. Gen 2:6; 1 Sam 28:13 where the verb עלה is used), hence "they will come up from the underworld" refers to Israel's national revival; (3) some interpreters separate Exod 1:10 from Hos 2:2; popular is Vriezen's suggestion that in the latter text the verb עלה has the meaning "to grow up" (of a plant), hence the image of new Israel growing up as a plant under God's blessing.

In this commentary, we follow the ancient interpretation which relies on the basic meaning of עלה, "to go/ come up," taking ארץ as a reference to the place of captivity. Thus, the prophetic saying hints at a future "exodus" when both the Israelites and Judaeans united under one leader will return from captivity to their land. This time could have been the post-exilic period, after the decree of Cyrus (538 B.C.), when the exiles returned to the promised land under the leadership of Shesh-bazzar (= Shenazzar, 1 Chr 3:18) "prince of Judah" in 538 B.C. (Ezra 1:1-8) and Zerubbabel in 520 B.C. (Ezra 2:2f), both of Davidic lineage.[82]

This prophecy of increase in population, the restoration of the two united states under one leader, and their return from captivity may be also read as a typology. The last fulfillment of this prophecy will occur when the former "Not-My-People," the Gentiles,[83] will share God's blessings initially made to Abraham (Rom 9:24f.),[84] resulting in a great increase in number of the New Israel. Thus, united under one leader, Jesus Christ,[85] and by the power of his resurrection, the new community of faith will be able to rise again from the dust on the last day.[86]

This typological interpretation is found in most of the ancient Christian interpreters. Having observed that this prophecy was spiritually (πνευματικῶς) fulfilled in Christ, Cyril of Alexandria[87] explains: "'They come up out of the land,' namely, they will live the life of the saints (τῶν ἁγίων) as well, 'for great is the day of Jezreel.' For, indeed, great is the day of Christ, when he will raise to life all the dead. In fact, he will descend (καταβήσεται) from heaven, and he will sit on his glorious throne. 'And he will give everyone according to his works' [Mt 16:27]. Therefore, if one wishes to understand by day the time of the visitation (τῆς ἐπιδημίας), when the remission of the sins is given by (παρὰ) Christ to the Greeks and Judaeans, and to those who have sinned (πεπλημμεληκόσι) against him, this will not deviate from the true words. For David too indicated the time of the coming of our Savior by saying, 'This is the day that the Lord has made; let us be glad and rejoice in it' [Ps 118:24]."[88]

3. The Last Warnings before Separation (2:4/2-15/13)

4/2. Rebuke[89] your mother! Rebuke! For she is not my wife and I am not her husband. Let[90] her remove her whoring from her face, and her adultery from between her breasts! 5/3. Lest[91] I strip her naked and expose her as on the day of her birth. And I will make her like a wilderness, and turn her into a parched land, and let her die of thirst. 6/4. And upon her sons I will have no mercy, for they are sons of whoredom. 7/5. For their mother has played the whore; she who conceived them has acted shamefully. For she said, 'I will go after my lovers who give me my bread and my water, my wool and my flax,[92] my oil and my drink.'[93] 8/6. Therefore I will hedge up[94] her[95] way with thorns; and I will build a wall against her so that she cannot find her paths. 9/7. She shall pursue her lovers, but not reach them. And she shall seek them, but not find (them).[96] Then she shall say, 'I will go and return to my first husband. For it was better for me then than now. 10/8. She did not know that it was I who gave her the grain, the new wine, and the fresh oil, and who lavished upon her silver and gold that they made into Baal.[97] 11/9. Therefore I will take back my grain in its time, and the new wine in its season; and I will remove my wool and my flax, which were to cover[98] her nakedness. 12/10. Now I will uncover her shame[99] in the sight of her lovers. And no one shall rescue her from my hand. 13/11. I will put an end to all her exultation, her feasts, her new moons, her sabbaths, and all her appointed festivals.[100] 14/12. I will lay waste her vines and her fig trees, of which she said, 'These are my pay,[101] which my lovers have given me.' I will make them a forest,[102] and the beasts of the field[103] shall devour them. 15/13. I will punish her for the feast days of the Baals, when she offered incense[104] to them, and decked herself with her ring and jewelry, and went after her lovers, and forgot me, says Yahweh.

The pericope 2:4/2-15/13 represents a prophetic speech (Wolff: "kerygmatic sermon") delivered by Hosea around 750 B.C. when Israel was going both internally and externally through a relatively calm period. These peaceful times were brought to an end by the Syro-Ephraimite war against Assyria (733 B.C.).

The setting of this section is probably a family quarrel between Hosea and his unfaithful wife. Wolff[105] suggests a quite different setting, a legal lawsuit held at the city's gate before the elders, but nothing in this pericope supports such a bold view. The term ריב, which might have a legal resonance ("to accuse") can also have a much milder connotation ("to rebuke, call to account"). And since the key players of this drama are all members of one and the same family one may conclude that a domestic rather than a legal setting is behind this intricate simile.

First, the children are asked by Hosea to take his side in rebuking their sinful mother (v. 4/2a). The three children stand as a *memento* before the mother telling her by their very presence that her perverted way hurts them ultimately. On the covenantal level, the mother refers perhaps to present Israel whereas the children designate the future generations (so ibn Ezra). Allegorizing, Theophylact of Bulgaria[106] identifies the "mother" with the old synagogue, and the children with "the apostles who followed Christ, who will sit on twelve thrones judging the twelve tribes of Israel [Mt 19:28]."

"For she is not my wife (אִשְׁתִּי), and I am not her husband (אִישָׁהּ)" (v. 4/2a) was considered by some scholars (so, e.g., Wolff) an official divorce formula. As Macintosh[107] noticed, no strong evidence can be found in either Akkadian or Hebrew texts. For Cyril of Alexandria,[108] these words suggest a crisis of intimacy between husband

and wife: "For she has not preserved the genuiness of love toward me, but rather she denied the intimacy (οἰκειότητα), and underestimated the purity of the spiritual communion with me, nor was she willing to bring forth the fruits of my will." Note that Hosea picks here the word אִישׁ "man" instead of a more technical term, בַּעַל "master, lord, husband," probably in order to avoid any sound connection with the odious god's name "Baal"; or to underscore woman's sense of belongingness to her man. (Same word-play ʾîš "man" — ʾiššā "woman" is first attested in the Yahwistic story of Paradise; cf. Gen 2:23).

The prophetic speech now takes on an exhortative tone. Hosea asks Gomer to remove "her whoring (זְנוּנֶיהָ) from her face, and her adultery (וְנַאֲפוּפֶיהָ) from between her breasts" (4/2b) or otherwise she should be well prepared to bear dire consequences (v. 5/3). The two abstract plural nouns ("whoring" and "adultery") may refer either to Gomer's bad behavior or to some distinguishing marks or jewelry worn by a prostitute.[109]

"Lest I strip her naked" (v. 5/3). According to Ezek 16:4-5, the "stripping" is an act of humiliation preceding capital punishment in case of an adulteress (cf. Lev 20:10; Deut 22:22: no exposure).[110] The text is silent as to whether or not Hosea has stripped his unfaithful wife exposing her naked in the eyes of her lovers. Perhaps this threat meant that Israel would experience humiliation and exposure during the Assyrian exile. The Israelites would be taken into captivity leaving behind their homeland which, due to a massive abandonment, would quickly turn into "wilderness" (מִדְבָּר) and "parched land" (אֶרֶץ צִיָּה) — a desolate place (cf. Ezek 19:13; Ps 63:2) dying of "thirst" — where fertility comes to an end.

Hosea's attempt to change Gomer's moral profile by drawing the children into the marital quarrel seems to have had failed. Such failure can be deduced from v. 6/4 where the children were shown no mercy because they were בְּנֵי זְנוּנִים "sons of whoredom" (cf. Hos 1:2) — inheritors in a sense of their mother's inclinations toward disobedience. At the historical level, the new association "mother—children" points to a moral-religious decadence on the part of the young generation following their forefathers' footsteps. The threat issued against the children is in the same vein as the old saying "The parents have eaten sour grapes, and the children's teeth are set on edge" (Jer 31:29).

Turning to Gomer, the prophet points out that her extra-marital affairs were not accidental but calculated acts (v. 7/5). The initial "she said" and the phrase "my lovers who give me [presents]" suggest that Gomer took a decision out of her free will, based on the conviction that the "lovers," rather than Hosea, are going to fulfill her needs. The series of presents "bread, water, wool, flax, oil, drink" offers a complete picture of Gomer's needs, starting with food and clothing as basic needs, aiming at life's preservation, and ending with cosmetics and drinks, as luxury items.

"I will go after my lovers" refers in a historical setting to the Israelites' frequent forays into the realm of idolatry. The plural "lovers" probably indicates various manifestations of the god Baal with respect to its different sanctuaries (Wolff). One may nevertheless add that the sin of idolatry as described in this prophetic book does not translate into a clear-cut separation from Yahwism. Hosea paints a rather intricate picture of religious life during the last years of Jeroboam II's reign, marked by syncretism. As in the case of Gomer, who has probably never left for good her house and husband, likewise Israel has never abandoned Yahweh for Baal, but features proper to the latter were transferred onto the "God of the fathers." Although the text does not say it, one can suppose that the faithless wife, while still living at Hosea's home, was "thinking of" (one of the meanings of אָמְרָה "she said") her past and potential "lovers," interweaving them with her real husband into the composite portrayal of an imaginary spouse.

The presence of the first person singular suffix on the gifts (i.e., "my bread," "my water," etc.) mirrors Gomer's selfishness and arrogance. Looking for things to satisfy her future needs, she is always inclined to forget Hosea's past and present love toward her. Similarly, the Israelites are ready to embrace passionately the new cults of fertility rather than holding strongly to the old Yahwism.

Starting with v. 8/6, the focus of this parable switches from the family to the realm of history. Three preventive measures (so Macintosh), rather than penalties (so Rudolph, Wolff), are issued by Yahweh with respect to the idolatrous people, i.e., blocking Israel's access to various sanctuaries, cessation of natural abundance, and an end to all cultic celebrations. These measures, triggered by Israel's deliberate decision to follow her "lovers" (v. 7/5), represent a final warning before the judgment.

The first measure aims at obstructing (שָׂךְ) the paths leading to the wife's "lovers," or, in Israel's case, to the sanctuaries of Baal, with a wall of thorns and a stone fence (גָּדֵר).[111] Yahweh is described here as a loving husband who sets obstacles in his wife's sinful way so that she may eventually return to her first love.

"She shall pursue her lovers, but not reach them." The faithless wife makes a last effort to follow her "lovers" but, due to husband's first measure, her action is fruitless. Then she comes to her senses, and makes the decision (note the use of the same אָמְרָה "she said" as in v. 7/5) to go back to her first husband.[112] The reason for such a return sounds quite pragmatic: "For it was better for me then than now." In Hosea the "past" (here אָז "then") represents an ideal time for Yahweh-Israel relationship—the period of the wilderness (2:16/14), before the settlement in Canaan (11:1ff.). Jerome[113] sees in this prophetic passage a parallel to the parable of the prodigal son, more precisely to the son's observation, "How many of my father's hired hands have bread enough and to spare, but here I am dying of hunger!" (Lk 15:17f.): "From this one understands that the evils befall us always by God's providence, so that we may not have whatever we desire, and oppressed by various calamities and miseries of this life, we may be compelled to serve God again."

According to ibn Ezra,[114] the phrase "she did not know" (v. 10/8) implies "until this time" when Gomer returned to her senses. Yahweh presents to Israel his natural gifts, grain versus bread, new wine versus fermented wine, and fresh (olive) oil versus oil. The absence of the first person singular suffix on these items (compare Gomer's soliloquy, v. 7/5) proves once more God's tenderness toward his people. His lordship does not manifest itself in boastful words and rushed judgments but rather in an almost stubborn, passionate, and sacrifice-oriented love toward Israel. Yet, in spite of all these tokens of divine bounty, "they" (perhaps a reference to the "sons of whoredom," the Israelites) have used the gifts of silver and gold to manufacture idols ("Baal").

In response to Israel's arrogant, self-centered behavior, Yahweh will take back his gifts (grain, new wine, wool, and flax) (v. 11/9). Interestingly enough, when withdrawn,[115] the gifts are accompanied by the first person singular suffix ("my grain," etc.). This means that Yahweh, not the people, is the true owner and giver of the natural goods. "Time" (עֵת) refers to the harvest time (cf. Ps 1:3; Jer 5:24; Job 5:26) whereas "season" (מוֹעֵד "appointed time, festival") could indicate one of Israel's festivals (perhaps "Succoth": "Booths"—the harvest festival). The "wool" and the "flax" are snatched away from Gomer so that she could not cover her nakedness. Desolation of the land is the keyword on the historical level.

"Now" (v. 12/10) as elsewhere in Hosea betrays a sense of urgency. The threat launched in v. 5/3 is now fulfilled. In a little while Yahweh is going to shame Israel by leaving her without any support before the very eyes of her impotent lovers (perhaps a reference to imported idols and foreign nations). Her naked exposure (lack of fertility in Israel's case) draws but the contempt of her lovers. A similar idea, though with respect to Jerusalem, is found in Lam 1:8, "Jerusalem sinned grievously, so she has become a mockery; all who honored her despise her, for they have seen her nakedness."

"No one"[116] will be able to save Israel from the punishing hand of God. These words echo God's self-portrayal in Deut 32:39: "See now that I, even I, am he; there is no god besides me. I kill and I make alive; I wound and I heal; and no one can deliver from my hand."

There is a logical connection between v. 12/10 and v. 13/11: the lack of fertility is immediately followed by a cessation[117] of all celebrations. The "feast" (חַג) opening this list refers probably to the festival of harvest held at the end of the year (Exod 23:16). The "new moon" (חֹדֶשׁ), which marked the beginning of the month, appears here and elsewhere (cf. 2 Kgs 4:23; Am 8:5; Is 1:13) besides the weekly "sabbath" (שַׁבָּת).[118] מוֹעֵד "Appointed festival" (from root יעד "to appoint [a time/place]") is a generic term for all Israel's festivals ("sabbath"—Lev 23:2; "new-moon"—Ps 104:19; "Passover"—Lev 23:4f.; "Succoth"—Deut 31:10).

Note that all these feasts, encompassing the main divisions of the calendar (year, month, week), are labeled Israel's "exultation" (מְשׂוֹשָׂהּ) rather than Yahweh's festivals due to the secularization of the Israelite worship and its syncretistic orientation. These are Israel's feasts (note the repetition of "her" with each festival) dedicated to Baal rather than to Yahweh. It is Yahweh, the source of all goods and joy who will eventually put an end to these caricatural festivals.

Yahweh retrieves the natural resources, puts an end to Israel's festivals, and is now going to lay waste the vine and the fig tree, two long-time symbols of peace and tranquility.[119] This prophetic word could be a reference to the gloomy days of the Assyrian conquest and later deportation which would come upon Israel in a little more than two decades (722/1 B.C.). The fact that the wild animals will devour them shows that humans were just a few and thus unable to resist.[120]

Israel, the unfaithful wife, was inclined to believe that vine and fig-trees were "wages" (אֶתְנָה)[121] from the Baals, her lovers, rather than an offering of love from Yahweh, her husband.

The word "Baals" (v. 15/13) refers to various manifestations of god Baal rather than to many deities with the same name "Baal." Israel will be punished for offering incense on the "days of Baals."[122] The phrase "days of Baals" points to the festivals listed in v. 13/11. Originally consecrated to Yahweh, these festivals have been, during the divided monarchy, tainted by Baalism. Note the use of the imperfect ("she used to do") which underscores the repetitive aspect of Israel's idolatrous acts of cult.

By putting the jewelry[123] on herself, and having gone after her lovers, Israel was taking active part in the syncretistic services held at different Israelite shrines. At the end of v. 15/13 Hosea emphasizes the personal dimension of Israel's sin. It is not only a paragraph of law that Israel ignored by her faithless attitude, but the Lord himself (אֹתִי "me," in Yahweh's speech) whom she forgot.

4. A Date in the Wilderness (2:16/14-25/23)

16/14. "Therefore I myself will allure her and lead her to the wilderness[124] and talk to her heart.[125] 17/15. And I will give her from there her vineyards,[126] and the Valley of Achor as a gate of hope.[127] And she shall sing[128] there as in the days of her youth, as on the day when she came up from the land of Egypt. 18/16. On that day, oracle of Yahweh, you[129] will call out 'My husband,' and you will no longer call me 'My Baal.'[130] 19/17. And I will remove the names of the Baals from her mouth and they will not be mentioned any more by their name.[131] 20/18. And I will make a covenant for them on that day with the beasts of the field, with the birds of the sky, and the creeping beings of the ground. I will abolish[132] bow, sword, and weapons from the land, and I will make them rest[133] in safety.[134] 21/19. And I will betroth you to myself forever; I will betroth you to myself in righteousness and justice, in mercy and compassion. 22/20. I will betroth you to me in faithfulness and you will know Yahweh.[135] 23/21. On that day, I will sing,[136] oracle of Yahweh, I will sing with the heavens, and they[137] will sing with the earth. 24/22. And the earth will sing with corn and new wine and fresh oil, and they will sing with Jezreel. 25/23. And I will sow her for myself in the land and I will have mercy on 'Without-Mercy' and I will say to 'Not-My-People': 'You are my people.' And he will say: 'My God.'"[138]

This collection (vv. 18-25) of a "loosely knit series of sayings" (Wolff) was probably put together around 733 B.C., when Tiglath-pileser III of Assyria captured and transformed most of the north-Israelite territory (2 Kgs 15:29; cf. Is 9:1) into three provinces, Dor, Gilead, and Megiddo. King Pekah was left only with the hilly region of Samaria.[139]

The tone of the prophetic discourse changes unexpectedly from threat (v. 15a) to hope (vv. 16ff.) in a special relationship between God and his people described in terms of a new betrothal (vv. 21-23). Theodore of Mopsuestia[140] points out that when Hosea "mixes together" (καταμίγνυσιν) the "transition to a better (situation)" with the "announcement of punishment, he follows the custom of other prophets and of David the Psalmist [Ps 30:9, 22 (LXX)], who speak of "misfortunes" (τὰς συμφορὰς) and "deliverance" (τὴν λύσιν) within the same pericope.

It is Yahweh who realizes that his previous threats have been of no avail; thus, he adopts a new attitude toward the unfaithful people. God behaves as he were a cheated husband yet still in love with his unfaithful wife. In a last effort, he tries to "allure" (מְפַתֶּיהָ)[141] her, to attract or persuade his wayward wife by offering something pleasant. Jerome[142] interprets "I allure her" (*lactabo eam*) as a reference to God's "caressing" (*blandietur*) his people. Relying on the LXX, the Greek Fathers have insisted a great deal in their interpretations on the semantic nuances of πλανῶ[143] "to lead astray, mislead, deceive," the rendition of Hebrew פתה (Pi'el). Cyril of Alexandria[144] writes: "'Behold I will mislead (πλανῶ) her' not from what it is necessary (ἀναγκαίου) and useful (χρησίμου) to life in order not to be in this way, but from the things which are shameful (αἰσχιόνων) and harmful (ἀδικεῖν πεφυκότων) to the fulfillment of any enjoyment (ὄνησιν)."

Theodore of Mopsuestia[145] interprets v. 16/14 as a reference to the captivity: "I will hand her over to the captivity (αἰχμαλωσίᾳ), he says, and, deprived (ἔρημον) of all goods, she is wandering (πλανᾶσθαι) through the ways, which she previously was unaware of, but now, in distress, she is compelled to run through." A similar interpretation is found in Theodoret of Cyrus[146]: "I will make the one who became captive (αἰχμάλωτον) to stray (ἀλᾶσθαι) and wander (πλανᾶσθαι), and I will deprive (ἔρημον) her of all these goods. Nevertheless, I will allure (ψυχαγωγήσω)[147] her while she is in all these afflictions (ἀλγεινοῖς)." For Theophylact of Bulgaria,[148] πλανῶ may indicate either "leading" into captivity or "removing" from idolatry and evil, with respect to Israel as object of the divine intervention.

For ancient interpreters such as Cyril of Alexandria, God being the subject of "misleading" is a quite difficult proposition. That is why, Cyril[149] explains that "misleading" is only the wife's perception, God being in fact at work for her good: "And as her ways are usefully hedged around with thorns so that she may not lay hold of her lovers, in the same manner now running down hill toward ruin and destruction, she believes (δοκεῖ) herself to be led astray (πλανᾶσθαι) by the mercy of God, while she is brought to desire virtue, and having received the light of the knowledge of God in mind and heart, as I said, she is no longer able to find her old path."

The threatening words of the past made the wife come to an incipient realization (v. 9b) but they were unable to rekindle any spark of love in her heart so that she may take the first step in the right direction. We are not told how he is going to get her seduced, but it seems obvious that this thing did happen. Jer 2:2, one of the earliest interpretations of Hos 2:16/14f., suggests that the wife has been seduced in the "wilderness": "I remember ... your love as a bride, how you followed me in the wilderness." The motif of "wilderness" (מִדְבָּר) reappears in Song 8:5 where it designates a dating-place of lovers: "Who is coming up from the wilderness, leaning upon her beloved?"[150]

On a historical level, "leading" to the "wilderness" means going back in time and place to the beginnings of Israel as Yahweh's people, while they were wandering through the wilderness in search for their religious identity.[151] Such an interpretation is found in Julian of Eclanum. The fact that in Latin there are two verbs *lacto*, (I) "to milk" and (II) "to mislead, allure" explains Julian's[152] allegory on *lactabo eam* "I will allure her": "Since he calls the time of liberation from Egypt the birth of the Synagogue, then the suckling (*lactatio*) may indicate the sustenance of Manna." Jerome[153] writes: "I will draw [her] out (*educam*) from misfortunes, in the same manner as I had previously drawn [her] out from Egyptian slavery."

For Cyril of Alexandria,[154] the "wilderness" is the new "look" designed by God for Israel to keep the demons' "desires" away from her: "Since she [Israel] is accessible (βάσιμον) like a well-watered land (ἔνυδρον γῆν) to the herds of demons, he [the Lord] promises to arrange (τάξειν) her as a wilderness (ἔρημον), teaching that he will display (ἀποφανεῖ) it to their desires (θελήμασιν) as an austere, untrodden and waterless place, so that finding no resting place (ἀναπαύλης) they would despise it and depart." In support of this interpretation, Cyril brings forth the saying of Jesus on the unclean spirit who finds no resting place in the "waterless regions" (Mt 12:43-45).

The goal of "leading" the wife to the wilderness is to "talk to her heart." Far from the city's distracting cacophony, in the midst of an austere environment, despised even by the unclean spirits, the wounded husband begins to caress his wife with loving words.[155] For Jerome[156] this heart-to-heart conversation consists of "soothing words, words of comfort that I might temper sorrow with gladness ... so that grief may be replaced by joy." Likewise, Theodore of Mopsuestia[157] insists on the idea of comfort: "Thereafter, I will comfort (παρακαλέσω) her, he says, who is wrestling with inconsolable evils."

But the mention of "heart" may allude to the "New

Covenant" inscribed in the hearts of the faithful rather than on tables of stone as was in the case of the Old Covenant (Jer 31:31; Ezek 36:26-27). Julian of Eclanum[158] explains: "Speaking directly to the heart indicates the promulgation of the law, which shaped the hearts of the listeners." On the other hand, Cyril of Alexandria[159] distinguishes between "mind" (νοῦς) or the reception of the law, and "heart" (καρδία) or the knowledge of it, the latter being described as the source of the virtuous life: "And we, who have Christ, the author of necessary things (ἀναγκαίων) dwelling inside the heart, were at once enriched in every kind of virtue (ἀρετῆς) and in the abundant and inalienable possession (κτῆσις) of the spiritual gifts (χαρισμάτων).... He promises to speak in (εἰς) her heart (καρδίαν). For the Synagogue of the Judaeans will be called to awareness (ἐπίγνωσιν) by taking into mind the divine laws inscribed through the Spirit, exactly as the Church from the nations." For Theophylact of Bulgaria[160] "to speak to one's heart" leads to the perception of both God's glory and man's sinfulness: "I will make her understand my glory and power as well as their own trespasses.... Here, when God speaks to the heart of those who once were rejected, he promises grace (χάριν) through Christ."

The return of the "vineyards" (כְּרָמֶיהָ) destroyed by Yahweh (v. 14: נַפְנָה) punctuates the renewal of the covenantal life. But the "vineyards" in v. 17 cannot designate Israel (cf. Is 5) as Jerome[161] suggests, because Israel herself is the recipient of this divine gift. Julian of Eclanum[162] sees here an allusion to the "excellent fruit of the vine" brought by the twelve scouts sent to investigate the land of Canaan during Israel's wandering through wilderness (Num 13:23).

The Greek interpreters, following the Septuagint, deal with "possessions" (τὰ κτήματα) rather than with "vineyards" in their interpretations. Thus, Cyril of Alexandria[163] explains that the "heavenly wealth" (ὁ πλοῦτος οὐράνιος) consists of "whatever is necessary for life and understanding of God's knowledge in Christ, through whom and in whom we saw the Father, enriched in unfading hope [1 Pet 5:4], as I said, in glory, pride of adoption, grace, and of reigning together with Christ himself. These are the possessions (κτήσεις) of the saints; this is the heavenly wealth." On the other hand, Theodore of Mopsuestia[164] points to a new "exodus" when Israel will enjoy again God's blessings.

Ancient interpreters such as Cyril of Alexandria[165] saw in "from there" (LXX: ἐκεῖθεν; MT: מִשָּׁם)[166] an important detail pointing to realities beyond the visible world. Cyril explains: "Her possessions will be from that place (ἐκεῖθεν) rather than from here (ἐντεῦθεν), that is to say, from this reality (πράγματος)."

The "valley of Achor" (עֵמֶק עָכוֹר)[167] once a place of human rebellion and divine judgment becomes a "gate of hope" (פֶּתַח תִּקְוָה)[168] for Israel. Both phrases steer one's attention backwards, to the period of conquest. Josh 7 shows how the Israelite conquest of Canaan was delayed by Achan's sin (the theft of booty from Jericho). Found guilty, Achan is executed and buried in a valley named in remembrance of this incident the "valley of Achor."[169] Hosea uses Achan's story to show Israel how serious is the sin of "greed" while urging her to get rid of the "gifts" she has illicitly received from her lovers (2:7/5).[170] The change in name, from "valley of trouble" to "gate of hope," will probably occur with the occasion of Israel's return from captivity (cf. Is 65:10).[171] Julian of Eclanum[172] interprets the valley's new name as a reference to Israel's "fertility" (*felicitatis*). Both elements of the new name "gate of hope" point to a kind of foretaste, rather than a full enjoyment, of the future blessings God will pour upon Israel.

Commentary: Hosea 1-3

Speaking of the "valley of troubles turned into an entrance (*ostium*) of hope, or opening (*aperiendam*) of hope," Jerome[173] insists on the purifying role of the misfortunes (*supplicia et tormenta*) which should be patiently endured "so that through these she [Israel] may achieve prosperity." And Jerome goes to say: "There is obvious hope in the place where had been despair."

The Greek Fathers, relying on the Septuagint interpretative translation (διανοῖξαι σύνεσιν αὐτῆς "to open her understanding," for MT: לְפֶתַח תִּקְוָה), dwell rather on the illuminating function of suffering. Thus, Theodoret of Cyrus[174] writes: "Just as those, at that early time, have learned through Achar's [sic: Achan] punishment (τιμωρίας) how serious is the transgression of law (παρανομία), in the same manner these will come to the realization of their own trespasses (πλημμελημάτων) through the captivity (αἰχμαλω-σίας)."

With the occasion of this new beginning marked by hope in God's benevolent intervention, Israel acts as a young woman who fell in love for the first time. She is so mesmerized by her lover's tender words, that her first reaction is singing.[175] She starts singing out of and for love, and her tune as wordless as it might sound, becomes the sheer expression of peace, safety, and genuine happiness of a woman in love.

The "days of her youth" (כִּימֵי נְעוּרֶיהָ) stands in synonymous parallelism with "the day when she came up from the land of Egypt," thus they should refer to the Exodus and/or the later events. Cyril of Alexandria[176] interprets the former phrase as an allusion to the promulgation of the law on Mt. Sinai: "She [Israel] will be humble (ταπεινή) and obedient (εὐήνιος) just as in the beginnings, when she was born to the knowledge of God (θεογνωσίαν) through the law, she gladly received the decree of the divine adoption. Accordingly, he calls the regeneration to the knowledge of God through the law the 'days [of her youth].'"

One may add that there is a certain similarity between Miriam (Exod 15:21: וַתַּעַן "she started singing") and the new Israel (Hos 2:17: וְעָנְתָה "she shall sing"), which goes beyond the lexical choice. Both the sister of Moses and the personified Israel are lauding Yahweh for his wondrous works while standing on the threshold of a new covenant with God.[177]

Both "there" (שָׁמָּה) and "on that day" (בַּיּוֹם־הַהוּא)[178] point to a certain place and time in the fulfillment of the "word of Yahweh" (נְאֻם־יְהוָה). While the "valley of Achor," somewhere in the neighborhood of Jericho, represents the scene or rather the "gate of hope" to a new life, the return from the Assyrian captivity describes the time when Israel draws near to her Creator with the "tender love" (חֶסֶד) of a bride (Jer 2:2). Overcome with joy, she starts singing the endless melody of youth, and from time to time, to caress her lover, she addresses him with such an intimate title as "my husband" (אִישִׁי).[179] Her reluctance toward the legal term "my lord (Baal)" (בַּעְלִי) is matched in intensity only by the repulsion of the prophetic circles against the religious syncretism of the eighth-century Israel.[180]

By allowing Israel to call him "my husband" (אִישִׁי), God reveals his willingness to start all over again. The Lord is ready to get rid of his own prerogatives and titles, in order to regain nothing else but the tainted love of Israel. He is approaching his wayward spouse not as her "owner" (בַּעַל) but rather as an equal partner of communion, as one who is about to spell out the unsaid and unheard thought: "I need you!" God's genuine lordship giving place to a candid humbleness prefigures Christ's *kenosis* magnificently chanted by Paul in Phil 2:7ff. ("But he [Christ] emptied himself, taking the form of a servant, being born in the likeness of men") and vividly exemplified by Jesus at the Last Supper by calling his apostles "friends" rather than "servants" (Jn 15:15).

To the wife's first step, Yahweh responds with another token of love, by removing the names of "Baals"[181] from the cultic repertoire of his people (cf. Zech 13:2).[182] Israel's return to Yahweh, even though it comes at the end of a series of misfortunes culminating with the captivity, is not exclusively Israel's. It rather reflects a wonderful yet intricate alchemy between God's powerful intervention along the lines of human history (2:8/6, 19/17) and people's free and deliberate decision to abandon sinful ways (2:9/7). Just as in case of Yahweh's singing with the heavens (vv. 23/21-24/22), it is difficult to decide whether God's song is an echo to Israel's tune (v. 17/15) or a divine tone given to the entire universe, including Israel, to carry on the Master's love song. Likewise, in case of the people's return there is no way to determine where this process of conversion started or how much either partner should be credited for.

"That day" is mentioned again to show us that the new relationship between God and his people can and will not remain at the level of the first tunes uttered by a young, mesmerized woman. Now it is time that these wordless tunes receive some lyrics, even though the genuine tunes are still heard and reinforced by God's own melody (v. 23/21). These are the lyrics of the new covenant (בְּרִית)[183] concluded with the entire creation[184] and expressed in terms of peace[185] and safety (בֶּטַח)[186] in the land (v. 20/18).

Starting with v. 21/19 the new covenant is described in terms of a betrothal (אָרַשׂ)[187] which, oddly enough, lasts "forever" (לְעוֹלָם).[188] There is no wedding ceremony, just an endless engagement,[189] a special "relationship" (οἰκειότης) with God, as Theodore of Mopsuestia[190] calls it. The basic idea is that Yahweh wants to be eternally engaged to Israel. Instead of simply restoring the previous union (the Sinai covenant), Yahweh treats Israel as a brand new entity and by consequence he betroths her. This means that God is willing fully to forgive and to forget Israel's sinful past. If in a re-marriage there is still the danger of bad memories surfacing from time to time, a betrothal is based on a pure love with no prejudices at all (the same idea is found in Hos 14:5/4). Jerome[191] has a rather keen description of such an unusual betrothal: "How great is God's mercy! A prostitute who fornicated with many lovers, and because of her offense was handed over to the beasts, after she returns to her husband, she is said not at all to be reconciled to him, but rather to be betrothed. Now, notice the difference between God's union and that of men. When a man marries, he turns a virgin into a woman, that is, a non-virgin. But, when God joins with the prostitutes, he changes them into virgins."

"I will betroth you to me (לִי)" (repeated 3 times; vv. 21/19-22/20). Cyril of Alexandria[192] considers "to me" (ἐμαυτῷ) to point to a personal relationship between God and humanity: "For we are united (ἑνούμεθα) with God in Spirit, and became rich by participation (μέθεξιν) to his divine nature (φύσεως)." This covenant, adds Cyril, will not be administered by angels or humans (as the old covenant by the ministry of Moses) but by Christ the Lord, "through (δι') whom and in (ἐν) whom we are united with God."

By juxtaposing covenant and betrothal, Hosea launches a new paradox which, on the one hand, speaks of "righteousness" (צֶדֶק),[193] "justice" (מִשְׁפָּט),[194] "mercy" (חֶסֶד),[195] "compassion" (רַחֲמִים),[196] and "faithfulness" (אֱמוּנָה),[197] as covenantal gifts or parameters,[198] but, on the other hand, leaves the door open to initiative, suspense, and passion as basic ingredients of any betrothal-like relationship. While offering these gifts as tokens of love, God gives content and direction to his covenant with Israel. Jerome[199] detects in this list of gifts three types of betrothal: "First, he [God] betrothed her [Israel] in Abraham or rather in Egypt, so that he may have an everlasting spouse. Secondly, on Mt. Sinai in the betrothal, giving her the equity (*iustitiam*) and judgment (*iudicium*) of the law, and the compassion (*misericordiam*) added to the law, so that whenever she should sin she would be given up into captivity; whenever she should show penitence, she would be brought back to [her] homeland, and she would gain compassion.... By his crucifixion and resurrection from the dead, he [Jesus] betroths [her] not in the equity of the law, but rather in faith (*fide*) and grace (*gratia*) of the Gospel." Thus, beyond the concrete historical meaning intended by Hosea, God's gifts prefigure his saving grace (χάρις) offered in Christ to the whole humanity (Jn 1:14-18; Rom 3:24-26; Eph 2:8-9).

The picture painted here is that of a quintet interpreting a love song. The sweet melody is quite contagious. It "starts" (although this is not the best word describing a choir) with Israel and "ends" (or better "restarts") with Jezreel (יִזְרְעֶאל), referring to the people (cf. the symbolic name of Hosea's first son in 1:4).[200] And in the "center" or more precisely inside this quintet, Yahweh himself makes a rather unexpected appearance, not in front, not at the end, not even in the center, but on the second spot. He joins other singers ("Israel," the "heavens" [הַשָּׁמַיִם], the "earth" [הָאָרֶץ], the natural elements[201]—"corn" [הַדָּגָן], "new wine" [הַתִּירוֹשׁ], and "fresh oil" [הַיִּצְהָר]),[202] not as a choir director but as a singer (אֶעֱנֶה). "On that day"—the endless day of the betrothal—the whole creation is in love again with its Creator, and the latter finds once more his handiwork attractive.[203]

In v. 25/23, Israel, the "Not-My-People" (לֹא־עַמִּי) is

renamed by Yahweh "My people" (עַמִּי) and the former addresses the Lord with "My God" (אֱלֹהָי). These titles are part of a covenant terminology meant to provide the betrothal-like relationship with a certain consistency. For the same purpose, God promises that he will "sow" (וּזְרַעְתִּיהָ)[204] Israel for himself (לִי "for myself"—perhaps a hint at the previous betrothal imagery; cf. 2:21/19-22/20). Cyril of Alexandria[205] interprets "for myself" (ἐμαυτῷ) in v. 25/23 as an expression of God's direct relationship with his people: "I will personally take care of her [Israel], just as I myself, not through another one, will sow that fertile and good land." The place of this "sowing" is the "land" (אֶרֶץ), probably a reference to Israel's return from captivity to the fathers' land.[206] For Theodoret of Cyrus,[207] the things said in v. 25/23 "occurred under Zerubbabel as a type (τυπικῶς), but in truth (κατ' ἀλήθειαν), happened after the incarnation of the Lord Christ, when he betrothed the Church for eternity. For at that time, those who believed in him were in truth called faithful people (λαὸς πιστός) and he himself was simply called the God of those who believed in him." The key point of this verse is that the covenant, with all its blessings and gifts, represents the solid framework of a betrothal-like, otherwise volatile, relationship between God and his people.

By comparing the relationship between Yahweh and Israel with a love tune sung by the two partners along with the entire creation, Hosea may be considered the spiritual predecessor of Jeremiah (31:31-34)[208] who coined the famous phrase "new covenant" (בְּרִית חֲדָשָׁה), probably sometime after the destruction of Jerusalem in 586 B.C., when the old covenant was deprived of its political and cultic (sacrificial) framework. For this reason, the "new covenant," says Yahweh, will be inscribed on the hearts of the faithful rather than on tables of stones as the

Sinai covenant. There are two features in this covenant which bring Jeremiah close to Hosea. First, the new set of titles, "their god" (לָהֶם לֵאלֹהִים) and "my people" (לִי לְעָם) in Jer 31:33, echoes Hos 2:25/23. Secondly, the stated goal of the covenant, namely to "know"[209] Yahweh in Hos 2:22/20 (וְיָדַעַתְּ אֶת־יְהוָה "and you will know Yahweh") parallels a more personal conclusion in Jer 31:34 (כִּי־כוּלָּם יֵדְעוּ אוֹתִי "For all of them will know me").

5. Love and Abstinence (3:1-5)

1. And Yahweh said to me: "Go again, love a woman who loves[210] a friend and is an adulteress, just as Yahweh loves the children of Israel, though they turn to other gods and love cakes of raisins."[211] **2.** So I bought her[212] for myself for fifteen shekels of silver, and a homer of barley and a lethech of barley.[213] **3.** And I said to her: "For many days you shall remain as mine;[214] you shall not play the whore, you shall not belong to another man; so will I also be for you."[215] **4.** For the children of Israel shall remain for many days without king or prince, without sacrifice or pillar,[216] without ephod or teraphim.[217] **5.** Afterward the children of Israel shall return and seek Yahweh their God, and David their king, and turn trembling[218] to Yahweh and his goodness in the latter days.

Chapter 3, written in the autobiographical style,[219] should not be read as another version of chapter 1 (a biography) or as referring to Hosea's second marriage to a woman other than Gomer.[220] In any case, Hos 3 describes events which occurred after the facts narrated in Hos 1. Jerome[221] rightly notices that in Hos 3:1 "'again' means that he [Hosea] has previously loved a whore, who now is an adulteress." With respect to the date of composition, chapter 3 may have chronologically preceded chapter 1, being a continuation, in terms of theme, of chapter 2, or more precisely a conclusion to 2:4/2-17/15 (compare, for instance 3:3f. with the measures in 2:8/6).²²²

In v. 1a, Hosea is ordered²²³ by Yahweh to "go again" (עוֹד לֵךְ)²²⁴ and "love" (אֱהַב)²²⁵ a woman. The emphasis falls here on "love" which contrasts with the first divine command to "take [in marriage]" (קַח) Gomer (cf. 1:2). This time the prophet is commanded not to "take" or remarry Gomer (such a thing would have legally been impossible, cf. Deut 24:1ff; Jer 3:1), but to "love" his wayward wife; not to reproach her for moral decadence; not even to show compassion on her, but to simply love and receive her with no second thoughts. The betrothal imagery (2:21/19-22/20) is brought back on stage by the "love" theme which marks out the entire chapter 3. That "love" for the ongoing wayward wife does not come easily is seen in the use of the imperative: Hosea is commanded to love. He has no other choice but to deny his own feelings and place God's word as his first priority. Yet, the hardest thing is not to "love" a wife whose past acts are reprovable while her present attitude moves in the right direction, but to love an active adulteress, "a woman who loves a friend (רֵעַ),"²²⁶ that is to say, a woman caught up in a series of adulterous acts with a member of the same community, probably a person whom Hosea knew. If that person was in reality Hosea's "friend" or acquaintance so much the more bitter would have been his marital drama. Note that in chapter 1 Gomer is presented as a "wife of whoredom" (אֵשֶׁת זְנוּנִים) while in chapter 3 she is called an "adulteress" (מְנָאָפֶת). This shift in terminology mirrors the transition from a kind of stifled (latent?) fornication to a rather overt adultery. For Cyril of Alexandria,²²⁷ the adulteress points to the "faithless crowd who did not choose the heavenly Bridegroom (νυμφίον) [Christ] and who rejected the one who wooed (μνώμενον) it in faith."

As one can notice in v. 1b, Hosea shares in a mysterious way God's own suffering. Yahweh "loves the children of Israel" in spite of their constant acts and signs of idolatry.[228] His behavior is similar to that of a loving husband about to caress his wayward wife but she would spitefully turn her face from him. Instead of loving God, the Israelites "turn (פֹּנִים)[229] to other gods" and make "love cakes of raisins." The phrase "other gods" (אֱלֹהִים אֲחֵרִים)[230] refers to the "Baalim" (cf. 2:15/13, 19/17; 11:2). "Cakes of raisins" (אֲשִׁישֵׁי עֲנָבִים)[231] served at cultic festivities (2 Sam 6:19; 1 Chr 16:3; Is 16:7) or used as an aphrodisiac (Song 2:5) stand here in parallel with "other gods" because the Israelites considered these delicacies, as other natural resources, gifts of the Baals (cf. 2:7/5).[232] Cyril of Alexandria[233] suggests that the "cakes" (πέμματα), perhaps "a round cake" (πόπανα) or "honey cakes" (μελιττούτας), were brought as an offering to "demons" (δαίμοσι). One may add here Jerome's[234] allegorical interpretation based on the Vulgate's rendition, *vinacea uvarum* "grape skins," namely, "which have no wine and they have lost their previous grace (*pristinam gratiam*), just as the demons who having fallen from their own dignity, and possessing nothing of the old grace, are arid and feeble because of their aged dryness." Then Jerome notices that according to Aquila (παλαιὰ "old") and Symmachus (ἀκάρπους "fruitless"), "these are not only grape skins but also old (husks) pointing to old offenses."

From v. 2 we learn that Hosea had first to redeem his wife for himself.[235] From whom? There is no definitive answer to this question. Some scholars[236] suggest that Gomer was redeemed from cult prostitution. Others[237] assume that Hosea paid for his wife's emancipation from domestic slavery. In any event, the main idea is that for Gomer's transition from adultery to a new relationship with Hosea a price had to be paid. Hosea "bought"[238] her for "fifteen shekels of silver,[239] and a homer of barley and a lethech of barley" which means thirty shekels of silver.[240] The intricate way in which the payment was done sheds some light on Hosea's modest financial status and, at the same time, underlines the event's historicity.[241] Hosea was not a man of substance, otherwise he would not have to combine barley and money in order to come up with the full price for his wife's redemption. He would rather have paid either in barley or money. Based on the LXX rendition of the price, Cyril of Alexandria[242] offers an allegorizing interpretation. First, he considers "silver" a type of the "instructive word"; then, he divides "15 (pieces) of silver" into 7 (a reference to the Sabbath or the seventh day, and the Old Law), and 8 (indicating Christ's resurrection which occurred on the "eighth day," and the New Law), hence the whole number may represent the Old and New Testaments;[243] "barley," animals' food, points to Israel's inclination toward "carnal things" (τὰ σαρκικὰ), people's life being similar to that of the beasts;[244] and, finally, a "pitcher of wine" may echo the state of "drunkenness" (μέθη) or "darkness" (σκότῳ)[245] in which Israel was living. On the same allegorizing path, Jerome[246] considers 15 shekels an allusion to the fifteenth day of the month Nissan when the Egyptian first-born were killed, and the people of Israel were led out of Egypt (Exod 12:2-51). For Theophylact of Bulgaria,[247] 15 pieces of silver by which the prophet "hires" (μισθοῦται) his wayward wife refer to "five legal books" (νομικῶν τευχῶν) and "ten precepts" (ἐντολῶν). With respect to the historical level of the parable, Theodore of Mopsuestia[248] remarks: "Likewise, by great gifts (δωρεαῖς) and rewards (μισθοῖς), God bound the Jews to himself."

Back at home, once again, the wayward wife is asked to live for a long, yet indefinite, period of time (יָמִים רַבִּים

"many days")[249] in a sort of seclusion or separation from other men, with no extra-marital relations (v. 3). During this period of purifying abstinence, she had to belong to Hosea and the latter would reciprocate, namely, he would be faithful to her. For Cyril of Alexandria,[250] this reciprocal pledge of fidelity points to Hosea and Gomer as "being conjugally united" (οἰκειώσασθαι γαμικῶς) or "one" (ἕν) according to Gen 2:24. Among the ancient Christian interpreters, Theodoret of Cyrus[251] represents an interesting case since he suggests that Hosea too abstained from his wife: "For this reason, the prophet lived with the prostitute, and even dwelt together with the woman, but he abstained (ἀπείχετο) from any conjugal relationship (γαμικῆς ὁμιλίας)." Thus, Gomer's return coincides with the beginning of a period of abstinence for both partners. But neither the text nor the context supports such an interpretation.[252] On a historical level, v. 4 speaks of Israel as being deprived during the captivity only of her former paramours (both political and cultic) and not of Yahweh's presence. Theodore of Mopsuestia[253] explains that "for a long time God wanted to draw the Jews to himself and promised them his assistance (κηδεμονίαν)." In other words, God's providence never abandoned Israel.

Like Gomer, Israel will be forced to live without her "lovers." The list in v. 4 includes three pairs of paramours with which the people "played the whore," or historically, committed the sin of idolatry: king (מֶלֶךְ) and prince (שָׂר),[254] sacrifice (זֶבַח)[255] and pillar (מַצֵּבָה),[256] ephod (אֵפוֹד)[257] and teraphim (תְּרָפִים).[258] Hosea depicts both the political and cultic institutions of his time as being corrupt and contrary to the will of God. As Jacob notices,[259] Hosea who focused much on the value of the symbolism did not intend to get away with it in the name of a "disincarnate spiritualism." The prophet wanted these cultic and political symbols to remain as they were and not to become goals in themselves. Thus, a sincere return to Yahweh must be preceded by a complete separation from the paramours of the past or more precisely from a wrong perception of traditional institutions.

"Afterwards" (אַחַר) means after a period of abstinence, namely the captivity, the sons of Israel will "return" (יָשֻׁבוּ) and "seek" (וּבִקְשׁוּ) Yahweh. Thus, the captivity does not represent God's final word but only a prelude to a new relationship with him. Yahweh's love toward Israel surpasses all people's transgressions and the subsequent judgment (3:1, 4).[260]

In contrast to her previous momentary and emotional attempt to return (וְאָשׁוּבָה "I shall return"), while never translated into action due to people's simultaneous idolatrous escapades (2:9/7), Israel's present conversion is sincere and fruitful since it is a consequence of the disciplinary abstinence imposed by God (v. 4). "At that time," Theodore of Mopsuestia[261] interprets, "consider-ing their own sufferings, they [the Israelites] will change their mind, and they will zealously pursue the knowledge and worship of God."

Israel's return is paralleled by her "seeking." The verb בקשׁ "to seek" with its cultic resonance appears after the verb שׁוב "to return" in 7:10, but in this verse both verbs are negated. The object of this "seeking" is twofold—"Yahweh their God and David their king." The second object does not indicate the Davidic monarchy[262] (in this case one should have the "house of David") but David as a type of Messiah the King (cf. Jer 30:9; Ezek 34:23, 24). That this text is a messianic prophecy may be supported by the juxtaposition of David and Yahweh.[263] Cyril of Alexandria[264] shows that at some time Israel, once rejected, "will be called, and by faith she will return and know the God of all and David along with him, that is, the one who is from the seed of David, Christ according to flesh, the Lord and the King of all." In 5:6 where בקשׁ "to seek" appears again, Israel's quest for God is fully reduced to an external worship ("they will go to seek Yahweh with flocks and herds"). On the contrary, in 3:5 the return and quest for God are placed under the sign of a profound religiosity on Israel's part expressed by the verb פחד "to tremble."[265]

The object of this sacred "tremor" is "Yahweh and his goodness." The latter term, "his goodness" (טוּבוֹ), may have either a concrete (crops, property)[266] or abstract (goodness of God) connotation. In our view, here, since it stands besides Yahweh, "goodness" should be taken in its abstract sense as referring to God's person. Jerome[267] considers "good" a divine attribute when he mentions that "the good Son is born from the good Father." Slightly different, Theodore of Mopsuestia[268] connects the "good things" (ἀγαθῶν) with the "divine providence" (προνοίας), while Cyril of Alexandria[269] identifies the former with God's "kindness" (φιλοτιμίας) and "grace" (χάριν). In other Old Testament texts where טוב "goodness" has an abstract meaning, it is paralleled by חֶסֶד "mercy, love, kindness" (Is 63:7; Ps 25:7) and צְדָקָה "righteousness" (Ps 145:7), both notions defining God in relationship with Israel.[270]

Summing up, Israel's spiritual journey, as viewed by Hosea, begins with a pragmatic attitude toward God, emphasizing the "good" side of the past (2:9/7), and concludes with the search for the source of the gifts, the "goodness" or the Provider himself (3:5). While turning to God's "goodness," Israel notices that in the depth of her soul is something "good" (טוֹב) which may be accepted by God as an offering or rather as a pledge for a new life (cf. 14:3).[271]

The last phrase, "in the latter days" (בְּאַחֲרִית הַיָּמִים), points to the final phase of history (Is 2:2; Mic 4:1; Jer

23:20). According to Theophylact of Bulgaria,[272] this time, marked by Israel's conversion, will occur when the "complete number (πλήρωμα) of Gentiles" forming Christ's Church will be reached. Quite different is the view of Theodoret of Cyrus[273] who sees in this phrase a mere reference to the period following Israel's "seventy-year [Babylonian] captivity."

Hosea's insistence on an inner, genuine quest for God as opposed to people's search for material abundance through the idolatrous channels prefigures Jesus urging his disciples not to follow the Gentiles who seek anxiously all the things necessary to life: "But seek (ζητεῖτε) the kingdom (βασιλείαν) of God and his righteousness (δικαιοσύνην), and all these things shall be yours as well" (Mt 6:33). Notice the similarity in terms of object between these texts: "Yahweh and his goodness," in Hosea's line and "the kingdom of God and his righteousness," in the New Testament passage.

The main idea of this chapter is that God loves us not because we were worthy of his love, but simply because he is a loving God. This is the pure, unconditional, and, to a certain point, incomprehensible, love of God towards men.

Notes

[1] MT: תְּחִלַּת דִּבֶּר־יְהוָה lit. "the beginning of that Yahweh spoke..." ("when Yahweh first spoke"). According to Kimchi (cf. Macintosh, *Hosea*, 7), דבר is a noun like שָׁלֵם (Deut 32:5), hence the same sense, "the beginning of Yahweh's speaking to Hosea." We follow here the LXX: Ἀρχὴ λόγου Κυρίου "the beginning of the word of the Lord," which reads דְּבַר word" (construct state); cf. θ; Tg: שריות פתגמא; but note α': Ἀρχὴ ἦν ἐλάλησε.

[2] MT: בְּ "in, with, through"; LXX: πρὸς "to" but a few

LXX mss.: ἐν "in"; V: *in*; S: ᵓ*l* "to"; Tg: בְ.

³ MT: לוֹ "to him"; the pronoun is absent in four MT mss. (3 Kennicott and 1 de Rossi mss.) and in two LXX mss. Cf. Macintosh, *Hosea*, 13. The pronoun is not present in V. The absence of the pronoun may be explained as an attempt to harmonize v. 3 with vv. 6 and 8 where the pronoun is not represented. Cf. Wolff, *Hosea*, 8.

⁴ One Hebrew ms. (K 224) has אֵלִי "to me," which, according to F. S. North ("Hosea's Introduction to his Book," *VT* 8 [1958]: 430-31), is the original reading (cf. Is 8:3). More probable seems Wolff's explanation (*Hosea*, 8), for whom this reading is an abbreviation of אליו "to him." See also Macintosh, *Hosea*, 19.

⁵ MT: יִזְרְעֶאל; LXX: Ἰεζραὲλ; LXXⱽ: Ιεσραελ; cf. OL *israhel*; V: *Iezrahel*; Tg: מבדריא "scattered ones" as a reference to God's scattering of Israel in exile.

⁶ Some LXX mss. read Ἰούδα "Judah"; cf. OL *iudae*. Jerome (PL 25, 825) explains this peculiar reading as due to the translator's unfamiliarity with the less common name "Jehu." Having mentioned that some mss. have "Judah," Theophylact of Bulgaria (PG 126, 581) observes that "Jehu" is required by the "meaning" (ὁ νοῦς). Cyril of Alexandria in his commentary on Hosea (*Commentarius in Oseam prophetam*, PG 71, 37) uses a ms. with Ἰούδα, labeling it ἡ τῶν Ἑβδομήκοντα, "the Septuagint." He also cites a different "version" (ἔκδοσις) which reads "Jehu." Macintosh's suggestion (*Hosea*, 19) that "Judah" was due to a Judaean "appropriation" of Hosea's book seems unlikely since the context centered on a definite act, requires the reading "Jehu" rather than a general term like "Judah." The word יהודה (especially its abbreviated form יהוד) might be easily confused with יהוא. Cf. G. H. Patterson, *The Septuagint Text of Hosea*, 16.

⁷ MT: וַיֹּאמֶר לוֹ; LXX (the Lucianic recension) adds κύριος; cf. S: *mry*ᵓ.

⁸ לֹא רֻחָ֑מָה; LXX: οὐκ ἠλεημένη; LXX (the Venetian recension): οὐκ ἠγαπημένη; S: *lʾ ʾtrḥmt;* V: *absque misericordia;* Tg: דלא רחימין.

⁹ MT: כִּי־נָשֹׂא אֶשָּׂא לָהֶם; LXX: ἀλλ' ἢ ἀντιτασσόμενος ἀντιτάξομαι αὐτοῖς; α': ἐπιλήσομαι αὐτῶν; S: *mšql šqlʾn lhm;* V: *sed oblivione obliviscar eorum;* Tg: משבוק אשבק להון. *BHS*'s suggested reading שָׂנֹא אֶשְׂנָא "I will utterly hate (them)" cannot be supported by LXX ("but I will surely set myself in array against them") since the Greek version always uses μισεῖν "to hate" in order to render Hebrew שׂנא. V and α' presuppose נשׁה "to forget," but the Hebrew verb is commonly followed by the accusative rather than ל as it is in our example. Tg ("to forgive") relies on one of the meanings of נשׂא "to lift; to forgive." However, this meaning contradicts what is said in the preceding clause, "I will not show love," even though D. A. Garrett (*Hosea, Joel* [The American Commentary 19A; Broadman & Holmans, 1997], 59ff.) explains this "contradiction" as an example of God's paradoxical response to Israel. S ("to carry off") is close to MT. We follow here Wolff's proposed translation (*Hosea*, 8-9) which accounts for the adversative meaning of כי "on the contrary" following a negative clause (cf. Gen 3:5; 17:5; Is 7:8), attested by LXX (ἀλλ'). The direct object of the verb נשׂא ("to carry off, withdraw"; cf. Jer 49:29) is implied in the preceding verbal form אֲרַחֵם "I will show love," hence the translation "on the contrary, I will withdraw it (i.e., my love) from them."

¹⁰ With the exception of the ms. Vaticanus of LXX and the ms. Berlin of Tg, which omit the name "Judah," all other versions, including the Qumran ms. 4Qᵈ, attest this name. Cf. D. Barthélemy, *Critique textuelle de l'Ancien Testament. 3. Ezéchiel, Daniel et les 12 Prophètes* (Éditions universitaires Fribourg/Suisse; Göttingen: Vandenhoeck & Ruprecht, 1992), 497-98.

¹¹ MT: וַתַּ֫הַר; the additions of LXX: ἔτι and S: *twb* do not

presuppose a עוֹד "again" in the Hebrew text, but they are there perhaps because of a tendency to harmonize this verse with v. 6. Cf. Macintosh, *Hosea*, 29.

[12] Wolff (*Hosea*, 9) points to the symmetry of this passage based among other literary devices on the triple repetition of the command "Call the name" קְרָא שֵׁם followed each time by "for" כִּי, announcing a threat.

[13] For a discussion on this topic, see Wolff, *Hosea*, 11.

[14] This is the view of the great majority of scholars, including the interpreters of the patristic Age (Theodoret of Cyrus, *Enarratio in Oseam prophetam*, PG 81, 1553; Cyril of Alexandria, PG 71, 24; Theodore of Mopsuestia, PG 66, 128; Theophylactus of Bulgaria, PG 126, 577; Julian of Eclanum, PL 21, 963). The "beginning" was understood by ancient Jewish interpreters in a broader sense, as the starting point of the classical prophecy. Thus, Rabbi Johanan (*Baba Bathra*, 14b) considers Hosea much older than Amos, naming him "the Elder." A similar interpretation is found in Jerome, PL 25, 822: "In addition, others are reluctant to consider Hosea the first among all the prophets from that which is said: 'The beginning of the Lord's speaking in Hosea'; but I showed that these things which follow, the Lord first spoke to Hosea."

[15] The preposition בְּ meaning "through" is found in other similar contexts (Hos 12:11; Num 12:2; 1 Kgs 22:28); see KBL, 104a, no. 13.

[16] PL 25, 822.

[17] PG 71, 24 A.

[18] The plural abstract noun זְנוּנִים (cf. Gen 38:24) does not designate a common prostitute for which the Hebrew Bible uses אִשָּׁה זוֹנָה (Josh 2:1; Judg 11:1). The whole phrase, a *hapax legomenon*, may be compared with other constructions containing a plural abstract noun such as, אִישׁ הַדָּמִים "bloody man" (2 Sam 16:7); אֵשֶׁת מִדוֹנִים [מִדְיָנִים] "contentious wife" (Prov 25:24).

[19] Cf. KBL, 92a; 261b. On the other hand, Jerome (PL 25, 822) notices that the plural noun points to the intensity of the promiscuous act: "The Hebrew word *zanunim* does not mean prostitute and prostitution, as most people believe, but many prostitutions"; cf. BDB, 276a.

[20] See note 111.

[21] J. Coppens, "L'Histoire matrimoniale d'Osée. Un nouvel essai d'interprétation. Festschrift Nötscher," BBB 1 (1950): 38-45.

[22] Wolff, *Hosea*, 15.

[23] PG 71, 28 A-B.

[24] *Contre les hérésies*, IV, 20, 12 (SC 2, 670-71).

[25] PL 25, 823.

[26] Cf. G. Blankenbaker, "Tradition and Creativity: Hermeneutical Use of Language in Hosea 1-3," *Seminar Papers Series* 21 (1982): 20ff.

[27] Rabbi Johanan (*Pesahim*, 87a-b) explains: "'Children of whoredom,' in other words, you [Hosea] do not know whether they are yours or of others"; cf. A. D. Tushingham, *JNES* 12 (1953): 157. In a similar context, Jerome (PL 25, 822) raises the following question: "Both can be understood either that he [the prophet] received the former children of the prostitute from [her] prostitution, or that he himself begot his own children by the prostitute, who must be called 'children of whoredom,' because they are begotten of the prostitute." An explanatory phrase such as, "and she will give birth to ..." inserted into the text would eliminate any doubt on the Hosean paternity of the children; cf. Wolff, *Hosea*, 15.

[28] Garrett (*Hosea, Joel*, 53-54) adds that even though Hosea's children bear only the stigma of promiscuity, "the people were themselves promiscuous."

[29] Or: "Israel and its descendants in those days" (Kimchi); see Macintosh, *Hosea*, 8. According to Jerome (PL 25, 824), the "land" refers to "Samaria and Israel, namely, the

ten tribes, which at the time when these things were being said had gone away from the Lord." For Clement of Alexandria (*Eclogae ex scripturis propheticis*, III, C [GCS, 137-55]), the land does not designate the "element" (τὸ στοιχεῖον) but "those who are on the element, having an earthly reason (γηγενὲς φρόνημα)."

30 Cf. GK §119ee-gg.

31 Concerning מֵאַחֲרֵי (lit. "from after"; cf. LXX: ἀπὸ ὄπισθεν), note the interesting combination between אַחֲרֵי "after" (i.e., after other gods; cf. Ex 34:15) and מִן "from" (i.e., far away from Yahweh), pointing to both the idolatry and apostasy of Israel.

32 PG 71, 36 C. A similar interpretation is found in Theophylact of Bulgaria, PG 126, 580 B: "The whole land of the Israelite tribes committed whoredom, that is, she turned away from following the Lord, and dedicated herself to the idols."

33 The Masoretic vocalization, "Gomer," relies on an old tradition since the same vowels are already found in LXX (Γόμερ).

34 In ancient Israel a name used for both male and female was not considered a problem; cf. Noth, *Personennamen*, 61.

35 PL 25 824-825. A similar explanation is found in ibn Ezra: "completed in promiscuity" (גמורה בזנות); cf. Macintosh, *Hosea*, 11.

36 Cf. Noth, *Personennamen*, 38. A similar toponym "Diblatayim" in Moab, is mentioned in Num 33:46 and Jer 48:22. Note "Beth-diblathen," line 30, in the Moabite stone; cf. Albright, *ANET*, 321). But, as Wolff (*Hosea*, 17 n. 89) shows, a misunderstanding is excluded by the fact that the place-names are constructed with בְּנֵי or בְּנוֹת rather than with בַּת as in Hosea's phrase.

37 PL 25, 824: "Debelaim [Diblaim] means παλάτας (i.e., Latin *palatha* "jam of dry figs"), which were in great quantity in Palestine, and which Isaiah commanded to be placed

on king Ezekiah's wound. In fact it is a lump (mass) of rich figs, which they tread over and combine shaping them in the form of bricks, in order that they may remain for a long time unharmed."

[38] Cf. E. Nestle, "Miszellen. 9. Gomer bath diblaim," *ZAW* 29 (1909): 233-34.

[39] *Hosea*, 12-13.

[40] In ancient Israel, the mother was usually involved in giving name to her children (Gen 4:1; Judg 13:24; Is 7:14). Note that there are a few instances when the father named his children (Gen 16:15 [Abraham]; Gen 35:18 [Jacob]; Exod 2:22 [Moses]; 2 Sam 12:24 [David]; Is 8:3 [Isaiah]).

[41] The "valley of Jezreel," called "Ezdraelon" by Josephus, was known to Hosea's contemporaries as a battle scene since the time of judges (Deborah: Judg 4-5; Gideon: Judg 6-7) and the beginning of monarchy (1 Sam 29:1).

[42] According to Wolff (*Hosea*, 18; cf. Alt, "Der Stadtstaat Samaria," *KSchr*, 3:268f.), the dynasty of Omri founded Jezreel as a second capital for the tribes of Israel in contrast to Samaria, the capital of the Canaanites. Note, though, that there is no archaeological/historical evidence to support such a view. On the contrary, recent studies by Ussinkin and Williamson suggest that Jezreel, strategically situated near the road from Megiddo to Bethshean, served as a military installation rather than a political or religious capital; cf. Macintosh, *Hosea*, 16-17.

[43] The plural דְּמֵי indicates a "blood guilt" (cf. Ex 22:1); אִישׁ דָּמִים (2 Sam 16:7) means "murderer."

[44] For Theodoret of Cyrus (PG 81, 1557), Theodore of Mopsuestia (PG 66, 129), and Theophylact of Bulgaria (PG 126, 581 B), "the blood of Jezreel" refers to the assassination of Naboth.

[45] Years after the Omride dynasty ended, the Assyrian sources still referred to Israel as the "House [Land] of Omri" (*bīt ḫumriya*). Cf. Bright, *A History of Israel*, 241.

⁴⁶ LXX has ἐκδικήσω "I will avenge." Note the LXX uses the same verb when the Hebrew text reads נקם "to revenge."

⁴⁷ See "Introduction: III. Hosea: the Man and the Prophet."

⁴⁸ PG 71, 40 D.

⁴⁹ PL 25, 825: "But the type of the seed of God and the revenge of his blood refer to the Lord's Passion. That is why it is said that the house of Judah and the kingdom of the whole Israel are to be overturned."

⁵⁰ This phrase appears in Hosea only two more times (2:18/16, 23/21), always with reference to an historical rather than metaphysical reality.

⁵¹ For Theophylact of Bulgaria (PG 126, 584 A): "By the valley of Jezreel, we should understand the condescension (συγκατάβασιν) of Christ, (his) humility (ταπείνωσιν) and being laid in the tomb."

⁵² The "broken bow" motif was used in curses cast by a deity on a guilty people, such as in the "Treaty of Esarhaddon with Baal of Tyre," where we read: "May Astarte break your bow in the thick of battle, and have you crouch at the feet of your enemy, may a foreign enemy divide your belongings"; cf. Reiner, *ANET*, 534.

⁵³ This interpretation, "bow" for military might (a metonymy), is found in Tg, ואתבר ית תקוף עבדי קרב ישראל "I will destroy the power of Israel's warriors"; cf. Theodoret of Cyrus, PG 81, 1557: "He (i.e., God) will put an end to the power (τὴν δύναμιν) in the valley of Jezreel."

⁵⁴ According to Wolff (*Hosea*, 19), v. 5, an "independent saying" of Hosea, was later (perhaps after the events of 733 B.C.) inserted into the original text. His arguments (e.g., different vocabulary, "Israel" instead of "House of Israel," vv. 4, 6; a different interpretation of "Jezreel") are not strong enough either to refute this verse as inauthentic (as he himself acknowledges) or to consider it a secondary material. As Garrett (*Hosea, Joel*, 57f.) well notices, it is difficult to as-

sume that such a short saying could be preserved independently. He also suggests that by omitting v. 5 the structure of the poem (vv. 4-5), based on the alternation of temporal clauses (e.g., "a little while," "on that day") with statements of doom (e.g., "put an end," "break") is lost.

[55] Macintosh (*Hosea*, 20) shows that the valley of Jezreel was since 1479 B.C., when Tutmose III reported a victory there, a reputable battlefield of Palestine, and then a synonym for a future battle. This development is comparable to that of Megiddo, which became the Armageddon of Christian apocalyptic.

[56] Cf. Wolff, *Hosea*, 19-20; Garrett (*Hosea, Joel*, 59) suggests that v. 5 may be a reference to both the end of Jehu's dynasty and the events of 733 B.C. As we said above, the assassination of Zechariah, the last representative of Jehu's dynasty, at Ibleam was already mentioned in v. 4; see the commentary on v. 4. Verse 5 seems just to reinforce the saying in v. 4 concerning the north-Israelite monarchy.

[57] PG 71, 44 D. According to Theodore of Mopsuestia (PG 66, 129), the "breaking of the bow" refers to the subjugation of Israel by the Assyrians.

[58] The translation used in this commentary is approximate since the symbolic name is a negated Pu'al perfect which may be translated "She does not receive mercy," from the denominative root רַחֲמִים > רחם "compassion, motherly feeling" < רֶחֶם "womb."

[59] Cf. Wolff, *Hosea*, 20. According to Macintosh (*Hosea*, 25), since there is no mention about Judah's captivity, one may assume that the interpolation of v. 7 was made before 587 B.C.

[60] According to Cyril of Alexandria (PG 71, 45), the prophecy in v. 6 points to the fall of Samaria in 721 B.C., followed by the deportation of the Israelites to different parts of the Assyrian empire.

[61] This interpretation is found both in rabbinic (ibn

Ezra and Kimchi; cf. Macintosh, *Hosea*, 25) and patristic interpreters (i.e., Julian of Eclanum, PL 21, 969; Theodoret of Cyrus, PG 81, 1560; Theodore of Mopsuestia, PG 66, 132; Cyril of Alexandria, PG 71, 45-47; Theophylact of Bulgaria, PG 126, 584-585; Jerome, PL 25, 826).

[62] PG 126, 585 B. Jerome (PL 25, 827) offers a similar interpretation when he writes that the Christians are saved "not by military power, but by preaching the Gospel."

[63] 2 Macc 7:27; cf. Gen 21:8; 1 Sam 1:24. The Egyptian writing "The Instruction of Ani" reminds a young man of the duties toward his mother, by making this observation: "Her breast was in thy mouth for three years"; cf. Wilson, *ANET*, 420.

[64] See the commentary on 1:6-7.

[65] This interpretation is found in Kimchi; cf. Macintosh, *Hosea*, 28-29. For Jerome (PL 25, 827), the "weaning" of Lo-Ruhamah coincided with the beginning of the Babylonian exile during which the Israelites, rejected by God, were forced to eat unclean food. A similar interpretation is found in Julian of Eclanum (PL 21, 969) who takes "Not-My-People" as a reference to Judah.

[66] The versions (LXX: καὶ ἐγὼ οὐκ εἰμὶ ὑμῶν; V: *et ego non ero vester*; and S: *wʾnʾ lʾ ʾhwʾ lkwn*) follow the MT reading. Note the paraphrase-translation of the T: "And my word was not in your support."

[67] *Hosea*, 21-22. Wolff brings into discussion the version of LXX which uses the possessive ὑμῶν, and the capital letters with personal names, e.g., Εἰμί, Οὐ λαός μου (v. 9). These details show that as early as the third century B.C. אֶהְיֶה was perceived as a proper name rather than a verbal form.

[68] Some of the LXX mss. have θεός before ὑμῶν; cf. Ziegler, *Duodecim prophetae*, 148.

[69] MT: וְהָיָה "and (the number) shall be"; the MT reading is supported by α', σ', and the context of 2:1f.; cf. Wolff, *Hosea*, 24. LXX tries to approach two units (MT: 1:2-9 and

2:1-2) by the formula καὶ ἦν (for Heb וַיְהִי "and it was"). Thus chapter 1 in LXX has 11 vv., whereas in MT only 9 vv. Hence, the different numbering with respect to chapter 2, i.e., v. 10 in LXX is identical to v. 1 of chapter 2 in MT.

[70] GK § 51c: *niphal tolerativum*. Both Niphal forms imply the idea of being unable to perform an action (i.e., "which cannot be measured, counted").

[71] MT: בִּמְקוֹם אֲשֶׁר. Kimchi remarks that this phrase (lit. "in the place where") may also mean "instead of"; cf. Macintosh, *Hosea*, 30. The literal sense is attested in LXX: ἐν τῷ τόπῳ οὗ; Tg. באתר ד; S: *bʾtrʾ b*. Origin (*Commentarii in Romanos*, PL 14, 1152) argues that the "place" where God speaks is not an earthly spot but rather the mind or heart of the man. For Andersen and Freedman (*Hosea*, 203), the "place" refers to the wilderness, an ideal meeting-place between Yahweh and Israel.

[72] MT: רֹאשׁ "head"; LXX: ἀρχὴν "beginning."

[73] Tg adds גלותהון "(the land of) their exile."

[74] LXX has both forms in singular: τῷ ἀδελφῷ, τῇ ἀδελφῇ, relating this verse to 1:6, 9, where two of Hosea's children are mentioned. Yet the context of 2:1f., V, and α' support the plural forms in MT.

[75] A similar expression is found in Is 9:3, כְּיוֹם מִדְיָן "as on the day of Midian," referring to Gideon's victory over the Midianites (Judg 7).

[76] Cf. the "Display Inscriptions" in Oppenheim, *ANET*, 285.

[77] See Wolff, *Hosea*, 26.

[78] Hosea's choice of אֵל־חָי instead of similar titles, אֱלֹהִים חַיִּים (1 Sam 17:26), אֱלֹהִים חָי (Is 37:17), underscores the contrast between Yahweh and the Canaanite god El. Cf. Garrett, *Hosea, Joel*, 72, n. 101.

[79] Note that in 3:5 when Hosea mentions the Davidic dynasty he picks up the classical term for king, "their king" (מַלְכָּם).

80 Thus Andersen and Freedman, *Hosea*, 209.

81 *Hosea*, 31ff.

82 A similar interpretation is found in Cyril of Alexandria (PG 71, 53-56) who shows that the Israelites were led to their land by Zerubbabel, the "leader" (ἡγουμένου) of the tribe of Judah. Cf. Theodoret of Cyrus, PG 81, 1560; Theophylact of Bulgaria, PG 126, 589; Theodore of Mopsuestia, PG 66, 132; Julian of Eclanum, PL 21, 971. On the postexilic period, see Bright, *A History of Israel*, 360ff.

83 Origen (PG 14, 1152) interprets the name "Not-My-People" as an allusion to the Gentiles called by the "living God" to become his sons; idem, "Homélies sur Jérémie," SC 232, 384; cf. Cyprian, *Ad Quirinum*, CCSL III/I, 19; Irenaeus, SC 100, 670.

84 Wolff, *Hosea*, 29.

85 As we saw above, in the commentary, "Jezreel" is a type of Christ, thus the "day of Jezreel" may refer to the day of his resurrection. See the commentary on 1:4, 5. For Theophylact of Bulgaria (PG 126, 592 B), the "day of Jezreel" points to both the cross (τοῦ σταυροῦ) and resurrection (τῆς ἀναστάσεως) of Christ.

86 According to Garrett (*Hosea, Joel*, 73), Ezek 37 functions in the same way, as both a reference to Israel's restoration and a type of the universal resurrection.

87 PG 71, 57 B.

88 For Jerome (PL 25, 829), "they came up out of the land" refers to Christians who will ascend "from the earthly senses and from the humiliation of the letter, and they will enter upon the great day of the seed of God."

89 The Hebrew root ריב means "to strive with," and followed by the preposition ב, as in this example, it should be translated "to rebuke, reproach, accuse" (cf. Gen 31:36; Ex 17:2; Judg 6:32). Although LXX (κρίθητε), V (*iudicate*), and S (*dwnw*), all have "judge," Tg (אוכחו) seems to be much closer ("reprove") to the context.

⁹⁰ As Wolff (*Hosea*, 30) well noted, the presence of "lest" (פֶּן) in v. 5a requires that וְתָסָר (jussive + *waw*) be treated as an exhortation. The reading offered by the LXX (καὶ ἐξαρῶ ... ἐκ προσώπου μου—with respect to Yahweh) pushes the divine threat back to v. 4.

⁹¹ MT: ("lest") is supported by α', σ', θ' (εἴ πως); LXX (ὅπως ἄν "in order to") does not fit the context.

⁹² LXX (τὰ ἱμάτια καὶ τὰ ὀθόνια "garments and linen clothes") points to an urban setting vis-à-vis the agricultural setting of MT (cf. α': ἔριον ... λίνον). See Wolff, *Hosea*, 30.

⁹³ MT: וְשִׁקּוּיָי "and my drink"; LXX: πάντα ὅσα μοι καθήκει; S: *wkl dmtbʿ ly* "all which is necessary for me"; Tg: כל פרנוסי "all my provisions"; all these versions do not suggest a different *Vorlage* (so Nyberg), but they represent "generalizations" with respect to the Hebrew text; cf. Prov 3:8 where LXX renders freely שִׁקּוּי by ἐπιμέλεια "care"; cf. Macintosh, *Hosea*, 50.

⁹⁴ The Dead Sea commentary on Hosea (4QpHos^a) leaves out the phrase ונדרתי את גדרה

⁹⁵ MT: דַּרְכֵּךְ "your way"; but LXX and S have a third feminine suffix ("her") which fits better in this context. The plural of S (*ʾwrḥth*) and Tg (אורחתיך) "ways" was probably dictated by the parallel form וּנְתִיבוֹתֶיהָ "her paths" in v. 8b.

⁹⁶ LXX (αὐτούς) and S (*ʾnwn*) presuppose a slightly different Hebrew text, i.e., תמצאם "find them."

⁹⁷ MT: וְזָהָב עָשׂוּ לַבָּעַל "and as for gold, *they* used (it) for Baal" (cf. 4QpHos^a where עשו and זהב are still visible); LXX: αὐτὴ δὲ ἀργυρᾶ καὶ χρυσᾶ ἐποίησε τῇ Βααλ "she made silver and gold [images] for Baal." The singular of LXX ("she") fits better in the context than the plural of MT ("they") which can hardly refer to Israel (feminine singular!) in v. 10a. Most of the biblical scholars (Wellhausen, Harper, Wolff) consider the last two words of v. 10 (MT) a marginal gloss describing the sin of Israel—making of idols from precious metals (cf. 8:4; 13:2). The feminine article τῇ preceding Baal

(LXX), a male deity (in later times represented as a heifer: τῇ Βααλ τῇ δαμάλει [Tob 1:5]; cf. Wolff, *Hosea*, 31), refers perhaps to ἡ αἰσχύνη (Hebrew בֹּשֶׁת) "shame," frequently used as a substitute for Baal; see Macintosh, *Hosea*, 54ff.

[98] MT: לְכַסּוֹת "to cover"; Tg (דיהבית לה לכסאה "which I gave her to cover") and S (*dyhbt lh* "which I gave her") insert the verb "to give" as a bridge between the noun and the infinitive. LXX (τοῦ μὴ καλύπτειν "so that she shall not cover [her nakedness]") is supported by the Dead Sea commentary on Hosea (4QpHos[a]): מלכסות.

[99] MT: נבלתה is a *hapax legomenon*; LXX: ἀκαθαρσίαν "impurity"; Tg: קלנה "shame"; V: *stultitia* "folly"; S: *pwrsyh* "nakedness," "pudenda"; ibn Ezra renders this word by ערוה "nakedness" due to the fact that the *hapax* is accompanied by the verb אֲגַלֶּה "I will uncover." Michaelis (more recently Wolff, *Hosea*, 31, "genitals"; cf. S) translates נבלתה *membrum pudendum*; cf. Akkadian *baltu* "genitals." As Macintosh (*Hosea*, 59ff.) remarks, in the present context the word designates the moral turpitude of Israel.

[100] MT: מוֹעֲדָהּ "her appointed festival" (sg.); 4QpHos[a] has a plural, מועדיה (cf. LXX, V, S); LXX reads all the nouns in plural.

[101] MT: אֶתְנָה is a *hapax legomenon* probably deriving, as אתנן (Deut 23:19; Hos 9:1), from the root תנה "to hire," and in our context it designates a prostitute's wages; LXX: μισθώματά "hire, price."

[102] MT: יַעַר "forest"; LXX (μαρτύριον "testimony") perhaps misread עֵד.

[103] LXX expands ("birds of the sky and the reptiles of the earth").

[104] According to Wolff (*Hosea*, 31), the MT תַּקְטִיר (Hiphil) should probably be vocalized as a Pi'el (תְּקַטֵּר); cf. Hos 4:13; 11:2; Am 4:5; Jer 1:16; 18:15. But Macintosh (*Hosea*, 68) points out that the Hiph'il of the root is already attested in pre-exilic writings.

[105] *Hosea*, 33. For the critique of Wolff's view, see Macintosh, *Hosea*, 40ff.

[106] PG 126, 592 C-D.

[107] *Hosea*, 41, note 3.

[108] PG 71, 60 B-C.

[109] Wolff (*Hosea*, 33f.) suggests that these terms could designate some marks/emblems (headbands, rings, necklace, etc.) worn by a woman while participating in Canaanite sex cults. Garrett (*Hosea, Joel*, 77) shows that the emphasis falls here on "face" (= personality) and "breasts" (= body, sexuality). Thus, the woman is asked to turn her whole person away from the wrong path.

[110] For Wolff (*Hosea*, 34), nakedness equals helplessness. If one of husband's duties is to provide his wife with clothing (cf. Ex 21:10) the divorce brings the end of such a duty. Thus, "stripping" would be a symbolic act by which the husband publicly ceases to take care of his former wife. As Macintosh (*Hosea*, 43, note 4) remarks, extra-biblical texts (e.g., Emar, Nuzi) adduced to support this interpretation refer to situations quite different from that found in Hosea. For instance, the Emar evidence concerns the remarriage of the widows rather than dealing with spousal separation as our passage does; cf. J. Huehnergard, "Biblical Notes on Some New Akkadian Texts from Emar (Syria)," *CBQ* 47 (1985): 431ff.

[111] G. Dalman, *Arbeit und Sitte in Palästina* II (Gütersloh, 1932), 59f., 319f; גדר is a fence of stone, one meter high, used to mark the boundaries of vineyards.

[112] For Wolff (*Hosea*, 36), the wife's desire to return supposes a divorce initiated by her. Yet Gomer's return may also indicate a dramatic change in her moral behavior. Moreover, as Wolff himself noticed, such a return after a legal divorce would be impossible according to the marriage laws (Deut 24:1ff.).

[113] PL, 25, 832.

¹¹⁴ Cf. Macintosh, *Hosea*, 55.

¹¹⁵ The phrase אָשׁוּב וְלָקַחְתִּי is an idiom that might be rendered: "I will take back (withdraw)"; cf. Deut 24:4; Jer 36:28; Andersen and Freedman (*Hosea*, 244) consider אָשׁוּב an ironic reference to Gomer's rushed decision: וְאָשׁוּבָה "and I will return" (v. 9/7).

¹¹⁶ The word אִישׁ "man" (negated—"no one") is used here as antithesis to "God": human limitations versus God's powerful acts; see Garrett, *Hosea, Joel*, 83 n. 147.

¹¹⁷ The Hiph'il וְהִשְׁבַּתִּי "I will put an end" is perhaps an ironic allusion to שַׁבַּתָּהּ "her sabbaths" perceived as "taboo-days," days of complete rest, during the reign of Jeroboam II (cf. Hos 2;13; Am 8:5); see Wolff, *Hosea*, 38.

¹¹⁸ According to some scholars (Harper, Driver), the "sabbaths," in pre-exilic times used to designate the new-moon festivals; see Macintosh, *Hosea*, 61; Wolff (*Hosea*, 38) disagrees with such a view.

¹¹⁹ 1 Kgs 5:5; Mic 4:4; since their harvest occurs in August-September (Mic 7:1), it is possible that the annual festival (חַג), v. 13/11, might refer to this time of year.

¹²⁰ See Garrett, *Hosea, Joel*, 84.

¹²¹ According to Wolff (*Hosea*, 38), Hosea's choice for the *hapax legomenon* אֶתְנָה, instead of the usual form אֶתְנַן, was dictated by the wordplay on תְּאֵנָה "fig tree."

¹²² We took the relative אֲשֶׁר as referring to "days," but it may also be related to "Baals"; the latter alternative is attested in the V (*quibus accendebat incensum*).

¹²³ MT חֶלְיָתָהּ is a *hapax legomenon* (root חלה "to adorn"); ibn Ezra: "necklace" (Song 7:2; Prov 25:12); Kimchi: "a type of jewelry"; see Macintosh, *Hosea*, 66.

¹²⁴ MT: וְהֹלַכְתִּיהָ הַמִּדְבָּר; LXX: καὶ τάξω αὐτὴν ὡς ἔρημον "I will make her as a desert"; according to Ziegler (*Duodecim prophetae*, 121), the LXX reading is due to an inner corruption, i.e., τάξω for κατάξω "I will lead"; and ὡς for εἰς "to."

¹²⁵ MT: וְדִבַּרְתִּי עַל־לִבָּהּ; Tg interprets: אמליל תנחומין עַל לבה "I will speak *comfort* to her heart."

¹²⁶ MT: כְּרָמֶיהָ "her vineyards"; LXX (τὰ κτήματα αὐτῆς "her possessions") reflects the transition from the agricultural setting [MT] to the urban setting characteristic to the Jewish community of Alexandria in the third century B.C.; but σ': τοὺς ἀμπελῶνας αὐτῆς; V: *vinitores* "vine dressers"; Tg: פרנסהא "leaders/administrators."

¹²⁷ MT: לְפֶתַח תִּקְוָה; LXX: διανοῖξαι σύνεσιν αὐτῆς "to open her understanding"; cf. S: *dtpth swklh* "that her understanding may be opened"; V: *et aperiendam spem*; Tg: לתחמודי נפש "for delights of the soul."

¹²⁸ MT: וְעָנְתָה; LXX: καὶ ταπεινωθήσεται "she shall be humiliated"; cf. σ': κακωθήσεται; S: *wttmkk*; all these presuppose ענה (III in BDB, 776) "to be bowed down, humbled"; but θ' (ἀποκριθήσεται) and α' (καὶ ὑπακούσει) assume ענה (I in BDB, 772-73) "to answer." V: *canat* points to ענה (IV in BDB, 777) "to sing."

¹²⁹ MT: תִּקְרְאִי "you (fem.) will call" (twice in v. 18/16); cf. θ', α', and σ', all have καλέσεις for the second occurrence of this verbal form; but LXX (καλέσει με), V (*vocabit me*), and S (*tqryny*), all presuppose תקרא לי "she will call me." Based on the MT *difficilior lectio* (which, according to exegetical methodology, would commonly represent a preferable reading), and context (vv. 4/2-17/15), one may assume that the second person reproduces the original text.

¹³⁰ MT: בַּעְלִי "my husband"; LXX (βααλιμ; cf. θ': βααλειμ "Baals") tries to harmonize v. 18/16 with the following verse where the plural "Baals" (MT: הַבְּעָלִים) appears; α' (ἔχων με "possessing me") simply translates the Hebrew form.

¹³¹ MT: בִּשְׁמָם "by their name"; LXX (τὰ ὀνόματα αὐτῶν "their names") harmonizes the end of v. 19/17 with its first part where the plural "names" occurs.

¹³² MT: אֶשְׁבּוֹר מִן "I will break from" (lit.) is a *constructio praegnans* (GK § 119ee-gg) which needs another verb, for

instance, "and I will remove"; cf. Wolff, *Hosea*, 46; Tg: אבטיל
"I will abolish" (cf. S: *ʾbṭl*); LXX (συντρίψω "I will break")
seems to be a literal rendition of the Hebrew verb; cf. V:
conteram.

¹³³ MT: וְהִשְׁכַּבְתִּים "I will make them rest"; LXX (κατοικιῶ
σε "I will make you [sg.] dwell"; cf. σ': κατοικίσω αὐτούς)
presupposes the Hebrew root ישב "to stay, dwell"; notice
the singular "you" in LXX for the MT plural "them."

¹³⁴ MT: לָבֶטַח "in safety"; cf. σ': ἐν εἰρήνῃ "in peace";
LXX (ἐπ' ἐλπίδι "in hope") is likely to be an interpretation
rather than a simple translation.

¹³⁵ MT: אֶת־יְהוָה "(you will know) Yahweh"; cf. LXX: τὸν
κύριον; yet 45 Hebrew manuscripts offer a different reading,
כִּי אֲנִי יְהוָה "(you will know) that I am Yahweh"; cf. Cyril
of Alexandria: ὅτι ἐγὼ κύριος; and V: *quia ego Dominus*.
According to Wolff (*Hosea*, 46; cf. idem, "Erkenntnis Gottes
im Alten Testament," *EvTh* 15 [1955]: 428ff.), the expanded
text represents probably an early interpretation of Hosea
in the light of the book of Ezekiel (and Deutero-Isaiah); cf.
Macintosh, *Hosea*, 85.

¹³⁶ MT: אֶעֱנֶה "I will sing" (our rendition); LXX and S miss
the first occurrence of this form. While Wolff (*Hosea*, 46-47)
considers MT reading secondary, Macintosh (*Hosea*, 89) tries
to support its authenticity on stylistic grounds.

¹³⁷ MT: וְהֵם "and they"; LXX: ὁ οὐρανός; but B reads
αὐτός; Ziegler (*Duodecim prophetae*, 152) considers B's
reading preferable.

¹³⁸ MT: אֱלֹהָי "My God!"; LXX (κύριος ὁ θεός μου εἶ σύ
"You are the Lord my God") offers an expanded confession;
cf. V: *Dominus meus es tu*.

¹³⁹ See "Introduction: I. Historical Background. The
Assyrian Expansion and the Last Years of Israel."

¹⁴⁰ PG 66, 140 B.

¹⁴¹ The verb used here, פָּתָה (Pi'el), usually describes a
deceit (1 Kgs 22:22; Ezek 14:9). It also may indicate enticement

(Exod 22:16: a virgin seduced by a man). The same root (Qal) is found in Hos 7:11: יוֹנָה פוֹתָה "silly dove"—easily seduced—with reference to Israel.

¹⁴² PL 25, 836.

¹⁴³ Of great importance for text criticism is Cyril's observation (PG 71, 81 A) that there were other manuscript variants of LXX, besides the one (with πλανῶ) used by him i.e., ἀποφέρω "to carry away," and ἀπατῶ "to deceive."

¹⁴⁴ PG 71, 80 D.

¹⁴⁵ PG 66, 140 A-B.

¹⁴⁶ PG 81, 1564 C.

¹⁴⁷ Note the use of the verb ψυχαγωγέω "to lead departed souls to the nether world"; "to allure, persuade" (metaphoric use), similar in meaning to Hebrew פתה (Pi'el) "to allure."

¹⁴⁸ PG 126, 609 D-612 A: "You will understand this in two ways: either to emigrate (μετοικίζεσθαι) from one place to another, either when she flees, or when she is led into captivity (αἰχμαλωτίζεται), I will deprive her of all my goods mentioned above; or when she races into evil things and gives herself to idolatry, I will lead her astray (ἀποπλανήσω), namely, I will remove (μεταστήσω) her from such a path, which thing will be the greatest benefit."

¹⁴⁹ PG 71, 80 D-81 A.

¹⁵⁰ In the Hosean passage, the accent falls on the "wilderness" as a place where man's dependence on God is tested. Jacob's wrestling with a mysterious "man" (Gen 32:24-31), Moses' call from the burning bush (Ex 3), Israel's wandering after the covenant-making (Ex 19-20), Elijah's quest for God (1 Kgs 19:10-18), John's appeal to repentance (Mt 3:1ff.), Jesus' thrice temptation (Mt 4), Paul's preparation prior to his mission (Gal 1:17), the thirst for spiritual life of the early Christian ascetics, or the apocalyptic flight of the "woman" from before the dragon (Rev 12:6), all these events occurred in the "wilderness," and all these persons wanted to be closer to God even though often they had to pass the test of

faith. See Garrett, *Hosea, Joel*, 88ff.

[151] Tg adds: "and I will work miracles and mighty deeds for her, as I did for her in the wilderness," and interprets the Hosean passage as a allusion to the time of Israel's wanderings through the wilderness following the Exodus-event. From this verse, it seems though that Hosea was unaware of Israel's "murmuring" traditions which painted the "wilderness" days in dark colors (cf. Ex 17:2f.); see Childs, *The Book of Exodus. A Critical, Theological Commentary* (OTL; 3rd impression; Louisville: Westminster, 1974), 254ff.

[152] PL 21, 977 D.

[153] PL 25, 836.

[154] PG 71, 81 A.

[155] "To speak to one's heart" (דבר על לב) is a Hebrew idiom designating an intimate conversation between a man and a woman (Gen 34:3; Ruth 2:13; Is 40:1).

[156] PL 25, 836.

[157] PG 66, 140 C.

[158] PL 21, 977 D-978 A.

[159] PG 71, 81 D-84 A.

[160] PG 126, 612 C-D.

[161] PL 25, 836.

[162] PL 21, 978 A. In Julian's view, the "wilderness" represents the time and the place marked by divine blessings while the opulent life of the city (e.g., Jericho's) is the expression of man's disobedience toward God (e.g., Achan's episode: Josh 7).

[163] PG 71, 84 A.

[164] PG 66, 140 C: "I will return her to the enjoyment (ἀπόλαυσιν) of the previous goods (τῶν προτέρων), by drawing [her] out from captivity (τῆς αἰχμαλωσίας)." According to Theophylact of Bulgaria (PG 126, 612 C-D), Israel's "possessions" (τὰ κτήματα) refer to the "lands" (χώρας) which the Israelites conquered from Canaan. Israel will possess again these lands after her return from captivity.

[165] PG 71, 84 A. For Theophylact of Bulgaria (PG 126, 613 A-B), "from there" means "from the one who speaks to (ἐπὶ) their heart. For from this we became rich in such possessions (τὰ κτήματα). Moreover, the possessions of everyone baptized in Christ are the remission of sins and the mansions (μοναὶ) above, which someone procures for himself, through the way which leads to each one of these. For there are as many ways as there are many different mansions. But the one who sins ceases to hold the possessions, and is deprived of them, while the divine word becomes silent (σιγᾷ) in him. Yet whenever he touches his heart he speaks in (ἐν) it, then he gives him those possessions from there, that is from the heart. For the kingdom of heaven is inside of us. Therefore, our heart either takes these goods away from us or he gives [them to us]."

[166] Macintosh (*Hosea*, 71) suggests that the context requires a temporal sense for מִשָּׁם ("from that moment"); cf. שָׁם "then" in Ps 132:17; Judg 5:11; Is 48:16.

[167] With respect to the location of the "valley of Achor" the scholars' views are divided. Wolff (*Hosea*, 42f.; idem, "Die Ebene Achor," *ZDPV* 70 [1954]: 76-81) suggests *Wadi en-Nuwēime* (north-west of Tell es-Sultan) bordered on its eastern side by the hills opposite the Jordan Valley at Khirbet el-Mefjer (Gilgal?). This location (near the fertile country) matches the valley's description as a "gate of hope." But Noth ("Beiträge zur Geschichte des Ostjordan-landes III: Die Nachbaren der israelitischen Stämme im østjordanlande," *ZDPV* 68 [1951]: 42ff.) argues for *Buqea*, situated near the Orthodox monastery Mar Saba, 9-12 miles south of Jericho, Khirbet Mird and Qumran. Yet, as Wolff pointed out in his critique of Noth, the text of Josh 7:24ff does not imply such a great distance from Jericho for the execution of Achan. Furthermore, the name "gate of hope" is not appropriate with this valley's location in the midst of a desert. More recently, the "valley of Achor" was identified with the lower end of

the Jordan valley; cf. Macintosh, *Hosea*, 74.

¹⁶⁸ The word תִּקְוָה "hope" may be taken as an allusion to Rahab's episode during the conquest of Canaan (Josh 2). Despite the order given by the king of Jericho, the prostitute Rahab hid the two Israelite spies; then, she let them down by a "rope" (חֶבֶל) through the window (2:15). The spies promise Rahab that the Israelites will spare her provided that she tie the same "crimson cord" (תִּקְוַת חוּט הַשָּׁנִי) in the window (2:18). Note the wordplay between תִּקְוָה "hope" (Hos 2:17) and the *hapax legomenon* תִּקְוָה "cord" (Josh 2:18), both nouns deriving from the same root קוה "to wait for" (cf. BDB, 875-76). But there is another common element, besides this wordplay, which links these two passages, namely prostitution. Both Rahab (mentioned among Jesus' ancestors, Mt 1:5) and Gomer are prostitutes about to be saved through God's wondrous providence; see Garrett, *Hosea, Joel*, 91.

¹⁶⁹ The author of Josh 7:25-26 explains the name Achor in relation to the Hebrew root עכר "to stir up, disturb, trouble," hence עָכוֹר could refer to the "trouble" Achan has caused by his deed. Note Cyril's original rendition (PG 71, 84) of "Achor" as "distortion, perversion" (διαστροφή) and its critique in Jerome's commentary on Hosea (PL 25, 836).

¹⁷⁰ See Garrett, *Hosea, Joel*, 91.

¹⁷¹ According to Rashi and Kimchi, the "valley of Achor" expresses the misfortunes of the exile; cf. Macintosh, *Hosea*, 75.

¹⁷² PL 21, 978 A.

¹⁷³ PL 25, 836-837.

¹⁷⁴ PG 81, 1565 A. Similar interpretations may be found in Theophylact of Bulgaria, PG 126, 614; Theodore of Mopsuestia, PG 66, 140.

¹⁷⁵ MT: וְעָנְתָה "And she shall sing"; here we opt for ענה (IV in BDB, 777) "to sing, utter tunefully" (Qal: Ex 15:21: Miriam's song of victory; 32:18: as in attack; Num 21:17; Ps

147:7: as in lauding; Jer 25:30: as in vintage; Pi'el: Ex 32:18: the sound made by the soldiers; Is 27:2: as in vintage; Ps 88:1: a lament). As one can notice, the contexts in which this verb appears are battle, vintage, and cult. Thus this verb might designate a sort of spontaneous tune or melody, probably with improvised lyrics or none at all. It is perhaps what the Septuagint wants to convey by its quite consistent use of ἐξάρχω "to start singing, to give the tone" for the Hebrew root ענה IV. Nonetheless, in Hos 2:17/15 the Septuagint reads ταπεινωθήσεται "she shall be humiliated" presupposing ענה (III in BDB, 776) "to be bowed down, humble," thus carrying on the idea of divine punishment evoked by the phrase "valley of Achor." Jerome (PL 25, 838) explains the Septuagint reading as follows: "'She will be humiliated' and 'she will be afflicted,' as the LXX and σ' translated, does not fit the time of joy unless indeed one seeks an analogy with Paul, who after he was called as apostle, cried for his old sins and said that he was unworthy to be called apostle since he persecuted the Church of God." Following LXX, the Greek Fathers are focusing primarily on "captivity" and all the humiliation Israel had to endure in order to realize the gravity of their trespasses and thus return to God (so Cyril, PG 71, 85; Theodoret of Cyrus, PG 81, 1565; Theodore of Mopsuestia, PG 66, 140-141). Theophylact of Bulgaria (PG 126, 616 B-C) explains: "They will be humiliated (ταπεινωθήσονται) by serving the Assyrians." And he goes on urging those who received the Christian baptism to be humble: "Let whosoever is an infant (νήπιος) in Christ, now born (γεννηθεὶς) from water and Spirit, be humble (ταπεινούσθω) and let him not exalt himself (ἐπαιρέσθω) concerning the gift of the remission of sins."

[176] PG 71, 88 A-B. But Theodoret of Cyrus, PG 81, 1565 B: "He calls the time spent in Egypt 'her childhood (νηπιότητα).'"

[177] The analogy between Miriam and Israel is found in

Julian of Eclanum, PL 21, 978 B: "For just as back then, with the waves divided, they crossed the sea on dry land, and Mary, the sister of Moses, grasping musical instruments, uttered praises of God with the choir accompanying, in this manner, they were singing while coming out from the Assyrian captivity"; cf. Jerome, PL 25, 837.

[178] Wolff (*Hosea*, 49) notices that the whole phrase וְהָיָה בַּיּוֹם־הַהוּא is followed here by an imperfect (cf. 2:23; Is 7:18; Jer 4:9; Ezek 38:10; Joel 3:18), but typical to the older prophetic literature is the use of a perfect consecutive (1:5; Am 8:9; Mic 5:9; Is 22:20). Wolff also shows (contra Robinson) that the grammatical choice alone cannot be considered a strong evidence for a later redaction in case of Hos 2:18. Even though it points to a certain historical event, one may not forget the eschatological dimension of "that day" (cf. Joel 4:18; and the "day of Yahweh" in Am 5:18). Cyril (PG 71, 88 B) sees here a reference to the Incarnation: "He calls 'day' the time of our Savior's epiphany (ἐπιδημία) for properly and truly one could call 'day' the time of Incarnation (ἐνανθρωπήσεως) of the Only-Begotten (Μονογενοῦς), when the mist in the world was dispelled and the darkness disappeared."

[179] On אִישׁ "man, husband" and בַּעַל "lord; Baal," see the commentary on 2:4. One may add that Theodoret of Cyrus (PG 81, 1565) distinguishes between the two terms, suggesting by the insertion of "inmate, spouse" (σύνοικον) into his commentary that "man" points to marriage: "In captivity she will get rid of idolatry, and will call me man and spouse." Differently, Jerome (PL 25, 838-839) shows that both terms, in Hebrew as well as in Syriac, designate "husband." In support to his view, Jerome brings forth Aquila's rendition of "Baal," ἔχων "the one who has," explaining "the one who has me means the one who has me in marriage." For Jerome, the only reason for which "Baal" is not used in the conversation between God and his people is its syncretistic-cultic connotation.

[180] The clearest evidence of religious syncretism is found in personal names. Thus in Samaria Ostraca, dating from the eighth century B.C., eleven names have Yahweh as a component whereas ten names are composed with Baal (Albright, *Archaeology and the Religion of Israel*, 41, 160). But, as Wolff (*Hosea*, 49) noted, syncretistic tendencies were already present at the beginning of the monarchy. "Jonathan" = "Yahweh has given" (1 Sam 13:16) and "Eshbaal" = "Man of Baal" (2 Sam 2:8) were both Saul's sons. The Elephantine Papyri of the fifth century B.C. show that in the Jewish colony of Elephantine in the Nile Delta, Yahweh was worshipped along with a female deity named "Anathyahu" ("Anath is Yahweh") or "Anathbethel" ("Anath of Bethel"). The name "Bealiah" (בְּעַלְיָה) = "Yahweh is Baal (Lord)" (1 Chr 12:6), encapsulating both divine names, Yahweh and Baal, describes an advanced stage of syncretism marked by confusion between Yahweh and the Canaanite god of fertility; cf. Noth, *Personennamen*, 120f.

[181] The plural "Baals" (הַבְּעָלִים) refers here, as in v. 15, to the local manifestations of the god Baal rather than to distinct deities. According to Cyril (PG 71, 88 D), "Baalim usually indicate idols (εἴδωλα)"; cf. Theodoret of Cyrus, PG 81, 1565.

[182] Theodore of Mopsuestia (PG 66, 141 B) sees in God's action of removing the "Baalim" from Israel's cult a powerful blow against syncretism: "Thus, they will apply (ἐπιθήσουσι) no more my name to the Baalim"; and Theophylact of Bulgaria (PG 126, 617 A) adds: "Nor will they say that God is Baal." Julian of Eclanum (PL 21, 979 A) concludes: "So that she [Israel] may not ascribe my name to the Baalim, that is to say, to the idols."

[183] The formula כרת ברית "to cut a covenant" (literally) in the Old Testament designates the "making of a covenant." The verb כרת "to cut" refers probably to an ancient ritual of cutting animals in two. By passing through the halves

of sacrificed animals, the person who initiated the covenant promises to observe it. Otherwise his fate would be as those animals' (cf. Gen 15:9f.). Wolff (*Hosea*, 50f.) suggests that in the Hosean passage Yahweh is not the partner of Israel but rather a mediator of a covenant between his people and the animal world. The fact that God includes within this covenant the animal realm does not necessarily exclude him from being Israel's partner in the new relationship designed and initiated by Yahweh himself. Macintosh (*Hosea*, 82) compares this covenant with God's promise in Gen 3:15 which concerns two other parties. Yet one may not forget that in Hos 2:20/18 God makes a "covenant," while in Genesis he only delivers a promise. This covenant is probably in the same vein as Is 11:6-7.

[184] For Cyril (PG 71, 89), the beasts and the birds included in Yahweh's covenant with Israel "may designate the enemies, Persians, Medes, and Babylonians, who ravaged the land of the Jews." According to Theodoret of Cyrus (PG 81, 1565 B), v. 20/18 "does not refer to the wild animals and birds, but to the beast-like (θηριωδῶν) men, and those who fly like birds, and to those who resemble venomous reptiles."

[185] The utter destruction of the military arsenal promised solemnly by God represents a dear ideal embraced by the Old Testament's prophets. Thus, for instance, Isaiah projects to a messianic future the long-awaited day when the nations "will beat their swords into plowshares and their spears into pruning hooks" (2:4); cf. 9:3; Mic 5:4; Zech 9:10.

[186] The ideal of a peaceful and safe life is expressed in a slightly different way, but still close to Hosea's theology, in Lev 26:6: "I will grant peace in the land, and you shall lie down untroubled by anyone (אֵין מַחֲרִיד)" (cf. Jer 23:6; Ps 4:9).

[187] The verb אָרַשׂ (Pi'el) designates the premarital period before paying the bride-price (מֹהַר) to the bride's father,

the last and the main act in acquiring a wife (Gen 34:12; Ex 22:15f.; 1 Sam 18:25). On the other hand, the verb לקח "to take" denotes in Hosea (1:2), as elsewhere in the Old Testament (e.g., Deut 20:7), the beginning of the marriage, after the bride left her father's house and stepped across her husband's threshold.

[188] According to E. Jenni ("Das Wort *ʿōlam* im Alten Testament," ZAW 64 [1952]: 235-39), לעולם "forever" is a technical term denoting a lifelong commitment (cf. Ex 21:6) made by the future husband by the payment of the bride-price.

[189] After showing that the old covenant was neither unbroken nor eternal, Cyril of Alexandria (PG 71, 92 C-D) describes the new covenant in terms of an eternal betrothal: "By the time of restoration, namely, at the time of Christ's epiphany (ἐπιδημίας), another type of betrothal appeared, eternal (διηνεκής), firm (ἀσάλευτος), much more radiant (λαμπρότερος) than the first one (πρώτου), and in a better condition than its foreshadow (σκιᾶς). For God of all, in the same manner as the one who lavishes his wife with the supply of fleshly service (σαρκικῆς δουλείας), through the foreshadow and figures (τύπων), called to a spiritual purification (ἀποκάθαρσιν). In addition, he determined (ἐμέτρει) the time for the betrothal (μνηστείᾳ). For the first one was not faultless (ἄμεμπτος), according to Paul, nor was it undecaying (ἀγήρως), nor far from being abolished. Thus, the place of a second one (δευτέρας) was sought, namely, of a new one (νέας), which, by Christ, brought to us the gift (δωρεᾶς) and the grace (χάριτος), neither temporary, nor for carnal freedom. For he enlisted us among the children of God and gave us the promise (ἀρραβῶνα) of the Spirit, and prescribed eternal laws." In the same vein, Theodoret of Cyrus (PG 81, 1565 D) interprets "forever" (εἰς τὸν αἰῶνα), as a reference to the "Church, gathered from among the Jews and Gentiles ... waiting for the eternal goods." Theophylact of Bulgaria (PG 126, 620 B) shows that the first covenant was

not eternal because the "service (λατρεία) of the law was transient (πρόσκαιρος)."

¹⁹⁰ PG 66, 141 D.

¹⁹¹ PL 25, 840.

¹⁹² PG 71, 93 A. Similarly, Theophylact of Bulgaria (PG 126, 620 B) writes: "For it was not an angel or an elder who saved us, but the Lord himself."

¹⁹³ Or "equity" designates a sort of social assistance for those less fortunate (Hos 10:12; Judg 5:11; Am 5:7, 24; 6:22; Ps 98:2); cf. K. Fahlgren, S^{e}daka (Uppsala, 1932), 78. For Theodore of Mopsuestia (PG 66, 141 D), δικαιοσύνη (LXX) refers to God's future intervention, "punishing (κολάζων) those who did harm to you [Israel] during the captivity."

¹⁹⁴ "Justice" denotes the societal order reached by observing the legal precepts (Hos 5:11; 6:5; 10:4; Am 5:7, 24; Ezek 20:11).

¹⁹⁵ Or "steadfast love, kindness" indicates a tender and thoughtful attitude toward the other members of the community (Hos 4:1; 6:4,6; 10:12; 12:7/6; Jer 2:2). Relying on LXX reading (ἐν ἐλέει "in mercy"), Theophylact of Bulgaria (PG 126, 620 D) explains: "He showed mercy (ἔλεον) and compassion (οἰκτιρμοὺς) to all men, whom he saved not by [their own] works, but according to his mercy, through the bath of regeneration and the renewal of the Holy Spirit."

¹⁹⁶ Or "pity"; on the meaning of this term, see the commentary on 1:6.

¹⁹⁷ Or "Steadfastness" emphasizes the idea of reliability, integrity, stability, with respect to Yahweh's personality; Deut 32:4 portrays Yahweh as אֵל אֱמוּנָה a "faithful God." LXX reads ἐν πίστει "in faith," hence Cyril's interpretation (PG 71, 96 B): "We were called through faith (διὰ πίστεως) to a spiritual intimacy (οἰκειότητα) [with God]. Having been called thus, we learned to know him who is God in essence (φύσει)." Similarly, Theophylact of Bulgaria (PG 126, 621 A) explains: "For knowledge of God comes from faith."

¹⁹⁸ We have here a series of bridal gifts Yahweh gives Israel, who plays the father's role as well. The particle בּ (*beth pretii*), prefixed to each term of this series, introduces in the conjugal law of the Old Testament the bride-price (מֹהַר; cf. 2 Sam 3:14), usually equivalent of 50 silver shekels (Deut 22:29). For Cyril (PG 71, 93), these items represent the "manner" (τρόπος) in which God's "union" (συναφείας) with Israel will occur.

¹⁹⁹ PL 25, 840.

²⁰⁰ Such an interpretation is found in LXX text variant used by Theodore of Mopsuestia (PG 66, 141-144) which has "Israel" (Ἰσραήλ) for "Jezreel." In his commentary, Theodore speaks of "Israel" as the recipient of all goods including a second habitation of her "own land," but makes no mention of "Jezreel." Similarly, Julian of Eclanum (PL 21, 980 B) identifies "Jezrahel" with the "people" (of Israel). For Theophylact of Bulgaria (PG 126, 621 C), "Jezreel" refers to both "the son born by the prostitute, and the previously idolatrous people." Cyril of Alexandria (PG 71, 100 A) has a rather typological interpretation: "Jezreel may be explained 'God's offspring,' that is the Son, who from the Father according to nature and in an ineffable way was born." And as Jezreel symbolizes Israel's fertility, in the same manner, shows Cyril: "The fruit of the saints' life is in the glory of Christ." A similar interpretation is found in Jerome, PL 25, 841. After translating "Jezreel" by "seed (offspring) of God," Jerome alludes to Christ's sacrifice: "For the seed of God is sown in the ground, so that it may bring much fruit."

²⁰¹ Wolff (*Hosea*, 53f.) rightly notices that in the ancient Orient, Israel alone, freed from the burden of mythological thinking (cf. Gen 1), could venture into a free study of nature. Thus, Hos 2:23/21-24/22 offers a sort of "scientific" description of the relationships within nature, rather than a simple enumeration of items as, for instance, in the miracle stories of the ancient Near East.

²⁰² On the series "corn, new wine, and fresh oil," see the commentary on 1:10. Cyril of Alexandria (PG 71, 97 C) explains: "The corn is the type of life; the wine stands for gladness; the oil stands for cheerfulness and vigor."

²⁰³ During the exile, Deutero-Isaiah (Is 62:5) would spell out Hosea's barely detected thought about God who finds delight in his bride: "As the bridegroom rejoices over the bride, so shall your God rejoice (יָשִׂישׂ) over you."

²⁰⁴ The verb זרע "to sow" alludes to "Jezreel" (one of Israel's designations) mentioned in 2:24/22. The name of Hosea's first son, "Jezreel," formerly announcing the end of the monarchy and the beginning of the captivity (1:4), is now (2:25/23) loaded with a hope-giving prophecy concerning the return from captivity of Israel and her inhabiting the land. This drastic shift in Israel's name and fate speaks of the wondrous redemptive work of God, who is willing and able to change the sin-caused misery into blessedness for those who are ready to repent; see Macintosh, *Hosea*, 88.

²⁰⁵ PG 71, 100 B.

²⁰⁶ According to Wolff (*Hosea*, 54), v. 25a refers to the return of the inhabitants of the Jezreel Valley who had been deported by Tiglath-pileser III in 733 B.C.

²⁰⁷ PG 81, 1568 B.

²⁰⁸ Cf. Mays, *Hosea*, 50f.

²⁰⁹ In the Hosean passage, the verb ידע "to know" conveys the idea of acknowledging God as the Giver of all gifts; see Wolff, "'Wissen um Gott' bei Hosea als Urform der Theologie," *EvTh* 12 (1952-53): 548f. Note, though, that in the Old Testament, the same verb describes the wide spectrum of intimate, sexual relations (Gen 19:8; Num 31:17; Judg 11:39). By using "Yahweh" as direct object instead of "me" (as in 2:15: אֹתִי שָׁכְחָה "she forgot me"), Hosea underscores the theological significance of the personal name "Yahweh" ("He will be"), that is to say, the active presence of God in the midst of his people.

²¹⁰ MT: אֲהֻבַת רֵעַ "beloved of a friend" (passive participle of אהב "to love"); α′, σ′ (ἠγαπημένην τῷ πλησίον / ἀφ' ἑτέρου); V (dilectam amico); and Tg (דרחימא על בעלה "which is beloved of her husband"), all presuppose the MT; LXX (ἀγαπῶσαν πονηρά) and S (rḥmʾ byštʾ) read the same consonants as the MT, but with different vowels, i.e., רָע / אֹהֶבֶת רָע "who loves evil things" (active participle of אהב). The active participle (LXX, S) is required by the context: in v. 1b the Israelites' attitude stands in parallel to Gomer's activity in v. 1a.; see Patterson, *The Septuagint Text of Hosea*, 7. Note Jerome's remark (PL 25, 842) with respect to the LXX reading, πονηρά "the evil things," that the Hebrew word רע (unvocalized!) may be translated either "evil" or "friend"; note also Theodore of Mopsuestia (PG 66, 144 C) who in his commentary goes further than the Greek version by depicting Gomer as a "worker (ἐργάτιν) of all sorts of evil things."

²¹¹ MT: אֲשִׁישֵׁי עֲנָבִים; LXX: πέμματα μετὰ σταφίδων "cakes of raisins"; S: *dbwšʾ dʾpštʾ* "honey (loaves) of raisins"; V: *vinacea uvarum* "grape skins"; Tg: ויהון דמן לגבר דאשתלי "they shall be like a man who has made a mistake"; as Macintosh (*Hosea*, 99) notices, Tg's interpretative translation is perhaps due to the similarity in sound between אשישי and אִישׁ "man."

²¹² MT: וָאֶכְּרֶהָ "and I bought her"; LXX: καὶ ἐμισθωσάμην "I hired [her]." Following the Greek version, Theodoret of Cyrus (PG 81, 1568 C) suggests that the "prophet offered a payment (μισθὸν) to the woman"; V: *et fodi eam* "I dug her in"; Jerome (PL 25, 843) explains: "When he says 'I dug,' one should understand the vineyard God planted, which in many places in the scriptures indicates the Jewish people"; S: *wzbnth* "I redeemed her"; Tg: ופרקתינון "I redeemed them."

²¹³ MT: וְלֵתֶךְ שְׂעֹרִים "and a lethech of barley"; LXX: νεβελ οἴνου "a pitcher of wine" (νεβελ is the translitera-

tion of Hebrew נֵבֶל "skin, skin-bottle, pitcher") points to a different *Vorlage* than that of the MT. For Epiphanius of Cyprus (PG 43, 272f.), "lethech" was an explanation of "homer": "Lethech (λεθέκ) is mentioned in prophet Hosea, 'for I hired [her] for myself for a lethech of barley,' but in some manuscripts, there is only 'a homer (γόμορ) of barley'; for these indicate 15 measures"; see Patterson, *The Septuagint Text of Hosea*, 32-33. According to Barthélemy (*Critique textuelle*, 502), LXX reading was probably influenced by 1 Sam 1:24 or 2 Sam 16:1, where νεβελ οἴνου concludes similar lists of provisions; V: *et dimidio choro hordei* "half a cor of barley"; cf. Jerome's commentary (PL 25, 842): "And for *nebel vini* Hebrew reads 'lethech seorim,' which other interpreters translated ἡμίκορον *hordei*, namely, half a cor, which represents 15 measures."

²¹⁴ MT: תֵּשְׁבִי לִי "you shall stay for myself"; LXX: καθήσῃ ἐπ' ἐμοί "you shall remain for me"; V: *expectabis me*; σ': προσδοκήσεις "you shall wait for me."

²¹⁵ MT: וְגַם־אֲנִי אֵלָיִךְ "and I also to you" (literal); Rosenmüller noticed that ibn Ezra and Radaq added לֹא אָבוֹא, hence the sentence "nor will I come to you," supported by the parallelism with the previous sentence; Meinhold, *BHS*, Weiser, Wolff and Mays inserted לֹא אֵלֵךְ "I will not go"; van Hoonacker rightly remarked that וְגַם־אֲנִי אֵלָיִךְ corresponds to תֵּשְׁבִי לִי rather than to וְלֹא תִהְיִי לְאִישׁ. Thus God's attitude toward his wife should match that of the latter toward her Lord; cf. Barthélemy, *Critique textuelle*, 506; Hoonacker's remark is supported by LXX: ἐγὼ ἐπὶ σοί "and I for you"; V: *sed et ego expectabo te* corresponds to *expectabis me*, V rendition of תֵּשְׁבִי לִי in v. 3a; S: w'n' 'hw' lwtky "and I will be to you"; Tg: ואף אנא עתיד לרחמא עליכון "then I too will have compassion on you."

²¹⁶ MT: מַצֵּבָה "pillar"; but LXX (θυσιαστηρίου), S (*mzbḥ'*), and V (*altari*), all presuppose מִזְבֵּחַ "altar."

²¹⁷ MT: תְּרָפִים "teraphim"; LXX (δήλων "manifestations")

and Tg (מחוי "proclaiming" [or "idolatrous oracles"; cf. M. Jastrow, *Dictionary of the Targumim, the Talmud Babli and Yerushalmi, and the Midrashic Literature* (New York: The Judaica Press, 1992), 758]) may be considered interpretative translations.

²¹⁸ MT: וּפָחֲדוּ אֶל "and they shall return trembling to": a *constructio praegnans* as in 1:2b; cf. Wolff, *Hosea*, 57; see the commentary on 1:2; LXX: καὶ ἐκστήσονται ἐπί "and they shall be amazed at"; S: *wnd'wn* "and they shall know"; Tg: ויתנהון לפולחנא דיוי "and they shall be present for the worship of the Lord."

²¹⁹ According to Wolff (*Hosea*, 57f.), ch. 3, along with the call accounts, belongs to the literary genre called *memorabile* (ἀπομνημόνευμα) concerned primarily with facts and their significance. The *memorabile* of symbolic action should be differentiated from a parable or an allegory, both making use of "imaginary elements," since the *memorabile* relies on an historical event. In Wolff's view, the emphasis does not fall on the autobiographical aspect of the ch. 3, but rather on God's command concerning symbolic action. The *memorabile* consists of three basic elements: (a) God's command (v. 1); (b) account of its realization (vv. 2f.); and (c) the interpretation (vv. 4f.).

²²⁰ For instance, Cyril of Alexandria (PG 71, 101) thinks that the woman "charged with adultery" is different from the "lustful woman" (Gomer) who was evicted; cf. Theophylact of Bulgaria, PG 126, 624. On the relationship between ch. 3 and chs. 1 and 2, see the "Introduction. 5. Conjugal Drama of Hosea. Preliminaries."

²²¹ PL 25, 842.

²²² Cf. Wolff, *Hosea*, 59.

²²³ According to Theodore of Mopsuestia (PG 66, 144 C), "'The Lord said to me' means that this is the voice of God who speaks, which is divinely (θειόθεν) revealed to him."

²²⁴ "Again" (עוֹד) belongs to the autobiographical account

(so Macintosh) rather than to a later editor. Hosea uses this adverb in reference to the events occurring later in his life compared to those marking the beginning of his ministry (1:2ff.). That "again" should be taken together with "go" (cf. Zech 1:17; 11:15) rather than with "he said" is obvious from LXX, V, and S. That both עוֹד "again" and אֵלַי "to" are marked with accents may mean that for the Masoretes the question with which word "again" should be taken had perhaps no great value.

225 Yahweh's command to "love" seems quite odd since actions rather than feelings are commanded (cf. M. Buber, *The Prophetic Faith* [translated by C. Witton-Davies; New York, 1949], 112). According to Wolff (*Hosea*, 60), here, as elsewhere in Hosea, "love" (אהב) is not a euphemism for intercourse, nor a term for marriage, nor a word designating a feeling, but an act, which may be translated: helping (11:1), healing (14:5), building a relationship (3:1).

226 "Friend" may designate a member of community (Ex 20:16) or a lover or paramour (Jer 3:1. 20; Song 5:16). In this context where Gomer is described as an "adulteress," the verb אהב "to love" has obviously a sexual connotation.

227 PG 71, 101 D. For Theophylact of Bulgaria (PG 126, 624 D) the "first wife" is a type of the "idolatrous generation prior to captivity," while the "second wife" (the adulteress) represents a "type of those brought into captivity."

228 Cyril (PG 71, 104) explains that this "stubborn" love of God toward faithless Israel stems from his "innate kindness (ἐμφύτου χρηστότητος)."

229 The verb פנה "to turn" denotes the sin of apostasy (cf. Deut 29:17; 30:17).

230 Wolff (*Hosea*, 60) notices that "other gods" (cf. Ex 20:3) shows Hosea's familiarity with the Decalogue (12:10; 13:4; 4:2). Although absent in Amos, Isaiah, and Micah, this phrase appears in Deuteronomy (e.g., 5:7; 6:14; 7:4; 8:19; 11:16).

[231] According to Theodore of Mopsuestia (PG 66, 144 D), these cakes are "loaves of wheat-bread (ἄρτους) prepared in various ways by mixing up raisins and dried fruits."

[232] Mays, *Hosea*, 57. Compare the "cakes" (כַּוָּנִים) offered by the Israelites to the "queen of heaven" (Jer 7:18; 44:19).

[233] PG 71, 104. Similarly, Theophylact of Bulgaria (PG 126, 625 A) explains: "They offered to demons cakes (πέμματα), namely, loaves of wheat-bread (ἄρτους) from the finest flour with raisins."

[234] PL 25, 842.

[235] "For myself" (לִי) in Hosea first-person speech conveys the same idea of direct, personal intervention as in the case of Yahweh betrothing Israel to himself; see the commentary on 2:21f.

[236] So H. Schmidt, "Die Ehe des Hosea," *ZAW* 42 (1924): 245ff. For Tushingham (*JNES* 12 [1953]: 150-59), Gomer was a cult prostitute under the supervision of a temple official called "friend" in Hos 3:1.

[237] So K. Budde, "Hosea 1 und 3," *Theologische Blätter* 13 (1934): 337f.

[238] The Hebrew root כרה "to purchase, buy" (II in KBL, 497), probably related to Arabic *kry* (VIII) "to hire" (cf. LXX: καὶ ἐμισθωσάμην "I hired [her]"), is found in a few other places in the Old Testament (Deut 2:6; Job 6:27; 40:30). For Jacob ("Osée," 36), the meaning of this root contains the idea of speculation. According to Macintosh (*Hosea*, 100), the verbal form אֶכְּרֶהָ derives from the root נכר "to regard, recognize" (already suggested by ibn Ezra) and indicates the legal transition from one authority to another. The Qal imperfect in Hos 3:2 should be translated "I gained possession of her" or "I gained the legal recognition that she was mine." This last sense is generally supported by Tg and S, both pointing to the idea of "redemption."

[239] "Silver" (כֶּסֶף) stands for "shekels of silver" (שֶׁקֶל כֶּסֶף), pieces of silver used in trade (Gen 23:15).

Commentary: Hosea 1-3

[240] A "homer" (חֹמֶר) is a dry measure equivalent to ten *ephahs*. In Jerome's estimation (PL 25, 842-843), a "lethech" (לֶתֶךְ) (*hapax legomenon*) is half of a "homer." According to 2 Kgs 7:1, 16, 18, in times of war one could buy 2 seahs of barley for 1 shekel; in times of peace the estimated price amounted to 0.3 shekel for 1 seah; in this case, 1.5 "homer" of barley would cost 15 shekels. Thus the full price paid by Hosea for his wife's redemption was 30 shekels, the value of a slave (cf. Ex 21:32; Joseph was sold for only 20 shekels; cf. Gen 37:28). But the difficulty with this computation lies in the lack of precision in determining the value of "lethech."

[241] Wolff, *Hosea*, 61; see "Introduction. 5. Conjugal Drama of Hosea: Preliminaries." Theodore of Mopsuestia (PG 66, 145 A) sees in the "minute way of speaking" (ἀκριβολογία) a proof that the events narrated really happened.

[242] PG 71, 105 A.

[243] A similar interpretation is found in Jerome, PL 25, 843.

[244] Similarly, Theophylact of Bulgaria (PG 126, 625 C) interprets: "Barley hints at the irrational (ἄλογον) food they feed on, meaning nothing spiritual (πνευματικὸν) or worthy of rational souls." "Barley" and "wine" taken together designate dry food and liquids necessary to life.

[245] Following Cyril's commentary, Theophylact of Bulgaria (PG 126, 625 C) uses here a different word, "going aside" (παραφορὰν), probably as an explanation of "darkness" (σκότῳ).

[246] PL 25, 843.

[247] PG 126, 625 C.

[248] PG 66, 145 A.

[249] For "eternity," Hosea uses לְעוֹלָם (2:21). According to Jerome (PL 25, 845), "many days" could be a reference to the period between Christ's mission and the long-awaited conversion of the "barren (*infelix*) Synagogue" to his teachings.

[250] PG 71, 104.

[251] PG 81, 1569 A.

²⁵² This view is found in ancient interpreters and modern scholars (e.g., ibn Ezra and Kimchi, *BHS*, Weiser, Mays, Wolff, Macintosh). Or, as MT, LXX, and other versions (V, S, Tg) show, the abstinence concerns only Gomer with respect to her paramours. Hosea's attitude toward Gomer will be in accord ("I will also be for you") with the latter's faithfulness toward him ("you shall remain as mine"); see McComiskey, *The Minor Prophets*, 53.

²⁵³ PG 66, 145 B.

²⁵⁴ "Prince" designates a military or royal court official; Hosea considers these officials as misleading (7:3, 16; 8:4, 10; 13:10) as the king (5:1; 8:4, 10; 10:15; 13:10f.). According to Cyril of Alexandria (PG 71, 109 A), "princes" refers here to the "priests" (ἱερεῖς).

²⁵⁵ Macintosh (*Hosea*, 105f.) translates it rather "feasting," as indicating acts of worship and banquet in the presence of Yahweh (cf. 6:6; 8:11, 13).

²⁵⁶ "Pillar" may refer to either a memorial (Gen 28:18, 22; 31:13; Ex 24:4) or a stela (of stone: basalt or limestone) with a cultic function (Ex 23:24; Lev 26:1; Deut 7:5), erected (cf. Hiph'il of נצב "to set up, erect") as a pillar. Although forbidden by Deuteronomy (16:22), the pillars are described in Isaiah's sayings (Is 19:19) as part of the Yahwistic worship.

²⁵⁷ "Ephod" designates one of the cultic vestments of the high priests; it was equipped with a pocket for the sacred lots Urim and Thummim (Ex 28:6f.; 39:2f.). Yet, according to some texts (1 Sam 2:28; 23:6), the ephod seems to be an oracular instrument carried from place to place. Macintosh (*Hosea*, 106f.) shows that originally the ephod was a breast-plate attached to an idol (cf. Judg 8:27). Later it came to indicate a priestly vestment (1 Sam 2:18) and eventually the garment (a sort of mantle) worn by the high priest (Ex 28:6f.).

²⁵⁸ "Teraphim" were household cultic objects (Gen 31:19ff.), probably anthropomorphic (1 Sam 19:13ff.), used, along with the ephod, in divination (Ezek 21:26; Zech 10:2).

C. Van Dam, *The Urim and Thummim. A Means of Revelation in Ancient Israel* (Winona Lake: Eisenbrauns, 1997), 149f., points out that LXX connected the "urim" and "thummim" (oracular devices) with "teraphim" by translating the latter term in Hos 3:4 with δήλων "manifestations," the word used usually to translate "urim" (Num 27:21; Deut 33:8; 1 Sam 28:6). This is an interesting case of interpretative translation because commonly LXX either transliterates "teraphim" (Judg 17:5; 18:14) or translates "idols" (Gen 31:19) and "carved images" (Ezek 21:26). The fact that "teraphim" in Hos 3:4 is not construed with אֵין "no" like the other items in the series shows that this term is closely associated with "ephod" (cf. McComiskey, *The Minor Prophets* [Grand Rapids: Baker, 1992], 53-54). Cyril of Alexandria (PG 71, 108 D-109 A) sees in "manifestation" (δήλωσις) and "truth" (ἀλήθεια), the two stones included in the "ephod," a "type for Emmanuel" (Christ) who is both the revelation of the Father (Jn 15:15) and the truth (Jn 14:6).

[259] "Osée," 36.

[260] Contrary to Rudolph who contests the authenticity of v. 5 as a whole, Wolff (*Hosea*, 62-63) recognizes only two late Judaean additions to this verse: "David their King" (messianic element; this phrase appears only in Jer 30:9) and "in the latter days" (eschatological element; cf. Is 2:2; Mic 4:1; Jer 23:20; Ezek 38:16). Macintosh (*Hosea*, 111) observes that "in the latter days" does not fit well here with "afterwards" at the beginning of v. 5. It is our view that the sole reference to Judah or David cannot be considered a solid argument for a Judaean origin. As a prophet of Yahweh, Hosea addresses at times not only the Northern Kingdom but also Judah, by urging her inhabitants to change their lives in order to avoid Israel's fate; see Jacob, "Osée," 37; see also the commentary on 1:7. Similarly, if a phrase such as "in the latter days" is attested in writers originally from the south, it does not necessarily mean that it could not be used by a northern

prophet as Hosea.

[261] PG 66, 145 C-D.

[262] Thus Theodoret of Cyrus (PG 81, 1569 B) sees in "David their king" an allusion to the "prince Zerubbabel who had sprung from the Davidic tribe, from whom they [the Israelites] received the enjoyment (ἀπόλαυσιν) of the good gifts of God," namely, the return from Babylonian captivity. A similar interpretation is found in Theodore of Mopsuestia, PG 66, 145 C-D; Theophylact of Bulgaria, PG 126, 629 A; and Jerome, PL 25, 845.

[263] Cf. Garrett, *Hosea, Joel*, 104.

[264] PG 71, 109 B; cf. Theophylact of Bulgaria, PG 126, 629 A-B; Jerome, PL 25, 845.

[265] The same verb פחד "to tremble," followed by אֶל and יהוה, appears in one of Hosea's contemporaries, Micah (7:17; cf. Jer 2:19). Note the synonymous verb חרד in Hos 11:10.

[266] For Macintosh (*Hosea*, 111), Yahweh's goodness refers to "staple crops of the land" (2:24/22; cf. Gen 45:18; Is 1:19; Jer 31:12; Neh 9:35).

[267] PL 25, 845. Note Jesus' description of God as "good" (ἀγαθός, Mk 10:18) and "perfect" (τέλειος, Mt 5:48); see Jacob ("Osée," 37) who compares Hos 3:5 with Jer 33:9, found in a similar eschatological context, equating "goodness" with "perfection"—the main purpose of God's work.

[268] PG 66, 145 D.

[269] PG 71, 109 B.

[270] One might add that the adjective "good" (טוב) was chosen by the author of Genesis 1 to describe the harmonious relationship between God's will and the end product of his creative work (vv. 4, 10, 12, 18, 21, 25, 31).

[271] In 14:3 "good" is used in reference to God's image present in every human person no matter how immoral this might be. See the commentary on 14:3.

[272] PG 126, 629 A-B.

[273] PG 81, 1569 C; cf. Theodore of Mopsuestia, PG 66, 145 C-D.

II. ISRAEL BETWEEN PUNISHMENT AND FORGIVENESS (4-11)

1. Yahweh's Dispute with Israel (4:1-3)

1. Hear the word of Yahweh, O sons of Israel, for Yahweh has a dispute with the inhabitants of the land. For there is no trustworthiness or mercy, no knowledge of God in the land. 2. Cursing, cheating, murdering, robbing, and adultery break out;[1] bloodshed follows bloodshed. 3. Therefore the land shall wither[2] and all who live in it shall languish,[3] with the beasts of the field[4] and the birds of the sky; even the fish of the sea shall disappear.[5]

The second part of the book (4-11), consisting exclusively of prophetic sayings, begins with a brief assessment of the moral status of northern Israelite society as a whole. The initial phrase "Hear the word of Yahweh" (שִׁמְעוּ דְבַר־יְהוָה) points to the solemn character of the following sentences (cf. Num 12:6; 1 Kgs 22:19; Am 3:1; 4:1; 7:16; Mic 3:1; Is 1:10). Yahweh addresses the whole country, people and leaders alike, under the generic label "sons of Israel" (בְּנֵי יִשְׂרָאֵל). He is in "dispute"[6] with the inhabitants of the country because of the lack of moral integrity.[7] Cyril of Alexandria[8] interprets the first verb, κρίνεται "(God) is in dispute," as evidence that "none was sentenced, nor did he (God) file mere charges against those who treated him impiously," but rather the Lord warned Israel to stay away from what is evil.

The absence of three virtues, "trustworthiness" (אֱמֶת),[9] "mercy" (חֶסֶד),[10] "knowledge of God" (דַּעַת אֱלֹהִים),[11]

ushers the people into the socio-political and natural chaos described in vv. 2-3. Based on the LXX reading, Cyril of Alexandria[12] offers an original description of Israel's life deprived of these virtues: "To say that there was no truth (ἀλήθειαν), suggests that in those days everybody committed calumny, perjury, deceit and treachery, the greatest disgrace of evils. For the fact that they were without mutual love and unmerciful, stiffnecked, stubborn and hardhearted indicates that there was no mercy (ἔλεος).[13] The fact that they were seeking pleasure rather than God and were entirely devoted to false gods tells distinctly one more time that there was no knowledge of God on earth." According to Theophylact of Bulgaria,[14] all three virtues are to be found in Christ, and the absence of "truth" and "mercy" is determined by the fact that there is no "knowledge of God."

The list in v. 2 includes five transgressions of God's commands, all expressed in Hebrew by absolute infinitives. The first two wicked acts ("cursing" [אָלֹה] and "cheating" [כַּחֵשׁ]) match only in spirit the third[15] and ninth[16] commandments. The other three transgressions ("murdering" [רָצֹחַ], "robbing" [גָּנֹב], and "adultery" [נָאֹף]) correspond ad litteram to the sixth,[17] eighth,[18] and seventh[19] commandments of the Decalogue.[20] All these crimes "break out" (פָּרָצוּ)[21] "in the land" (cf. LXX: ἐπὶ τῆς γῆς) as a direct consequence or simply due to the absence of the three main virtues. Thus, no matter how inoffensive it might look, the absence of these virtues in itself has a bad effect on the human person, because sooner or later man's wicked acts will fill the emptiness left by these virtues. Theophylact of Bulgaria[22] interprets: "Therefore, because truth does not exist, there is curse (that is, abuse [λοιδορία]), calumny, and lie; because there is no mercy, there is murder, and slaughter mixes with slaughter; because there is no knowledge of God, there are these things, and theft and adultery." Theodore of Mopsuestia[23] underlines the fact that Israel repaid the "providence" (κηδεμονίαν) of God with great evils.

Hosea concludes the description of moral decadence with an observation, "and bloodshed follows bloodshed" (וְדָמִים בְּדָמִים נָגָעוּ), which may be interpreted as a fulfilment of one of his early prophecies concerning the punishment of Jehu's dynasty (cf. 1:4).[24] For Julian of Eclanum[25] this picture, far from being exaggerated, refers to Elijah's times (cf. 1 Kgs 19) when "they [the Israelites] filled all the places of the once holy region with murders so that due to the great number of killings blood mingled with blood." Cyril of Alexandria[26] interprets: "For having murdered the holy prophets, they included among them the Lord of the prophets himself." Similarly, Theophylact of Bulgaria[27] writes: "They mixed his [Christ's] blood with the blood of the prophets, and after that, they mixed the blood of the apostles."

"Therefore" (עַל־כֵּן) (v. 3) commonly introduces God's punishment. Far from being a direct and fulminant intervention, God's punishment, as described by Hosea, is rather an inner process, inside the nature, something similar to a cause-and-effect relationship.[28] Thus, the immediate consequences of the moral decline appear in surrounding nature. Both Cyril of Alexandria[29] and Jerome[30] see in this degraded nature (i.e., beasts, birds, and fish) a reference to people's aggressivity, pride, and lack of right judgment. Inside nature, the absence of virtues translates into the absence of life. The picture in v. 3 is that of a serious drought where the land "withers" (תֶּאֱבַל),[31] and people and animals "languish" (אֻמְלַל).[32] The situation is so tragic that "even" (וְגַם) the fish start "disappearing" (יֵאָסֵפוּ),[33] so that, as Julian of Eclanum[34] notices, "food may not be found even in waters." Jerome[35] explains this prophecy through the prism of the captivity when "even the speechless elements will feel the wrath of the Lord." The theme of solidarity between men and nature in both punishment and redemption is found elsewhere in the prophets (Is 16:8; 24:3-6; Jer 12:4; 23:10; Am 1:7; Zeph 1:2-3; Joel 1:10; and in the New Testament, Rom 8:22).[36]

The main idea of this pericope is that between the three distinctive facets of life, moral-religious (or theological), social, and natural, there is a close and continuous interdependence. When the theological relationship between God and men is disturbed then all the other relationships in society and nature are in decline.[37] Thus, the three main virtues listed in 4:1 ("trustworthiness," "mercy," "knowledge of God") may be compared to the three "theological" virtues ("hope," "love," "faith") in 1 Cor 13:13, which coordinate both man's relationship with God and his neighbor.

2. God's Dispute with the Priests, Prophets, and People (4:4-19)

4. Yet let no one rebuke and let no one reproach; for my dispute is with you,[38] O priest. **5.** And you shall stumble in the day(light),[39] and also the prophet shall stumble with you at night,[40] and I will make your mother perish.[41] **6.** My people perish[42] for lack of knowledge. Because you have rejected knowledge, I reject you[43] from being a priest for me. You have forgotten the instruction of your God, and so I too will forget your sons. **7.** The more they increased, the more they sinned against me. I will exchange[44] their glory for ignominy. **8.** They feed on the sin[45] of my people; they[46] are greedy for their iniquity. **9.** And it shall be the same for priest and people; I will punish him for his ways and repay him for his deeds.[47] **10.** They shall eat, but not be satisfied; they have played the whore, but they will not multiply.⁴⁸ For they have forsaken Yahweh to devote themselves to 11. whoredom⁴⁹ and wine, and new wine, which take away my people's understanding.⁵⁰ 12. They consult their wood;⁵¹ and their staff⁵² answers them. For a spirit of whoredom has led them astray,⁵³ and they have played the whore away from their God. 13. On the tops of the mountains they sacrifice, and on the hills they burn incense, under oak, poplar, and terebinth, because their shade is pleasant. For this reason your daughters play the whore and your daughters-in-law commit adultery. 14. I will not punish your daughters because they play the whore, nor your daughters-in-law because they commit adultery. For they themselves go aside⁵⁴ with whores and sacrifice with sacred prostitutes.⁵⁵ Thus a people that does not understand shall be ruined.⁵⁶ 15. Though you play the whore, O Israel, let Judah not become guilty.⁵⁷ Do not enter Gilgal, or go up to Beth-aven,⁵⁸ and do not swear,⁵⁹ "As Yahweh lives!" 16. For like a stubborn heifer, Israel is stubborn. Should Yahweh now feed them like a lamb in a broad meadow? 17. Ephraim is joined to idols — let him alone.⁶⁰ 18. When their liquor is gone,⁶¹ they play the whore all over again; they love⁶² dishonor more than their pride.⁶³ 19. A wind has wrapped them⁶⁴ in its wings, and they shall be ashamed because of their altars.⁶⁵

If in 4:1-3 Yahweh was in dispute with the people of Israel, in this pericope (4:4-19), he is rebuking both leaders (priests, prophets) and people.

"Yet (אַךְ)⁶⁶ let no one rebuke (רִיב), and let no one reproach (יכח)" (v. 4).⁶⁷ In spite of Israel's moral decline and environmental disaster, no one has to rebuke or reproach his neighbor, because a certain priest (כֹּהֵן)⁶⁸ is primarily guilty of the gloomy situation described in vv. 1-3. Who was this priest? A comparison with Amos (7:10) makes one assume that this mysterious person might have been one of the high representatives of the north-Israelite hierarchy, appointed over an important sanctuary, comparable, for instance, to Amaziah, the priest of Bethel.[69] As A. Neher remarks,[70] far from questioning the legitimacy of the Northern priesthood as a class, Hosea rebukes only those priests who failed to fulfill their duties. Julian of Eclanum[71] presents the priest in a rather favorable light, and Israel as an idolatrous people arguing with the priest, rejecting the holy services and admonitions, and thus going away from the genuine priesthood. On the contrary, Cyril of Alexandria,[72] following the Septuagint, shows that in the Old Testament a "disputed priest" (ἀντιλεγόμενος ἱερεύς) was that priest unfitting for the sacred duties for various reasons (e.g., bodily impairment). In captivity, deprived of her cultic and political institutions, Israel will be as a "disputed priest," namely unfitting and thus excluded from serving the Lord. Similarly, Theodore of Mopsuestia[73] notices: "My people are like a priest who is contradicted, who has fallen from his previous dignity and does not appear worthy for any reason. Just as if some priest who falls into controversy would be set aside and dishonored by everyone. 'And he will be weak by day.' To the greatest extent, he will become weak because of the upcoming evils."

In v. 5 the divine judgment against the priest is both revealed and extended to an anonymous prophet (וְנָבִיא). Except for this occurrence, Hosea has a positive attitude towards the prophets (6:5; 9:7f.; 12:10, 13).[74] That is why, Theodoret of Cyrus[75] explains that Hosea refers here to a "pseudo-prophet." Theodore of Mopsuestia[76] adds that these prophets deceived Israel through false predictions: "The ones who first made use of false predictions to deceive you, most will also themselves become weak, because of the calamity which holds them back, as if they were wrapped up in some kind of night darkness they see the pursuit of deceit which was useless for them."

The priest "stumbles" (כשל)[77] in "daylight" (הַיּוֹם), and the prophet stumbles "by night" (לָיְלָה). The mention "by night" may be a hint at some oneiric revelations received by the prophet at night (cf. Mic 3:6; Jer 23:25; Zech 1:8),[78] or, along with "in day(light)," it may designate the idea of perpetuity ("all of the time").[79] For Theodore of Mopsuestia,[80] "by night," when everything is surrounded by darkness, anticipates a national "calamity." Based on the Septuagint reading, Cyril of Alexandria[81] sees in "(for) days" (ἡμέρας) a reference to the temporary character of the judgment: "One says that Israel will be weak (ἀσθενήσειν) not forever (οὐκ εἰς ἅπαν) but for days (εἰς ἡμέρας). For it has been reserved for her a time (καιρός) of salvation and return to faith." Jerome[82] renders the Hebrew form היום by *hodie* "today" explaining: "Today means either the present time or you will be led into captivity in daylight, not deceitfully and insidiously."

There are at least two interpretations concerning the act of "stumbling." This may indicate a current wrongdoing of Israel's leaders (so Sellin, Harper) or a future judgment, a direct consequence of sin, as in the environmental crisis mentioned in 4:4. The use of the verb כשל in Hosea's book (5:5; 14:2) supports the latter interpretation.[83] This is also the understanding of the ancient Christian interpreters. Thus, Theodoret of Cyrus[84] writes: "For many days (πολλαῖς ἡμέραις), you [i.e., the Israelites] and the prophets who prophesied lies to you will be handed over to this chastisement (παιδεία)." Jerome[85] defines "stumbling" more closely: "Therefore today (*hodie*) you are falling (*corruitis*), that is, you are being brought into captivity and are losing the kingdom of Israel."

The divine punishment against the priest includes his immediate family, "mother" (v. 5) and "sons" (v. 6).[86] The context refutes a metaphorical interpretation, i.e., "mother" for place of origin (the cities were called "mothers in Israel"; cf. 2 Sam 20:19), or for nation (cf. Hos 2:4/2; Ezek 16:44). For Julian of Eclanum,[87] the "mother" is the "crowd of elders, which I have called your mother, that made much noise just before with garrulous profanity, but during the calamity's night became silent." Similarly, Jerome[88] identifies the "mother" with the "people, the whole multitude of the Hebrew nation." The Greek writers, such as Theophylact of Bulgaria,[89] relying on the Septuagint reading, resorts to an allegorizing interpretation: "The mother of the people is the synagogue, which, since it is covered by the darkness of ignorance and did not receive the radiance of God's knowledge, may be compared to the night."

"My people perish (נִדְמוּ)[90] for lack of knowledge (הַדָּעַת)"[91] (v. 6). This lament-like[92] accusation echoes the observation in 4:1 concerning the "knowledge of God." Responsible for spreading "the knowledge" are the priests (cf. Deut 33:10; Mal 2:7). Instead of doing their duty, the priests have "rejected" (מאס)[93] "the knowledge" and have "forgotten" (שׁכח) the "instruction" (תּוֹרָה). Jerome[94] notices that, since the object of "the knowledge" is God's law, the people "became silent" (cf. V: *conticuit*) for they failed to know the law and observe its precepts. Similarly, Cyril of Alexandria[95] equates "the knowledge" with "the guidance (ποδηγίαν) through the law."

Even though there is not final agreement among scholars with respect to the precise content of the "instruction" (תּוֹרָה) we may assume that this term refers to the Pentateuch (the "Torah"), the five-volume collection traditionally attributed to Moses. Hos 8:12 suggests that a written "instruction" was extant during the eighth century. In addition, 4:2 alludes to several commandments of the Decalogue.[96]

The divine sentence matches the way the priests behaved: God is going to reject the negligent priest from the "priesthood" (כהן)[97] and to throw his "sons" (בָּנֶיךָ)[98] into oblivion.[99] Theodore of Mopsuestia[100] explains: "Just as you rejected (ἀποβεβλήκατε) my knowledge (γνῶσιν), in the same manner I will reject you from my worship (θεραπείας), removing you through captivity from those places where it was fitting for you to offer a priestly service (ἱερατεύειν) to me." For Cyril of Alexandria,[101] the knowledge is Christ: "Since you expelled the knowledge, that is Christ, through whom, and in whom the Father is at the same time approachable and known, you will be thrown out (ἐξωθήσῃ) from being holy (ἱερός), and from offering sacrifices, as impure (βέβηλος)." With respect to the "instruction" (LXX: "law"), Cyril interprets: "And since you forgot the divine laws (θείων νόμων), you will not understand the Mosaic laws spiritually, nor will you comprehend the teachings of Christ subtly and diligently, and I also, as if I were swimming under the oblivion, I will not remember your sons, and I will refrain myself from considering them worthy of (my) attention (φροντίδος)." Jerome[102] connects the loss of priesthood with idolatry: "For she [i.e., Israel] rejected God's law, and therefore she lost the priesthood forever, worshipping the golden calves at Dan and Bethel; since she [Israel] has forgotten the law of God and inside Egypt surrounded herself to the idols, therefore the Lord will forget his sons, handing them over into eternal captivity."

Even though beginning with v. 7 the object of the accusations is not the "priest" but "they" (i.e., the "priests") there is no need to separate vv. 4-6 from vv. 7-10.[103] Already in 4:6 Hosea refers to a priest ("you"—masculine singular) and his "sons" thus creating a smooth transition from singular to plural with respect to the addressee of his sayings.

The increase in number (רֻבָּם)[104] of priests is paralleled by an increase of "sinning" (חטא)[105] (v. 7). Note the personal touch introduced by the pronominal suffix לִי "against me." In Hosea's view, any sin is an act of rebellion against the divine person (cf. 2:15/13). The mention of increase in the number of priests may be a reference to the economic prosperity experienced by Israel under king Jeroboam II. We may add that the connection between the increase in number and the apostasy from Yahweh is a Hosean feature (8:11; 10:1; 13:6; cf. Deut 8:13; 32:15).[106] Jerome[107] interprets: "Therefore, I will turn their glory in which they boasted themselves, preferring the idols to God, into ignominy, so that both people and priests be afflicted." For Theodore of Mopsuestia,[108] Israel's "sin" was that they failed to see in God's providence the cause of the people's proliferation.

Yahweh's response is that he will "exchange (מוּר)[109] their glory (כְּבוֹדָם)[110] for ignominy (קָלוֹן)."[111] In other words, priests once highly respected individuals within their communities will be scorned by the same people who held them in great esteem. Applying this prophecy to the people rather than the priests, Cyril of Alexandria[112] explains the way God will turn people's glory into ignominy: "How would this be possible? They will loose the glorious achievements in reference to the great multitude, when the war and the warriors will consume all (their) time. For empty houses and cities will be left behind." Theophylact of Bulgaria[113] points out that this prophecy was fulfilled during the captivity when "the exiled kings of the Hebrews held the glory and riches in greater contempt."

The list of charges against the members of the hierarchy continues in v. 8. Instead of handing over the "instruction" (תּוֹרָה), the priests are more interested in the moral decadence of the people. They feed on the sin (חַטָּאת) of Yahweh's people, looking greedily after their iniquity (עֲוֹנָם).[114] The phrase נשׂא נפשׁ "to raise the throat"[115] describes the idea of eagerness and greediness (cf. Jer 22:27; Ps 86:4). Although it is not clear whether in Hosea חַטָּאת indicates a sin-offering, we may assume that the priests, as the recipients of the sin-offerings (Lev 6:19; 7:7; 10:17), were eager to see their people sinning and then bringing such offerings.[116] Cyril of Alexandria[117] explains: "They used to sacrifice goats for sin, for this reason the sacrifice was called sin. By offering a goat on the altar, the priests at the right time, used to bring the intestines and the lard, and they ate the rest, this was ordered by the divine law [cf. Lev 3:3].... 'They eat the sins of my people' means they eat the offerings brought for sins." What is punishable in the priests' attitude is their selfishness for petty gain (cf. 1 Sam 2: the case of Eli's sons), combined with total negligence in fulfilling the basic duties of their sacred office. This is also the interpretation of Theodoret of Cyrus[118]: "Since, according to the law, they [i.e., the priests] used to receive a good portion from the sacrifices which were offered for sins and trespasses, since they benefitted from this worship, they were reluctant to accuse those who used to live in sin." In the same vein, Jerome[119] notices: "And for this reason, they are feasting on the sins of my people, approving the crimes of the sinners. For when they behold them sinning, not only do they not argue, but they also praise and extol them calling them fortunate."

"People" (עָם) and "priest" (כֹּהֵן)[120] are equally guilty for the moral morass, and thus both punishable (v. 9). Jerome[121] explains: "Wherefore both people and priest, and both those who are taught and those who have taught, will be bound with an equal judgment." God will punish the priest the same way he treated the people, namely he will leave him with no providential care. For

Theophylact of Bulgaria,[122] the priests are as corrupt as the people because out of greed they approved the wicked deeds of the latter. Theodore of Mopsuestia[123] suggests that the captivity will blur the distinction between priests and people: "They will be in such a great confusion and calamity because of the captivity, as if there was not a single distinction between being a priest and being under the priesthood; inasmuch as there was no one of those who then belonged to the divine priesthood, but all were bound in the same manner by the calamity of captivity."

The two verbs used here, פָּקַד followed by preposition עַל "to visit X for either punishment or reward" (cf. 1:4) and שׁוּב (Hiph'il) "to return," point to the idea of bringing one's deeds upon oneself. Given the parallel with מַעֲלָלָיו "his deeds," we should take דְּרָכָיו "his ways" in sense of behavior (cf. 1 Kgs 2:4; Prov 10:9; Jer 3:21). Thus, Cyril of Alexandria[124] writes: "Seemingly, he calls 'ways' the walkings in works (ἔργοις), and 'counsels' the faults (πταίσματα) from the outrageous thoughts. Then, he says, she [Israel] did not go rightly, having turned aside from the straight road; as if marching the footpath of all profanity, they devised the most shameful and absurd things, dishonoring the God of all while turning towards idolatry." In addition, Theophylact of Bulgaria[125] interprets: "By calling the deeds (πράξεις) ways (ὁδοὺς), he says, that I will bring over them all the judgment and punishment for their deeds. And I will not punish the deeds only, but also 'his' counsels [cf. LXX: διαβούλια], namely, of the people. For we will suffer punishment not only for the deeds but also for the outrageous thoughts (λογισμῶν)." Similarly, Jerome[126] explains: "For he will visit not only their deeds, which are called 'ways,' in which they were engaged, but also the thoughts [cf. V: *cogitationes*] they bore, thoughts according to which they acted. For not only the deed but also the thought of an evil deed is punishable."

In Hosea's view there is a close correspondence between deeds and punishments or rather the consequences of these deeds (cf. 4:3). Cyril of Alexandria[127] explains: "'I will punish him' means I will give judgment proportionally with (their) trespasses." Similarly, Julian of Eclanum[128] writes: "When, he says, the avenging judgment begins to work, these measures of griefs, which they [i.e., Israel] had made in sins, will be filled, so that they may experience in punishments what they have achieved in desires."

Satiety (שׂבע) and fertility (פרץ)[129] sought in the realm of idolatry[130] will never be reached because Israel has "forsaken" (עזב)[131] Yahweh, the Giver of all goods; the one who can both provide and withdraw his gifts from an idolatrous people (cf. 2:10/8, 11/9). For Cyril of Alexandria[132] this lack of "satiety" is related to the captivity: "A remnant from Israel has been preserved. Since the judgment does not go entirely to the priest, he adds, 'They eat but they will not be satisfied.' This means either emigration and captivity for those leaders of Israel, or, because of Christ, desolation (ἐρήμωσιν) of Judaea by the hands of Romans.... For among those Israelites brought then by Salmanasar [Shalmaneser] and Theglafalasar [Tiglath-pileser III] to Assyria and Media, very few could offer to the priests the things prescribed by the law." Theophylact of Bulgaria[133] offers an interesting interpretation of Israel's eating yet never being satisfied: "For as the insatiate ones who gnaw are not satisfied, in the same manner they [the Israelites] eat the fruits of their deeds, namely the punishments (κολάσεις), and just as those who do not eat and are not punished, they invite other punishments." Jerome[134] writes: "Desire is insatiable, and the more it is felt, the more it creates in those who enjoy it a greater hunger. On the contrary: 'Blessed are the ones who hunger and thirst for righteousness, for they will be satisfied' [Mt 5:6]. For righteousness satisfies, while wickedness because it has no substance deceives by fraud those who feed on vain things, and leaves the stomachs of those who raven empty. 'They played the whore continually [lit.: and they have not ceased].' In fornication they run out of strength and the ardent desire of the fornication does not make a pause. The ten tribes played the whore with the idols of Jeroboam son of Naboth."

In v. 10b the emphasis falls on God's person (cf. 2:15). God himself, rather than a paragraph of law, was in fact forsaken. People and priests have abandoned Yahweh to devote themselves (שׁמר)[135] to "fornication" (זְנוּת)[136] and "wine" (יַיִן), and "new wine" (תִּירוֹשׁ);[137] all these vices, Hosea notices, take away the understanding (לֵב "heart")[138] of Yahweh's people (v. 11). In his interpretation, Cyril of Alexandria[139] insists on the leaders' responsibility to steer Israel away from idolatry: "'They [i.e., Israel's leaders] kept the whoredom' means that they got ready to preserve the error (πλάνησιν) for those who were under their authority; yet, they had rather to remove and throw it from their midst. For it is the vigilance of the teachers, which should eagerly remove what hurts the people, and turn down without delay what is hateful to God. By refusing to do this, they allow to stay somehow and to keep the works of error; yet, they confirm rather the contrary, when the mind of those who teach receives altogether wine and drunkenness. For how well the disciples keep vigil, and how will they be able to point the eye of the understanding to God in nature and in truth, if the instructors and the teachers of useful things will still encourage them to err?"

Verse 12 should be read together with v. 11 in order to get a better understanding of Israel's ridiculous behavior—her tireless flirt with the art of divination which the terms "consult" and "answer" allude to. The word עֵץ means "tree, a piece of wood," hence the divination technique may be an oracle tree (Gen 12:6), a wooden idol (Is 44:13ff.; Hab 2:18f.), or even the Ashera (Deut 16:21; Judg 6:25ff.). The second tool used in divination is מַקֵּל which again may have more than one meaning: a twig (Gen 30:37), a staff (1 Sam 17:40), or a wand used in rhabdomancy (Ezek 21:21f.). The last sense is supported by the Septuagint (ῥάβδοις "staves") and the ancient Christian interpretation. Thus, Jerome[140] explains: "The Greeks call this method of divination rhabdomancy (ῥαβδομαντείαν)." Similarly, Cyril of Alexandria[141] writes: "To those from Israel who came to them, and, to some degree, to those who were eager to know their own things, they brought tidings to them not only by signs (συμβόλοις) but also by their rods (ῥάβδοις). This is another way of treachery, a sort of rhabdomancy (ῥαβδομαντεία), and perhaps an invention of the Chaldaeans' idle curiosity." Guilty of the sin of divination are, in Theodoret of Cyrus'[142] view, both those who ask for advice and the diviners: "Again, he lists their lawbreakings (παρανομίας), he charges them with drunkenness (οἰνοφλυγίαν), and worship of idols; for he calls the latter 'fornication' (πορνείαν). He adds the ridiculous divination (μαντείαν), teaching that, the first group inquired of those who promised to deliver an oracle, and the other group answered in same way."

Israel's behavior is the result of two interfering factors: Israel's own deeds or more precisely her "addiction" to fornication and alcohol (v. 11), on the one hand, and a "spirit of whoredom" (רוּחַ זְנוּנִים), a mysterious force working from inside but in the same time distinct from people's personality, on the other hand; cf. similar expressions "spirit of confusion" (Is 19:14), "spirit of deep sleep" (Is 29:10), where the second element of the construct indicates the effect of the force ("spirit") upon the human subjects. For Jerome,[143] as for most of the ancient interpreters, the "whoredom" is just another term for "idolatry." According to Theodoret of Cyrus,[144] this "spirit" refers to a "strong desire" (ὁρμὴν) for "whoredom" (idolatry). Cyril of Alexandria[145] sees in the "spirit" rather an allusion to the evil spirits: "He wisely teaches that all these things are not done apart from the unclean and evil spirits. For every form of wickedness is due to them, and none of the most shameful deeds is done without design by those who chose to fulfill (their) thoughts." For Mays[146] the source of the "spirit of whoredom" is the "blandishments of these 'lovers' [Baals]," ready to take over Israel's perverted understanding. So powerful is this "spirit," that it may make Israel "go astray" (הִתְעָה), and, what is even worse, "away" (מִתַּחַת) from (lit. "from under") Yahweh's providence and lordship.

The list of Israel's wickednesses continues (v. 13). Yahweh's people, represented here by "daughters" (בָּנוֹת) and "daughters-in-law" or "young wives" (כַּלּוֹת), which designates the younger generation, is still undecided. They take part in the acts of cult labeled "whoredom" (זנה)[147] and "adultery" (נאף), in the same way as their forefathers offered "sacrifices" (יְזַבֵּחוּ)[148] on the "mountain tops" and "incense" (יְקַטֵּרוּ)[149] on the "hills," under the "pleasant" (טוֹב)[150] shade of the trees (oak, poplar, terebinth). Jerome[151] notices that the Israelites "deprived of the fig-tree and vine, under which the pious man is said to rest, sacrifice under oak, poplar and terebinth, which are fruitless trees." According to Theodore of Mopsuestia,[152] the Israelites considered the "shadow" of the trees a sign of holiness: "Therefore, they [i.e., the Israelites] used to run up to the mountains and to the hills, offering there sacrifices to the demons, singling out the tallness and shadiness of the trees to fulfill there their own deception (ἀπάτην), judging the size of the shadow from the trees to be something great and holy."

Cyril of Alexandria[153] plays on the word νύμφη which means "daughter-in-law" or "nymph," interpreting v. 13 as a reference to a worship of wood-nymphs: "For they offered sacrifices, laying hold of mountains and hills, and serving the base demons on the earthen elevations. Therefore becoming excited on the raised places under the oak-tree and the white poplar, they offer libations, honoring the nymphs (νύμφαις), perhaps the wood-nymphs (ἁμαδρυάσι), according to the Greek myths. For the distinguished Greek poets and authors say that the unclean demons, called by them nymphs, are in love with trees and woods. Thus, it seemed to them that is right to be satisfied with the shadows and be corrupted by the flowery forests, praising and saying 'good is the shady place.' For this reason, the one fond of pleasure (φιλήδονος) cannot be a God-loving person. For Paul brings testimony saying that they are more fond of pleasure than God-loving persons [2 Tim 3:4]. Therefore, 'blessed are those who mourn' now [Mt 5:4], as the Savior says, and we should most of all honor and love patience in useful toils."

Offering sacrifices on these "high places" (בָּמוֹת)[154] had become a common thing in Israel, but people's relentless flirt with such Canaanite memorabilia reached a dangerous point, the beginning of the end in terms of Israel's apostasy. Jerome[155] remarks that "by loving the high places, Israel has forsaken the High God." The phrase "for this reason" (עַל־כֵּן) links v. 13b with vv. 13a and 12b, explaining the idolatrous behavior of the younger generation as a continuation of the forefathers' inclinations, but in the same time as an effect of that powerful force called "spirit of whoredom."

Unexpectedly, Yahweh announces (v. 14) that he will not punish the young women for their promiscuous acts

(Exod 20:14; Deut 22:13ff.), perhaps, because they have acted under special circumstances (i.e., forefathers' influence, pressure from that "spirit of whoredom"). "They themselves" (הֵם, i.e., the older generation) are rebuked for their "going aside" (פָּרַד)[156] with "whores" (הַזֹּנוֹת), and "sacrificing" (זבח) with the "hierodules" (קְדֵשׁוֹת),[157] both actions depicting Israel's total immersion in the murky waters of idolatry.

In the view of Theophylact of Bulgaria:[158] "'Whores' (πόρνας) refer to the priestesses (ἱερείας) of Beelphegor. This was the idol, called by the Greeks 'Priapos,' a guardian of the licentiousness reflected in its very shape. Those women who worship such a shameful abomination are entirely playing the whore." Based on the Septuagint reading (τετελεσμένων "initiated, consecrated"), Theophylact defines then the second group of prostitutes (Hebrew קְדֵשׁוֹת) mentioned in v. 14: "He calls 'initiated' (τετελεσμένους) the ones who are initiated in holy things (or priests of the mysteries: ἱερομύστας) and belong to the same idol, the ones who are worthy of the secrets pertaining to the rites of the initiation.... Thought to be males, they were effeminate persons (θηλυδρίαι), using cymbals, with womanish loud cries [i.e., sounds used by women to invoke a god], going around in the public places, accomplishing the secret rites (μυστήρια) of Beelphegor." Theodoret of Cyrus[159] points out that the secrecy of these cultic acts will not last forever: "For whatever you undertook secretly, I [i.e., God] will allow it to become public." On God's decision not to judge the sins of the "daughters" and "daughters-in-law," Cyril of Alexandria[160] offers this interpretation: "And when these things will occur, he says, I will remain calm, and I will not lay charges. Because of the misfortunes of the war and the troubles of the captivity, it seems right that all that will happen be predicted to the sinners. For they, who once captured and overcame others, will do with the captives as they like, making use of power without bridle, and shamelessly attacking whoever agrees with them, neither taking into account the law, nor considering what is likely or proper, but hardened, and extremely wild in soul, they refuse to refrain from any kind of wretchedness. Therefore, he clearly showed that the young children will be exposed to the enemies because of the insult and shameless conduct of the fornicators."

"A people that does not understand (לֹא־יָבִין)[161] shall be ruined (יִלָּבֵט)"[162] comes as a conclusion to the gloomy picture painted in vv. 11-14a. Although, as motif and terminology, v. 14b belongs to the Wisdom repertoire (cf. Prov 10:8, 10), by its occurrence within a lament-oracle, the same line sounds as a passionate saying of doom.[163] We may note the emotional shift from "my people" (v. 12) to "a people" (עָם) which perhaps indicates that Israel is no longer Yahweh's people, but only "a people" among others. Jerome[164] interprets: "'A people that does not understand will be flogged (*vapulabit*)' means that Israel will be flogged in captivity and be afflicted with various plagues, so that by suffering she may receive instruction."

The author launches a warning to Judah while addressing primarily Israel (v. 15). He urges the inhabitants of the Southern Kingdom to stay away from idolatry and not to follow Israel's example. The mention of "Judah" has made many scholars consider this verse a Judaean gloss. But, this is not the only time when Hosea refers to Judah (cf. 5:5, 10, 13f.; 6:4). According to Cyril of Alexandria,[165] the mention of Judah is not odd at all since the idolatry is the sin of entire people, not only of Israel: "Speaking in the present about both and either one, he thoroughly refutes the people's malady." Hosea, in his quality of prophet preaching in Israel, has the moral responsibility to warn Judah, for, as Julian of Eclanum[166] puts it, "Israel not only embraced the audacity of profanity within its own borders of character, but also she aimed at the defilement of her brother as for some benefit." With respect to the similarity between v. 15 and Am 5:5, introduced as an argument for the Judaean redaction of v. 15 (i.e., a calque on Am 5:5), this may be well explained as a free adaptation of an older text done by Hosea himself while warning Judah.[167]

Any pilgrimage to the places of worship tainted with Baalism such as Gilgal or Beth-aven is utterly forbidden. "Ghilgal" (today *Khirbet el-Mefjer*) was an important Israelite sanctuary located in the Jordan Valley (Josh 4:19). Yet, for Hosea, this place of worship had a bad reputation (9:15; 12:11; cf. Am 4:4; 5:5). Theodore of Mopsuestia[168] mentions that in Galgala (Gilgal) there was "a set up idol" competing with the true God. Theophylact of Bulgaria[169] remarks that in Gilgal, the city which commemorates the miraculous crossing of Jordan (cf. Josh 5:2), the Israelites offer now sacrifices to the idols. "Beth-aven" (בֵּית אָוֶן) "house of wickedness" (5:8; 10:5) is a nickname, borrowed probably from Amos (5:5), for "Beth-el" (בֵּית אֵל) "house of God" (12:5 [MT]). Cyril of Alexandria explains:[170] "He calls Bethel the 'house of the wrong-doing' [cf. Theodotion: ἀδικίας]. For what reason? For 'Bethel' means 'house of God.' When they [i.e., the Israelites] have been somehow corrupted, it became the house of an idol, hence this surname .... Thus, the house of God became, as I said, the house of an idol." Jerome[171] adds that "after the [golden] calves were set up there, the city was named Beth-aven, namely, the useless house [cf. Aquila, Symachus: ἀνωφελοῦς] and the house of an idol." Theodoret of Cyrus[172] explains the Septuagint reading οἶκον Ὤν "house of On": "'On' is the name of the idol of Bethel. It does not mean, as some believe, 'the eternal one' (ἀίδιος), namely, 'the one who exists' (τὸν ὄντα), since this is a Hebrew rather than a Greek name." The "royal sanctuary" (Am 7:13), as the shrine of Bethel (today *Beitin*, about 9 miles north of Jerusalem) came to be known, was built by king Jeroboam I toward the end of the tenth century B.C. to rival the temple of Solomon in Jerusalem (1 Kgs 12:28-32). There is no way to say whether the Judaeans used to visit these north-Israelite sanctuaries located near Judah's border,[173] or whether in fact Hosea's saying should be read as an indirect warning to Israel.

In his dispute with Baalism, Hosea urges the Israelites not to use the traditional oath by the life of Yahweh (Ruth 3:13; Judg 8:19; 1 Sam 20:3, etc.) since the mere mention of its words "As Yahweh lives!" (חַי־יְהוָה) could create confusion by Yahweh's association with Baal, the god of fertility, who was thought of coming back to life with each spring.[174] Cyril of Alexandria[175] notices: "It is such a strange thing to take an oath by God, having the living Lord on your tongue, and at the same time being addicted to the idols and adoring lifeless calves." Jerome[176] interprets: "Your mouth should not mention my name, since it is defiled by the remembrance of idols." Similarly, Julian of Eclanum[177] writes: "Let not Judah be deceived by this familiarity of words [i.e., of the oath]; first let it begin not to fear calves and thereafter let it begin to swear oaths."

Verses 16-19 form a unity centered on the judgment of Israel/Ephraim for their wickedness in the cultic realm. During her tense relationship with God, Israel became as "stubborn" as a "stubborn heifer" (פָּרָה סֹרֵרָה);[178] cf. Jer 31:18: "untrained calf." Theodore of Mopsuestia[179] interprets: "Like a heifer by the motion of physical desire you incline toward disorderliness, you went away from my service and with an intemperate judgment you inclined toward the service of idols." Now, Yahweh is wondering whether he "should feed (רָעָה) Israel as a lamb (כְּבֶשׂ) in a broad meadow (מֶרְחָב)" (v. 16). Both "to feed" and "broad meadow" (lit. "wide space"; cf. Hab 1:6) are used to describe a good situation (Ps 18:20; 31:9/8; 118:5). Thus, in this setting of judgment, v. 16b should be read as a rhetorical question. The main idea is that Israel, the "stubborn heifer," will be abandoned as a powerless "lamb" in a vast area; Yahweh will not any longer take care of her. Cyril of Alexandria[180] insists on the lamb metaphor, identifying the Israelites brought into captivity with the lamb: "For the captives are always humble and fearful, seized with fear for prolonged suffering, and initiated in the greediness of the conquerors. The land of Persians and Medes is called 'wide' (ἐρύχωρον), thus one says: 'She will dwell in a wide and immense land, and she will change many regions and without having the same master always but changing them along with the regions." Jerome[181] shows that, because of their inclination toward idolatry, the Israelites "will be fed in a wide and spacious way, which leads to death, and the long-suffering of the Lord, the good shepherd, will nurture them toward destruction." Theodore of Mopsuestia[182] points to the idea of helplessness: "Therefore, I will disperse them, leading them here and there by the attack of their enemies, so that they do not differ from a lamb running through a vast countryside, wandering and seeking his mother."

With the passage of time, the sin of idolatry turns into an addiction:"Ephraim is joined (חָבוּר)[183] to idols (עֲצַבִּים)."[184] Theodore of Mopsuestia[185] remarks: "They [i.e., the Ephraimites] chose the communion (κοινωνίαν) with the idols." The imperative "Let him alone!," probably addressed by Yahweh to Hosea,[186] shows that there is no hope in Ephraim's return (v. 17). "Ephraim," the name of the most prominent north-Israelite tribe to which king Jeroboam I belongs (1 Kgs 11:26), stands for the more common name "Israel" (Hos 5:3, 5; 11:8). According to Jerome,[187] the mention of "Ephraim" beside "idols" echoes Jeroboam I's connection with the golden calves of Bethel and Dan: "Therefore, O Judah, if Israel plays the whore, let Judah, at least, not become guilty, listen to my advice, do not despise the words of the prophet. Since Ephraim is once and for all a friend and a partaker of the idols, leave him, do not follow his impiety, whose cult, religion, and sustenance is disjoined from your table. For they, once and for all, serve idols, and offer sacrifices to demons, and daily they play the whore."

"When liquor (סָבְאָם)[188] comes to an end (סָר),[189] they play the whore all over again" (הַזְנֵה הִזְנוּ),"[190] turning the entire worship into a place and occasion of endless orgies. In Hosea's book fornication is closely associated with alcoholic intoxication (cf. v. 11); both vices make Israel love "dishonor" (קָלוֹן), i.e., idolatry and promiscuous life, more than "their pride" (מָגִנֶּיהָ; cf. emended text), that is Yahweh (v. 18). In the view of Theodore of Mopsuestia,[191] idolatry is the source of all disgraceful deeds: "Indulging in much madness and arrogance against me, they chose the worship of idols, which will be the protector (πρόξενος) of every dishonor (ἀτιμίας) for them."

Israel is wrapped in the wings of a "wind" (רוּחַ), which may be an allusion to the "spirit of whoredom" (v. 12), since the word רוּחַ means both "wind" and "spirit." If in v. 12 this powerful "spirit" made Israel "go astray," now it is "wrapping" (צָרַר)[192] her in its wings, making her inactive. Cyril of Alexandria[193] interprets: "For they will not be called free; but rather they walk in wantonness and dishonor and they will be under cruel despots. Otherwise if the most insane multitude of Ephraim is subjected to all of these, nevertheless, O Judah, you became as a blast of wind [cf. LXX: πνεύματος συστροφή] in the wings of a bird. It is obvious by all means and at any rate that the birds, pushing against the strong wind, and straining, they fly more swiftly. Therefore, Israel ran headlong, she turned towards apostasy. But you became compared to her 'a blast of wind in the wings.' How? For after she saw you, being instructed in the law, sitting by the divine temple, and offering sacrifices according to the law, leaving off work and being entangled in the same trespasses, she departed more quickly." Jerome[194] notices: "They [i.e., the leaders] imbued them with the disgrace of the idols, instead of the worship of God, and the devil's spirit bound them up in his wings, and they are carried around by all the wind of the [his] teaching." Theodore of Mopsuestia[195] sees in this line a reference to Isreal's captivity: "For as a bird in flight which beats the air with its wings, and high above this world is taken in flight, in the same manner, carried away by my wrath, as if being high in the air, they will be taken away with much violence into captivity." In the end Israel, abandoned by Yahweh (v. 16b), left only with "their altars" (מִזְבְּחוֹתָם; cf. emended text), will experience humiliation and disappointment because of their flirtation with idolatry (v. 19).

3. Leaders and People on a Wrong Path (5:1-7)

1. Hear this, O priests! Pay attention, O house of Israel! O house of the king, hearken! For the judgment pertains to you;[196] for you have been a trap at Mizpah,[197] and a net spread upon Tabor,[198] 2. and a pit dug deep in Shittim;[199] but I will chastise[200] all of you.[201] 3. I myself know Ephraim, and Israel is not hidden from me; for now, O Ephraim, you have played the whore;[202] Israel is defiled. 4. Their deeds do not permit them[203] to return to their God. For a spirit of whoredom is in their midst, so they do not know Yahweh. 5. Israel's pride[204] testifies[205] against her; and Israel and Ephraim stumble in their

iniquity; Judah also stumbles with them. 6. With their flocks and herds they shall go to seek Yahweh, but they will not find him;[206] he has withdrawn from them. 7. It is Yahweh they have betrayed,[207] for they have borne bastard sons. Now the new moon[208] shall devour them along with their fields.

This new pericope (5:1-7) which continues listing Israel's (people and leaders) cultic[209] wickedness opens with a triple exhortation to listen to Yahweh's word (vv. 1, 2): "Hear" (שִׁמְעוּ), "pay attention" (הַקְשִׁיבוּ), and "hearken" (הַאֲזִינוּ). The exhortation is addressed to Israel's leaders whom Yahweh's "judgment" (הַמִּשְׁפָּט) pertains to, "priests" (כֹּהֲנִים) (cf. 4:4: "a priest"; 4:6: the anonymous priest and his "sons"), "house of Israel" (בֵּית יִשְׂרָאֵל),[210] and "house of the king" (בֵּית הַמֶּלֶךְ).[211] For Cyril of Alexandria,[212] the accused priests are "pseudo-priests, not belonging to the tribe of Levi, but having a 'bought' priesthood; they bought with money the right to worship idols.... For they devised and set up the structure of idolatry, erecting altars, offering libations and sacrifices, and extending the path of perdition for the people who are deceived. However, the kings are the innovators (εὑρεταὶ) of the error (πλάνης)." Jerome[213] offers a different interpretation concerning the identity of these "priests": "The priests of the ten tribes, and the kings are called to judgment, not because the priests are from the tribe of Levi, but because the priests are designated by the people." That is why "Israel, i.e., the people, is also called to judgment." The charges brought against Israel's leaders concern their association with the idolatrous worship performed in three of the northern sanctuaries: Mizpah,[214] Tabor,[215] and Shittim.[216] Their specific sins are defined with the help of three metaphors from the sphere of hunting: "trap" (פַּח), used primarily for birds (Am 3:5; Prov 7:23; and as a metaphor Ps 140:6), "net" (רֶשֶׁת), prepared for birds (7:2), but also for lions (Ezek 19:8), and "pit" (שַׁחַת; cf. emended text), dug for all kinds of game. Theophylact of Bulgaria[217] interprets: "And 'net,' not as Christ's disciples and fishermen used to have, that is engaged in the miracles, but like those with which the hunting demons have always fastened the spiritual prey." "They dug deep" (הֶעְמִיקוּ) or "(a pit) dug deep" is an irony telling of the passion of the wicked leaders who wanted to make sure that Israel was once and for all trapped in the deep pit of idolatry. Jerome[218] writes: "'And you lowered the victims into the depth' [cf. the Vulgate's reading] so that no one might repent, neither raise the bowed head."

The sentence-like conclusion, "But I will chastise (מְיַסֵּר; cf. emended text)[219] all of you" (v. 2) points to the fact that Yahweh will definitively chastise all who mislead his people (vv. 1-2). The accent falls here on correction/instruction (cf. LXX: παιδευτής "corrector") rather than on legal punishment. Jerome[220] explains: "I am your master (*magister*), or rather (your) instructor (*eruditor*), who wishes to correct (*emendare*), rather than to punish (*punire*); to save (*salvare*), rather than to lose (*perdere*)." A certain vacillation between harsh "punishment" and "instruction" is found in Cyril of Alexandria's[221] interpretation: "He will be their instructor (παιδευτής), promising that soon he will impose the evils (τὰ κακά) from his anger and wrath." Similarly, Theophylact of Bulgaria[222] writes: "I will impose correction (παιδείαν), that of the captivity, upon you and upon the whole people, which he called 'Israel.'" We may add that the theme of instruction (7:12, 15; 10:10; cf. Deut 8:5; Prov 4:1; 19:18) is an important component of Hosea's theology of redemption through judgment (2:6/4f., 14/12f.; 3:3ff.).[223]

Verses 3-4 are built around the theme of "knowledge" (יָדַע). In v. 3a Yahweh "knows" Ephraim,[224] that is to say, he takes notice of their "fornication" (זְנוּת)²²⁵ or "defilement" (טָמֵא)²²⁶ for nobody, including Israel, can "hide" oneself (כחד) from his omniscience. Cyril of Alexandria²²⁷ writes: "Who is that person that, by holding his words together in the heart, thinks he could hide his intentions from me?" "Fornication" and "defilement" point to apostasy and idolatry, as Theodore of Mopsuestia²²⁸ interprets: "I saw them finally going away from me, and being defiled by the worship of idols." Theophylact of Bulgaria²²⁹ considers God's instruction the sheer expression of his love towards Israel, explaining the divine knowledge through the prism of the same virtue: "That I 'know' means I 'loved' is seen from God's words: 'I instruct them, because I loved (ἠγάπησα) Ephraim and I did not remove Israel from me. For though she plays the whore in idolatry, nevertheless I would not reject her, but I will be with her.' This is in harmony with what the prophet was told in the beginning, when he was ordered to marry a whore. Who would not love an instructor, who corrects with love rather than with anger? This is also the instruction [promoted] for every leader, to chastise (κολάζειν) not for anger but for education and assistance." Jerome²³⁰ identifies "Ephraim" with king Jeroboam I when he writes: "I, he says, I know Ephraim, that is, Jeroboam, who deceived the people, and all the kings who followed him in dignity and folly; and Israel is not hidden from me, that is, the people of the ten tribes; since the king plays the whore, Israel is defiled."

In v. 4 Israel is unable to know Yahweh due to two adverse factors, "their deeds" (מַעַלְלֵיהֶם)²³¹ which do not "permit" (נתן)²³² her to "return" (שׁוּב) to God, and, again, that mysterious and almost irresistible entity labeled "spirit of whoredom" (רוּחַ זְנוּנִים). First, there was an outside "spirit" misleading Israel "far from their God" (4:12); then the "spirit" became a storm-like frightening force enwrapping a people without understanding "in its wings" (4:19); and now the same promiscuous "spirit" is in "their midst" (קִרְבָּם),[233] paralyzing Israel in their attempts to know Yahweh (5:4; cf. 4:1).[234] Jerome[235] interprets: "First, the king [i.e., Jeroboam I] chose to play the whore away from the worship of God, wishing to adore golden calves, and the people followed him willingly, with equal zeal they accomplished equal ungodliness. They do not return to the Lord, for they found, what they were looking for, and the spirit of whoredom which, according to the apostle, 'works in the sons of distrust' [Eph 2:2], holds their hearts captive; as long as it governs, they will not know the Lord. In fact, they forgot their creator.... They, whoever advance in ruin, do not have thoughts of penitence. For the spirit of whoredom, by which they played the whore in the church, and by which they went away from the true marriage, dwells in their midst; that is why, they did not know the Lord." For Theophylact of Bulgaria[236] the "spirit of whoredom" leads to both "idolatry" (εἰδωλολατρικῆς) and "carnality" (σωματικῆς), two fundamental sins which prevent the people from knowing the Lord. Julian of Eclanum[237] writes: "The reason nobody thought of correction was that the unclean spirit, that demon or love for impiety, was dwelling in their midst. For if they did wrong from a distance, the unclean spirit was believed to draw close to them. But now, since they devote all the time of their life to sins it is rightly said that the author of the impiety is not at all their neighbor, but in their midst. Therefore, as long as he is rooted in their hearts, they do not think of correction, and thus they are subject to ruin."

In vv. 5-7 Hosea takes a closer look at the correspondence between Israel's wrongdoings and the subsequent punishments. Israel's "pride" (גְּאוֹן)[238] has become her own accuser. Here "pride" does not designate Yahweh

(4:18: emended text; cf. Exod 15:7; Is 24:14; Mic 5:3), but Israel's arrogance and over-confidence in her economic prosperity during Jeroboam II's reign.[239] Theophylact of Bulgaria[240] notices: "'Insolence' (cf. LXX: ὕβριν) means contempt (καταφρόνησίν) of God and defection (ἀποστασίαν) from him, which happened to a certain degree to the captives; or the boastfulness (ἀλαζονείαν) the prosperous had with respect to the wealth. Therefore, they will see openly of what sort is the fruit of impiety and boastfulness. For he refers to this, when he says: 'In his face.' The 'insolence of Israel' means otherwise idolatry. For wood-worship, since it is rational, is insolence and the greatest disgrace." "Testify against" (ענה ב) is taken perhaps from the trial terminology (cf. 1 Sam 12:3; 2 Sam 1:16). The line "Israel's pride testifies against her" is found again in 7:10a. Julian of Eclanum[241] interprets: "Fittingly, he says, zeal (*industria*) will respond, that is, in such a way that they, who commonly boasted themselves with respect to their offenses, will feel ashamed under calamities."

"Israel and Ephraim shall stumble in their iniquity." Here, as in two other places in Hosea's book (4:5; 14:2), the punishment, indicated by the verb כשל "to stumble," is intrinsically linked to Israel's "iniquity" (14:2; עָוֹן; cf. 4:8). Thus, Israel and Ephraim will stumble in their own arrogance (cf. Prov 16:18). If in 5:3 "Ephraim" may be explained as another term for the Northern Kingdom, here "Ephraim" looks quite distinct from "Israel." While ancient Christian interpreters, such as Jerome,[242] see in "Israel" a reference to the ten tribes and in "Ephraim" an allusion to their kings, most of the modern scholars take "Ephraim" either as a gloss or dittograph.[243]

Hosea concludes that Judah "stumbles" (כָּשַׁל)[244] with her sister in the north. According to Jerome,[245] Judah will imitate Israel's "wickednesses" (*scelera*) and, by consequence, her "punishment" (*poenam*), the captivity. Theodoret of Cyrus[246] notices that "Judah rightly comes at the end since she endured the captivity after those [i.e., Israel and Ephraim]."

Verse 6 is another example of correspondence between iniquity and punishment. The reference to "flocks" and "herds," followed by the verb "to seek" (בקשׁ),[247] introduces the reader to a cultic setting dominated by Israel's quest for Yahweh. Note that this "seeking" is external, relying exclusively on sacrificial means (cf. 4:8, 13) with no moral connotations (cf. 6:6) which, partly, explains its failure. Cyril of Alexandria[248] interprets: "Therefore, even if the Israelites would offer legitimate sacrifices, imploring for the dismissal of the faults done by them in an unholy manner, or seeking the fellowship with God, they will not reach it, neither will they profit by finding God; in this way, nothing will be accessible to the penitents. For these things are reached only by the life which is in Christ, whose approach would make them comprehend the word of faith and, besides this, the saving baptism, which procures spiritual fellowship with God." Since, in the past, Israel has chosen to go astray far from God and to participate in idolatrous acts of cult (4:12-13), they are now unable to find him (contrary to the promise of Deut 4:29).[249] Theophylact of Bulgaria[250] notices that the main reason for such a failure is Israel's oscillation between Yahweh and the false gods: "Why did not the Lord appear to those who offered sacrifices? For they did not do it from all their soul, but heartlessly and for a while. Yet, the law commands to love God with the whole heart, the whole soul, and the whole mind. Or because they march out to the false gods, in the same way as to the Lord. They will not find the true Lord, for they used to address the idol as 'living Lord.'" Hosea ends v. 6 with the observation: "Yahweh himself has "withdrawn"

(חָלַץ)[251] from them, thus sentencing Israel's apostasy. With respect to God's "withdrawal," Julian of Eclanum[252] suggests that in fact God has not disappeared, but rather this was Israel's perception: "Not because God was able to be withdrawn, but because his assistance occurred nowhere in this way to them, perhaps, they saw him as entirely 'withdrawn.'" On the other hand, Jerome[253] emphasizes the idea that God himself has in fact withdrawn from Israel: "That is why they do not find the Lord, for he is withdrawing (*aufertur*) from them, and is departing afar (*procul*)."

The greatest iniquity of Israel is encapsulated in Hosea's brief remark "It is Yahweh they betrayed (בָּגָדוּ)" (v. 7). Theophylact of Bulgaria[254] explains this third-person divine speech as an indication that the Spirit addresses the prophet: "When the Spirit says these words in the prophet, he uses the third person." The root בגד "to act or deal treacherously, to betray" is used here in the same way as in the passages describing the deception of a husband by a wayward wife (Exod 21:8; cf. Jer 3:20). For Jerome,[255] "they have dealt false-ly" (cf. V: *praevaricati sunt*) points to idolatry, "for they played the whore with the idols." Similarly, Theodore of Mopsuestia[256] notices: "Since they left him [i.e., God] for these things, they devoted themselves entirely to the idols."

The "betrayal" translates into giving birth to "bastard sons" (בָּנִים זָרִים), who most probably cover the same entity as the "children of whoredom" (1:2). These "bastard sons" may be either a new generation of Israelites devoted, as their parents, to the idolatry,[257] or the sons born to the Israelites by their foreign wives.[258] Cyril of Alexandria[259] sums up both interpretations taking no side: "'Foreign sons,' he says, are those who, from the womb, and from their swaddling-clothes, were dedicated to the worship of idols, perhaps when the fathers offered the thanksgiving and sacrifices for births to the demons. Therefore, 'foreign sons' are the ones who are not in God. Or, according to another interpretation, the ones from the foreign wives. For the Israelites mingled thoughtlessly with the daughters of the nations, even yet idolatrous, although the law manifestly says that they should not unite in marriage with the foreigners [Deut 7:3-4]." Similarly, Jerome[260] lists the two views, while suggesting that the religious explanation (i.e., an idolatrous people) would fit better into the context: "Since they played the whore, they produced sons not for God but for demons. Others believe that this refers to later times, mentioned in Ezra, when they married foreign women, having sons from them, and then they were forced to drive them [i.e., the women] away. Yet, at this juncture it is better to admit that 'foreign sons' designate the ones who were born in the error of idolatry, or more accurately those whom they consecrated, through fire, to the idols."

Verse 7b is one of the more obscure lines in the entire book of Hosea. The punitive action, the "new moon" (חֹדֶשׁ) devouring (אָכַל) Israel's "fields" (חֶלְקֵיהֶם), speaks of a country completely abandoned by Yahweh.

There are two ways of dealing with the controversial form, חֹדֶשׁ, in this line: (1) to leave the MT unchanged, or (2) to resort to one of several emendations proposed thus far.

(1) If one follows the MT reading, the "new moon" (cf. Is 1:3) by metonymy could designate religious practices; thus, these practices tainted with Baalism will eventually lead Israel to her ruin.[261] Given the number of versions (V, Aquila, Symmachus, Theodotion) which support the MT reading, we consider this reading and the related interpretation plausible. However, there is no satisfactory answer as to how a "(new) month" could be one of Yahweh's punitive instruments against Israel. In search for an an-

swer, Jerome[262] replaces "months" with "enemy" for the subject: "Every single month, the enemy will arrive and will devastate everything." According to Jerome, v. 7b refers to Tiglath-pileser III's ("the enemy") invasion in 733 B.C., followed by the deportation of Samaria's inhabitants to different provinces of Assyria. For the ancient Jewish interpreters, such as Rashi and ibn Ezra, the devouring "month" mentioned here is *Ab*, the traditional month of the destruction of the Jerusalem temple in 587 B.C. This interpretation was probably triggered by the reference to "Judah" in v. 5b.[263]

(2) If one changes the vowels of חֹדֶשׁ to *ḥādāš* "(someone) else," then the meaning of this line would be something to the extent that the outsiders (cf. 8:7) will grasp Israel's territory.[264] Another alternative would be to follow the emendation proposed by the Septuagint (ἡ ἐρυσίβη "red blight," the LXX common rendition of the Hebrew word הֶחָסִיל "locust"), and to substitute חֹדֶשׁ with the word for "locust," hence the translation "Now the locust shall devour their fields."[265] Based on the Septuagint reading, Theodoret of Cyrus[266] identifies the "red blight" with the foreign enemies: "Red blight (ἐρυσίβην) designates that disease that occurs to the fruits of the earth due to an imperfection of the air; figuratively (τροπικῶς), it indicates the enemies (πολεμίους) who destroy everything after the manner of the red blight." According to Cyril of Alexandria,[267] this line suggests that the war is inevitable: "The war will not be postponed or ceased, but rather it is at once and on the track."

In one way or another, either one reads "month" with the Latin writers, or "red blight" as the Greek fathers do, the meaning of v. 7b remains the same: a foreign enemy will devastate the whole country. The destruction is imminent and complete.

4. Ephraim and Judah in Conflict (5:8-15)

8. Blow the horn in Gibeah,[268] the trumpet in Ramah![269] Shout the alarm in Beth-aven![270] After you, Benjamin![271] 9. Ephraim shall become a desolation on the day of chastisement. Among the tribes of Israel, I declare what is sure. 10. The princes of Judah act as those who move the landmark. Upon them I will pour out my fury like water. 11. Ephraim is oppressed,[272] justice is crushed, because willingly[273] he followed vanity.[274] 12. But I am like pus[275] to Ephraim, and like rottenness[276] to the house of Judah. 13. When Ephraim saw his sickness, and Judah her wound, then Ephraim went to Assyria and sent to the great king.[277] Yet he, he cannot heal you or cure your wound.[278] 14. For I am like a lion to Ephraim, and like a young lion to the house of Judah. I myself will rend and go away; I will carry off, and no one can rescue. 15. I will go back to my place until they bear punishment[279] and seek my face. In their distress, they will seek me early.[280]

If the chapters 1-3 and 4:5-7 date to the end of the prosperous reign of king Jeroboam II, the new pericope (5:8-15) mirrors the tumultuous events occasioned by the Syro-Ephraimite war.[281] In 733 B.C. Rezin of Aram and Pekah of Israel attack Judah to replace king Ahaz who refused to join them against Assyria. Ahaz appeals to Tiglath-pileser III of Assyria who intervenes and puts an end to the conflict between Israel and Judah (2 Kgs 16; cf. Is 7). A great part of Israel's population was then deported, and the territory, except for Samaria and the mountainous region of Ephraim, was occupied by the Assyrian troops and transformed into four provinces. King Pekah was murdered by Hoshea who became the last king of Israel in exchange for an annual tribute paid to Assur (732-724 B.C.).[282] This section underscores the idea, already outlined in 5:5 (cf. 4:15), that "Ephraim" (the name of the Northern Kingdom throughout this pericope) and "Judah" are equally guilty, and the sufferings experienced by them during the Syro-Ephraimite war are the fitting punishment for having betrayed Yahweh (cf. 5:7).

Verse 8 introduces a new setting, different from the previous one dominated extensively by Israel's worship. Now the setting is the battlefield where control over the territory of Benjamin should be decided between the two sister-kingdoms, Judah and Israel. Jerome[283] interprets: "Every single month—or rather, rust—will devour Ephraim and Israel and Judah along with their districts. Therefore I advise you who are listening that you make a noise not with uplifted voice but with loud horn. For a loud sound is needed so that all on the periphery may hear [it].... The Kingdom of Israel then will be in desolation, and the captivity, that has already befallen the neighbors, is approaching." Yet, for Theodoret of Cyrus[284] the scene described in v. 8 is dominated by the idolatrous cult: "Lay hold of the highest hills [cf. LXX: βουνούς], on which you were offering every kind of worship to the idols. Let them give you their help at the necessary time!" Similarly, Cyril of Alexandria[285] writes: "Therefore, when he says to sound the trumpet on hills, elevated places, and in the house of On, you should understand places of the idols.... Thus, we may suppose, indeed, that the prophetic word asked them to sound the trumpet, not only on hills and elevated places, namely, not only against Israel's idolatry, i.e., that of the ten tribes in Samaria, but also against the one in Jerusalem, beside Judah and Benjamin. For there, they adored the sun ('On' is the sun), throwing God out and turning away from his holy things."

Benjamin had been a bone of contention for more than a century and a half. During the period of Judges, this tribe was depending on the northern tribe of Ephraim (Judg

5:4: Song of Deborah). At the time of the great schism (ca. 922 B.C.) between north and south, Benjamin joined Judah (cf. 1 Kgs 12:20ff.). During the Syro-Ephraimite war, one may assume that the territory of Benjamin fell again under Israel's influence as the joined troops of Rezin and Pekah were victoriously marching southward to Jerusalem. When the Assyrians made their appearance in the theater, the Judaeans captured the much disputed territory (cf. 5:10). According to Theophylact of Bulgaria,[286] "Benjamin" refers here to Judah, hence his interpretation focusing on Jerusalem: "Those in Jerusalem went away (ἐξέστησαν), namely, they moved from the center, they perished utterly, just as they were acting impiously."

"After you, Benjamin!" (אַחֲרֶיךָ בִּנְיָמִין) should be read, as Macintosh[287] suggests, in the light of Judg 5:14 (Song of Deborah) where this cry of solidarity is recorded for the first time ("From Ephraim came they whose roots are in Amalek; after you, your kin Benjamin"). Hosea asks the watchmen in the towns of Benjamin to raise the alarm[288] for the invader is approaching. In these circumstances, the inhabitants of the Northern Kingdom might have said, "We Ephraimites are behind you, Benjamin." The bitter fate experienced by the Benjaminite towns (Gibeah,[289] Ramah,[290] Beth-aven[291]) reoccupied by the Judaeans is going to be shared by Ephraim, the old ally of Benjamin, now at the whim of Tiglath-pileser. This interpretation fits well with Hosea's objective view of the Syro-Ephraimite war: both kingdoms are guilty and deserving punishment (5:12). For Julian of Eclanum[292] "behind Benjamin" (*tergum Benjamin*) indicates the position of the localities in reference to Judah: "[D]esolation will take possession of entire Ephraim. All the places, which he said, namely 'behind Benjamin,' which tribe was bordering the territory of Judah—Gabaa, Rama and Beth-aven—we infer, were close to Judah's borders."

Commentary: Hosea 4-11

In v. 9a "Ephraim" refers to the Northern Kingdom (5:11; 7:8, 11) or, more precisely, to what was left after Tiglath-pileser III's quick intervention in 733 B.C. Theodore of Mopsuestia[293] writes: "'Benjamin' refers to the Kingdom of Judah, while 'Ephraim' designates the ten tribes. He does not say that the one is amazed (ἐξέστη), and the other utterly destroyed (ἀφανισμὸν); but here he says that both of them will be amazed and utterly destroyed."

Yahweh declares among the "tribes of Israel" (שִׁבְטֵי יִשְׂרָאֵל), i.e., to the whole nation, "what is sure" or already "established" (נֶאֱמָנָה):[294] Ephraim will become a "desolation" (שַׁמָּה) in the day of "chastisement" (תּוֹכֵחָה).[295] Cyril of Alexandria[296] explains: "I showed my words as sure and true. For they, as I have already predicted, were not deceived by any of my words. And since they went away from the former customs, and lost their good mind, they were expelled even from their territory; similarly, they were banished from God's kindness and every prosperity." Theodore of Mopsuestia[297] interprets: "By bringing forth these words for them, I will prove the truth and validity of my threats, which they would not believe, even though they came through the prophets. But they will learn from experience that all the sayings were trustworthy and truthful." For Theophylact of Bulgaria[298] the "day of disproof (ἐλέγχου)" points to crucifixion of Jesus: "But he showed trustworthy things in the days of cross and resurrection, when he shook creation and through this refuting them, on the one hand, and presenting his divinity as trustworthy, on the other hand." Jerome[299] writes: "In the day of reproof and suffering of the ten tribes, I showed my words, I threatened through prophets, as trustworthy; thus, what I predicted by word, I proved by deed." Hosea's critical attitude toward Pekah's alliance with Rezin of Aram against Judah accords with Isaiah's harsh words to Ahaz whereas his asking Tiglath-pileser III for help against Israel (Is 7:1ff.).[300] Israel's wrong conduct is punishable. Ephraim's "desolation" refers probably to the Assyrian invasion in 724 B.C.

Verse 10 deals with Judah whose "princes" (שָׂרֵי), i.e., the military leaders, are guilty of moving the "landmark" (גְּבוּל). This saying may be an allusion to the Judaean advance into the Benjamite territory occasioned by the intervention of Tigalth-pileser III in 733 B.C. But Judah's "princes" do not stop at Benjamin; they begin to pluck portions out of the Ephraimite territory which never belonged to the Southern Kingdom.[301] This wrongdoing committed by the Judaean troops is compared with the crime of those individuals who move the boundary markers (cf. Deut 19:14; 27:17; Prov 22:28). Yahweh announces that he will pour out his "fury" (עֶבְרָה)[302] like the waters upon them. "Waters" refer to the waters of the sea (Am 5:8) and the whole imagery used here is taken from the flood tradition.[303] Cyril of Alexandria[304] writes: "For hard to bear and insufferable, and entirely irresistible are the things stemming from the divine wrath; like a disagreeable, strong and excessive rush of waters." Theophylact of Bulgaria[305] notices that God will pour out his wrath upon the leaders of Judah, "just as the water of the Red Sea came upon Pharaoh, who often lied, and was kept, due to his unrepentant heart, for the display of God's might. For God is not mocked." Julian of Eclanum[306] interprets: "Namely, at the time of the Assyrian captivity, when he drove the ten tribes out of their boundaries, the leaders of Judah, who should have been moved to tears by the brother's calamity, and to think carefully of their behavior, so that they perhaps not fall into similar troubles; not only felt nothing of fear or compunction, but they even made public their parricide intentions, obviously rejoicing that large territories might be added to theirs as a result of their brother's expulsion." Jerome[307] adds: "Therefore, the Lord says: 'And the Babylonians will come over the very leaders of Judah; and they will fall upon them as the rush of water; not by their own strength, but by my indignation.'"

In v. 11a the attention turns back toward Ephraim punished by Yahweh for his alliance with Aram against Judah during the Syro-Ephraimite war. "Ephraim is oppressed (עָשׁוּק), justice (מִשְׁפָּט) is crushed (רְצוּץ)."[308] The political fiasco and social morass experienced by Ephraim are due to both the invasion of Tiglath-pileser III in 733 B.C. and the Judaean incursions into Benjamite and Ephraimite territories. But the real cause of Ephraim's troubles is that "he willingly followed vanity" (v. 11b). "Vanity" refers to the Kingdom of Aram with which Israel made an alliance in order to stand up against the common enemy Assyria. Eventually, this pact proved itself to be worthless and even dangerous for the fate of the Northern Kingdom. Hosea underscores that Ephraim made this political step "willingly," hence the gravity of his transgression. For Cyril of Alexandria[309] the "vanity" points to idolatry: "The origin of such a suffering, he says, is holding the vain things in honor, and following the idols. For it is impossible to follow at the same time God and the evil and unclean spirits." Similarly, Theodoret of Cyrus[310] explains: "The cause of his [i.e., Ephraim's] wrong-doing was the worship of idols. For, if he knew me, he would have learned what is proper from my law." And Theodoret of Mopsuestia[311] writes: "They accomplished these [i.e., vain things] from the time when they willingly chose the worship of idols, inasmuch as they still failed to follow my laws and will." Theophylact of Bulgaria[312] clearly equates the "vain things" (μάταια) with the "idols," noticing, that the cause of Ephraim's injustice is his "attachment (σχέσις) to and following (ἀκολούθησις) of idols." In the same interpretative vein, Jerome[313] notices that to go after "dirt" (cf. V: *sordem*) means "after idols which may be compared to dirty things." But Jerome offers also a military explanation of the first part of v. 11 when he writes: "Ephraim is being oppressed by the Assyrians, first by Phul, next by Teglathphalasar [Tiglathpileser III], then by Salmanasar; not that those were just, who oppressed him and therefore he was handed over to them; but that those who were once my people are being handed over to punishment after I deserted them."

The saying in v. 12 concerns both Ephraim and Judah. Yahweh's judgment is impartial: both kingdoms are guilty (vv. 10, 11) and thus punishable. To avoid the wrong conclusion someone might draw—that he is absent on the historical scene, and by consequence the distress experienced by the Israelites and Judaeans is due to external causes (political and military)—Yahweh declares that he is like "pus" (עָשׁ)[314] to "Ephraim," and "rottenness" (רָקָב)[315] to the "house of Judah." Nowhere in the entire Old Testament does Yahweh introduce himself with such shockingly bold metaphors. Hosea makes here an interesting point: behind the visible phenomena it is Yahweh himself[316] who works against the sinful nations. Cyril of Alexandria[317] interprets: "For Ephraim, or rather the ten tribes were greatly cast into confusion, because of the war which fell upon them, partly from the neighboring Syrians, partly from the Persians and Assyrians; Judah suffered severely; she was beyond measure frightened. For she expected to experience shortly the same evils perhaps, or much worse." Julian of Eclanum[318] writes: "Judah, you made public such cruelty of your soul, that in the wicked deeds, for which Israel has been convicted, you appear rougher and more inveterate. Whence, due to the difference in faults, the method of my sentences is sharpened; thus, I will renew Ephraim like a moth, but I will devour you [i.e., Judah] as an inherent decay. One may note by how much less destruction are those things which the moth bites consumed than those things which decay pervades." Jerome[319] interprets: "Therefore, just as the moth (*tinea*) consumes clothing, and the decay (*putredo*) or dry-rot (*caries*), wooden things (which both occur over a long time), in the same manner God, giving a place of penitence over a long time to the ten tribes and then, afterwards, to the two tribes, summoning to salvation those who treasure for themselves wrath for the day of wrath, becomes like a moth or like rot."

Verse 13 is built around three observations: (a) Ephraim and Judah notice their "sickness" (חָלְיוֹ) and "wound" (מְזֹרוֹ);[320] (b) instead of returning to Yahweh who loves them in spite of their apostasy (3:1), they appeal[321] to the "great king" (מֶלֶךְ יָרֵב) of Assyria for help; (c) but "he" (הוּא)[322] cannot "heal" (רפא) them or "cure" (יִגְהֶה)[323] their wounds. Jerome[324] interprets: "Judah under king Ahaz begged Teglathphalasar [Tiglath-pileser III], the Assyrian king, for help, but the Assyrians could not liberate them while God opposed [it], nor untie the bond (*vinculum*) of captivity. We propose *vinculum* for Hebrew *mezur*, while Aquila rendered ἐπίδεσιν or συνδεσμόν, namely, tie or league; this concerns the time, when Rasin and Phasee, son of Romelia, destroyed many thousands of men from the tribe of Judah, because Judah asked in vain for the Assyrian help, rather than God's, against the two kings."

At the historical level, Ephraim's "sickness" refers to the invasion by Tiglath-pileser III of the Northern Kingdom at the end of the Syro-Ephraimite war (733 B.C.), while Judah's "wound" may be a hint at the unsuccessful siege of Jerusalem done by the allied kings Rezin of Aram and Pekah of Israel (2 Kgs 16:5; Is 7:1). If this is true, then the "great king" is no one else but Tiglath-pileser III. Judah's "sending" messengers[325] to the "great king" for help (2 Kgs 16:7-9) reflects king Ahaz's lack of faith in Yahweh's assurance, delivered by prophet Isaiah, that Jerusalem's capture "will never happen" (Is 7:7). Ephraim's "going" to Assyria refers probably to king Hoshea who, after he murdered Pekah (2 Kgs 15:30), paid tribute to Assyria and became a vassal.[326] According to Cyril of Alexandria,[327] who relies on the Septuagint reading, Ephraim's "sending" messengers to the Assyrians alludes to the end of the Syro-Ephraimite war, while king "Iareim" (Ἰαρείμ) is Tiglath-pileser III: "Taking Damascus by force, he [i.e., Tiglath-pileser III] brought Rezin out of its midst. As for Ephraim, he went to the Assyrians buying with money and supplications the delay of the attack. Although he sent messengers to king Iareim, literally, the one who avenges (ἔκδικον) or the vindication (ἐκδικητὴν) (for this is the meaning of Iareim), nevertheless they could not overpower the divine wrath, nor will they be over God, for such an apostasy reclaims judgment. For he, convinced with money, was not able to make you rest briefly, nor could any of the hirelings heal you. The sting (κέντρον) of grief will never cease." For Theodoret of Cyrus,[328] "Iareib" (Ἰαρείβ) was the king of Egypt: "When the Assyrians came again against you, you sent messengers to the king of Egypt, asking for help from him, nevertheless you received no aid from him, but you were delivered to one suffering after another. That he calls king Iareib the king of Egypt is easily understood from what follows [cf. Hos 7:11].... For it was proper to ask for my help, since it is powerful and is very near to him, he continued going around, here and there, seeking for powerless aids; but he will receive no profit from their help."

Assyria's failure to heal the disease of Ephraim and Judah is due to Yahweh's harsh intervention against these nations (v. 14). The repetition of the independent pronoun "I" (short אֲנִי and long אָנֹכִי forms) shows Yahweh's resoluteness to punish both kingdoms left alone with no "rescuer" (מַצִּיל).[329] The situation depicted here is that of Israel being reduced to Ephraim, with most of the territory (i.e., Gilead and Galilee) turned into Assyrian provinces (733 B.C.). The metaphors used for Yahweh, "lion" (שַׁחַל) and "young lion" (כְּפִיר),[330] are similar in terms of boldness to those found in v. 12. This theriomorphism (Yahweh as a "lion" appears again in 13:7; cf. Is 31:4) is meant to emphasize the actuality of Yahweh's anger.[331] Theophylact of Bulgaria[332] explains: "By panther [cf. LXX: πάνθηρ] one may understand that the evils will come upon them quickly and suddenly. For the panther is swift and light. The lion designates what is great and dreadful." In v. 14, as in v. 12, Hosea tries to convey the idea that Yahweh, although working in a hidden way, is the Lord of history.

Verse 15 continues the foregoing imagery while anticipating the confession in 6:1-3. Yahweh does not return to his "place" (מָקוֹם) until he sees the result of his actions. Theodoret of Cyrus[333] writes: "For it is the habit of those beasts, after they hunt something to return to their usual places, and to rest awhile from the toil caused by the hunting. Thus, I, he says, like a panther and lion, come against you through enemies, then I will be by myself, and consider you unworthy of care." Paradoxically, God "withdraws" so that he cannot be found (5:6), but at the same time he is waiting to be sought.[334] Cyril of Alexandria[335] encapsulates this paradox in his explanation: "For the divinity is altogether unlimited (ἀπεριόριστον) by any place. But it said to be present in certain places, when he shows [his] grace; but [it is said] in turn to be absent from among those who have sinned, when he turns away from them, by driving [his] kindness back. For one speaks of

God in human terms, but this is not understood as truly befitting him." Jerome[336] writes: "By 'my place' we have to understand God's place, his splendor and majesty; so that by no means according to the dispensation does he descend to men, become angry, merciful, forgetful, become as a panther, turn into a lion, change into beasts; on the contrary, he disdains human things and allows those whom he once protected to be cast to enemies, so that they may languish, disappear, and be destroyed, and seek eventually the face of the Lord.... Others consider God's place the heaven where God returns after being offended by the inhabitants of the earth; and he makes go to ruin those who, due to the multitude of their sins, turned the mercy of the Lord into the rage of beasts toward them." Ephraim and Judah will seek Yahweh's "face" (פָּנַי) only when they will experience the punitive sufferings. Cyril of Alexandria[337] offers a typological interpretation: "It seems that the saying refers very suitably to the mystery of Christ, and the redemption through him, pointing to the conversion to God. For God's sought face signifies most certainly the Son himself 'who is the image, and the radiance, and the very seal of the Father's nature' [Heb 1:3]. Thus, the true face of God and Father is the Son, inasmuch as he is recognized in him, 'and who saw him, saw the Father' [Jn 14:9]. The divine cantor thus calls him, when he cries out to God of all, saying: 'Cause your face to shine upon your servant' [Ps 118:135]. Indeed, just as from the person of those who believed, and were already transformed according to the Son through the Spirit: 'The light of your face, O Lord, has been marked upon us' [Ps 4:6]. Or as the prophet says: 'The light of our face, the anointed Lord' (Χριστὸς Κύριος) [Lam 4:20]."

The conclusion that they will "seek early" (שִׁחֵר)[338] the Lord in their "distress" (צַר), points to the pedagogical dimension of the divine punishment. By punishing

Ephraim and Judah, Yahweh aims to make them repent of their wrongdoings and return to him (cf. 2:9/7; 3:5). Punishment is not Yahweh's last word or purpose but only a means of divine instruction ("chastisement"; cf. 5:9). Cyril of Alexandria[339] writes: "'They seek early' seems to indicate here that they, as if awaken from the sleep of thoughtlessness which was in them, and further as if brought from night and darkness to light and day, will call out to one another, that it is fitting to return to the Lord. This is a return to senses (ἀνάνηψις) of those fallen into deception, and those taken up by the worships of idols. For the fruit of vigilance is at present seeking to get out of the gloom which is demoniac."

5. Repentance, Revival, and Yahweh's Response (6:1-6)

1. Come, let us return to Yahweh,[340] for he has torn and he will heal us; he has struck us[341] and he will bind us up. 2. He will revive us[342] after two days;[343] on the third day[344] he will raise us up[345] that we may live in his presence. 3. Let us know, let us strive to know Yahweh; as sure as the dawn is his going forth.[346] He will come to us like rain, like spring showers[347] that water the land. 4. What shall I do with you, O Ephraim? What shall I do with you, O Judah? Your mercy is like morning mist, like dew that vanishes early. 5. Therefore I have hewn them in pieces[348] by the prophets, I have killed them by the words of my mouth, and my judgment like light goes forth.[349] 6. For I desire mercy[350] and not[351] sacrifice, the knowledge of God, rather than burnt offerings.

There are at least three main interpretations of vv. 1-3.[352] Some scholars (Wolff, Mays, Rudolph, Jacob) consider these verses a reproduction of a song of penitence sung by priests or people in times of national calamities (e.g., the critical period after the Syro-Ephraimite war). Other commentators (Marti), see in 5:15-6:3 a later, post-exilic, addition to the Hosean text. Yet, both views are unable to explain the obvious similarities in content and form between vv. 6:1-3 and the surrounding context. The basic idea in 5:12ff. and 6:1ff. is that Yahweh is for Israel her chastiser and healer at the same time. The similarity in language is given by key verbs such as, רפא "to heal" (5:13; 6:1), טרף "to tear apart" (5:14; 6:1), and שוב "to return" (5:15; 6:1).

The third interpretation, followed in this commentary, belongs to three ancient versions, the Septuagint, *Peshitta*, and Targum. According to this view, between 5:15 and 6:1-3 there is a close connection. People's penitence in vv. 1-3 is in fact a part of the divine speech which precedes it. This explains the interpretative gloss, "saying" or "they say," inserted by the ancient versions at the end of 5:15. Thus, the last part of the divine speech sounds like a prophecy concerning people's penitence: "In their distress, they will seek me early, saying, 'Come, let us return to Yahweh.'" This interpretation accounts for the similarities between 6:1-3 and the preceding and following texts. But if vv. 1-3 mirror the ideal penitence in Yahweh's view, how should one read Yahweh's harsh criticism with respect to Israel in vv. 4ff.? A possible explanation: What Yahweh criticizes in vv. 4ff. is not the content of people's confession (vv. 1-3) but the way Israel fulfills the divine prophecy. Instead of translating her inner penitence into moral deeds, as Yahweh wants (6:6), Israel remains at the level of good intentions and promises[353] as transitory as the mist and the dew (6:4), or reduces everything to an external worship dominated by animal sacrifices (5:6).

Verse 1 represents the first of two exhortations by which an afflicted nation recognizes that only Yahweh, the one who chastises (cf. 5:12ff.), is able to heal its wounds (cf.

Deut 32:39; Job 5:18). Thus, punishment is not a goal in itself but a way chosen by Yahweh to instruct the people, to bring them back to him. Theophylact of Bulgaria[354] interprets: "For when God snatches away, or strikes, no one can heal. Thus, in the calamity they remembered God. These may refer to those among the Hebrews who afterwards came to believe in Christ. In such a thirst and long captivity, they will seek the face, namely, the Son. For he is the mark of the Father's hypostasis (person). Those who turn to the Son are stripped of the veil which lies on their heart." In the same vein, Theodore of Mopsuestia[355] writes: "Due to the troubles occurring to them, they will quickly run to me, believing firmly that I, who struck them, will completely heal them, and similarly, cure their wounds, and I will quickly and easily restore their things." Cyril of Alexandria[356] offers a rather spiritual explanation of God's paradoxical intervention: "If one ought to extend the meaning of the prophecy to all mortals, we are going to extract this sense. In the beginning, he seized Adam's human nature; for he at once declared it accursed, ascribing it to death and corruption. Thus, the wrath has struck, but grace plugged the wound with lint. For Christ has brought the healing; he invited [us] to know the true divine revelation, he confirmed through the Spirit to observe the commandments; he showed us again zealous followers, by placing us beyond corruption and freeing us from the previous infirmities, namely, sin and passions." The cohortative "let us return" (נָשׁוּבָה) echoes 2:9/7 where again Israel takes the decision to return to Yahweh, her "first husband," but as in 6:1, her return did not become actual fact. In 5:4 Israel's wicked deeds do not allow her to return to God (cf. "pride" in 7:10), and in 11:5 Israel will experience captivity for they refused to return to Yahweh. Contrary to all these instances, the return in 3:5, projected in a future time (postexilic or eschatological), reaches its fruition. As in 6:1, in 3:5, Israel's return is preceded by a period of austerity. People's intention to return in 6:1 points also to Yahweh's decision to return to his "place" (5:15).[357]

The verbs "to tear" (טרף) and "to strike" (נכה) allude to the killing of a victim; thus, the picture painted in v. 1, that of a destroyed nation, anticipates and clarifies the language of resurrection in v. 2.[358]

"He will revive us (יְחַיֵּנוּ)" (v. 2a). Is this line referring to people's revival (resurrection) as Ezek 37? The answer depends on how one deals with another question: Is the nation in 5:14-6:1 ill or dead? Both verbs in v. 1, "to tear" and "to strike," point to the second situation. "To tear to pieces" means that the victim is lifeless, while "to strike, to give a fatal blow" suggests killing not maiming. In this case, "he will raise us up" (יְקִמֵנוּ)[359] presupposes a cessation of life. Moreover, "that we may live in his presence" (v. 2b) can barely parallel "to preserve alive," v. 2a (Wolff), since the image of a debilitated nation preserved in life as depicted by the latter clause would considerably diminish the vigor of the phrase "living in the presence of Yahweh" which points to a full personal relationship with God. Conversely, the imagery of the people's revival (resurrection) would match well such a vigorous relationship. Thus, the Pi'el of the verb חיה "to live" is better to be rendered "to make alive, to revive"[360] than "to preserve alive."

"After two days" (מִיֹּמָיִם) ... "on the third day." Alone, "the third day" indicates a short period of time (Gen 22:4; 40:20; Exod 19:11); here, connected with "two days," it looks oddly as a repetition since the prefixed מִן "after" (cf. Judg 11:4) points to the day after two days, "the third day," that is.[361] Probably, this period refers to the time when a revival was still possible, before the body begin to decompose (Jn 11:39; cf. Jon 2:1).[362] What could signify the recovery or even the revival of a nation after such a short interval of two days? This sequence of numerals remains meaningless unless the text is read as a messianic prophecy regarding Christ's resurrection: "two days" refer to the time the body of Jesus lay in the tomb and "the third day" points to his glorious resurrection. Writing to the Corinthians, St. Paul mentions that Jesus "was raised (ἐγήγερται) on the third day in accordance with the scriptures" (1 Cor 15:4), probably alluding to Hos 6:2.

The Targum interprets the Hosean text in connection with the final resurrection. Yet, due to the polemic with Christian circles, the author of the Aramaic translation replaced the references to the number of days with his own interpretation (here, in *italics*), "He will give us life *in the days of consolations that will come; on the day of the resurrection of the dead* he will raise us up and we shall live before him."

Among the Church's writers, Tertullian (third century A.D.)[363] is the first author to relate this passage to the resurrection of Jesus, more precisely, to the scene of the myrrh-bearing women who went "at early dawn" (Lk 24:1: ὄρθρου βαθέως; cf. Hos 5:15: ὀρθιοῦσι πρὸς μὲ [LXX] "they will seek me early") to their Master's tomb to anoint his body. Theodoret of Cyrus[364] explains: "For there is no need of a period of time for curing, but he will grant swift health. By these he designates the Savior's resurrection which occurred after three days, which mediated the universal resurrection, and granted all of us the hope of immortality made possible through the knowledge of God." Similarly, Cyril of Alexandria[365] hints at resurrection when writes: "These things [healing and restoration] will happen to mortals not for the first time, not even for the second time, but for the third time, namely, for the last and uttermost time. For all periods of time number three [phases], initial, middle, and last, when Christ appeared to us. That is why the very ones say from medical experience: the healing will happen after two days, as the prophetic word measures one day opportune for us.... We shall rise together with Christ; and since one died for all, we live his life, not removed from the eyes of God for transgression, nor cast behind for sin, but brought in sight and having boldness through him for the righteousness in Christ." Theophylact of Bulgaria[366] interprets: "Certainly, it alludes to the mystery according to nature. For he has stricken nature by death and gave those who sin to death. But he inserted (παρενέβαλε) his Son in the stricken nature like some precious thing, who, since he was in the wound of death, he healed us and rose (ἀνέστησε) on the third day. For by raising the acquisition (πρόσλημμα) he assumed from us, he bestowed upon us all the resurrection (ἀνάστασιν), which each one of us will have it in his own time (εἰς καιροῖς ἰδίοις), and we will live. For if one died for all, that same one also rose for all, and we will, since we are not far off from him since we are seen in his face, we have a more perfect knowledge." But for Theophylact, the "third day" has also a spiritual meaning: "We shall rise on the third day, when the third part of the soul, the reasoning faculty (τὸ λογιστικὸν) will be quite clearly illuminated (φωτισθῇ) through spiritual contemplation (θεωρίας). For at that time, we shall live in the very presence of God, that is, contemplating him face to face." Jerome[367] writes: "Therefore, God smites and heals us; for 'God reproaches him whom he loves, and chastises every son whom receives' [Heb 12:6]; not only does he cure, but also he gives life after two days, and on the third day, rising again from the lower regions, raises along with him the entire humankind. And after he has healed those beaten and given life to those healed, and raised those given life, then we shall live in his sight, in whose absence, we lay dead. But we shall live in his presence; we shall know him and attend him with all zeal so that we may know the Lord, who rose on the third day, and therefore we arose. In these sayings one explains what often we were told, that Israel and Judah, namely, those ten and two tribes, would have one shepherd, king David, at the time when they should believe in the resurrected Lord; but the Judaeans in vain are offering themselves dreams for one thousand years, while the salvation of all was guaranteed in return on the third day, when the Lord rose from the lower regions. The Hebrews interpret the second day for the coming of their Christ, and the third day for the judgment, when they are to be saved. So that we may concede this, let them tell us what is the first day, this is the first advent of the Savior. And as they were unable to answer, let us urge that the first day was according to their view, the coming in humility of the Savior, the second in glory, the third in the posture of the judge. But those who mistrust the second and the third, they declare that they lost the first, for the second and the third cannot be named without the first." According to Theodore of Mopsuestia,[368] the prophet speaks of Israel's restoration to a former prosperous situation, rather than a transition to a brand new life: "He heals us in such a short time that he will restore (ἀποκαταστῆναι) us again to the ancient prosperity in two or three days at the most."

Historically, Hos 6:2 may be read as a reference to Israel's future restoration following a short (cf. the metaphor "two days") captivity (cf. Ezek 37:1-14). But typologically this text foreshadows Christ's resurrection. The transition from historical to typological is possible since Christ in his life and activity embodied Israel. For instance, the forty days Jesus fasted in the wilderness parallels Israel forty-year journey. Thus, the Lord's resurrection is a "typological embodiment" of Israel's revival which will be literally fulfilled at the end of time when the New Israel, all who believe in Christ, will be raised up (1 Thess 4:13-17).[369]

Verse 3 introduces the second exhortation centered on the "knowledge" theme (cf. 4:1; 6:6). "Let us know" in this context, and according to Hosea's theology, means "acknowledging" Yahweh as the Lord of life and death. This "acknowledgment" is based on concrete experiences such as the national calamities occasioned by the Syro-Ephraimite war (cf. 5:14-6:1). "Let us strive to know" alludes to the tragic situation from which a frightened nation struggles desperately to escape. Theodoret of Cyrus[370] dwells on one of the first gifts of resurrection, that is the knowledge of God: "For after resurrection, the Apostle says, I shall know fully as I have been fully known: 'For now I know in part, then I shall know fully, even I have been fully known' [1 Cor 13:12]. Thus, then we shall receive a more precise knowledge of things." For Theodore of Mopsuestia,[371] the knowledge translates into the enjoyment of more excellent things: "The phrase 'And we shall know' stands for: We shall be in the enjoyment of better things. Just as 'You acquainted me with the ways of life' (Ps 15:11) stands for: 'You established me in life.'"

The second part of v. 3 spells out the people's trust in Yahweh's bounty. His intervention (i.e., "his going forth" [מוֹצָאוֹ][372] probably from his "place"; cf. 5:15) is as sure as the breaking of the "dawn" (שַׁחַר)[373] and Israel's visitation by Yahweh is likened to the benefic rains (of winter [December-February] and spring [March-April]) watering the land. Jerome[374] compares this line with Ps 19:5: "And he comes forth from his pavilion like a bridegroom," noticing, "He [God] is called not only at morning or dawn, or daybreak (*diluculum*); but he will come to us as an early and late rain to earth. We accept Christ as an early rain, when the foundations of the faith are laid within us, and we shall take him as a late rain, when after the crop is ripened we grasp eternal fruits, and store them up in the master's barn." Julian of Eclanum[375] writes: "Let us know and search him, who as the morning light expels the nights of our troubles and sufferings, and penetrates as a timely and overdue rain into the supplies to be distributed." Theodoret of Cyrus[376] interprets: "For as the daybreak does away with the darkness of night, in the same manner he will deliver us from the imminent temptations, and will offer the ray of his providence (προνοίας)." With respect to the "rain" metaphor, Cyril of Alexandria[377] writes: "For I suppose that he waters upon us, who received faith, and have known rightly his manifestation (ἐπιφάνειαν), in two ways. On the one hand, he reveals knowledge in the spirit of the old and legal, and in addition to these, prophetic teachings. In my view, this is the early rain. On the other hand, he adds to this the late [rain], the interpretation (νόησιν) of the Gospel's teachings, and the most desirable (τριπόθητον) grace of the apostolic preachings (κηρυγμάτων)." Theophylact of Bulgaria[378] offers a typological interpretation: "Therefore, God will come to us as an early rain, when he will begin to liberate us from captivity. And like the late [rain], when reestablishing us in our homeland, he treats us with great care, and he is anxious for us. After his resurrection, Christ revealed himself early in the morning to the women, and in the evening, although the doors were shut, to the disciples [Jn 20:26]. There is an early rain in every soul, when he [God] reveals the knowledge (γνῶσιν) of the Old [Testament], which rose first from the knowledge of God (θεογνωσίας). But there is a late [rain], when he grants the comprehension (σύνεσιν) of the Gospel, which beamed forth late in the last times." Since Israel is still lingering in the realm of nature, possibly under the influence of Baalism,[379] ignoring Yahweh's intervention in history, her "return" to Yahweh remains an empty attempt to build a personal relationship with him.³⁸⁰

Yahweh's response to Israel's penitence begins with v. 4. As we noticed above,³⁸¹ vv. 6:1-3, a prophecy on Israel's penitence, belong to Yahweh's saying in 5:12-15. In his response to this penitence (6:4-6), Yahweh does not criticize the content of Israel's confession nor her good intentions but rather people's fickleness. In his omniscience, God knows that both exhortations (6:1, 3) will remain at the level of people's inflamed words or, in the best scenario, they would make Israel move toward a predominantly sacrificial worship tainted with Baalism (5:6; cf. 6:6).

In v. 4 Judah appears again besides Ephraim (5:14; cf. 4:15: in parallel with Israel). Here, as elsewhere in Hosea's book where it occurs, the reference to Judah should not be considered a later gloss but rather a part of the original writing. As a prophet of God, Hosea addresses the two nations on the brink of their national tragedy. The basic idea of this lament is that both peoples are equally guilty of instability and inconsistency. On the one hand, Israel proclaims Yahweh's reliable intervention in case of need (v. 3), but on the other hand, she does not follow her Master, for Israel's "mercy" (חֶסֶד)³⁸² is as transitory as the "morning mist" (עֲנַן־בֹּקֶר) and the "dew" (טַל). Theodoret of Cyrus³⁸³ writes: "Your repentance (μεταμέλεια) is temporary, and not lasting, and it resembles the brief dew which is removed and consumed by the sun, and the cloud which appears early in the morning, and is scattered by the sun's rays. Compassion (ἔλεος) is measured by repentance." Cyril of Alexandria³⁸⁴ interprets: "The meaning of the prophecy fits well especially with the gift (δωρεᾷ) through Christ. For he is the rain-producing cloud, the fertilizing dew. Early, namely, after the night which indicates the diabolic mist and gloom, he comes down from heaven. For the Word (ὁ Λόγος) comes to us from above, from the Father (παρὰ Πατρὸς). 'Which passes' (πορευομένη), for he goes through everything beneath the sky. For the saving preaching is exceedingly widespread all over the world beneath the sky, while the law become humble embraces only one region of the Judaeans. According to the psalmist, 'For known is God in Judaea' [Ps 75:2]. All together know the Savior and Redeemer of all, that is Christ." Theophylact of Bulgaria[385] compares Israel's transient compassion with that of God, noticing, "But the Hebrews did not accept the Son, who being the compassion of the Father (through whom mercy was shown us), departed as a cloud because of the materiality (παχύτητα) of his body."

"Therefore I have hewn them in pieces (חָצַבְתִּי)[386] by the prophets (נְבִיאִים)" (v. 5). The perfects used in v. 5 point to Israel's past which is a confirmation of people's present fickleness. The word "prophets" refers probably to the former prophets beginning with Moses (cf. Deut 18:18), and including Elijah, Elishah, Micaiah son of Imlah, and Samuel.[387] These prophets, from heralds of Yahweh's word, charged with the proclamation of "the words of his mouth," become instruments[388] of his punitive measures against Israel (cf. Am 7:10; Is 9:7; Jer 23:29). Thus, Yahweh's powerful word is not only informative but formative as well. Since it comes from the Lord of history, Yahweh's word is quite active, for it does not return to the one who uttered "without effect" (cf. Is 55:11). In v. 5, its effectiveness is seen in the "killing" (הרג), rather than total annihilation, of both Ephraim and Judah, an allusion to the disastrous outcome of the Syro-Ephraimite war. (The suffix "them" designates the two nations.) Julian of Eclanum[389] interprets: "I brought up the axes of the prophetic menacings, and I described the evils to be inflicted with such great increase, that they were easily terrified at the hearing itself of every thing."

Verse 5b proclaims Yahweh's unwavering "judgment"

(מִשְׁפָּט) with respect to both nations. The divine "judgment" is as the "light" (of the sun)[390] which goes forth with each breaking "dawn" (cf. v. 3).[391] Behind Israel's fickleness, and a step further from Yahweh's justified wrath, lies his eternal "judgment" or will. Cyril of Alexandria[392] interprets: "Therefore, he says, 'My judgment like light will go forth,' that is, my will (θέλημα) is not overshadowed by riddles, but will be plainly (γυμνῶς) and openly (ἀκρύπτως) in the thoughts (διανοίαις) of all. For Emmanuel having come at the right time (κατὰ καιροὺς), he will not transfer the legal worship over the deceived (πεπλανημένους), nor will he persuade to honor those things still in figures (τύποις) and shadows, but rather he leads back to equity, kindness, and good heartedness, reciprocal love, and to true and unerring knowledge of God."

This eternal will of Yahweh is revealed in v. 6. "For I desire (חָפַצְתִּי)[393] mercy (חֶסֶד) and not sacrifice." Note that "mercy" is followed by "knowledge of God" (דַּעַת אֱלֹהִים) as in 4:1. Both virtues reflect the will or the delight of God in promoting a profound relationship with Israel. Yahweh is the Lord, and in this quality, he sets the moral standards and principles pertaining to the covenantal relationship with Israel. Yahweh does not reject worship as a whole but he criticizes the way Israel perceives it. Instead of a means to enter the relationship with God and to foster community ties, the worship becomes gradually a goal in itself (cf. Am 5:21ff.; Mic 6:6ff.). A similar explanation may be found in Theodoret of Cyrus[394]: "For I do not require sacrifices, I accept these sacrifices, condescending to the weakness of your mind. But I demand these two things: good-will (εὔνοιαν) toward me, and love (φιλανθρωπίαν) for your neighbor (πέλας)." Instead of cultivating the "knowledge of God" and "mercy," Israel is more interested in bringing sacrifices (or sacrificial meals) and burnt offerings. Between the two basic virtues listed in v. 6 there is a close relationship with the observation that the final position of "knowledge of God" underlines its priority. Thus, "mercy" stems from the "knowledge of God"; when someone "acknowledges" Yahweh as Lord of his life and people's history he is more inclined to maintain good, friendly relations with his neighbor who is now seen as a member of Yahweh's people. Jesus quotes twice this text when he criticizes the hypocrisy of his opponents (Mt 9:13; 12:7). Cyril of Alexandria[395] identifies "mercy" with "love" when he underscores the relationship between the two virtues: "For most of all, worship (τίμιον) of God displays the love (τὴν ἀγάπην) .... For truly, the compassion from beside the Father is Christ, as he takes away the sins, dismisses the charges, and justifies by faith, and recovers the lost, and makes [them] stronger than death. For, what is good and he does not give? Therefore, the knowledge of God is better (ἀμείνων) than sacrifice and holocausts, as it is brought to perfection (τελουμένη) in Christ. For by him and in him we have known the Father, and we have become rich in the justification (δικαίωσιν) by faith." Theophylact of Bulgaria[396] explains: "Compassion indicates the active (πρακτική) [life], while knowledge [designates] spiritual contemplation (θεωρία)." Theodore of Mopsuestia[397] emphasizes the prophets' role in bringing the people to the knowledge of God: "For I kept sending you prophets, as one who prefers to make clear to you the worthiness of your sacrifices and holocausts, and to lead you to knowledge of me." Jerome[398] interprets: "I hewed them by prophets, I killed them with my mouth's words, I uttered grave threats, in order to show mercy to those who repent, and to stretch my hand out to both those who have fallen and rise. For I do not find delight in sacrifices and victims, and in the hosts of holocausts.

My sacrifices and holocausts, the salvation of the faithful,
is the repentance of the sinners."

6. Turmoil in Israel (6:7-7:2)

7. But like Adam[399] they transgressed the covenant; there they betrayed me. 8. Gilead is a city of evil-doers tracked with blood.[400] 9. As robbers wait in ambush,[401] so does a gang[402] of priests. On the way to Shechem they commit murder; indeed, they carry out an evil plan. 10. In Israel's house I have seen a horrible thing;[403] Ephraim's whoredom is there, Israel is defiled. 11. For you also, O Judah, a harvest is set.[404] When I would restore my people's fortunes, 7:1. when I would heal Israel, then the guilt of Ephraim is revealed, and the wicked deeds[405] of Samaria; for they deal falsely: the thief breaks in,[406] the robbers raid outside.[407] 2. But they do not consider[408] that I remember all their wickedness. Now their deeds surround them, they are before my face.

The new section 6:7-7:2 is an investigation deep into the moral fabric of Israel's life. As in 4:1-3, the absence of "mercy" and "knowledge of God" leads to an increase in number of the moral and social evils (vv. 7ff.). Unlike the former section, Israel's wickedness is this time linked to concrete localities. Another similarity between the two pericopes is that both concern the priesthood (an anonymous "priest" in chapter 4, several "priests" in chapter 5, and the present section). The charge raised against the priests is even greater (i.e., robbery and murder) than in chapter 4 (negligence in fulfilling the priestly duties). The occurrence of the key verb בגד "to betray" in both 5:7 and 6:7 links together the sections 5:1-7 and 6:7-7:2. In addition, the independent pronoun וְהֵמָּה "they" (6:7) marks off the beginning of a new pericope pointing backwards to the priests mentioned early in 5:1-7.[409] As for the his-

Commentary: Hosea 4-11

torical situation reflected in this section, the general view is that nothing in these verses presupposes the Syro-Ephraimite war. Therefore, the events referred to might have occurred in the short interval between Jeroboam II (784-743 B.C.) and Menahem (743-737 B.C.), when two kings, Zechariah son of Jeroboam II and Shallum son of Jabesh, were murdered (cf. 2 Kgs 15:8-15); or better this section echoes Pekah's rebellion in 736 B.C., when supported by fifty Gileadites (2 Kgs 15:25), Pekah succeeded in overthrowing king Pekahiah.[410] The latter interpretation seems to be more plausible since it accounts for Gilead in v. 8.

Verse 7 opens the list of transgressions committed by the priests (already mentioned as a group in 5:1-7) by emphasizing the role of the spiritual leaders (note the pronoun "they") in transgressing (עבר) the "covenant" (בְּרִית). Surprisingly, the word "covenant" appears without article or pronominal suffix ("my"), which might make one see here a political alliance rather than the covenantal relationship between Yahweh and his people. But this explanation ignores the fact that in v. 7b the transgression of the covenant is qualified by "betrayal" (בגד) of Yahweh (cf. 5:7). Thus, the "covenant" refers to the relationship between Yahweh and Israel inaugurated by the exodus from Egypt (11:1; 12:10; 13:4). For Theodoret of Cyrus,[411] "covenant" equals "laws": "Likewise, by despising my long-suffering (μακροθυμίας), they transgressed the laws (νόμους) laid down for them."

With respect to *ʾādām* (אָדָם) there are at least two major interpretations. (1) The first interpretation (found already in V: *sicut Adam*; LXX: ὡς ἄνθρωπος "like a man"; cf. S and perhaps Tg) follows the MT reading, "like Adam" or "like a man" seeing here a reference to the first man created by God out of the dust and placed by him in the garden of Eden "to till it and tend it" (Gen 1:26-28; 2:15).

In this case, the transgression of the covenant would be the sin of rebellion committed by Adam who, at Eve's request, took from the forbidden tree (Gen 2:16-17; 3:6).

Having distinguished between the Hebrew reading ("as Adam") and that of the Septuagint ("as a man"), Cyril of Alexandria[412] interprets: "The Israelites' transgression was as that of Adam. For he could have communion with God, and persevere in incorruption, and glory himself in the delicacies of the paradise; but since he took no care of the divine commandment, and forgot the things I dishonor, he was unexpectedly deprived of the original [things]. In this manner, the Israelites, I say, having the gracious and loving God of all, the one who saves (σώζοντα) and intercedes (προεστηκότα) .... They became indifferent concerning the useful things for them, and those profitable for happiness and honor, and they despised the omnipotent God of all .... Like Adam, they slid away into apostasy, and they will utterly fall outside the one who knows how to gladden [them]. For they have transgressed the covenant." And Cyril goes on offering a spiritual explanation: "If one understands the prophecy (χρησμώδημα) in a more mysterious way (μυστικώτερον), as referring to Christ, again we say this, clarifying the meaning of the sayings. From heaven, God the Father sent the Son, the one who enlightens the Israelites, and makes his judgment manifest, so that he might move the ancient sacrifices and legal holocausts toward cessation, and to show compassion, justifying by faith, and to invite to knowledge of the true God. For by him and in him we may behold the Father, and we obtain access, as somewhere [Eph 2:18; Rom 5:2] the Holy Scripture says. Yet, the Israelites became 'as a man who transgresses a covenant' [cf. LXX: ὡς ἄνθρωπος]. And this is anything I could say. Differently, one who transgresses a written covenant [will] or who does not accept the inheritance assigned by the one who wrote this [covenant].... The Judaeans have been in such a situation with respect to Christ. How or in what way? For God the Father gave authority over the nation to the Son as a splendid and exquisite share of inheritance.... They [the Judaeans] transgressed the covenant of the Father when they despoiled the heir. By refusing the inheritance given to them by God, they did not come to the grace." Thus, says Cyril, a "new covenant" was promised (Jer 31:31-32): "But the New Covenant (ἡ Καινὴ Διαθήκη), namely, the inspired words (θεσπίσματα) through Christ called up to divine adoption by faith, incorruption, everlasting life, participation (μέθεξιν) in God through the Spirit, and to the kingdom of heavens. But they did not want to have the share of inheritance assigned to them by the God the Father through the Son. By disobeying the covenant and the heir, they have upset both of them, as I said, expelling the share of inheritance given to them by the Father, and thus being excluded from the gifts given by God in Christ." Jerome[413] explains: "They imitated Adam. So what he had done in Paradise, neglecting my covenant and laws, they did on earth. And there, that is in Paradise, they all have betrayed me, in the likeness of Adam's betrayal. For it is not to be wondered at if what preceded in the parent, also be blamed in the sons."

Scholars have raised a few objections against this Adamic interpretation: (a) Hos 6:7 is the only place outside the Genesis alluding to Adam's fault; (b) ʾādām without article does not mean "Adam," the first man's name but "men" in general; (c) God did not conclude a covenant with Adam; and (d) שָׁם "there" requires a place name rather than a person name in v. 7a.

(2) The second interpretation considers ʾādām a place name, the city "Adam" mentioned in Josh 3:16 (modern ed-Damiyeh, on the eastern side of Jordan) where the

waters of the Jordan river separated themselves so that the Israelites could "cross" the river near Jordan. This interpretation supported by one ms. DeRossi, reading בְּאָדָם "in Adam" instead of כְּאָדָם "like Adam" (MT), and by the presence of שָׁם "there" in v. 7b., is embraced by most scholars (among others, Weiser, Wolff, Rudolph, Mays, Jeremias).[414]

In this commentary we follow the first interpretation which leaves the MT unaltered, and accounts for the other textual witnesses, V, LXX, S, Tg. The objections raised above are solvable:[415] (a) there are other texts outside the Genesis referring to Adam's sin (e.g., Ps 82:7; Job 31:33; Is 43:27); (b) 'ādām without article designating the name of the first man is typical of the later phases of the Hebrew language; (c) God did not conclude a formal covenant with Adam, but the probation under which the latter was placed (cf. Gen 2:15-17) hints at a sort of covenantal relationship between the Creator and his rational creature; in addition, Hos 8:1 ("they rebelled against my instruction") interprets any rebellion, including Adam's, against God's instruction as the sheer expression of transgressing Yahweh's covenant; (d) "there" does not refer to "like Adam" but to "Gilead" (v. 8).[416]

In v. 8 Gilead is described as a city of "evil doers" (פֹּעֲלֵי אָוֶן)[417] a locality "tracked (עֲקֻבָּה)[418] with blood." In the past, Gilead, the mountaneous Transjordanian region, was the place where Laban caught Jacob accusing him of betrayal (Gen 31:22-42); the place where Jacob prepared to meet with his brother Esau on the eve of his wrestling with God (Gen 32). References to a city with such a name are few (besides v. 7, Judg 10:17; 12:7). The city of Gilead was identified with *Khirbet Jal'ad*, 6 miles south of Jabbok.[419] More probably, Gilead alludes to Pekah's rebellion (736 B.C.) against Pekahiah when fifty Gileadites took Pekah's side in overthrowing the former king (2 Kgs 15:25).[420]

The priests are formally mentioned in v. 9 which tells that a "gang of priests" (חֶבֶר כֹּהֲנִים)[421] wait in ambush (חַכֵּי)[422] as robbers carrying out an "evil plan" (זִמָּה):[423] "they commit murder" (יְרַצְּחוּ)[424] on the way to Shechem.[425] The priests' crime is quite grave for they have an "evil plan" in their minds: to detour those who might want to come to the untainted sanctuary of Shechem, a "competitor" to the shrines at Bethel and Dan (cf. Deut 27:11ff.).[426] Relating a story from Hebrew sources, Jerome[427] offers a similar explanation: "The priests of Bethel, or rather the fanatics of Beth-aven, during the Passover, Pentecost and the feast of Tents, when the pilgrims had to pass through Shechem (today Neapolis), to go to Jerusalem, the only place where it was permitted to sacrifice the victims, stationed robbers to wait in ambush for passersby, so that they adore the golden calves at Dan and Bethel rather than God in the Temple of Jerusalem." Similarly, Cyril of Alexandria,[428] expanding the Septuagint reading[429] to "The priests have hidden the way of the Lord," explains "For while hiding the way of the Lord, they killed the Shechemites [i.e., those who intended to go in pilgrimage to the Temple in Jerusalem], bringing them under the hands of robbers." For Theodore of Mopsuestia, the murders committed on the Shechem way are an echo of the atrocities that occurred in the past:[430] "This comparison shows their wickedness. For your fathers (i.e., Levi and Simeon, Jacob's sons), he says, when they learned that their sister was raped, were so irritated at what happened, that they dealt secretly and cunningly with the Shechemites, by mimicking friendship; that is why he says, 'They have hidden the way'; at the right time, they killed them all for their deed."

If v. 9 continues the description of Pekah's rebellion (v. 8), one may assume that this conspiracy initiated by armed troops from Gilead had the support of a group of priests who committed crimes on the way to Shechem, located on the opposite side of the Transjordanian Gilead.[431] But since there is no way to determine the priests' participation in Pekah's rebellion one should accept tentatively the cultic interpretation.

Verse 10 should be read together with v. 11a. "The house of Israel" refers probably to the Northern Kingdom (in 1:4 and 5:1 the same expression is connected with the northern monarchy) where the sanctuaries of Dan and Bethel were located.[432] Ephraim and Israel are here synonym terms for the Northern Kingdom. Some commentators[433] consider v. 11a a Judaean gloss simply for it mentions Judah, but even the difficulty of this verse suggests that Judah cannot be treated as a "conventional gloss."[434] These lines sound like a lament uttered by Yahweh deeply moved by what he saw in the "house of Israel": a "horrible thing" (שַׁעֲרִירִיָּה),[435] (cf. Jer 5:30; 23:14) Israel's propensity to idolatry, that is. Because of this "horrible thing," defined as "whoredom" (זְנוּת), Israel became "defiled" (נִטְמָא)[436] or unfitted for Yahweh's worship. "There" (שָׁם) refers probably to the sanctuaries of Dan and Bethel where the cult of the golden calves, the "horrible thing," was practiced. Yahweh announces that a "harvest" (קָצִיר)[437] is set (שָׁת)[438] for Judah (v. 11a). Jerome[439] interprets: "For what could be more horrible than ten tribes suddenly crossing over to idolatry?" And then, with respect to Judah's "harvest," he writes: "For not much later, you [Judah] will be led captive to Babylon, and the time of your harvest will come. And when the Chaldaeans have harvested you, I will turn my people's captivity around, and under Cyrus, king of Persians, and Artaxerxes, I will bring back my people. And note how distinctly the captivity and return of Judah alike are prophesied; but about Israel, i.e., about the ten tribes, no word, and when prosperity is mentioned, it is postponed for the coming of Christ. But in the house of the heretics daily we see horrible things; teachers fornicate, and the people seduced by them defiled. He warns Judah, namely, the Church, that he will prepare a harvest for her because of her sins, when the time of judgment arrives. But the latter the Lord forgives and promises his grace, for whom he loves he chastises, and 'punishes every son whom he receives back,' so that he may store in his treasure-chambers what is tried and cleansed." Cyril of Alexandria[440] writes: "For anyone is exceedingly astounded seeing the chosen and holy nation turning away from love toward God, and not only that, they will invent idols for others, but they will prevent them from loving the divine things." Theodore of Mopsuestia[441] interprets: "Now in the whole Israel I saw things filled with shuddering (φρίκης), the whoredom of all the peoples connected not to the body but to the ruin of the soul and departure from God."

In vv. 11b-7:1 Yahweh's willingness "to heal" (רפא)[442] Israel, by "restoring" (שׁוּבִי שְׁבוּת)[443] her to the original state, faces the latter's stubbornness on the path of evil. Israel's capital, Samaria (10:5, 7; 14:1), paralleled by guilty Ephraim, is seen as a source of "wicked deeds" (רָעוֹת).[444] "They deal falsely" (פָּעֲלוּ שָׁקֶר)[445] may refer in this cultic context to the shallow penitence outlined by Israel (6:1-3).[446] According to Theophylact of Bulgaria,[447] "lies" (ψευδῆ) equal "idols." Other "wicked deeds" are "stealing" (גנב)[448] and "robbery" (פשׁט)[449] inside and outside, namely everywhere. "My people" (עַמִּי) points to a lament-like saying (cf. 4:6, 8, 12; 5:10). Cyril of Alexandria,[450] interprets 7:1 as an allusion to the robbers who tried to despoil the pilgrims heading for Jerusalem. According to Cyril, this line may also apply to the beginnings of the Church: "The Judaean leaders rejoiced when those who believe in Christ were attacked, and they joined other invaders and robbers, exulting over the persecuted believers, and accepting in heart and mind that robber, Satan, the one who deprived the mind of any piety, so that they may have their heart in harmony with him." Jerome[451] relates 7:1 to Jn 10:8 where Jesus calls those who came before him "thieves and robbers," observing: "We ought to understand as the thieves and robbers who came before the Lord not Moses and the prophets who are always praised by the mouth of the Savior, but the pseudo-prophets, and afterwards the heretics who were not sent by the Lord, but came of their own will." Theodoret of Cyrus[452] writes: "Since they neglected the true knowledge of God and bound themselves to the error of the idols, enemies will come upon them as robbers and thieves, they will set on fire and sack some, they will bind others, and they will deprive them of all goods."

Verse 2 may be read as an indirect response to Israel's superficial penitence exposed in 6:1-3. In spite of Yahweh's frequent attempts to heal and restore Israel, the latter does not recognize that Yahweh remembers all their wickedness. Thus, while Yahweh is ready to intervene in his people's favor, their deeds, always before God, surround them as a fence. Yahweh's intervention has no effect as long as Israel is reluctant to make a real penance by confessing her sins. Note that in 6:1-3 there is no mention of Israel's state of sinfulness. Cyril of Alexandria[453] writes: "As it is said, they were besieged by their own thoughts and unholy considerations. For by their guile and fraud, when they murdered the Shechemites, and now, as robbers, they turn even against God. Moreover, the offenses, beyond any description, are before me, for I shall not overlook such evils, nor are they removed from my sight; I shall be rather a slow chastiser." Julian of Eclanum[454] interprets: "Enemies surrounded them, and their masters, by the right of victory, so diligently scrutinized everything, as if either the thieves entered the inner chambers of the houses, or robbers went into the open fields." Theodoret of Cyrus[455] observes: "But for 'deliberations' (διαβούλια), Aquila and Symmachus have 'pursuits' (ἐπιτηδεύματα), which means almost the same thing. For the Septuagint assumes by 'thoughts' (λογισμοὺς) the first movement of the soul, while Aquila and Symmachus, the 'pursuits' and deeds born from these."

7. Political Instability (7:3-7)

3. By their wickedness they gladden a king, and by their lies officials. 4. They are all adulterous like an oven heated by the baker;[456] he ceases to stir the fire, from the kneading of the dough until it is leavened. 5. The officials began[457] the day of our king[458] by being inflamed[459] from wine; he stretched out his hand with scoffers.[460] 6. For they are kindled[461] like an oven, their heart burns within them; all night their anger[462] smolders; in the morning it blazes like a flaming fire. 7. All of them are hot as an oven, and they devour their rulers. All their kings have fallen; none of them calls upon me.

Hosea paints here the gloomy picture of Israel, a moribund kingdom marked by political instability. This literary unit deals with the same historical period as the pericope 6:7-7:2. The simile used by the prophet to describe the passionate battle for power is that of a baker's oven (תַּנּוּר; cf. vv. 4, 6, 7). In biblical times, almost every Israelite household used to have such an oven, cylindrical in form, open at the top, on whose inner walls flat cakes were baked (cf. Lev 26:26). Since only the palaces had professional bakers (cf. Gen 40:1; 1 Sam 8:13),[463] the mention of the "baker" (אֹפֶה) in v. 4 makes one think of the royal palace in Samaria as the central scene for conspiracy and assassination. (In twelve years four kings have been murdered: Zechariah, Shallum, Pekahiah, and Pekah.)

Verse 3 shows that the conspirators ("they") by "wickedness" and "lies" gladdened a king and his court. Perhaps "king" (מֶלֶךְ) mentioned here refers to Pekah who rose to power by assassinating king Pekahiah in his palace in Samaria, 736 B.C. (2 Kgs 15:25). For Jerome,[464] this line deals with king Jeroboam I and his court. Hosea uses "king" without the definite article to underscore the fact that Pekah was just one in a series of kings-assassins in the final days of the Northern Kingdom. "Wickedness" (רָעָה) and "lies" (כַּחֲשֵׁי) describe the hypocrisy of Pekahiah's subjects who after they had conspired against their own king made the usurper Pekah and his court feel good. According to Theodore of Mopsuestia,[465] "lies" refer to idols: "Since they repudiated my knowledge (γνῶσιν) they adopted the false and guileful worship of the demons." Theodoret of Cyrus[466] interprets: "Since they were ready for destruction through their own transgression of law (παρανομίαν), they became the heralds of joy for their enemies." Cyril of Alexandria[467] writes: "The saying truly refers to those who crucified Emmanuel. For while lying and calumniating him, they gladdened Herod and Pontius Pilate, and the leaders of the Synagogue. For the divine Peter says to God and Father of all: 'For truly in this city there were gathered together against your holy child Jesus whom you did anoint, both Herod and Pontius Pilate, with the Gentiles and the peoples of Israel' [Acts 4:27]."

In v. 4 (usurper) king, royal court, and conspirators altogether are labeled "adulterous" (מְנָאֲפִים), another term for wickedness and deceit (v. 3), here probably with a political connotation.[468] Furthermore, they are likened to a heated oven. As the baker in the simile, who ceases to stir the fire from the kneading of the dough until it is leavened, they fuel no longer the fire of rebellion and conspiracy, but they just wait for the fitting time to make their wicked plans come true. Cyril of Alexandria[469] writes: "The Judaeans have treated Christ in the same way. For speaking falsely against his glory, and gradually drawing the multitudes away from his love, the Scribes and Pharisees played the whore in a spiritual way (νοητῶς), removing from him the whole herd." For Jerome[470] the "leaven" designates false teachings (Mt 16:6: "Take heed of the leaven of the Pharisees").

With v. 5 the focus of the unit shifts to "officials" (שָׂרִים) who begin the king's day by being intoxicated with wine. Hosea distinguishes between "our king" (perhaps Pekahiah who acceded to the throne peacefully) and "their kings" (v. 7; cf. "king," v. 3), probably the kings, including Pekah, who grasped the power by violence. The king's "day" could be the coronation day (rather than the birthday) of king Pekahiah. This is Jerome's[471] interpretation although he thinks of Jeroboam I as the celebrated king in this verse: "This is the day of Jeroboam our king; this is the festal day our king has appointed for us; let us celebrate and sing, let us exult and laud, let us worship the golden calves on this day." The conspirators take advantage of the king's officials drunkenness drunk and act accordingly. Deprived of his supporters, the king stretches out his hand (in a sign of friendship?)[472] to the "scoffers" (לֹצְצִים), i.e., his assassins.[473] According to Theodoret of Cyrus,[474] λοιμῶν "pestilent fellows" (cf. LXX) refer to those "accused of brutal outrage (λύμης) and injury (βλάβης). For as the pestilence (λοιμός) when it touches someone, damages the ones which come close on account of him, in the same manner the people who live together with those familiar with wickedness will be ravaged." For Theophylact of Bulgaria[475] this line points figuratively to the betrayal of Judas: "And the disciple

Judas stretched out his hand, when he received the silver for handing [him] over, agreeing with the pestilent fellows (λοιμῶν) of the Pharisees and Scribes, when they were lying in ambush to tear in pieces and apprehend the Lord."

In v. 6 the conspirators are compared again to an oven. While "smoldering" (יָשֵׁן) all night long, their "anger" (אַף) turns into a "flaming fire" (אֵשׁ לֶהָבָה) in the morning. Julian of Eclanum[476] interprets: "He [i.e., the baker] did not remove the fire set below, but although having stuffed the oven with wood, free from care he allowed himself by falling asleep, knowing that their drunkenness and wickedness would cook the whole night." Theophylact of Bulgaria[477] allegorizes: "The one who sins, sleeps the whole night of his life, lacking perception. That is why Paul urges the true child of day Timothy: 'Keep vigil always' [2 Tim 4:5]." As long as "their heart" (לִבָּם)[478] burns in them with passion, their wickedness and anger are unknown to their contemporaries. But on the king's day, their anger blazes as a fire and their hidden plans are discovered.

Verse 7 is a conclusion to vv. 3-6. The conspirators are burning as an oven devouring "their rulers" (שֹׁפְטֵיהֶם). The mention of "rulers" alludes to the period of "judges," the charismatic leaders of Israel, when faith in God rather than political plots and military alliances was the right attitude toward the foreign invaders. Yahweh notices that "all their kings" (כָּל־מַלְכֵיהֶם) have fallen. They fell because "none" of them called upon God. For Cyril of Alexandria[479] to call upon God has a broader meaning than simply looking for help: "For none of them desired to worship (προσκυνεῖν) me, and to fervently supplicate the God of all, and to glorify himself in the knowledge of God." Hosea criticizes here the political system of the Northern Kingdom for lack of faith in God, the only one

8. Failed International Politics (7:8-16)

8. Ephraim mixes himself with the peoples. Ephraim is a cake not turned. 9. Foreigners devour his strength, but he does not know it. Even gray hairs are sprinkled upon[480] him, but he does not know it. 10. Israel's pride testifies against her; yet they do not return to the Lord their God, nor seek him, for all this.[481] 11. Ephraim is like a dove, easily deceived and without sense. Upon Egypt they call, to Assyria they go. 12. As they go, I will cast my net over them. Like birds of the air I will bring them down. I will chastise[482] them according to the report of their evil.[483] 13. Woe to them, for they strayed from me! Destruction to them, for they have rebelled against me! And I, I would redeem them, but they speak lies against me. 14. And they do not cry to me from the heart, but they wail upon their beds; for grain and new wine they gash[484] themselves; they rebel[485] against me. 15. And I, I trained[486] and strengthened their arms, yet they planned evil against me. 16. They turn to nothing;[487] they are like a slack bow; their officials shall fall by the sword because of the rage of their tongue. This is because of the mockery in the land of Egypt.

This pericope describes the relationship between Ephraim and the foreign powers, Assyria and Egypt. The period following the reign of Jeroboam II (784-743 B.C.) is marked by Israel's inconsistency in the domain of the foreign affairs. In 738 B.C. Menahem pays a heavy tribute to Assyria to consolidate his reign (2 Kgs 15:19f.). Around 733 B.C., Pekah king of Israel allies with Rezin king of Damascus in an anti-Assyrian coalition, trying to convince Ahaz, king of Judah to adhere to their cause. (This episode is known as the Syro-Ephraimite war.)

In 732 B.C. Hoshea, the last king of the once-Northern Kingdom, accedes to the throne by paying tribute to Assyria (2 Kgs 15:30). Later, after the death of Tiglath-pileser III (727 B.C.), same Hoshea will seek help from Egypt against Assyria.

In v. 8 "Ephraim" refers to the mountainous region of Israel which has preserved its independence after the Assyrian intervention in 733 B.C. When the prophet says that Ephraim "mixes himself" (יִתְבּוֹלָל)[488] with the "peoples" (עַמִּים), i.e., Assyria and Egypt, he probably refers to religious syncretism. Ephraim's inhabitants have lost their identity by importing religious ideas and cultic practices alien to their ancestors' beliefs.[489] Furthermore, Ephraim "has become" (הָיָה)[490] "a cake" (עֻגָה)[491] not turned, uncooked on one side, burnt on the other side, hence worthless. This is Cyril of Alexandria's[492] interpretation "He says that Ephraim is a bread not turned like the loaves baked on stones which, if they are not turned, they entirely burn to ashes and further they appear useless (ἀχρείους) and in the midst of flames what is eatable suffers damage." For Julian of Eclanum,[493] this metaphor points to Israel's foolish and impudent behavior: although troubles befall the people, nevertheless they persist in apostasy; they even call upon their ravagers and devourers. Jerome[494] explains: "The kingdom of the ten tribes has become like any other nation because they went away from the Lord; and he [Ephraim] is like a bread beneath the ashes, which is not turned, that is, he does not repent." Theodoret of Cyrus[495] writes: "He [Ephraim] persisted in wickedness and did not accept at all a change for the better."

The Ephraimites do not realize that the "foreigners" (זָרִים), i.e., Assyria and Egypt,[496] devour his "power" (כֹּחַ)[497] (v. 9). This line alludes to the territorial amputation effected by Tiglath-pileser III in 733 B.C.[498] A similar interpretation is found in Cyril of Alexandria.[499] The north-Israelites are also unable to read the first signs—symbolically represented by the first "gray hairs" [שֵׂיבָה] "sprinkled" [זָרְקָ][500] on one's head—of the future tragedy. The image used in vv. 8-9 is that of an aging nation losing its power and worth. Jerome[501] sees in Ephraim's old age a metaphor for the "final captivity." Cyril of Alexandria[502] interprets "Ephraim became gray" as a reference to the long period of time elapsed until the citizens of the Northern Kingdom were able to realize the dramatic situation that confronts them.

Verse 10 continues the accusation in vv. 8-9. Israel's arrogance (גְּאוֹן)[503] is her own accuser and also an obstacle for people's "return" (שׁוּב) to Yahweh. Jerome[504] interprets: "Israel's pride will be humbled not long after, but now also in the present; that is why it says 'in her face'; she was humbled however because she had elevated herself but trusted not in God; rather she trusted the multitude of troops; and because 'God opposes the proud but he accords his favor to the humble' [Jas 4:6]." Cyril of Alexandria[505] writes: "For the pride of Israel, namely, the apostasy (ἀπόστασις), that she contrived from arrogance (ὑπεροψίας) and through which she turned toward other gods, dishonoring the true God, will turn against her." Due to their arrogance the Israelites, though deprived of power, are nevertheless reluctant to return to Yahweh. One may note the cultic dimension of Israel's attitude underlined by the use of the root בקשׁ "to seek."[506]

In v. 11 Ephraim is compared to a "dove" (יוֹנָה) easily deceived (פֹתָה)[507] by his own illusions with respect to Assyria and Egypt. The second part of this verse speaks of Ephraim's oscillation between the two great powers while trying to regain his lost security. In the view of Theodoret of Cyrus,[508] Ephraim is a "foolish (ἄνους; cf. LXX) dove," for having been punished by God, he does not repent but rather he seeks help from his enemies. Julian of Eclanum[509] shows that the same simile may attain different purposes within a divine speech; for instance, the simile of the senseless, easy to seduce, dove underscores in Hosea the simplicity and foolishness of Israel, while in the words of Jesus the dove stands for innocence (cf. Mt 10:16). For "simplicity without judgment is foolishness," adds Jerome.[510] This line may refer to the events occurring after 733 B.C., when king Hoshea switched from paying tribute to Tiglath-pileser III to appealing to Egypt for help (2 Kgs 17:4) against Assyria (727 B.C.).[511]

The image of the fluttering bird continues in v. 12. God's punishment comes upon Israel while they are oscillating between Assyria and Egypt. Jerome[512] writes: "One may ask: Why was Ephraim compared with a dove and not with other birds? The other birds hurry to protect their offspring even at the risk of life; and when they see a bird of prey, snake, raven, or crow approaching their nest, they fly to and fro, and attack with their beak, and wound with their claws, and with a crying voice show the parent's suffering; only the dove does not grieve for or miss (its) robbed offspring; Ephraim is rightly compared with this bird, because he does not suffer for his devastated people, but he is indifferent to its salvation."

Yahweh is depicted in v. 12 as a fowler casting his "net" (רֶשֶׁת) over the Israelites. For Theodore of Mopsuestia[513] the image of the senseless bird brought down by the fowler points to Israel's captivity as punishment for her lack of trust in God. Julian of Eclanum[514] interprets: "And for that reason you should not believe that in this migration you will be free from all dangers; behold I foretell that even in that place you will endure the net of my revenge, nor will you be able to escape my wrath, unless you correct those endeavors that caused it." Based on the Septuagint reading (τῆς θλίψεως "of their affliction"; in contrast

Commentary: Hosea 4-11

to MT: לַעֲדָתָם "to their assembly"), God's chastisement (יסר) is according to Israel's wickedness (emended text: לְרָעָתָם "[to the report] of their evil"). Cyril of Alexandria[515] explains: "The rumors preceded the very experience of future events, and when the inhabitants of Samaria heard of the terrible things they were terrified. Therefore they were educated, by hearing about the future tribulation which has not yet occurred. For those who were wise this was enough to return. But exceedingly hard-hearted are those who having a stubborn, hard, unbroken, and very sick mind, were not put to shame by the experience itself." Theophylact of Bulgaria[516] writes: "The net of God, his multifaceted wisdom, by which he foresees whenever we are going to do evil, casts hindrances; and he brings down and humbles those who are proud like the demons of the air. And he announces beforehand Gehenna and the worm which does not go away and the fire which is not extinguished, and he educates them by hearing as the lover of humankind." In this verse wickedness points to Israel's lack of trust in God. Jerome[517] interprets: "I will drag (them) down not to ruin, but so that I strike them like sons; and I will strike them not with many penalties, but with fear, so that they will improve merely by hearing the terrible news about the former sufferings."

In v. 13 God laments[518] Israel's going astray (נדד),[519] another metaphor for religious syncretism. Theodoret of Cyrus[520] explains: "First, I will educate them through the thread of sufferings; then I will catch all of them like birds placing around them a cloud of enemies like a net. And having said these, he does not forget his love for mankind but he offers a dirge from fatherly love for them." The punishment for Israel's rebellion (פשע)[521] is severe: national "destruction" (שד).[522] Although God is willing[523] to change the verdict against Israel, the latter keeps on speaking "lies" (כְּזָבִים)[524] against him. Israel's treacherous behavior makes God's attempts to redeem (פדה)[525] his people fail. Jerome[526] equates Israel's rebellion with the worship of golden calves: "Therefore they will be devastated and in distress, and always fearful and terrified, because they conspired against God, worshipping golden calves, and abandoning the one who redeemed them from Egyptian servitude, and brought them out with a high arm. They themselves told lies against the Lord when they said about the idols: 'These are your gods, O Israel, who brought you out of the land of Egypt'! [Exod 32:4]; they did not cry out to the Lord in their heart, but they turned to the whoredom of idolatry."

Instead of crying (זָעַק) to Yahweh from their heart, the Israelites "wail" (יְיֵלִילוּ)[527] upon "their beds" (מִשְׁכְּבוֹתָם),[528] resorting to idolatrous practices such as lacerations (גדד)[529] to gain fertility ("grain and new wine") (v. 14). Cyril of Alexandria[530] explains: "'They did not cry to me from their heart' means that they have asked nothing from me, yet they believed and they were convinced that I was the giver and provider of any good thing. From these we know that God does not need a loud cry (βοή), but rather the disposition (διάθεσις) of the heart and mind." For Theophylact of Bulgaria,[531] this line refers to a purely external worship: "They honored me only with their lips, but their heart was far away from me, or that they did not acknowledge me, but the idols, as a benefactor." Julian of Eclanum[532] explains: "For where there is no disposition of a sincere mind, a supplication flowing from (drink) intoxication is rightly called wailing." Theodore of Mopsuestia[533] interprets: "Although they entered the promised land and gained the rest which was given by me (for this is called "their bed"), yet they did not observe any of my words; instead they occupied themselves in the worship of demons, crying out and cutting themselves according to their custom. When they accomplished these things, they attributed to them the prosperity of the good things which were given to them by me." All these endeavors are labeled rebellion (סרר)[534] against God. The ritual of bodily lacerations links this line to the episode with the prophets of Baal on mount Carmel (1 Kgs 18:28). Gushing of blood for dead was forbidden by the law (Lev 19:28; Deut 14:1). Perhaps Israel believed that God is dead like Baal and only by screaming and gushing of blood could they bring him back to life.[535] At any event, Israel's obsession with the fertility of the land described in this line echoes the loss of the fruitful valley of Jezreel during the invasion of Tiglath-pileser III in 733 B.C.

Verse 15 introduces Yahweh as the one who strengthens (יסר)[536] Israel's arms (cf. 2:10/8; 11:1ff.), as a pedagogue who takes care of his children, while Israel plans (חשׁב) evil against her Maker. Theodore of Mopsuestia[537] explains: "I was the one who gave them the whole strength against the enemies. Yet they pursued everything that is strange and full of impiety, while they were sinning against me." Julian of Eclanum[538] writes: "When the time came to march to battle, I fulfilled the duty of a prompt teacher, so that their arms might be strengthened for combat and they might taste the sweet grace of victory. Yet they used my gifts against me, they immediately exercised the firmness of their hearts which they had acquired by despising the law, and because they averted the hostile yoke, they refused to be submissive to me." Theodoret of Cyrus,[539] considers "arms" a metaphor for "strength" (δύναμις) and Jerome[540] equates "evil" with the "arrows of blasphemy" shot at God. In almost the same vein, Theophylact of Bulgaria[541] writes: "Although I showed them genuine warriors strengthening their arms, nevertheless they thought about me that I am not God." The same idea of Israel's ingratitude toward Yahweh is expressed in v. 13. Israel's reaction to God's goodness is that of thinking perversely of her Provider.

While oscillating between Assyria and Egypt in search for help, the Israelites turn to "nothing" (לֹא),[542] i.e., things and persons of no avail (v. 16). Both idolatry and foreign powers are implied in this line. The futility of Israel's attempts to gain fertility and security is rendered by the simile "slack bow" (קֶשֶׁת רְמִיָּה), denoting a bow whose arrows do not reach the target (cf. Ps 78:57). For Jerome,[543] "the untrustworthy (*dolosus*) and perverse (*perversus*) bow is the bow that shoots the archer and wounds its owner. Or more accurately, they became as a bent bow, always ready for fight and disputes, for the ruin of the listeners." Guilty of Israel's deplorable situation are the "high officials" (שָׂרִים); they will fall by sword because of the "rage" (זַעַם) of their tongue by which, explains Jerome,[544] "they ventured to call the golden calves gods." Cyril of Alexandria[545] interprets: "The angry feelings will be not only against the leaders of the subjects, but they will include very quickly those who were accustomed to revel in the highest honors. 'They will fall by the sword' for the impudence (ἀσελγής) of the tongue will be the alleged cause (πρόθασις) of their suffering. For truly there is a sign of ignorance (ἀπαιδευσία) to say to the wood: 'You are my God'; and to the stone: 'You gave me birth'[Is 2:27]. This refers to Emmanuel, against whom the scribes and Pharisees set in motion an ignorant (ἀπαίδευτον) language, although he educated and strengthened them, certainly in a spiritual way. Some of them took nothing into account and turned to nothing (οὐδέν). They turned to the teachings and laws of the men, and they became like a bow turned to the opposite direction (ἀντεστραμμένον), striking wickedly against their Master, whom they needed to excel as a whole, and to obtain victory over adversaries, as genuine disciples of those who believe." By appealing to Egypt for help the high officials have blasphemed Yahweh the Lord of history.[546] The "mockery" (לעג) or the blasphemy in the land of Egypt reflects probably Hoshea's policy of allying with Egypt against Assyria (727 B.C.).

9. Ephraim's Unfaithfulness (8:1-14)

1. Set the horn to your lips![547] As a vulture (it comes) over Yahweh's house, because they transgressed my covenant, and rebelled against my instruction. 2. To me they cry: "My God![548] We, Israel,[549] know you!" 3. Israel rejected the good. An enemy shall pursue her.[550] 4. They make kings, but without my consent. They set up officials,[551] but without my knowledge. With their silver and gold they make idols for themselves, so that it shall be destroyed.[552] 5. Reject[553] your calf, O Samaria! My anger burns against them. How long will they be incapable of purity? 6. For [they are] from Israel![554] That, a craftsman has made. It is not God. Yes, the calf of Samaria shall be[555] broken to pieces.[556] 7. For they sow the wind, and they shall reap the whirlwind. The standing grain with no head yields no flour. If it were to yield, foreigners would swallow it. 8. Israel is swallowed up. Now they are among the nations as an unwanted[557] vessel. 9. For by themselves they have gone up to Assyria. A wild ass [wandering] alone for himself, Ephraim pays off its lovers. 10. Even if they bargain[558] among the nations, I will now gather them up. They shall soon writhe[559] under the burden[560] of king and officials. 11. For Ephraim has multiplied altars—for sinning.[561] They became to him altars for sinning. 12. Though I write for him the multitude of my instructions, they are regarded as a something strange. 13. Though they offer choice[562] sacrifices, though they eat flesh, the Lord does not accept them. Now he will remember their iniquity,

and punish their sins. They shall return to Egypt.[563] **14. Israel has forgotten her Maker, and built palaces. And Judah has multiplied fortified cities. But I will send fire upon her cities, and it shall devour their castles.**

In this pericope Yahweh is addressing his prophet Hosea immediately after the conclusion of the Syro-Ephraimite war (733 B.C.). God charges Ephraim with unfaithfulness in the realm of religious-political life. Idolatry, political plots, and lack of trust in Yahweh with respect to the foreign relations, all these make the inhabitants of Samaria consider Yahweh's instructions a strange thing. For this reason, God's punishment is near: Israel, the unwanted vessel, will be brought into captivity. Judah will experience the same fate because of her arrogant attitude toward Yahweh.

Verses 1-3 form a unity centered on the motif of an unexpected enemy menacing Israel for her sins. People's arrogance reflected in the transgression of the covenant is doubled by Israel's rebellion against God's instruction.

In v. 1 Yahweh orders his prophet to blast[564] the "horn" (שֹׁפָר) (cf. 5:8) as a signal of alarm that an enemy is approaching "Yahweh's house" (בֵּית יְהוָה), a Hosean phrase for the land of Israel (cf. 9:8, 15).[565] Julian of Eclanum[566] interprets: "In your throat let there be a trumpet, that is, your throat, like the trumpet, will exclaim because he [the enemy], as an eagle, a ferocious predator, will come upon God's house, i.e., the temple in Jerusalem." Theophylact of Bulgaria[567] writes: "The war trumpet will sound and the king of Babylon will come upon Lord's house hissing and swiftly as an eagle. For Nebuchadnezzar, after he dispatched the troops, burnt the temple." The "enemy," or as Theodoret of Cyrus[568] puts it, the "king of the enemies," more probably Assyria than Babylon, is as swift and dreadful as a "vulture" (נֶשֶׁר).[569] But this enemy is only an agent chosen by

Commentary: Hosea 4-11

Yahweh to punish Israel, or as Theodoret of Cyrus[570] suggests, "the king of the enemies." Cyril of Alexandria[571] rightly points toward Assyria as the Eastern-most terrible enemy: "For the tyrant of Assyria, he says, the one who will take them captives, will come with a numerous multitude of fighting-men.... He will come as an eagle in the house of the Lord, that is, he will fly quickly and powerfully over the Lord's temple, and he will attack the kingdoms of Judah and Jerusalem, seizing without toil and taking them captive into his own [kingdom]." It is Yahweh who controls human history. According Jerome,[572] this line refers to the events of 586 B.C. "Raise your voice as that of a trumpet, so that many may hear it, for many have sinned. Whenever you raise your voice, this means with a loud cry, as an eagle over the Lord's house; this signifies: Nebuchadnezzar will come with his entire army so suddenly, so swiftly, that he will imitate the speed of an eagle rushing to its prey; and he will come not to another place but to Jerusalem, where the temple of the Lord is located, in order to destroy and overthrow it." The first two verbless clauses convey the urgency of the events as well as the prophet's emotions (cf. 5:8).[573] This saying should be dated after the loss of Galilee (including the sanctuary of Dan) to Tiglath-pileser III in 733 B.C.[574] Theodore of Mopsuestia[575] explains: "As the eagle comes unexpectedly upon the wild beasts, in the same manner the enemies will come, destroying the people and setting the divine house [temple] on fire." The conjunction יַעַן "because" introduces the reason for such an imminent danger: the Israelites transgressed (עבר) Yahweh's "covenant" (בְּרִית)[576] and rebelled (פשׁע) against his "instruction" (תּוֹרָה). Since "instruction" (including written material [8:12], and the ten commandments [4:2]) in the book of Hosea is the expression of God's will toward his people, any rebellion against this "instruction" is primarily against God's person (4:6; 6:7). The juxtaposition in this verse between "covenant" and "instruction" makes one think of "instruction" as the concrete content of the "covenant."[577]

Verse 2 reproduces Israel's over-confident confession that they know Yahweh. The theme of "knowledge of God" (cf. 2:22/20; 4:1) surfaces again, this time in a setting of judgment. To cry out to God claiming that you know him means to confess your loyalty toward him.[578] The clumsy exclamation "My God!" (אֱלֹהַי)[579] (cf. 2:25/23) uttered by the Israelites underlines the intimacy between the latter and their Maker or reflects the prophet's personal touch inserted in Israel's general ("we") confession. If one reads this line in the light of 7:14 ("they do not cry to me from the heart") one may conclude that Israel's confession is shallow and insincere. According to Jerome,[580] this cry will be uttered by Israel "in a time of want and distress, when the captivity will occur." Theodoret of Cyrus[581] writes: "For when they will be experiencing those evils, then they will seek my aid." Similarly, Theodore of Mopsuestia[582] explains: "Then, under the circumstances and the punishment laid upon them, they will unwillingly confess my power." For Julian of Eclanum,[583] the Israelites, inspite of being "defiled with profane pursuits, dare to say: 'Our God freed us, who alone in the whole world know you, and in the name of Israel, given by you, we pride ourselves.'"

The main accusation against Israel is that she "rejected" (זָנַח) the "good" (טוֹב), i.e., Yahweh (v. 3).[584] According to Julian of Eclanum,[585] the "good" refers to the "worship of holy religion." If the goods Israel enjoys abundantly, observes Cyril of Alexandria,[586] depend on the latter's close relationship with God, then "rejecting" these goods equals the sin of apostasy. That is why an "enemy" (אוֹיֵב) shall chase (רדף) Israel.[587] This unnamed "enemy" may allude to Assyria, as Jerome[588] suggests: "Since Israel rejected the good, an enemy, namely, Assyria, will attack and occupy her." Hosea uses here an indefinite substantivized participle to emphasize the fact that the foreign enemy is only an instrument of God's wrath and the chase lasts as long as the people are spurning God and his goodness.

Verse 4 shows the way Israel rejected Yahweh from both politics and religion. Politically, Israel went away from the charismatic monarchy according to which Yahweh as supreme king was to appoint his visible representatives (cf. Deut 17:15) through the office of the prophets (e.g., prophet Elisha and king Jehu, 2 Kgs 9). To the contrary, the Israelites appointed their kings and officials (Hiph'il of מלך and שׂרר) without God's knowledge (ידע) and approval. This line, though alluding to the series of murders surrounding the Israelite throne (cf. 7:1-3), is not a rejection of the monarchic system as a whole. Jerome[589] interprets this line in reference to the northern monarchy beginning with Jeroboam I found at fault for Israel's split into two states in 931 B.C. Similarly, Theodore of Mopsuestia[590] underscores both the political and religious aspects of the schism: "They abolished the kingdom which I established and the service concerning the law, when they established their own kingdom (he is speaking about what happened with the tribes which began with Jeroboam, who first made the heifer for them), and when they accomplished the things which follow on the strangeness concerning the choice of the kingdom, the many different idols, some made from gold, some from silver." Theodoret of Cyrus[591] offers a slightly different explanation: "This accusation he makes against the ten tribes who appointed Jeroboam king, without consulting the God of all, whether they ought to do it. But let no one among those who have read the books of the Kings think that this is contrary to those referred there. For he [God] did not send Ahijah the Shilonite to the people but to Jeroboam [1Kings 11:29ff.]. Thus those who attribute for themselves the election of the king are not worthy of forgiveness." Religiously, Israel used her prosperity for manufacturing idols (עֲצַבִּים).[592] Hosea warns that the punishment will not tarry: "it shall be destroyed [cut off]" (יִכָּרֵת); the verb in singular may be an allusion to the calf in v. 5,[593] or a hint at wealth as an abstraction from precious metals (cf. 2:10/8; 9:6).[594]

Verses 5-6 represent a small literary unity centered on the theme of idolatry. The "calf" (עֵגֶל) mentioned here refers to one of the two golden calves set up by Jeroboam I (931-910 B.C.) in the sanctuaries at Bethel and Dan (1 Kgs 12:26-33). This episode reminds us of Aaron's moral support for calf-worship at Sinai (Exod 32). From a pedestal for the invisible Yahweh (as a north-Israelite replica to Yahweh's ark in the temple of Jerusalem), the golden calves came to represent Canaanite deities such El and Baal. Such a calf image was probably made of wood plated with gold, hence it could be burned (Exod 32:20) or broken to pieces (Hos 8:6). As the sanctuary of Dan had already fallen into the Assyrians' hands in 733 B.C., the only calf left was that in the "royal sanctuary" of Bethel (Am 7:13).[595] If "Samaria" (שֹׁמְרוֹן) stands for the north-Israelite capital (cf. 7:1), the prophetic saying concerns its inhabitants, who are asked to reject (זָנַח)[596] the ill-famed idolatrous emblem of Israel in favor of the "good" (i.e., Yahweh) (cf. v. 3a: זָנַח). Mentioning the Septuagint reading, Jerome[597] remarks that "Samaria refers to all ten tribes, and not to a single city; in fact, the calves were set up not in the city of Samaria but rather in Dan and Bethel." Cyril of Alexandria[598] interprets: "How rightly and truly he says 'Reject!' (ἀπότριψαι), as in presence of a stain or defilement and extreme impurity! For truly this matter of the unclean idolatry makes the soul disgusting, ill-smelling, and odious before God. Thus he, as prone to pity and good, urges them to change for the better and to make away with anger, and further to take care of the causes of future events, and to cut short sufferings by acts of repentance, and eventually they will come to their senses."

Yahweh's "anger" (אַף) burns against the Ephraimites who have transgressed the second commandment of the Decalogue (cf. Exod 20:4-5 where Yahweh reveals himself as אֵל קַנָּא "impassioned God"). The phrase "How long?" (עַד־מָתַי), reminiscent of the lament language (Is 6:11; Zech 1:12; Ps 6:4; 13:2), underlines Yahweh's consternation with respect to Ephraim's stubbornness. Despite Yahweh's anger burning against them, the Ephraimites are not capable of "purity" (נִקָּיֹן).[599] Theodore of Mopsuestia[600] explains: "So, did not the long time teach you duty? Did you not put aside the stain of such impiety? Do you gape at the idols made by human hands? When would they even be considered gods, since they have such a cause of their existence?"

Based on Septuagint evidence, Wolff[601] suggests that the elliptic nominal clause "For [they are] from Israel" should be read together with v. 5b as a prophecy of hope. The Ephraimites belong to the covenantal Israel. Since they are not completely assimilated to the Canaanites, a return to God is still a possibility. As for the calf idol, a "craftsman" (חָרָשׁ) made it. And since it is not God, the "calf of Samaria" will be "broken to pieces" (שְׁבָבִים).[602] Theodoret of Cyrus[603] comments: "He satirized quite appropriately the weakness of the idols. For in order to exist they require material and skill. Taking the material from the earth, such as wood, stone, gold, silver, or tin, and borrowing the form from art, they deified the handmade images of animals."

In v. 7 Hosea uses two Wisdom sayings to exemplify Israel's senseless behavior. The first saying is a proverb which may be summarized as follows: to any deed there is a corresponding reward due to a rational principle which governs man's life (cf. Prov 11:8; 22:8; Gal 6:7: "you reap what you sow"). The one who sows "wind" (רוּחַ) (indicating emptiness and futility; cf. Prov 11:29; Job 7:7), will reap "whirlwind" (סוּפָתָה) (a metaphor for punishment and destruction; cf. Ps 83:16; Job 27:20; Is 29:6). If the Epraimites sow the wind of idolatry, they will experience the whirlwind of the final destruction (722/1 B.C.). Note the similarity in sound between *sûpātāh* "whirlwind" and *sûp* "to come to an end."

The second saying is a pseudo-sorites, "a form of non-logical logic,"[604] used to create an emotional climax. The main idea conveyed by this rhetorical device is that early failures anticipate a gloomy future or that calamity follows calamity so that nobody can be saved. Hosea says that there will be no harvest, and if such a thing would occur, the foreigners (זָרִים) (cf. 7:9; "enemy" in v. 3) will "swallow" (בלע) Israel's crops. Cyril of Alexandria[605] explains: "He names 'foreigners' (ἀλλοτρίους), those who falsely are called gods. Therefore our unpaid zeal for those [idols] who upset God, and the kind manners which fall short from pursuing the good will always and entirely be reproved by him." Historically, Israel's openness for syncretism and political alliances to solve her problems led the nation to final ruin. One may add that this saying is construed on rhyme (*ṣemaḥ* "[grain] head" — *qemaḥ* "flour"), a rare device in Hebrew poetry. Theodore of Mopsuestia[606] writes: "For it [the idolatry] does not differ at all from those sprouts, which dried up and destroyed by the warm wind, are entirely unfit for man's food. For on the one hand, ruin and destruction succeed these; on the other side, they are useless to men for they are not able to yield flour fit for sustenance." Similarly, Theodoret of Cyrus[607] explains: "For you pluck no fruit from the idols' service, but their bundles are like those ears of wheat destroyed by the wind, which show full stalks from outside, but which internally have no grain. Such is the nature of idolatry; for on the one hand it can take the image of a man or a woman, or a lion, or a different animal from art, but on the other hand, it is deprived of any strength or energy." Theophylact of Bulgaria[608] interprets: "He says this about idols that they have no substance (ὑπόστασιν); if they seem to have, the coming enemies will take them away, since they are gold and silver. Further, they [idols] have no power to help otherwise, but they appear to have power to make the enemies richer through their own material."

Verse 8 is linked to the preceding line by the catchword בלע "to swallow." "Now" (עַתָּה) it is Israel herself which is swallowed up by the foreigners. The Ephraimites "are" (הָיוּ) as an "unwanted" (אֵין־חֵפֶץ; cf. Jer 22:28, of king Jehoiachin in exile) vessel among the "nations" (גּוֹיִם), i.e., Assyria and Egypt. These lines echo the events of the year 733 B.C.: the annexation of Gilead and Galilee to Assyria, and Israel's submission to the latter which translates into her loss of value in the eyes of other nations.[609] Theodore of Mopsuestia[610] explains: "For you will undergo complete disappearance because of these, since you will be taken captive by the Assyrians. You will be among the foreigners as an entirely useless vessel, worthy of no word (λόγου)." According to Jerome,[611] "unclean" (*immundum*) or "useless" (*inutile*) vessel designates Israel intermingled with foreign nations and their idols. Theodoret of Cyrus[612] interprets: "Although they asked for help from the Assyrians, they will be handed over into slavery to them, because they neither fulfilled the worship to God, nor did they keep the festivals according to the law." Cyril of Alexandria[613] explains: "For having been carried off to Assyria and Media, he became entirely useless (ἠχρειώθη) anyway being quickly forced to think what it seemed good to those people. Rather, he became a useless (ἄχρηστον) vessel, in this way he was swallowed up (κατεπόθη), and getting rid of his fortune, he passed to the nations." Theophylact of Bulgaria[614] writes: "As if shipwrecked, they have been swallowed up by some great sea of their sins."

The first line of v. 9 alludes to king Hoshea who, at the beginning of his reign (732 B.C.), paid tribute to Assyria. The pronoun הֵמָּה "they" underscores the deliberative character of such a political move on Israel's part. Hosea employs a play on words between "Ephraim" (*'epʻrayim*) and "wild ass" (*pereʼ*) to convey people's stubborn isolation from Yahweh.[615] Jerome[616] explains: "And since [Israel] became an unclean vessel, they will go up to Assyria as a lonely wild ass; not at all as sheep pastured by the Lord, but as those who abusing wickedly their freedom are brought into captivity." Julian of Eclanum[617] writes: "The people of the Judaeans accepted no orders from the foreigners, but [were] as a wild ass unknowing the yoke and the burdens." In the last line, Ephraim is compared with a prostitute who, instead of receiving gifts, "pays off" (Hiph'il: הִתְנוּ)[618] her "lovers" (אֲהָבִים). This line refers probably to the receipt by Tiglath-pileser III of 1000 talents from Hoshea of Samaria.[619]

Verse 10 describes Yahweh's judgment as unavoidable. God will gather up (Pi'el: קָבַץ) the Ephraimites for judgment (cf. Joel 4:2) even if "they bargain" (Qal: יִתְנוּ) among the "nations" (גּוֹיִם). Theodoret of Cyrus[620] explains: "She [Israel] did not fill herself with good things, but kept on desiring more; that is why she will be handed over into the slavery." "Now" (עַתָּה) followed by imperfect "I will gather" (אֲקַבְּצֵם) emphasizes God's determination to render judgment.[621] Theophylact of Bulgaria[622] writes: "In the past, he says, I permitted them to live as unquestioned und unjudged, quite clearly due to my love for men, and hope for repentance. But 'now I will receive them,' i.e., to judge them, and I will call them for judgment, and I will demand penalties. 'Now' means quickly or in the enemies' region." The second line alludes to the tribute paid by Israel to the Assyrian king and his officials. This tribute is a "burden" (מַשָּׂא) which makes the Ephraimites "writhe in pain" (וַיָּחִילוּ).[623] For Jerome,[624] v. 10 refers to Israel's desperate attempts at freedom and her "final servitude" in Assyria. Based on the Septuagint reading ("[they shall cease in a little while] to anoint [a king]"), Theodore of Mopsuestia[625] writes: "For they will cease to institute those kingdoms and realms which are contrary to the law, when they will be chastised with captivity and weakened by their own iniquity." Similarly, Cyril of Alexandria,[626] identifying the "king and princes" with idols, notices: "Therefore, having received the chastisement, they ceased to anoint further king and princes. For while they were slaves to the Assyrians and Medes, what sort of spare time did they have to fulfill the works of apostasy, since they kept on bewailing (κατοιμώζοντες), and lamenting the unexpected calamity? It would to be known that after Cyrus the son of Cambyses [sic!] set Israel free from captivity, they did not anoint in Samaria those from the tribe of Ephraim, but they all were under one yoke, since those from the tribe of Judah reigned in Jerusalem."

In vv. 11-13a Yahweh charges Ephraim with two transgressions: over- preoccupation with the external worship and disregard of Yahweh's law. The verdict (v. 13b) is as harsh as brief: the Ephraimites "shall return" (יָשׁוּבוּ) to Egypt.

Verse 11 concerns the expansion of the altars. This

saying is not against the worship *per se*, but it targets a wrong attitude with respect to cultic life. The altars and sacrifices were considered ends in themselves rather than means of communion between Israel and Yahweh. From places where expiation of sins could be obtained, Ephraim's altars became an occasion to get away from Yahweh and thus for "sinning" (לַחֲטֹא).[627] Though not explicitly mentioned, the religious syncretism (i.e., importation of Canaanite elements into Israel's worship) is implied in this accusation.[628] Jerome[629] shows that the Israelites will suffer the distress of captivity because "Ephraim, their leader, multiplied the altars, not to bring sacrifices to the Lord, but to join sins to sins—these altars, namely the structures for sacrifice (*arae*), will turn back against him as a crime (*delictum*); so that the more there are, the more his wicked deeds (*scelera*) will increase.... Whatever they did, imitating the order of the sacrifices and rites, whether they gave alms, or promising chastity, or they imitate humbleness, and with falsehood and flattery deceive the artless people. God will not accept this kind of sacrifices." Theodoret of Cyrus[630] writes: "Rightly, he says, I will put an end to his lawless kingship, since through this [kingship] he ran headlong into the multitude of idolatrous altars, and plucked the impiety from there, ardently disposing himself around the lawless altars." Theophylact of Bulgaria[631] adds: "For when he reigned over them, Jeroboam misled them to multiply the idolatrous altars, which became for them an occasion for many sins. For they sinned against my honor, and they committed every other kind of sins." Cyril of Alexandria[632] reads this line as a reference to Jeroboam I and his successors who "erecting altars to the demons on every mountain and hill, persuaded the Israelites to offer sacrifices."

The consequence of Ephraim's obsession with the

multiplication of altars is presented in v. 12. The bridge between v. 11 and v. 12 is built by the word-play *hirbāh—rubbô* "multiply—multitude." Since Ephraim multiplied his altars, focusing exclusively on the sacrificial aspects of religious life, he came to disregard Yahweh's law. The Ephraimites were looking at God's precepts as if they were a "strange thing" (כְּמוֹ־זָר) or coming from an alien deity.[633] One might add that this saying is one of the earliest evidence that, as early as the eighth century B.C., the Torah (the instructions written by Yahweh; cf. Exod 24:12; 34:1) circulated, at least partially, in a written form.[634] Jerome[635] explains: "I will write again the laws (*leges*) I had formerly given through Moses. Yet what would be the benefit to write in addition different [laws], when he disregarded those he previously received? Or is it not contempt for God that when I order that there be one altar to be in Jerusalem, idols have been made throughout all mountains and hills by which they irritated the Lord?" Julian of Eclanum[636] writes: "Therefore my laws which once were promulgated and are primarily preserved in the book of Deuteronomy, I will write for them in many different ways (*multipliciter*), i.e., I will show and multiply them. Thus, for you, so that we may remember briefly many things, the saying concludes in this way: That if you do not want to listen to God's voice, so that you keep and execute all his precepts and the rituals which I teach you to perform today, those curses will come upon and seize you." Theodore of Mopsuestia[637] interprets: "I shall place this multitude of altars and new laws which they invented with respect to the worship of the idols against them like a just written accusation, bringing forth a sentence against them for so many violations of the law."

Verse 13 deals with the topic of animal sacrifices. Though the Ephraimites offer sacrifices (זִבְחֵי),[638] followed by traditional meals (Lev 3), Yahweh finds no delight (רצה) in them. From means of communion between God and his people, the sacrifices, as the altars, became goals in themselves, objects of love and veneration. Theodoret of Cyrus[639] writes: "For God needs none of these [i.e., animal sacrifices], but he demands the disposition (διάθεσιν) of the soul." In the same vein, Theodore of Mopsuestia[640] observes that "none of these [sacrifices] offers remission of sins to them." For Jerome,[641] this line condemns Israel's material aspirations related to worship: "As the Lord spoke in the Gospel: 'Truly, truly, I say to you, you seek me, not because you saw signs, but because you ate your fill of loaves' [Jn 6:26]. For they have only one desire, to devour the sacrifices, rather than to please God through them; nor will God accept these [sacrifices] they offered not to him but to their stomach and gullet." Cyril of Alexandria[642] interprets: "For what they sacrifice, he says, is not offered by them to God but rather to the sacred precincts of the idols. Even if they keep festival after the sacrifices, filling themselves full of food or drink, this is nothing for God. For they did not perform the festival for him." That is why, God now remembers (זכר) Ephraim's iniquity (עָוֹן) and punishes (פקד)[643] his sins (הַטָּאוֹת).[644] The Ephraimites will be brought into captivity or, in Hosea's words, they will return (שׁוּב) to Egypt. The final line may be understood in two ways: either figuratively as a reverse of the Exodus event and by consequence to an Assyrian captivity or historically as a reference to an Egyptian exile (cf. 9:3; 11:5). Most scholars incline toward the second interpretation: v. 13 alludes to Hoshea's pro-Egyptian policy (around 727 B.C.) which anticipates and, to some degree, prepares Yahweh's punishment on Israel, i.e., the Assyrian captivity. Theodore of Mopsuestia[645] writes: "In those terrible circumstances, they will ask help from Egypt, but they enjoyed no assistance from them at all; instead they were taken captive and brought to Assyria."

The pericope concludes with a lamentation (v. 14). Israel and Judah are equally guilty. Israel built palaces (הֵיכָלוֹת: royal palaces or temples) and forgot (שׁכח)[646] her Maker (עֹשֶׂה) (cf. Is 44:2; 51:13) while Judah multiplied the fortified cities (בְּצֻרוֹת). Both kingdoms have relied on political and military means of defense instead of trusting God. Therefore Yahweh will send fire (cf. "enemy" in 8:3) which will destroy the objects of their trust. Cyril of Alexandria[647] observes that "when the Babylonians set the cities of Judah on fire they were ministers (ὑπουργοί) of divine wrath." Jerome[648] interprets: "Israel forgot her Maker, and disregarding the Creator, she devised for herself another god. Also Judah, the *vir ecclesiasticus*, with wicked deeds or even by a wrong interpretation of the Holy Scriptures, built fortified cities for herself, not with God's assistance, but by an artful deception; the Lord says that he will kindle them with the fire of his spirit, and will devour his βάρεις [cf. LXX], namely their great houses built in the way of high buildings with tower (*turrium*); and he will overthrow the badly set foundations so that they may not be able to erect impious sanctuaries (*delubra*) against God." Similarly, Theodoret of Cyrus[649] interprets: "On the one hand, he will teach Judah, when the cities are in flames, not to trust in city walls, but rather in me; on the other hand, he will teach Israel not to build shrines to the demons, but rather to follow my worship according to the law."

10. On Exile and Prophecy (9:1-9)

1. Do not rejoice, O Israel! Do not exult[650] like the peoples! For you have played the whore away from your God. You have loved a harlot's fee on all threshing

floors of grain.[651] 2. Threshing floor and winepress shall not know[652] them; the new wine shall deceive them.[653] 3. They shall not dwell in Yahweh's land. Ephraim shall return[654] to Egypt, and in Assyria they shall eat unclean food. 4. They shall not pour out wine to Yahweh, and their sacrifices[655] shall not please him. Like mourners' bread [it shall be] for them; all who eat of it shall be defiled. For their bread shall be for themselves alone; it shall not come into Yahweh's house. 5. What will you do on the day of assembly, on the day of Yahweh's feast? 6. For behold, they have gone from destruction,[656] Egypt shall gather them in, Memphis shall bury them. Precious is their silver—weeds[657] shall inherit them; thorns [shall be] in their tents. 7. The days of punishment have come, the days of retribution [are here]. Let Israel know[658] it! "The prophet is a fool, the man of the spirit is mad!" Because of your great iniquity, your hostility[659] is great. 8. The watchman[660] of Ephraim is with God;[661] [he is] a prophet. A fowler's snare is on all his ways, hostility in the house of his God. 9. They have become deeply corrupt[662] as in the days of Gibeah.[663] He shall remember their iniquity, he will punish their sins.

These sayings were delivered at one of Israel's main shrines (Gilgal, Bethel, Samaria?) during a fall festival (Sukkoth?), in the years following the military intervention of Tiglath-pileser III (733 B.C.). The focus of the pericope is on Ephraim's syncretistic worship which promised fertility and security but in fact brought destruction and exile. The shift from the third (singular and plural: vv. 2-4; 6-9) to second person (vv. 1, 5, 7) with respect to Israel represents the evidence of a dialogue between prophet and his audience, at times interrupted by the prophet's personal remarks. The Ephraimites will be carried away into a foreign land where they will be unable to offer fitting sacrifices to Yahweh. Instead of Ephraim's twisted image on the prophet (i.e., "the prophet is a fool"), Hosea proposes his own definition: the prophet is rather a "watchman" appointed by God to see and reveal things his contemporaries cannot see.

In v. 1 Hosea asks his audience to stop "rejoicing" (שׂמח) and "exulting" (גיל)[664] according to the custom of the "peoples" (עַמִּים), for their festival is another occasion to play the whore away from God. According to Julian of Eclanum,[665] Israel should not rejoice because "through cultic uncleanness [she] went away from the covenant of the law." Jerome[666] interprets: "Israel said she is one of the many nations (*gentibus*) when she goes away from God's law and worships idols; she is rejoicing and exulting since she has gone away from acquaintance with God and become a nation mixed with others, and therefore he seizes them; and he says: 'Do not rejoice, nor exult, nor consider yourself to be such as the other nations. For the one who is ignorant of God and the one who leaves God are punished differently, for the servant who knows the will of his master and does not fulfill it will greatly be flogged." Theodoret of Cyrus[667] explains: "It does not fit for you to rejoice like the foreign nations. For they received no teaching through the prophets. But you, though you continually enjoyed these things, culled no use thence, you offered (first-fruits) sacrifices to the demons of the goods given to you by me." Theodore of Mopsuestia[668] writes: "Therefore, it is not fitting for you to rejoice and exult like the rest of the peoples. For they did not receive any teaching which might lead them to piety, but you, after much instruction and knowledge of God, rebelled against the knowledge which had been given to you because of the depravity of your opinion, and turned to the worship of the idols."

The use of name "Israel" rather than "Ephraim" (i.e., the inhabitants of the region with the same name) points to the people as a cultic community (cf. 4:15; 8:2, 3, 6).⁶⁶⁹ The mention of "threshing floors" (גָּרְנוֹת) of "grain" (דָּגָן) makes one think of a harvest festival held on a threshing floor. In biblical times, on the threshing floors, located near the city's gate, were held religious, legal, and political gatherings (Judg 6:37; 2 Sam 6:6; 24:18; 1 Kgs 22:10). Theophylact of Bulgaria⁶⁷⁰ accordingly interprets: "Although you enjoyed my goods, you gave them as presents to the idols, offering to them the first-fruits of the threshing-floor." Theodore of Mopsuestia⁶⁷¹ writes: "You offered the first-fruits to the demons, considering them the source of the gifts." The festival mentioned in this section could be the "Booths" (סֻכּוֹת) or the "festival of Yahweh" (חַג לַיהוה) (Lev 23:41; Deut 16:13ff.; Judg 21:19ff.), a seven-day celebration marked by joy and exultation. "Harlot's fee" (אֶתְנָן) refers to natural resources (grain, wine, and oil) the wayward wife has considered gifts from the Baals, her lovers (2:10/8ff.). Cyril of Alexandria⁶⁷² interprets: "In which way did they play the whore? She loved the gifts, he says, not those from God, but rather those from heifers and Baal, though the latter gives nothing to those who ask. Where did she seek the gifts from them? 'On all threshing floors of grain.' For it seemed to them unholy and inconsiderate to ask fruitfulness from the fields, as he said, from vain objects of worship. Therefore Israel sought the gifts from the idols."

At the harvest festival the threshing floor and winepress will not provide Israel with grain and wine; they do not want to recognize her as the beneficiary of these natural products. Moreover, the new wine will deceive Yahweh's people in their expectations (v. 2). Read along with the following lines (v. 3), this verse may allude to foreign enemies who will deport Israel's population and spoil its crops.⁶⁷³ According to Julian of Eclanum,⁶⁷⁴ the economic crisis Hosea mentions here characterized the years of exile. Theodoret of Cyrus[675] explains: "For I will despoil you of the goods usually supplied by me." Theodore of Mopsuestia[676] sees in the "carrying off (ἀφαίρεσιν) of the fruits" a fitting penalty for Israel's transgressions. Theophylact of Bulgaria[677] interprets: "Since you offered the fruits to the idols, you will no longer cultivate anything, neither grain nor vine. Yet you will even see abundant vines, but at the time of new wine you will be cheated of your hopes." Cyril of Alexandria[678] writes: "There is no disputed point among those with zeal for knowledge, that pestilences, long barrenness, and drought, occurred in Samaria. Thus she lost hope when she did not receive the things she demanded."

"Ephraim" in v. 3 designates the central part of the Northern Kingdom which remained independent after the quick intervention of Tiglath-pileser III in 733 B.C. The prophet announces that the people will cease to dwell in the promised land which, according to Lev 25:23, belongs to Yahweh, hence the phrase "Yahweh's land" (אֶרֶץ יהוה) used here for the first time in the Old Testament (cf. "my land" in Jer 2:7; 16:8). Ephraim's "return" to Egypt (cf. 7:16; 8:13; 9:6; 11:5) may be a reference to those groups of Ephraimites fleeing to Egypt (cf. Mic 7:12), whereas the last part of v. 3 hints at the Assyrian exile during which the deportees would eat "unclean" (טָמֵא) food (i.e., food eaten in a land which does not belong to Yahweh but rather to other gods; Ezek 14:3). Jerome[679] explains: "When they will be in Chaldea with no temple and no altars they will not offer wine to the Lord but to the demons; and he will not find delight in them for they offer libations to foreign gods and are kept in captivity and among the Assyrians share the sacrifices offered to the idols (*idolthyta*), becoming as the mourners' loaves." Theodoret of Cyrus[680] interprets: "Since they loved the transgression of the law in the promised land, they will live in a lawless way in the land of Assyria."

Verse 4 indicates that the Ephraimites will be unable to offer proper libations (cf. Num 15:1-2; Exod 29:40) and sacrifices in the lands of exile. On the one hand, because there are no Yahwistic shrines, on the other hand because the foreign lands are under the control of deities other than Yahweh. The matter of these sacrifices is compared to the "mourners' bread" (לֶחֶם אוֹנִים), a defiled food (any contact with the deceased made one unclean: Num 19:11ff.), which cannot be used in a sacrificial setting; it may serve only as physical (lit. "for their gullet" [לְנַפְשָׁם]) sustenance. Jerome[681] explains the phrase "mourners' bread" by relating it to the Greco-Roman cultic practices: "The Greeks call the mourners' dinners περίδειπνα, whereas we may designate them as paternal [dinners] (*paternalia*), because they are offered to the deceased parents." Theodore of Mopsuestia[682] writes: "They showed such haste and ambition with respect to the offerings of the idols, as to give them first-fruits from each threshing-floor. But to God the giver of all goods, they do not want to offer libations of wine, nor to do anything that might please God." Ephraim's sacrifices shall not "please" (יֶעֶרְבוּ)[683] Yahweh and thus they will not enter "Yahweh's house" (בֵּית יהוה), i.e., one of the shrines (not the temple of Solomon)[684] consecrated to Yahweh. Theodoret of Cyrus[685] compares this offering with that of Cain and concludes that God rejected both offerings because they were not brought with a sincere heart. According to Julian of Eclanum,[686] God's refusal of Israel's offering was determined by the latter's numerous crimes. Cyril of Alexandria[687] explains: "Having collected the fruit of the vine into the wine-vats, they offered the firstlings as a libation to the demons, and not to the God who gave them. They also offered loaves of bread as first-fruits of the harvest. Except that the sacrifice will become for them defiled and impure, he says, and the offerings will be considered as mourning breads, that is, disgusting, impure, and odious. For what reason? For, the law considered unclean anyone who approached a dead body either by blood relationship or rather by the very touching of the body. Therefore it was easy for the relatives or friends of the dead person to become unclean during mourning, since they handled the dead body, and since they were willing to do for him what was customary. And whatever they touched became unclean. Therefore the mourning bread is that bread which was at hand as food for those who were mourning for the dead; for those who strive to avoid contamination with a dead body it is considered terrible even to taste this bread. Wherefore even the breads themselves are defiled and rejected, even though they may have been offered as first fruits of the harvest. 'Those who eat them will become unclean.' They will be useful only to their souls (ψυχαῖς), that is, as a food (βρῶσιν) for them."

The question in v. 5 concerns the Ephraimites who, deprived of homeland and proper worship, are no longer able to celebrate "Yahweh's feast" (חַג יהוה) or the feast of "Tabernacles" (סֻכּוֹת) (cf. Lev 23:39; Judg 21:19).[688] This joyous festival originally held on the fifteenth day of the seventh month (1 Kgs 8:2) was observed in the Northern Kingdom starting with Jeroboam I in the eighth month (1 Kgs 12:32). God's punishment upon Ephraim will occur on the "day of assembly" (יוֹם מוֹעֵד), another name for "Yahweh's feast." According to Julian of Eclanum,[689] these lines refer to Israel's captivity marked by tenebra, bitterness and distress. Theophylact of Bulgaria[690] explains: "Compelled to serve and to be governed according to other laws, you will not be able to keep the divine festivals according to Mosaic legislation.

Some think that the day of celebration and feast are the time of war and through it of vengeance, as if when the Lord rejoices and celebrates over their destruction. These lines may also refer to those who intended to crucify the Lord, as when the prophet full of indignation exclaims: 'How do you intend to do such a thing on the day of Pascha!' The time then was the festival, when all the people got together, truly the festival of the Lord. For he instituted this when he sacrificed himself for us." Cyril of Alexandria[691] writes: "Therefore God calls his festival (ἑορτὴν) the time when Israel will be punished for the sins committed against him."

A thematic similarity exists between vv. 6 and 3: both verses mention Egypt as a place of refuge; but this place of refuge will eventually turn into a place of punishment. The Ephraimites will flee from "destruction" (שֹׁד) in their own land seeking deliverance in Egypt. (Note the play on words between "day of assembly" [v. 5] and Egypt's "gathering" [קָבַץ] the refugees for burial [v. 6].) Instead of salvation, they will get a burial place in one of Egypt's most famous necropolises, Memphis. Silver, the precious metal in which they put their trust, will be inherited by weeds; their abandoned "tents"[692] will be occupied by the thorns. Theodoret of Cyrus[693] writes: "They will pluck no delightful (ὀνησιφόρον) fruit. By these he indicated the punishment of the flight to Egypt." This is the picture of a desolate place left behind by the refugees heading for Egypt. Cyril of Alexandria[694] observes: "For the cities will reach such a desolation when they will be full of thorns. This is the sign of a inaccessible and desolated land." Jerome[695] connects this line with the events following the siege of Jerusalem (586 B.C.) and the murder of the newly appointed governor Gedaliah, when the prophet Jeremiah and other Judaeans sought refuge in Egypt (cf. 2 Kgs 25:25; Jer 42): "Behold, he says, with sufferings and destruction oppressing [them], and Assyria and Chaldea desiring to take them captives, they fled to Egypt." Theodore of Mopsuestia[696] interprets: "For after much suffering (ταλαιπωρίαν) that you endured in Egypt, where you fled as if some safety, the Assyrians will take you from there into captivity." Theophylact of Bulgaria[697] explains: "When Samaria was captured, the survivors fled to Egypt. Later, when Jerusalem was destroyed by Nebuzaradan, Gedaliah's murderers fled to Egypt while Jeremiah was trying to hinder them."

Verse 7 underscores the imminence of God's judgment expressed by the days of "punishment" (פְּקֻדָּה) and "retribution" (שִׁלֻּם)[698] which "have come" (perfect בָּאוּ) near. In the people's view, the "prophet" (נָבִיא) is a "fool" (אֱוִיל)[699] and the "man of spirit" (אִישׁ הָרוּחַ)[700] a "madman" (מְשֻׁגָּע).[701] Jerome[702] notices: "What we call 'fool' (*stultum*), the Septuagint interprets as pseudoprophet." One may infer from this characterization that the Ephraimites have ridiculed Hosea for pointing out the nearness of God's punishment. Cyril of Alexandria[703] writes: "It was the habit of the Israelites to repudiate the words of the holy prophets, and value as nothing those [words] from God, though often he prophesied to them their future sufferings." In spite of their scornful attitude, Israel will eventually know that Yahweh's prophet was right. The invasion of Tiglath-pileser III in 733 B.C. was just a preview of a more terrible event, the so-called "hostility" (מַשְׂטֵמָה)[704] which would befall Israel according to her "iniquity" (עָוֹן). Julian of Eclanum[705] remarks that Israel's fault is "certainly not a simple error but rather a repeated madness, i.e., to despise the spiritual leaders and those strong in prophetic distinction, especially at that time, as senseless and foolish, at which [time] they themselves were sustaining a lack of wisdom that they were considering gods those [idols] whom they were manufacturing." Similarly, Theodore of Mopsuestia[706] concludes that Israel added the multitude of idols to her madness. Theodoret of Cyrus[707] writes: "When the fruits of iniquity, which are near, will lay hold of you, you will be like a pseudo-prophet, who because of an indwelling spirit becomes mad, wandering hither and thither. Such a displacement (ἔκστασις) of mind will lay hold of you. The multitude of your iniquities brought this foolishness upon you."

For Hosea, the prophet is a "watchman" (צֹפֶה) appointed by God to supervise his people (cf. Hab 2:1); the word "watchman" is used in v. 8 (cf. Is 56:10; Jer 6:17; Ezek 3:17; Hab 2:1) as a prophetic title. Cyril of Alexandria[708] explains: "It is customary for the Holy Scripture to name as watchmen the leaders of the people, and those who are raised to a great height through honor, the persons someone should look to, if he wishes to live a righteous life beyond reproach." Although belonging to Ephraim by birth, the prophet is "with" (עִם) God by his ministry, i.e., in a special relationship with God (cf. Moses: Exod 34:28). According to Julian of Eclanum,[709] "Ephraim" alludes to king Jeroboam I who descended from that tribe. In the beginning, Jeroboam was like a prophet taking care of the religious life; later he ceased to do so bringing instead ruin and ensnarement for his followers. By naming the prophet's God "my God," Hosea gives a passionate tone to these lines. The prophet (Hosea?), Ephraim's "watchman," finds himself in a difficult situation: the "hostility" (מַשְׂטֵמָה) directed against him is at work in the "house of his God," i.e., in the land of Israel, while a "fowler's snare" (פַּח יָקוֹשׁ) is spread on all prophet's ways. According to Theodore of Mopsuestia,[710] the "madness" (cf. LXX: μανίαν) in the "house of his God" refers to the "idolatry with which you filled the whole promised land; for he calls the promised land 'God's house,' as inhabited by God." Jerome[711] interprets the "house of his God" as a reference to the shrine of Bethel where one of the two golden calves set up by king Jeroboam I was located; the "madness" (*insania*; cf. V) in Bethel designates this calf-idol. According to Theodoret of Cyrus,[712] "God's house" indicates the entire people appointed by God as watchman and prophet to the neighboring nations "so that by my providence toward you and your own way of life according to the law they [nations] may also come to know me."

In v. 9 Hosea indicates that the current hostility against the prophet has an antecedent in the crime committed by the Benjamites against the traveling Levite (a spiritual ancestor of the prophet)[713] in Gibeah (cf. Judg 19-21). Julian of Eclanum[714] so interprets the text. According to Theodore of Mopsuestia,[715] the phrase "days of the hills" (cf. LXX: ἡμέρας βουνοῦ) refers to the journey through the wilderness after the Exodus event when Israel had to deal for the first time with the idolatry (i.e., the episode of the golden calf; cf. Exod 32). Having showed that the toponym "Gibeah" means in Hebrew "hill," Theophylact of Bulgaria[716] connects the Hosean phrase to that episode from the time of Judges. Hosea's opponents are as deeply "corrupt" (שחת Pi'el) as the Benjamites in the "days of Gibeah." Yet God will "remember" (זכר) their iniquity and punish their sins. If the older crime brought the extermination of almost an entire tribe, Benjamin, the present persecution against Yahweh's prophet will lead to the destruction of Ephraim. Jerome[717] writes: "For that reason he will remember their iniquity, which now through long-suffering he seems to be unmindful of; he will visit their sins and wounds that for a long time decayed."

11. Baal-peor and Gilgal (9:10-17)

10. Like grapes in the wilderness, I found Israel. Like a first fruit[718] on the fig tree, in its first season,[719] I saw your[720] fathers. But they came to Baal-peor, and devoted themselves to Shame, and became detestable like the thing they loved.[721] 11. Ephraim's glory shall fly away like a bird—no birth, no pregnancy, no conception. 12. Even if they bring up children, I will bereave them to the last man. Indeed, woe to them also when I turn away from them![722] 13. Ephraim, as I have seen, has made his sons a hunter's pray.[723] Ephraim [was ready] to bring out his sons to slaughter.[724] 14. Give them, O Yahweh—what will you give them?—give them a childless womb and shriveled breasts. 15. All their wickedness is in Gilgal, for there I came to hate them. Because of the wickedness of their deeds I will drive them out of my house. I will love them no more. All their officials are rebels. 16. Ephraim is stricken, their root is withered. They shall yield no fruit. Even though they give birth, I will kill the cherished offspring of their womb. 17. My[725] God will reject them, for they have not obeyed him. They shall become wanderers among the nations.

Verse 10 begins a new pericope centered on three historical evocations. At the onset, Yahweh recalls the moment when he first met Israel in the wilderness. The surprise and joy of this initial encounter between God and his people contrasts with two other moments in Israel's past: Gilgal and Baal-peor. While the former toponym is wrapped in mist, the latter is linked to cultic and sexual transgressions recorded in Num 25. Barrenness of the women and death of the children rather than fertility and life are the divine response for those who sought fruitfulness in the realm of the sacred prostitution.

Given the "hostility" against Yahweh's prophets (after

733 B.C.) mentioned above, Hosea was eventually forced to withdraw from the public arena, and to continue his activity in the inner circle of his disciples. This shift explains the lament-like tone of the pericope.[726] One may notice that vv. 14, 17 anticipate by their bold language Jeremiah's "confessions" (e.g., Jer 15).[727]

Israel is compared to the grapes in the "wilderness" (מִדְבָּר), and the "first fruit" (בִּכּוּרָה) on the fig tree (v. 10). As grapes are rare in deserted places, and ripe figs appear exceptionally in May-June (Is 28:4; Jer 24:2) before the main season, i.e., August, Yahweh's first encounter with Israel is described as "finding" (מצא)[728] or "perceiving" (ראה) an unexpected treasure. These lines refer to Israel's journey through the wilderness. In Hosea's view, this was the ideal time of the relationship between God and his people (2:16/14ff.; 11:1; cf. Jer 2:2), the moment of divine election, as reflected in Cyril of Alexandria's[729] interpretation: "For I chose (ἐπελεξάμην) them as if finding a bunch of grapes in the desert, and as if grasping a ripe fig from a fig tree." According to Jerome,[730] the first grapes and figs allude to Abraham, Isaac, and Jacob, in whom God found a people: "And notice the rightness: the fathers are seen, the people are found, and in both cases there is a vine and a fig tree under which, one is told that the one who trusts the Lord finds rest." Similarly, Julian of Eclanum[731] writes: "When the nature of mortals, Abraham, Isaac, and Jacob, was neglected and covered by the thick thorn-bushes of impiety, sentences of kindness were pre-eminent: thus producing sweetness of the confession due God as grapes and figs; I did not despise their faith and virtue inproportionate its paucity but I considered it worthy of the greater honor and favor the more they despised the examples of the pagan nations." Theodoret of Cyrus[732] interprets: "In the same manner [i.e., as finding the grapes in the wilderness], when the people of old lived in impiety, I saw Abraham's virtue and plucked him for myself, and I made a covenant (συνθήκας) with him, and in the same way with his son and grandson." Theodore of Mopuestia[733] explains: "I showed such a disposition (διάθεσιν) for their fathers, as someone would have who sees a bunch of grapes in the wilderness beyond all hope, or figs appearing on the tree before their season." Yet Israel's faithfulness toward Yahweh proved to be short. As soon as they arrived at Baal-peor (the first contact with the cultivated land), Israel's forefathers "devoted" (נזר) themselves to "Shame" (בֹּשֶׁת) becoming detestable (שִׁקּוּצִים),[734] unclean, as the object of their worship, i.e., Baal of Mt. Peor (Num 23:28).[735] This last episode is narrated in Num 25 where the Israelites under the influence of the Moabite women embraced ("yoked themselves"—צמד) Baal's worship. Jerome[736] explains: "In fact, Beelphegor (an idol of violent sexual passion) means the one who has on the head, i.e., on top, leather, so that it may indicate the shamefulness of the man's member. And because they entered Beelphegor, they became deprived of God, handed over to their own confusion; that is, to the idol." Theodoret of Cyrus[737] writes: "They preferred the worship of Beelphegor to my worship, plucking from this only shame; for this reason, those who once were beloved became abominable."

The "glory" (כָּבוֹד)[738] of Ephraim, the remainder of the former Northern Kingdom, "shall fly (עוּף Hithpo'el)[739] away like a bird" (v. 11). The Ephraimites, like their fathers at Baal-peor (Num 25:1, 6, 8), gave themselves to various sexual rites in order to obtain fertility but what they found instead was complete barrenness from conception to birth.[740] Theophylact of Bulgaria[741] explains: "He flew away quickly from me without striving after those fathers [the patriarchs]. Or that he will be led hastily into captivity." Similarly, Theodoret of Cyrus[742] writes: "Thus they will be transferred swiftly into a foreign land. For they will not love the fame (κλέος) of virtue, but rather they will suppose fecundity as the greatest glory." Julian of Eclanum[743] interprets: "That people therefore who did not want to discern between pious and impious things but has become abominable in the same way as the [cultic] images themselves, deservedly will be brought into captivity with such rapidity that it will seem not to have walked but to have flown."

Verse 12 underscores the inexorable character of God's punishment. If Ephraim still rears children then this will be for a short while since God "will bereave (שׁכל) them to the last man (מֵאָדָם)" by deportation, famine, or war. The "woe" (אוֹי) of this situation, more unbearable than lack of fertility, comes from the fact that Yahweh, the source of life, turns away (שׂוּר) from Ephraim. Theodore of Mopsuestia[744] interprets: "They do not conclude that even if the children who are born reach full maturity, there will be nothing more for them from this. For they will be brought by the slaughter of war to childlessness." In Jerome's[745] view, these lines refer to the siege of Samaria by king Ben-hadad of Aram, which was marked by a terrible famine and much violence (cf. 2 Kgs 6:24-32). Mentioning the Septuagint rendition (σάρξ μου ἐξ αὐτῶν "my flesh is from them") Jerome observes: "If Christ is the head of the body, that is, of the Church, we all are members of Christ and of the Church. Thus, whoever goes away from the Church lacerates Christ's body." Similarly, Theodoret of Cyrus[746] interprets: "Nevertheless, you are not going to experience utter destruction until I take my flesh (σάρκα) from you. The blessed Paul clearly teaches this: 'For he [Christ] took Abraham's seed and not that of the angels' [Heb 2:16].... Therefore, he says, since my flesh that I assume is from them I will not utterly destroy them until I take my flesh and choose those who obey the call."

The text of v. 13 is one of the more difficult in the entire book. If we follow the Septuagint reading, which fits well into the context, a new image, that of hunting, makes its appearance. The saying of v. 13 represents the climax of the situation described in v. 12. Ephraim exposes his children as a "hunter's prey" to the "slaughter" (הָרֵג), a metaphor for Assyria. Probably Theodore of Mopsuestia[747] so understands it when he says that "they [the Israelites] will be delivered as a prey into the hands of the enemies." These lines may refer either to Ephraim's coalition with Damascus and their military advance against Jerusalem, which led to the Assyrian intervention in 733 B.C., or to Hoshea's pro-Egyptian policy triggered by the accession of Shalmaneser V to power in 727 B.C.[748] Theodoret of Cyrus[749] interprets: "Since they continue to offer these [offerings] to the idols, for this reason I will give those already born to the slaughter, and I will make the husbands sterile and the wives infertile." Theophylact of Bulgaria[750] writes: "For I see, he says, O Lord, that Ephraim, by the sins and impious acts he committed, himself exposed his sons to the hunt, namely, captivity, and to torture, which is to slaughter. For some were led into captivity and others were slaughtered by the enemies."

Verse 14 is the prophet's prayer to Yahweh regarding Ephraim's fate. Hosea holds a delicate position. On the one hand he is a member of Ephraim, on the other hand he is Yahweh's prophet. He begins his prayer on the people's side by asking Yahweh to bestow upon Ephraim (his blessings?): "Give them, O Yahweh...." Yet as Yahweh's messenger, he realizes that what Israel deserves is punishment rather than blessings from above. Thus after a brief pause, followed by a question (cf. Am 7:2; Is 6:11), "What will you give them?," he concludes on a rather submissive note: "Give them a childless womb and shriveled breasts" as the least (cf. 2 Sam 24:14) or the most lenient (cf. Lk 23:29) among the possible punishments (deportation, famine, war, and the worst of all, God's absence from the midst of his people). The mention of "childless womb" and "shriveled breasts" here may be a reversal of the blessing of Joseph, Ephraim's father in Gen 49:25: "Blessings of the breast and womb."[751] Theodoret of Cyrus[752] explains: "Since they have made a bad use of the gifts, I will put an end to their iniquity by the mean of infertility (ἀγονίᾳ)." Theodore of Mopsuestia[753] observes: "They endure this just and fitting penalty: to be encompassed by sterility and not be able to feed the children who are born." Cyril of Alexandria[754] interprets: "If the Israelites were intending not to know God, but rather to be dragged off to a unclean and irrational hope, and to think that they would be superior to their enemies on account of the great number of the children, and that they had a great war-like spirit, and for this reason there was no need to be aided by your hand, then let their women not at all bear their children for them. For this is a 'childless womb.'"

The root of Ephraim's "wickedness" (רָעָה) is in Gilgal (v. 15). According to Jerome,[755] the name Gilgal points to the inauguration of Saul's kingship (1 Sam 11:14f.). "There they went away from me by demanding a human king," explains Jerome. In fact, the northern monarchy is not infrequently accused in the book of Hosea (3:4; 7:3-7; 8:4; 10:3, 7, 15). Yet as Mays remarks,[756] the other passages in Hosea where Gilgal appears (4:15; 12:12; cf. Am 4:4; 5:5)[757] concern the worship rather than the monarchy. The "wickedness" refers more probably to some fertility rites performed in the sanctuary of Gilgal.[758] A similar interpretation is found in Julian of Eclanum,[759] who after observing that these lines refer to the idols set up in Gilgal, adds: "But some have thought that, because of Saul, the prophet might allude also to this place." Theodoret of Cyrus[760] perhaps agrees with the former view when he characterizes the inhabitants of Gilgal as workers of "impiety" (ἀσεβείας). Or Theodore of Mopsuestia:[761] "There [in Gilgal] they followed every kind of impiety, and those who committed such things were justly hated." Hatred (שׂנא) and expulsion (גרשׁ)[762] are God's response to the rebellion (סרר) of Ephraim's royal "officials" (שָׂרִים). Yahweh's "house" in v. 15 is the promised land (cf. 8:1; 9:8) from where the Ephraimites will be driven out. Yahweh's promise that he will no longer love his people echoes the saying of 1:6f. concerning Hosea's daughter Lo-Ruhamah. Thus Theophylact of Bulgaria[763] interprets: "I shall expel them from my house, namely, the land of Palestine, that they had from me as a house, or from my temple. For I will evict them." In the view of Cyril of Alexandria,[764] Israel's expulsion is not so much a physical relocation, but rather a weakening of the "relationship" (οἰκειότης) with God.

Verse 16 returns to the imagery of v. 12. Ephraim's offspring is condemned to annihilation. The people is compared with a felled (fig?) tree whose root is withered, and yielding no fruit (cf. Jon 4:7; Ps 121:6; Mt 21:19). Theodoret of Cyrus[765] interprets: "'Root' indicates the kingdom, that Salmanasar overturned utterly [lit. by the roots], when he devastated Samaria. After the siege of Samaria, the ten tribes remained with no king." Theodore of Mopsuestia[766] writes: "Using the metaphor of trees he says that they will be completely destroyed, in the same way that trees utterly wither and can yield no fruit when their root is destroyed." Jerome[767] explains: "He refers to Ephraim whose root withered because he lost God in whom he was established, or he was not worthy to have as his parents Abraham, Isaac, and Jacob, in whom he had put out his root; and that is why he did not yield the fruit of justice." "Even if" (גַּם כִּי) their wives give birth to children Yahweh himself, rather than one of his agents, will exterminate (Hiph'il מוּת) the "cherished offspring (מַחֲמַדֵּי) of their womb (בִּטְנָם)."⁷⁶⁸ Theophylact of Bulgaria⁷⁶⁹ interprets: "I will kill their children, handing them to the battle to the enemy, even though they [their parents] desired and loved them. For they themselves are not worthy on their own to be desired and loved; inasmuch as they are the fruit of their womb, are they dear to them." Note the pun אֶפְרַיִם—פְּרִי "Ephraim—fruit" which negates the former blessing of Ephraim in Gen 41:52.⁷⁷⁰

The prophet intervenes for the second time (cf. v. 14). "My God" in v. 17 (cf. "his God" in 9:8) underscores the special relationship between Hosea and Yahweh, on the one hand, and the increasing distance between the prophet and his contemporaries, on the other hand. God will reject (מאס)⁷⁷¹ Ephraim for they have not obeyed (שׁמע) him, and thus they will be wandering (נדד)⁷⁷² among the nations (cf. Deut 28:65)—a reference to the Assyrian exile (721 B.C.). Julian of Eclanum⁷⁷³ explains: "The captivity will devour them; in fact their offspring, compared with whom nothing is sweeter to their parents will be consumed by a multiple and various calamity." Theodore of Mopsuestia⁷⁷⁴ interprets: "For I will estrange all of them from my own providence (κηδεμονίας), since they do not want to listen to him, and to consider penitence (μεταμέλειαν). For this reason, they will be taken and will be captive among the foreigners (ἀλλοτρίοις), compelled by great need to go around and wander here and there." Cyril of Alexandria⁷⁷⁵ writes: "It happened that they suffered this; at that time they are carried off to Assyria; and now they are no less abhorred for their debaucheries against Christ."

12. Israel without Cult or King (10:1-8)

1. Israel is a luxuriant[776] vine that yields fruit[777] for herself. The more her fruit increased, the more altars she made. As her land was bountiful, she beautified his pillars. 2. Their heart is divided.[778] Now they are guilty.[779] He himself will wreck their altars and destroy their pillars. 3. Indeed, now they will say: "We have no king! For we did not fear Yahweh. What can the king do for us?" 4. Words are uttered,[780] perjuries are committed, agreements are cut, and justice sprouts like a poisonous weed[781] along the furrows of the field. 5. The inhabitants[782] of Samaria tremble[783] for the calf[784] of Beth-aven. Indeed, its people mourn over him, and his idol-priests[785] [wail] over him. They exult[786] because of his glory for it has departed from him. 6. Even it itself shall be borne to Assyria, as a gift for the great king.[787] Ephraim shall experience shame, and Israel shall be ashamed of her plan.[788] 7. Samaria is destroyed.[789] Her king is like foam upon water. 8. The high places of wickedness, Israel's sin, will be destroyed. Thorns and thistles shall grow on their altars. They will say to the mountains: "Cover us!" and to the hills: "Fall on us!"

The pericope, a collection of prophetic sayings, opens with a new metaphor of Israel as a luxuriant vine (v. 1). The prophet ponders on God's judgment concerning Israel's religious and political life. The wayward people will be left with no pillar and altar, no king and capital, no idol and high place. All these human means leading to transgression will be destroyed so that Israel may taste alone Yahweh's wrath. Israel's desperate cry begging for death ends this pericope (v. 8) whose emphasis falls on the worship tainted by Baalism and apostasy, specifically on the bull idol of Bethel (vv. 5-8). According to Wolff,[790] 10:1-8 belongs to a type of prophetic speech which may be labeled "didactic" or "reflective." This "didactic" speech was probably delivered to the small circle of disciples (cf. Is 8:16) a while after 733 B.C. when the people were able again to focus on cultic life (cf. vv. 1, 5).

Verse 1 introduces a new simile, Israel a "luxuriant (בּוֹקֵק)[791] vine (גֶּפֶן)"[792] (cf. "like grapes in the wilderness," 9:10). Mentioning the Septuagint reading, εὐκληματοῦσα, Jerome[793] explains: "That means having good shoots and fruit-bearing branches, she [Israel] produced many clusters, and the abundance of the grapes equaled the great number of the branches; but she who was of such a kind before offending God, afterwards turned the abundance of the fruits into a great number of offenses, so that the more people she had, the more altars she built, and she overmatched the abundance of the land by the number of the idols. Instead of images, the Septuagint interprets στήλας, that we call statues or inscriptions, which properly are of demons or dead men." Similarly, Julian of Eclanum[794] sees in the extended vine-branches metaphor a sign of prosperity which characterized Israel after her settlement in the promised land after the Exodus event. Having mentioned that many prophets used this designation, Theodoret of Cyrus[795] explains: "Hence he calls Israel 'a vine with many branches (εὐκληματοῦσα)' and its fruit 'abundant' (εὐθηνοῦντα), not because of piety or another virtue, but rather because of the multitude of the offspring." Cyril of Alexandria[796] writes: "When he says that Ephraim was smitten at his roots and that he would be fruitless and that these things happened from the savageness expended on them by the Assyrians, he necessarily shows how it was in the past and that he had been fruitful, when he wisely laid claim to a life according to the law." The metaphor Israel—the vine planted and tendered by Yahweh—is also found in Is 5:1-7 and Jer 2:21. "Israel" in v. 1 refers to the whole nation since its beginnings, and covers all its historical periods. This vine, though luxuriant, yields fruit for "itself" (לוֹ) and not for the vine dresser, i.e., God. The shrines are the fruit Israel yields for herself.[797] Israel's economic prosperity has a religious reverse, the increase of the idolatrous practices, from erecting "altars" (מִזְבְּחוֹת) to beautifying (Hiph'il טוֹב) the "pillars" (מַצֵּבוֹת).[798] For Hosea worship and economics constitutes a vicious circle: prosperity leads to a more sophisticated worship which, represented here by altars and pillars, is in turn the trigger of more prosperity which again spurs the proliferation of syncretism and idolatry.[799] Theodore of Mopsuestia[800] writes: "Although they enjoyed many goods of the earth, they erected columns in place of them, for the worship of idols." Cyril of Alexandria:[801] "For on account of the multitude of the goods which were given to them, he showed their iniquity as a certain companion and well matched in struggle against God." Hosea does not condemn the cultic symbols in themselves but rather their misuse. When these symbols lose their "transparency" turning into a screen between God and his people they should be removed.[802]

Some scholars see in v. 2 an early interpretation of v. 1, using the same catchwords "altars" and "pillars."[803] Israel's heart is "divided" (חלק)[804] between Yahweh and the Cannanite idols (v. 2). Julian of Eclanum[805] interprets: "Namely, they have been separated from me by all thought, and have turned aside from the law-veneration by firm judgment." Jerome[806] writes: "Their heart is divided, namely the heart of the king and people, and when there is no excuse left, they will be destroyed and brought into eternal captivity; for as soon as the people separate from the king, ruin comes." Theodore of Mopsuestia[807] explains: "So great was their madness for idols, that their mind was divided in their zeal for idols, some eager to worship these idols, some eager to worship other ones." "Now" (עַתָּה) they are found guilty. Thus "he" (הוּא),⁸⁰⁸ i.e., Yahweh, will punish Israel by "wrecking" (ערף)⁸⁰⁹ the altars and "destroying" (שדד)⁸¹⁰ the pillars. According to Cyril of Alexandria,⁸¹¹ it is not the Lord who speaks but rather the king of Babylon. "For it happened that they burned the shrines to ashes along with the cities in Samaria and they plundered the carved images (γλυπτά)."

In v. 3 the author switches from worship to monarchy citing the Ephraimites who notice that they have no king for they did not "fear" (ירא)⁸¹² Yahweh. This last observation implies a sign of remorse on the people's part. At the same time, they realize that a king is of no help. One may add that the situation depicted here is similar to that described in 3:4 (i.e., absence of king and pillars). In 732 B.C. king Hoshea killed Pekah and acceded to the throne by paying tribute to Assyria (2 Kgs 15:30). Later, after the death of Tiglath-pileser III (727 B.C.), Hoshea would seek help from Egypt against Assyria. According to 2 Kgs 17:4, the north-Israelite king was captured and imprisoned by Shalmaneser V. Hosea's words in 10:3 refer probably to these events and it is not unlikely that Hosea observing the end of Pekah was able to foresee the conclusion of Hoshea's reign.⁸¹³ A similar interpretation is found in Jerome:⁸¹⁴ "Now they will say—when they are devastated, when they realize that Hoshea, the last king, is taken from them—therefore the king is taken from us because we did not fear the Lord, the true king." Theodoret of Cyrus⁸¹⁵ explains: "For we have had, they say, no aid from the king. We should trust in God, the one who deems us worthy of all providence; instead we trusted in men who speak no truth, the ones who always devise excuses, and make agreements now with these and now with those." Cyril of Alexandria⁸¹⁶ writes: "For those among them who obtained the thrones of the kingdom expected that the golden heifers and security from the other idols would suffice as help for them, even if they had no divine law, or they chose not to observe the precepts given through Moses. But the experience showed that they are liars." Similarly, Theodore of Mopsuestia[817] interprets: "For now they will perceive their thoughtlessness, by which they chose a king against God's will. And since they did not fear God and founded an invalid and illegal kingdom, against David's succession which ruled according to the divine promise, their kingdom will be taken away, and all of them will be handed over into captivity; they had no advantage from the king. Nevertheless, using guileful words, he [king Jeroboam I] made a wicked agreement with them, so they went away from God, and they worshipped the heifers manufactured by him."

Verse 4 answers Israel's previous question: "What can the king do for us?" (cf. v. 3). Hosea offers a detailed list of transgressions committed during the monarchic regime. "Words" mean empty speeches; "perjuries" refer to the enthronement's vows which were never fulfilled; and "agreements" point to the covenant made by the king with the people on the day of enthronement (2 Sam 3:21; 5:3).[818] The main responsibility of the king was to maintain a climate of "justice" (מִשְׁפָּט) among his subjects. Yet, due to the political instability, justice began to "sprout" (פָּרַח) like a "poisonous weed" (רֹאשׁ) along the furrows of the "field" (שָׂדַי).[819] This simile suggests a perverted justice.[820] Jerome[821] writes: "Say what you want, sigh for the old mistakes, promise to yourselves the prosperous things, which will turn into opposite things, make a covenant, by no means with God, but rather with the untruth. And then the covenant, which the Septuagint translates 'testament,' will produce, for you not rich crops of wheat, but not even fodder for beasts of burden, that is barley, not various leguminous plants, not vines which make their fruit sweat into new wine, the trees will not produce fruits which turn the moisture of the land into various savors; but rather bitterness will appear to you, nay, the judgment of bitterness, or ἄγρωστις, which we translate into Latin as brush. For this type of grass is similar to a reed which through several knots sends a shrub upwards and a root downwards, and again these shrubs and bushes are the seeds of another grass, and thus in a short time if it is not dry up from its deepest roots, it makes all the fields like thorn-bushes. Finally, even if somehow a part of it is dry, provided that it has a knot, and falls upon tilled land, it fills everything with brush." Julian of Eclanum[822] observes that "because he had noted that they did not sin by negligence but rather by dedicated zeal; he called furrows the marks in an arable field, in which the bitterness of judgment, that is, the severity of vengeance, will be born." Theodoret of Cyrus[823] writes: "Just as the wild grass grows abundantly in a untilled field, without the mattock digging or the plough furrowing, so easily the punishment will be inflicted by me upon you." Cyril of Alexandria[824] explains: "He, as a herb (ἄγρωστις), takes hold of the heifer, namely, the idols worshipped in the temple, which is in Bethel, for this means 'the house of On.' Again other interpreters rendered, 'the heifer of the house Bethel.' But the Septuagint translated the 'house of On' for the 'house of Bethel.' Although we explained the reason above, nevertheless it does not hurt to repeat. The Egyptians, for whom 'On' (Ὤν) means 'sun,' fabulated a myth about Apis, the Moon's son and the Son's grandson. The heifer made by Jeroboam was an image (τύπον) of the Egyptian Apis. Thus as an herb taking hold of and conquering any obstacle, he says, my judgment (κρίμα) will come upon the 'heifer of the house of On,' namely, Bethel."

The theme of worship returns in vv. 5, 6, 8. The "inhabitants" (שָׁכַן)[825] of Samaria (the royal capital of the Northern Kingdom)[826] "tremble" (גּוּר)[827] for the calf-idol set up by Jeroboam I in Bethel (= "Beth-aven": "house of wickedness"; cf. 4:15).[828] The text in 1 Kgs 12:26-33 mentions a second golden calf in the sanctuary of Dan which was probably destroyed or taken as a booty during 733 B.C. Assyrian invasion, hence Hosea's silence on Dan's calf (cf. 8:5-6).[829] The worship given to the calf-idol[830] at Bethel is described as "mourning" (אָבַל)[831] on the part of its "people" (עַם)[832] as well as of its "priests" (כְּמָרִים).[833] People and priests gather at Bethel to lament over the calf-idol. Usually this lamentation was merely symbolic for the "death" of the deity during the hot season; this time, the worshippers tremble for the fate of the calf-idol itself.[834] Theodoret of Cyrus[835] interprets: "Not only that they had no assistance from it [the idol], but also they wept and lamented over it even when they saw it covered with dishonor (ἀτιμία)." Cyril of Alexandria[836] writes: "And Israel lamented when they saw the one they thought was God dispatched [as a tribute].... 'And its people mourned for them.' To what does 'its' refer? Or is it clear that it refers to "On," i.e., to Apis? Nevertheless, he says, as they seemed to embitter and dishonor it by sending it to others, in the same way they will rejoice over its glory. For they think that it will be more glorious when it is worshipped by many nations."

The worshippers "exult" (גִּיל)[837] over the calf-idol for his "glory" (כָּבוֹד)[838] "departed" (גָּלָה)[839] "from him," i.e., from the idol. Probably this line refers to the difficult situation, after 731 B.C. (2 Kgs 17:3ff.; cf. 2 Kgs 18:16) when the golden overlay of the calf was used to pay the heavy tribute to Assyria.[840] Andersen and Freedman[841] draw attention to the wordplay between *yāgîlû* and *gālāh* as anticipating the time of exile. There is a real problem here by juxtaposing "mourning" with "exulting" if one opts for the historical interpretation. Jerome[842] explains that at the deportation of the golden calf "they [i.e., the priests] rejoiced for their fraud [i.e., replacement of the golden calf with bronze calves] would never be disclosed or discovered."

Verse 6 is a continuation of v. 5. "It itself" (אוֹתוֹ), i.e., the calf-idol not only "its glory," will be "borne" (יִבָּל)[843] to Assyria as a "gift" (מִנְחָה)[844] to the "great king" (מֶלֶךְ יָרֵב).[845] As a conclusion, Hosea states that Ephraim/Israel will be "ashamed" (בּוֹשׁ) of her "plan" (עֵצָה). Israel's "plan" refers probably to the strategy of Jeroboam I to divert the attention of his subjects from the temple in Jerusalem to the two sanctuaries (Bethel and Dan) and the golden calves he set up in them.[846] Theodoret of Cyrus[847] interprets: "For when they saw its weakness, they made it in a cast, and brought it as a gift to the king of the Egyptians, pleading with them for help; but they will not enjoy any assistance from there." Cyril of Alexandria[848] explains: "The heifer was taken from Israel, and after they bound it up (the word is witty), they carried it away as a gift of friendship (ξένια) to king Iarim, that is, the Avenger. For he was invited to help, as if to revenge Samaria which was utterly destroyed by the Syrians. And Phul received the heifer as a gift from Ephraim; he calls the king of Israel Ephraim."

The theme of monarchy returns in v. 7 with the prophetic announcement that Samaria, the royal capital, is "destroyed" (נִדְמָה),[849] and her king[850] (a reference to the last monarch Hoshea ben Elah) helplessly carried away "like foam (קֶצֶף)[851] upon water." Jerome[852] explains: "Just as foam, which is upon the water, is quickly dissolved, so the kingship of the ten tribes quickly will come to an end; and the high places, that is 'bamoth,' will perish." Similarly, Julian of Eclanum[853] writes: "The king, that is his kingdom, they have compelled to be destroyed of quick end; thus, as the foam swims upon the currents of water so the impiety and dignity of the people slip away." According to Theodore of Mopsuestia,[854] the prophet refers here to both the king and people brought into captivity by the Assyrians. Theophylact of Bulgaria[855] interprets: "The kingdom will be easily (ῥᾳδίως) taken from Samaria, as a light chip of wood swept away by the water. Or he calls the king a calf, which they easily sent to the Assyrians, as he said." For Cyril of Alexandria[856] the "king" is another name for the calf-idol of Samaria: "Therefore he says, the Samaritans threw the heifer away, to which they gave divine and royal honors. It was thrown like a chip of wood (κάρφος) gliding in the whirlings of the waters, and then it would be carried by their force to any place whatever." This line hints at the end of king Hoshea who was captured and imprisoned by Shalmaneser V (2 Kgs 17:4).

Verse 8 focuses again on the syncretistic worship of Israel. The "high places" (בָּמוֹת), whose cult was probably described by Hosea in 4:11-13,[857] are labeled here "high places of wickedness (אָוֶן)." This characterization hints at the derogatory name of Bethel, Beth-aven "house of wickedness" (10:5; cf. Am 5:5f.), and indirectly to the calf-idol venerated there. Since the idol of Bethel was brought as tribute to Assyria (v. 6), the high places, "Israel's sin," will be "destroyed" (שׁמד)[858] and Israel's altars will be invaded by thorns and thistles. Left without king, capital, and worship, the Israelites will beg for death, pleading with the mountains ("Cover us!") and hills ("Fall on us!") in order to escape Yahweh's fury foretold by the series of events depicted in vv. 5ff. The last line of this verse is quoted by Jesus with respect to the dread of the last days (Lk 23:30; cf. Rev 6:16). Jerome[859] interprets: "Therefore, whatever is said against the ten tribes or against all Israel, let us know that τυπικῶς may be applied to the entire people, so when the Romans seized Jerusalem, and destroyed the Temple, or when the day of judgment has come, so that others mistrust and, seized with great fear, say 'to the mountains: cover us over; and to the hills: fall upon us,' wishing more to die than to see the things which will bring the death." Similarly, Theodore of Mopsuestia[860] writes: "Since they were under these, they will desire to endure a quick destruction, than to suffer one punishment after another." Cyril of Alexandria[861] wittily remarks that the mountains and hills upon which the Israelites set up their idols eventually will become their tombs.

13. Gibeah and Beth-arbel (10:9-15)

9. Since the days of Gibeah you[862] have sinned, O Israel! There they have remained. Shall war not overtake the sons of wrong[863] in Gibeah? 10. I have come[864] to chastise[865] them. Peoples shall be assembled against them when they are chastised[866] for their double iniquity.[867] 11. And Ephraim was a trained heifer that loved to thresh. When I passed by her fine neck, I wanted to harness[868] Ephraim, Judah would plow,[869] Jacob would harrow[870] for himself. 12. "Sow for yourselves according to righteousness, and reap according to mercy.[871] Break up the fallow ground of knowledge[872] and seek[873] Yahweh until the fruit[874] of righteousness comes to you." 13. You have ploughed wickedness, you have reaped injustice, you have eaten the fruit of lies. Because you have trusted in your chariots,[875] in the multitude of your warriors, 14. tumult of war shall arise[876] among your people, and all your fortresses shall be destroyed, as Shalman's[877] destruction of Beth-arbel[878] on the day of battle, when mother was dashed over sons. 15. Thus it shall be done[879] to you, O Bethel,[880] because

of your great[881] wickedness. At dawn the king of Israel shall be completely silenced.

This section is clearly delimited with respect to both the previous pericope (10:1-8) and the next section (11:1-11). The simile of Ephraim as a heifer within the farming imagery (vv. 11-13a) is intercalated between two units centered on the theme of a destructive war (vv. 9-10, 13b-15) and built around two toponyms (Gibeah: v. 9; and Beth-arbel: 14). The use of name "Israel" in the beginning and end (vv. 9, 15) and nowhere else in between adds to the internal unity of this section.[882] The central theme, the "war" (מִלְחָמָה) (vv. 9, 14; the term is nowhere else used by Hosea) as a consequence for sins,[883] may be considered another sign of unity.

As for the place where this unit was delivered, Samaria is perhaps the best choice given the hint at the leaders of the royal court in vv. 13-15. As for dating, the prophet begins this pericope with the same words he ended section 9:1-9 "days of Gibeah." Taking into account that for a while Hosea withdrew into his disciples' circle (cf. 9:10-10:8), one may conclude that 10:9-15 (addressed to a larger audience, i.e., "Israel," vv. 9, 14) dates to the period following Hosea's withdrawal, i.e., after 733 B.C. (His withdrawal did not last so very long given the same expression "days of Gibea" found in 9:9 and 10:9.)[884]

In v. 9 the past is mentioned as a lesson for the present. The phrase "days of Gibeah" (cf. 9:9)[885] refers to the crime of the Benjamites against the traveling Levite, followed by the near extermination of the Benjamine tribe by the confederation of Israel's tribes (cf. Jud 19-21). This is also Julian of Eclanum's[886] interpretation: "The reproach seems to be the same against those who sinned by incestuous obscenity and who considered their spiritual men foolish and senseless persons. Therefore, the captivity will be violent in the likeness of that destruction which had almost destroyed the Benjamites by extermination." For Theodoret of Cyrus,[887] the word "hills" (LXX: βουνοῖς) refers to Israel's capital transgression, idolatry, paralleled by apostasy from God. On the other hand, Cyril of Alexandria[888] sees here an allusion to Jeroboam I who set up two golden calves at Bethel and Dan, along with a whole host of idols on the mountains and hills of Samaria. They "remained" (עָמָדוּ) there, in Gibeah, in terms of sinfulness; they "remained unchanged" (cf. Lev 13:5; Jer 48:11; Dan 10:17);[889] "they persevered in error," explains Jerome.[890] Theodore of Mopsuestia[891] writes: "'They stood there.' The punishment put an end to their lawbreaking (παρανομία). 'It will not seize them on the hill' (= LXX). For captivity will deprive them of the zeal for the hills, nor will they any longer be found in the worship which they had in the hills, for they will be occupied with captivity's distresses." Cyril of Alexandria[892] explains: "'They stood there,' i.e., just as they say or at least think, worshipping the carved images (γλυπτοῖς) 'there,' they had the surety of health and happiness and that they stood upon stable goods." The people's present sin is only a repetition of the past transgression that occurred in Gibeah. For the sins committed unceasingly, the "sons of wrong" (emended text: בְּנֵי עַוְלָה),[893] Hosea's contemporaries will be overtaken by the "war" (מִלְחָמָה), the same way the wicked Benjamites have experienced the war in the "days of Gibeah." The shift from the second person to the third person with respect to Israel in the same verse is a Hosean feature (cf. 8:1-14).[894]

Verse 10 shows that the foreign "peoples" (עַמִּים for foreign nations; cf. 7:8; 9:1) gathered against Israel, as once the tribes against Benjamin (cf. Judg 20:8-11), are only the instrument of divine judgment; the real author of this judgment is Yahweh himself who solemnly declares that he came "to chastise" (יסר) his people. For Hosea,

Yahweh works in an invisible yet efficient way through concrete historical events. This theological interpretation of history is similar to that found in Isaiah (10:5).[895] The "double iniquity (עֲוֹן; Qere)" mentioned in v. 10 may be a reference to the past and present history of Israel tainted with injustice and violence.[896] Jerome[897] interprets: "Two injustices, for first they sinned in the idols of Micah, secondly in the calves of Jeroboam. Or certainly we are able to designate the two injustices of Samaria in Bethel and Dan, about which prophet Jeremiah speaks: 'My people have committed two evils; they have forsaken the fountain of living water, and have dug out for themselves worthless cistern that can hold no water' [Jer 2:13]. These two injustices are against the two precepts of the Decalogue, in which it is said: 'I am the Lord your God; you shall have no other gods before me.'" Theophylact of Bulgaria[898] explains: "They abandoned me, their benefactor, and they ran to the senseless and useless idols."

Verses 11-13a use agricultural terminology to present a tense relationship between Yahweh and his people.

In v. 11 Ephraim is likened to a "trained heifer" (עֶגְלָה מְלֻמָּדָה)[899] willing to thresh. If we take into account the fact that "Eglah" (עֶגְלָה) "heifer" was a favored female name (cf. David's wife; 2 Sam 3:5), by painting Ephraim as a "heifer," Yahweh expresses his genuine love for his people. The "threshing" (דוּשׁ) in the case of Ephraim does not imply a threshing sledge, but rather it should be viewed as simple activity of a heifer walking freely over the straw to be threshed. Yet, when God intended to harness that free heifer for more difficult and productive work in Canaan, he passed by the "beauty" (טוּב) of her neck (i.e., "her fine neck"), namely, he discovered that she could do more than threshing.[900] This was the very moment of Israel's election which occurred in the wilderness. Jerome[901] explains: "Since Ephraim does not want to accept the yoke of the law, I will pass over and mount upon the beauty of his neck, so that the obstinate and lewd cow may learn to work which it does not want. On the other hand, Judah will plough of her own will, for she has a temple; and she remains in law, so that all twelve tribes may eagerly prepare the fields for sowing." Theodoret of Cyrus[902] writes: "He [Ephraim] is compared to a heifer which does not accept the yoke, but who struggles against it." "Similarly, Theodore of Mopsuestia[903] explains: "Like a heifer which leaps away and desires to prevail over those who are trying to tame it, he [Ephraim] thus is revolting from God and does not yield to the yoke of the slavery.... I will dismiss Judah who is being tested by evils giving him no help at all." A different interpretation is found in Julian of Eclanum:[904] "I, he says, will break Ephraim's so far proud neck, so that the teacher and benefactor whom he despised, he at last may experience as avenger. Truly, pleasing success will not put away my judgment. For, however, much destruction subdues them, he will heal others through their example." "Harnessing" Ephraim may be an allusion to the promulgation of the Law on Mt. Sinai.[905] In Hos 9:10 election is described again in terms of a surprising discovery: Yahweh finds Israel as "grapes" in the wilderness. If "Ephraim" and "Judah" designate the two kingdoms, "Jacob" seems to be a generic title of the people of Israel. The three names are circumscribed by three agricultural activities: Ephraim is harnessed to thresh, Judah plows, and Jacob harrows.

Verse 12 continues the agricultural imagery by showing what kind of activity Israel had to perform once settled in Canaan. The emphasis falls on the relationship between Israel's work and God's gifts, which will eventually bring fruitfulness. Therefore "sowing" (זִרְעוּ) had to be done according to "righteousness" (צְדָקָה) and "reaping" (קִצְרוּ) in reference to "mercy" (חֶסֶד).[906] Theophylact of

Bulgaria[907] writes: "'Sow for yourselves.' For you are not of use to God but to yourselves. He calls 'righteousness' the true worship of God. For it is just to give worship to the Creator and Author and not to the idols." Jerome[908] explains: "Then he warns that they should sow for themselves through penitence, and sow in justice, that is in law, and reap in mercy, that is in grace of the gospel." "Breaking up the fallow ground" means ploughing an uncultivated, abonded land. More specifically, Israel is asked to plough the land of "knowledge"[909] and "to seek (דרש) Yahweh"; the last phrase indicates complete dependence on God. Theodore of Mopsuestia[910] interprets: "Until the time comes, seek after the knowledge of the truth, before the time of punishment, repenting to the extent possible in order to profit from the experience of evils." Thus, Israel's quest for righteousness, mercy and God implies a great deal of patience and persistence, "until the fruit of righteousness" reaches the diligent farmer. "Righteousness" is the result of an intense cooperation between people's fervent search and God's benevolent intervention in history.

As one can notice from v. 13, Israel failed to fulfill Yahweh's request. Instead of sowing righteousness, the people planted "wickedness" (רֶשַׁע), and in place of mercy, they reaped "injustice" (עַוְלָתָה). Thus they will feed on the fruit of "lies" (כַּחַשׁ) instead of the fruit of righteousness. Israel became the victim of her own false hopes and illusions. Theodoret of Cyrus[911] explains: "'False food' (βρῶσιν ψευδῆ) means empty hope. For though you trusted in the multitude of soldiers and in chariots, you got no use from them." Similarly, Cyril of Alexandria[912] writes: "'They ate the fruit of deception,' namely, they had a useless and senseless hope. For the true fruit is the one that can save and help, the love toward God, and the glory of righteousness. On the contrary, the false fruit would reasonably be considered impiety for in the end it altogether descends to what is abominable (τὸ ἀπευκτόν)."

Verse 13b shows of what these illusions consist: Israel "trusted" (בטח)[913] in their chariots[914] and "warriors" (גִּבּוֹרִים)[915] more than in Yahweh the Savior (cf. 8:14). The chariots were a powerful weapon especially in the Neo-Assyrian times. From the "Monolith-Inscription" (Sixth Year) of Shalmaneser III we learn that Israel of the king Ahab (middle of the ninth century B.C.) had almost 2,000 chariots and 10,000 foot soldiers.[916] Sargon II, who captured Samaria in 721 B.C., succeeded in seizing 50 Israelite chariots.[917] Jerome[918] writes: "Because, O Ephraim, you have relied upon the ways of your idolatry; for these are your ways: having hope not in God, but in the multitude of your forces and the might of the army."

In these circumstances marked by people's lack of trust in Yahweh, the war became unavoidable (v. 14). Jerome[919] interprets: "Therefore an uproar shall rise in the midst of your people, which in Hebrew is 'saon' [i.e., שָׁאוֹן], that is the noise and rushing of a howling army, and all your fortifications will be devastated by those who shout aloud." This line may be an allusion to the reign of Hoshea when what remained from the Northern Kingdom rebelled against Assyria. Israel's fortresses crumbling under the enemy's attacks echoes Beth-arbel's destruction by Shalman. The image of the mother "dashed" (רטש)[920] over sons represents the climax of such gloomy picture. The ancient Christian interpreters[921] identified Shalman with Zalmunna the king of Madian in the time of Gideon the judge (Judg 8:5). Some modern scholars took Shalman as an abbreviation of Shalmaneser V (727-722 B.C.) and the entire line as a reference to the attack on Samaria in 722 B.C. This date is too late for Hosea's prophetic ministry. More probably the conqueror of Beth-arbel should be identified with Salamanu of Moab who paid tribute to Tiglath-pileser III.[922] If Beth-arbel is the same as *Irbid* in Gilead, 12 miles north-west of Tell Ramit (Ramoth of Gilead) then the episode mentioned here could have been one of the border skirmishes in Transjordan (cf. Am 2:1-3).[923]

Verse 15 is a conclusion to this section. The destruction of Israel, here represented by Bethel[924] in parallel with Beth-arbel, is caused by her "great wickedness," a reference to Israel's overconfidence in military resources. According to Jerome,[925] Bethel, the "house of the idol," alludes to the golden calf set up by Jeroboam I. In addition, the king himself will be silenced at dawn, i.e., at the beginning of battle (cf. 1 Sam 11:9-11; Is 17:4). Historically, this line points to king Hoshea who was taken prisoner by Shalmaneser V prior to the fall of Samaria (cf. 2 Kgs 17:4). For Julian of Eclanum,[926] the dramatic end of the Israelite monarchy was determined by its very beginning when the people wanted to have a king "by analogy with the neighboring nations, without God's assistance." Theodoret of Cyrus[927] writes: "By these words he designated the immediacy (τὸ σύντομον) of the destruction. For the dawn lasts for a short time, then the rising of the sun produces the day." Cyril of Alexandria[928] interprets: "The rest of the translations, as well as the Hebrew text clearly said, 'They were thrown away like the early morning,' meaning by this, exactly as in a short time, or suddenly and without warning or preparation, Israel fell away from the intimacy (οἰκειότητος) with God. Indeed the time of the dawn is very short.... That is why like the dawn, that is, in a little, brief, and very much compacted span of time, the leaders were altogether rejected." Theophylact of Bulgaria[929] writes: "The king of Israel was cast out, namely he was exiled to Babylon [Assyria!]. He was cast out also [means] namely the Kingdom of Samaria came to an end." Jerome[930] explains: "He compares the king with a foam and bubbles floating on the top of the waters which promptly are dissolved.... For as the breaking of the dawn, the daybreak or beginning of the day, which is called morning, passes through the vicinity of dark and light, just as the night ends and the day grows bright, so the king of Israel, i.e., the ten tribes, will quickly pass."

14. God's Tenderness (11:1-11)

1. When[931] Israel was young, I loved him; out[932] of Egypt I called my son.[933] 2. The more I[934] called them, the more they went away from me.[935] They sacrificed to Baals, to idols they have burnt incense. 3. I myself taught[936] Ephraim to walk; [I][937] took them in my[938] arms, but they did not perceive that I cared for them. 4. With human cords[939] I drew them, with ropes of love. I was to them like those who lift[940] an infant[941] to their cheeks; I bent down to him that I might feed[942] him.[943] 5. He returns[944] to the land[945] of Egypt, but Assyria is his king! For they refuse to return [to me]. 6. The sword whirls[946] in his cities, it destroys the bars of their gates,[947] and devours[948] because of their plots. 7. My people are bent[949] on apostasy from me.[950] To Baal[951] they call,[952] but he does not raise them up[953] at all.[954] 8. How can I give you up, O Ephraim? surrender you,[955] O Israel? How can I make you like Admah? treat you like Zeboiim? My heart turns itself against me, my remorse[956] burns intensively.[957] 9. I will not execute my burning anger, I will not again destroy Ephraim. For I am God and not a man, the Holy One in your midst, I will not come into the city.[958] 10. After Yahweh they shall go; like a lion he shall roar. When he roars the sons shall come trembling from the sea.[959] 11. They shall come trembling like a bird from Egypt, like a dove from the land of Assyria, and I

shall return them[960] to their houses. Saying of Yahweh.

The same interest for historical past—an explanatory lesson for the present—marking this pericope may be found throughout Hosean writing. But chapter 11 represents a "review" of everything said previously on this topic. God reveals the goal of all his pedagogical interventions in Israel's history.[961]

There is no other Old Testament passage to match chapter 11 in terms of intensity of the metaphor Yahweh as a loving father willing to forgive and forget Israel his beloved son no matter how many times he had upset the father by transgressing.

Thematically, this chapter is close to chapters 2 and 3 since in both of them Yahweh shows his persistent love toward Israel. But if in these two previous chapters Israel's repentance plays a key role in her restoration, in chapter 11 the emphasis falls almost exclusively on God's love which alone and above all can save an idolatrous people from its ruin. Thus chapter 11 more resembles 14:4/3 where God's healing love is again foremost.[962]

The section 11:1-11, whose literary unity is secured by the presence of נְאֻם יהוה "saying of Yahweh" (v. 11), may be divided into four small units: 1-4 Yahweh's love and Israel's faithlessness in the past; 5-7 Israel's present rebellion and imminent exile; 8-9 God's suffering overwhelmed by his unconditional love; 10-11: Israel's return from captivity, an act of divine mercy.

Since there is no sign of disputation, these sayings seem to have been delivered in the inner circle of Hosea's disciples so interested in both past and future history of Israel. The most probable date of the passage is the first part of Shalmaneser's reign (727-722 B.C.) when Israel sought assistance in Egypt to rebel against Assyria (2 Kgs 17:4).[963]

Verse 1a describes Israel as a "lad" (נַעַר),[964] a dependent person (Gen 18:7; 1 Kgs 3:7; Jer 1:6), whereas v. 1b names it Yahweh's "son" (בֵּן) (cf. Exod 4:22: Israel—Yahweh's "firstborn" [בְּכוֹר]; Deut 14:1: בָּנִים "sons," of the Israelites; Is 43:6; Jer 3:14; Mal 3:17). Hosea switches here from the metaphor of "wife" (chapters 2 and 3) to that of "son." The portrayal of Yahweh as a father to Israel is also found in Deuteronomy (4:37; 7:8; 10:15; 23:6). In Hosea the emphasis falls on the historical aspect of this fatherly love; thus there is nothing mythological in the relationship between God and his people. The Exodus event from Egypt is the sheer expression of Yahweh's love (אהב) toward Israel. The people's election which coincides with the Exodus-event is an act of love, the very first in a long series. Cyril of Alexandria[965] interprets: "Because I loved him, for this reason I took his children out of the Egyptians' arrogance (πλεονεξίας). 'For I will show mercy upon thousands who love me' [Exod 20:6]. Why were they honored and chosen for the sake of their fathers? Why were they honored with the grace of freedom and released from slavery and hardships? They were not honored, were they? They have not through their good will (εὐνοίαις), being zealous, sought to gladden the protecting God, have they? Not at all, he says. For they ran away from the Master; they went away from the one who honored them; they cursed and insulted the one who called them." Theodore of Mopsuestia[966] explains: "He calls Israel a child (νήπιον) from the period when they were in Egypt, at which point Israel began to unite together and to enjoy the divine care (ἐπιμελείας). For, he says, I was at once the first one to take position and bring forth great providence (πρόνοιαν) so that I might draw them out of Egypt." Theodoret of Cyrus[967] applies these words to Israel's present behavior: "Because of lack of understanding and childish intelligence, he says, they endure such a punishment." "Calling" (קרא) is an election term which means "summon into a relation."[968] One may add that Yahweh has the initiative by choosing Israel as partner of communion.

The New Testament application of Hos 11:1b in Mt 2:15 concerns the return of Jesus, Mary and Joseph from Egypt. One might add that Matthew did not use the Septuagint version (τὰ τέκνα αὐτοῦ "his children"), but rather a Hebrew manuscript which had the singular "my son" (cf. MT: בְּנִי). Jerome[969] explained: "There is no doubt that from this place Matthew took testimony in accordance with the Hebrew truth (version) (*Hebraicam veritatem*). Thus the ones who deride our interpretation let them give the scripture, from which the evangelist took this testimony and interpreted as referring to the Lord Savior, when he was brought back from Egypt to the land of Israel." To Julian the Apostate (fourth century A.D.) who accused Matthew of playing around with the Gentiles' ignorance when he applied Hos 11:1, initially concerning Israel as a people, to Jesus of Nazareth, the learned writer responded: "Matthew was the first to produce the Gospel in Hebrew because they would not be able to read it unless they were Hebrews." Thus Matthew did not do it to ridicule the Gentiles. He only saw in Jesus the Messiah who fulfilled typologically Hos 11:1 by recapitulating Israel's history.[970] Jerome goes on, observing: "In fact this refers to Israel which is called out of Egypt, which is loved, which in that time after the error of idolatry is summoned somewhat like an infant or a child; yet perfectly is referred to Christ. For also Isaac was in the image of Christ because he had carried on himself the wood of future death.... However, one cannot accept that everything which the ones who partially (*ex parte*) were types of the Lord Savior are said to have done was done in his type. For the type represents a part; if a type surpasses the whole, then this is not a type, but rather a historical truth." In the same vein of typology, Theophylact of Bulgaria[971] observes: "But Christ himself is said to be Israel (for he saw God: 'For no one has seen the Father except the one who is from God' [Jn 1:18]). Accordingly, he became an infant and the Father called him, the truly beloved, out of Egypt."

In v. 2 the first example of Israel's past disobedience is introduced. God's later acts of providence are seen as a renewal of election.[972] To God's repeated invitations to communion, Israel used to respond by acts of apostasy, worshipping Baals (i.e., "sacrificing" and "burning incense").[973] The plural "Baals" may refer to either a multiplicity of Canaanite deities or various manifestations of a single god, Baal (e.g., Baal-peor, Num 25; Hos 9:10).[974] Julian of Eclanum[975] observes that the Israelites dedicated themselves to the "worship of various idols who were to be served with different rituals." For Jerome,[976] this line refers to all Israel's encounters with idolatry starting with the Baal-peor episode before the conquest of the promised land. Cyril of Alexandria[977] explains: "But the Israelites followed the Egyptian errors, not knowing yet the true God, i.e., me; rather they learned how to sacrifice to the Baalim, i.e., the idols, by offering incence to the carved images, i.e., to the objects which the native populace worshipped." Theophylact of Bulgaria[978] writes: "'Baalim,' as it is often said, designates the idols of Baal: carved images of other gods. He shows their madness, for while they abandoned him who liberated them from Egypt, they worshipped those [idols]. He reveals his own kindness from what follows." The word פְּסִלִים "idols" derives from a root פסל meaning "to hew, carve," hence any carved or hewn image (e.g., the "golden calf," Exod 32 in the past, or the "calf of Samaria," [Hos 8:6] in Hosea's day).

Verses 3-4 describe in anthropomorphic language

Yahweh's fatherly care (רפא)⁹⁷⁹ toward Israel. Yahweh as a loving father teaches his son to walk. When the son gets tired, the father takes him in his arms. But in spite of this care, Israel behaves as a prodigal son disregarding his father's love. Based on the Septuagint reading, Cyril of Alexandria⁹⁸⁰ interprets: "But, because I am kind (χρηστός) and good (ἀγαθὸς), I bound the feet (συνεπόδισα) of Ephraim, that is, the whole Israel (as it is obvious there from the reference to one tribe), although he was awkward. He himself declares why this is so: 'I will take them in my arms.' This image is from child-raising. For those who take infants in their arms, are those who bind their feet, bringing their feet together. For it is necessary, I think, that the thighs and knees of anyone who sits down should be drawn together. And in fact this is, 'I bound the feet,' as, for instance, it is written about Abraham, when he bound (συνεπόδισεν) his son Isaac, when he thought to bring him as a sacrifice to God. One must note that the Hebrew version and other versions do not have 'I bound the feet' but rather 'I became as one who nourishes (τιθηνὸς) Ephraim.'" Theodore of Mopsuestia⁹⁸¹ explains differently the Septuagint rendition συνεπόδιασα 'I bound the feet': "In my care, I will gather together those scattered under Egypt's hardships. 'And I will take him in my arms.' And according to my power I considered him worthy of [my] care." Theophylact of Bulgaria⁹⁸² writes: "I also acted thus, and as if binding their feet, that is drawing together the feet, I took him up to my right hand. This means that I did not allow them to move disorderly and lawlessly, but bound their movements by giving them a law, and I granted them my arm, that is, my power, as an ally in battles, which will carry their weakness."

Verse 4 continues the metaphor of v. 3. The father uses now cords and ropes as he keeps on teaching his son to walk. These devices have a double purpose, on the one hand they give the child more confidence in himself, and on the other hand they assist the father in directing and guiding his son. During the training sessions, the father lifts the infant up to his cheeks in a sign of tenderness. Then letting him down, he bends to feed him. Historically, these verses refer to the period of Israel's journey through the wilderness "where you have seen how Yahweh your God bore you as a man bears his son, in all the way that you went until you came to this place" (Deut 1:31). Yahweh bends down to the level of his partner guiding him by "human" (אָדָם)[983] and "loving" (אהב) means, a clear example of divine condescension. While providing the wandering Israel with food (*manna*: Exod 16; and "quails": Num 11), Yahweh is always attentive to his son's spiritual needs. Through laws and precepts, Yahweh lifts Israel up to his face. Jerome[984] interprets: "And as the lover of humankind, I will draw them to believing in cords of love, just as that which is written in the Gospel: 'No one comes to me unless the Father who sent me will have drawn him.' But they thought that my light yoke was very heavy; and I bent toward them leaving the kingdom of heaven, so that I may eat with them, having assumed the human form, or rather I gave them my body as food, I was both food and table companion." Theophylact of Bulgaria[985] explains: "'I stretched them out in the cords of my love.' The one who intends to bind someone's hands stretches them out for binding. He also says this here 'I stretched them out' for 'I prepared them' and I made them fit to be bound by my love."

Verses 5-7 point to Israel's present rebellion described in terms of political alliances and apostasy/idolatry. Israel's "return" (שוב) to Egypt alludes to king Hoshea's change in foreign politics. During the reign of Shalmaneser V (727-722 B.C.), Hoshea stopped paying tribute to Assyria and sent messengers to Egypt requesting military assistance in his bid for freedom (2 Kgs 17:4). Yet, despite his political maneuvers, warns the prophet, Assyria is still Israel's "king" (מֶלֶךְ)⁹⁸⁶ or the suzerain power; and this because Israel "refused" (מֵאֵן) to return in repentance to Yahweh. One may note the word-play on the root שׁוּב "to return" which appears again in the word "apostasy" (מְשׁוּבָה) (v. 7). Based on the Septuagint reading, Cyril of Alexandria⁹⁸⁷ interprets: "After he left behind, he says, the land that carried him as a booty, the wholly wretched Ephraim made the land of the Egyptians as his own [land], since he feared the calamities of war. But he became subject to Assur [Assyria] himself, and he placed his neck under foreign scepters.... For we will dwell (κατοικήσομεν) in Egypt, that is, we will be entirely and altogether immigrants and wanderers, not because we gave up the land which is percieved by the senses and moved to another land, but we gave up the portion of the holy ones. We will be under Assur [Assyria], namely, the ruler of this age [Jn 12:31]. To him we will be servants and captives, listening to his will, because our sword is weak and laid to rest."

The punishment upon Israel for designing these "plots" (מֹעֵצוֹת) instead of trusting God is a widespread, devastating war whose description is as brief as colorful: the Assyrian "sword" (חֶרֶב) "whirls" (חוּל) through cities, destroying the gates' "bars of gates" (בַּד)⁹⁸⁸ and devouring everything on its way. Verse 6 may refer to the campaign of Shalmaneser V against Israel (2 Kgs 17:4-5) which concluded with Hoshea's imprisonment and a three-year siege of Samaria.

In the midst of such a tragic situation the people do not become wise and do not return to Yahweh because they are unable to do so; they are "bent" (תלא) or addicted to "apostasy" (מְשׁוּבָה) (v. 7). Thus they "call" (קרא) to

Baal, but he does not "raise" (Po'lel רום) them up. There are two ironies here: Yahweh "calls" Israel repeatedly but they do not pay attention; this time they "call" Baal but he gives no answer. Second, Yahweh "lifts" (Hiph'il רום) his child up to his face tenderly embracing him (v. 4) while Baal is incapable of such a genuine love toward Israel. Based on the Septuagint reading, Theodore of Mopsuestia[989] explains: "For they will not remain in their own habitation (οἰκήσεως), nor will they have a safe abode on the spot, because they are all as hanging with no base; Assyria will bring into captivity the multitude she seized."

Verses 8-9 shed a few glimpses into the mystery of God. Yahweh has to solve a serious dilemma: Israel is guilty and thus she is going to be punished in the same way the ancient cities of Admah and Zeboiim were punished;[990] yet Yahweh loves his people with a fatherly love. It is the infinite, overwhelming love of God which finally triumphs. God's inner struggle is described almost dramatically: God's heart (i.e., emotions, feelings) "turns" (Niph'al הפך) against his just decision to punish the apostate people (cf. 10:8, 14-15). God's "remorse" (נחומים) (cf. Is 57:18; Zech 1:13) over his decision to punish "burns intensively" (Niph'al כמר); in the end his justified "burning anger" is fully replaced by the covenantal love for his people (v. 8). As Hosea who, at God's command, receives back his adulterous wife (chapters 2 and 3), likewise Yahweh is willing utterly to forgive his faithless people. Jerome[991] interprets: "Whenever he wanted to carry out his harsh and even cruel sentence, parental compassion prevailed, and he softens the severity of judgment with fatherly love.... It displeased me to blot my people out for good; for that reason I will not act according to the passion of my anger, nor will I be charged entirely from my compassion in order to ruin Ephraim.

For I do not smite to destroy for good, but rather to correct. My cruelty is an opportunity for penitence and piety. For 'I am God and not man.' Whereas a man punishes to destroy, God reproaches to emend." Theodoret of Cyrus[992] writes: "He imitates the father and the mother, who are by nature thrown into great confusion and for the most part unable to turn away from their children. But he says these words, not because now he wants this, and then he changes his mind, but rather he constructs his speech for wrath and love, for punishment and compassion, terrifying through the former, and persuading through the latter." Cyril of Alexandria[993] explains: "But I will not do this [i.e., destroy Ephraim], he says, though justly it should be done; but rather I will go to the other side (for I have changed my mind), and I will not use excessive wrath; I will not destroy Ephraim entirely even though he became wicked. For what reason? Did they not deserve to suffer this? Yes, he says, but I am God, not a man, that is to say, good, not one conceding victory to the angry emotions, for such passion is merely human. Why therefore do you chastise, he says, if you are God, who are not overcome by anger, but rather who follow the gentleness in your nature? I chastise, he says, for I am not only good as God but, in addition, I am also holy so that I hate iniquities and I turn back the defiled, I reject God's haters, and I make the sinner repent and cleanse the impure so that he may be again united with me."

Since Israel is unable to return in repentance to Yahweh, the latter takes the initiative revealing himself as a "merciful" (רַחוּם) and "gracious" (חַנּוּן) God (cf. Exod 34:6). Thus the divine partner goes beyond his wounded love and "returns" ("repents") to forgiveness.[994] Yahweh will not destroy Ephraim and the reason for such a radical decision is that he is "God not man" (cf. Ezek 28:2), the "Holy One" (קָדוֹשׁ) in Israel's midst. "Holy" probably points to the fact that God is "completely sovereign over his own actions."⁹⁹⁵ In any event, this is the great paradox of God of Israel. Although "holy" (i.e., transcendent in essence; cf. basic meaning of root קדשׁ "to cut, separate"), he is at the same time "Yahweh" (i.e., personally present in his people's history; cf. the meaning of the tetragrammaton יהוה "He is"). The conclusion of this small unit, Yahweh "will not come into the city," underscores the idea that God is circumscribed by no human structure (v. 9). Jerome⁹⁹⁶ explains: "I am not one of those who dwell in the cities, who live by human laws, who take cruelty for justice, for whom the supreme wickedness is the supreme authority; but my law and my justice is to save those who are reformed. But we may say differently: since Cain, the first murderer, built a city in the name of his son Enoch, in which sort of city, made of violence, blood, and murder, the Lord would not enter." Julian of Eclanum⁹⁹⁷ takes a critical position against Jerome who considers Cain the father of urban life and Hosea's saying an absolute indictment of this type of life: "Who considered such an interpretation without deriding? For our God, saying that he would not enter the city, did not express horror for all the cities in general, about which we read: 'The Lord loves the gates of Zion more than any dwelling-place in Jacob,' and 'God will not be agitated in her midst: he will judge her by her own face' [Ps 87:2]." For Julian, God's promise that he will not enter the city should be understood within the context where one mentions "the Sodomites and the neighboring cities, which we read in Genesis [Gen 19], that he [God] entered in order to destroy." Thus any appearance of the Holy One in a sinful city spells judgment and punishment. Cyril of Alexandria⁹⁹⁸ has a different interpretation: "And Judah proclaims: 'I will not enter the city,' namely, I will have God as a town-wall; I will make the hope in him an assurance; I will run under the right hand of the Savior. He alone will suffice for my salvation. I confess the entirely purposeless and useless expectation, given the war overrunning the land, that I will be saved should it enter the city. Therefore 'I will not enter the city.'" Theodoret of Cyrus[999] writes: "For I will not get angry like a human being, he says, nor will I remember for the most part the evil deeds. For I, God, am holy, and appear in the things around you, and I am superior to all earthly things; I am not forced like human beings to dwell in a place, but I am present everywhere and I am present for all."[1000]

Verses 10-11 deal with Israel's future, i.e., the return from captivity. Yahweh is compared with a "lion" (אַרְיֵה; cf. שַׁחַל another word for "lion" in 5:14; 13:7) at whose powerful "roaring" voice (שָׁאַג; cf. Am 1:2; 3:8) the "sons" (בָּנִים) (i.e., the Israelites; cf. "my son" v. 1) shall come from the "sea" (יָם), i.e., from the west (a reference to a deportation on the coastlands; cf. Is 11:11) and "go after" Yahweh. The phrase "going after a deity" means to take part in a cultic procession. The new exodus of Israel is depicted as a procession headed by Yahweh himself (cf. Is 40:3; 43:1; 48:20).[1001] For Jerome,[1002] "sons of the sea" are "those who are caught by the Lord's net, and are pulled away from the sea of this age." Theodore of Mopsuestia[1003] offers a different interpretation: "For if we would exhibit ourselves in this way, he will raise his voice over all those like a lion terrifying the flocks and herds; he will bring all who have suddenly come upon you like water in their great number into astonishment by his own fear." Theodoret of Cyrus[1004] writes: "For 'sons of the waters' means fish, like those that have the origin of life in water. In the same way, when the enemies are destroyed by the divine will." For Julian of Eclanum,[1005] the "sons of waters" designates the enemies of Israel who as the Egyptians at the Red Sea will try to destroy them.

Upon Israel's exodus from the lands of captivity, Egypt and Assyria, their attitude is marked by "trembling" (חרד; cf. 3:5: פחד), a genuine reverence toward Yahweh, their redeemer, who will return the wandering captives to "their houses" (בָּתֵּיהֶם). Jerome[1006] explains: "They will come to their nests, that is, their houses where the Lord will dwell with them." The main idea is that Yahweh is the Lord of history, the one who works Israel's salvation.[1007] These lines presuppose that part of the Israelites found refuge in Egypt during the Assyrian siege of Samaria (724-721 B.C.) while most of the inhabitants of the Northern Kingdom were eventually taken as captives to Assyria. According to Theodoret of Cyrus,[1008] v. 11 hints at Israel's return from the Babylonian captivity which occurred under the leadership of prince Zerubbabel. Similarly, Cyril of Alexandria[1009] connects the return from captivity with the edict of king Cyrus (539/8 B.C.): "'He will roar as a lion.' Who will roar? Cyrus, of course. It is as if someone should perhaps say: The war of Cyrus against the Babylonians will resound terribly and burdensome. When he roars and cries out as a lion against the enemies, the 'sons of waters will be amazed.' And he says 'they will be amazed' (ἐκστήσονται) in place of 'they will be stricken down' (καταπλαγήσονται). By the 'sons of waters' he means the Babylonians, who, since they were no less fearful than the children of the waters, that is, those who swim in the water, namely fish, they will be captured since they were easy to capture and unmanly on account of their experience of this."

Notes

[1] MT: פָּרְצוּ "they expand in number"; LXX (κέχυται ἐπὶ τῆς γῆς "abounded in the land") presupposes a Hebrew text with בָּאָרֶץ "in the land" which was probably lost

by homoioteleuton (cf. Wolff, *Hosea*, 65). According to Macintosh (*Hosea*, 131), the words ἐπὶ τῆς γῆς may have been added *ad sensum* to facilitate the translation of the verb. V: *inundaverunt* (= LXX); S: *sgyw* "they have increased."

² MT: תֶּאֱבַל; LXX (πενθήσει), V (*lugebit*), S (*ttb bʾblʾ*), all these versions read "it will mourn"; but Tg: תחרוב "it will dry up." As Wolff (*Hosea*, 65) points out, due to the parallel word אמלל, the verbal form תֶּאֱבַל should be connected to אבל II (cf. Akkadian *abālu* "to dry up") "to wither" (cf. Jer 12:4) rather than אבל I "to mourn."

³ MT: אֻמְלָל "it shall languish"; LXX omits this verb.

⁴ LXX adds καὶ σὺν τοῖς ἑρπετοῖς τῆς γῆς "and with the creeping beings of the earth," probably under the influence of 2:20/18.

⁵ MT: יֵאָסְפוּ "they shall disappear"; LXX (ἐκλείψουσιν "they will die") cannot presuppose יָסֻפוּ (so Nyberg); cf. Macintosh, *Hosea*, 134.

⁶ The form of these sayings is that of a רִיב "dispute" between Yahweh and Israel; on the meaning of this term, see the commentary on 2:4/2.

⁷ Defending the integrity of Hosea's book and the arrangement of the pericopes, Theodoret of Cyrus (PG 81, 1569 C) suggests that the author in 3:4-5 "presented beforehand" (προμηνύσας) the good things to come, while in 4:1f., he resumed the series of charges against those who behaved in an evil manner; cf. Julian of Eclanum, PL 21, 982 A-B.

⁸ PG 71, 112 B.

⁹ The word, found only here in Hosea, is probably a synonym of אֱמוּנָה "faithfulness" (2:22/20); see the commentary on 2:22/20. Thus אֱמֶת (frequently together with חֶסֶד, Ex 34:6; Ps 40:12; 85:11; Prov 14:22) may refer to the reliability of a man who is consistent in his actions; cf. Mays, *Hosea*, 62.

¹⁰ See the commentary on 2:21/19. None of this word's common renditions (e.g., steadfast love, grace, mercy, kindness, goodness) can encompass its entire meaning. Accord-

ing to Garrett (*Hosea, Joel,* 110), חֶסֶד refers to that kindness which goes beyond legal obligation, whether is husband's spontaneous love for his wife or the compassionate attitude of a person toward a stranger. In other words, when someone is willing to go an extra mile (Mt 5:41) (s)he, one may say, performs an act of חֶסֶד. Note LXX rendition "mercy" (ἔλεος).

¹¹ As Wolff (*EvTh* 12 [1952-53]: 537, 547) notices, the phrase "knowledge of God" is not Hosea's own creation; a good argument in support of such a view is the lexical variety in which this concept appears: דַּעַת אֱלֹהִים the "knowledge of God" (4:1; 6:6), הַדַּעַת "the knowledge" (4:6), ידע אלהים "to know God" (8:2; 13:4), יָדַע אֶת יְהוָה "to know Yahweh" (2:2; 5:4; 6:3). For Mays (*Hosea,* 63), the "knowledge of God" is Hosea's formula for "normative faith" based on the revealed "instruction" (תּוֹרָה) of God (4:6). "To know" God means to acknowledge him as Lord and to observe his commandments (1 Chr 28:9). In Prov 2:5 the "knowledge of God" is paralleled by the "fear of Yahweh" (יִרְאַת יְהוָה), which describes a profound religiosity. Responsible for the lack of the "knowledge of God" are the priests who failed to provide "instruction" to the people (4:6).

¹² PG 71, 112 C.

¹³ Theodoret of Cyrus (PG 81, 1569 C) is more specific, using "love towards men" (φιλανθρωπία) for "mercy" (ἔλεος); cf. Theodore of Mopsuestia, PG 66, 148 A.

¹⁴ PG 126, 632 B-C.

¹⁵ "You shall not take the name of Yahweh your God in vain (לַשָּׁוְא)" (Ex 20:7; Deut 5:11). As "cursing" (אָלֹה) implies taking an oath or invoking God's name (Ex 21:17; Lev 19:14; 20:9), this act may be indirectly considered a violation of the third commandment.

¹⁶ "You shall not bear false witness (עֵד שֶׁקֶר) against your neighbor" (Ex 20:16; Deut 5:20). The common feature which ties "cheating" (כחש) the neighbor (7:3; 10:13; 12:1) with the

ninth commandment is deliberate avoidance of telling the truth.

[17] "You shall not murder (רצח)" (Ex 20:13; Deut 5:17). In prophetic and wisdom literature, the verb רצח came to mean an intentional and violent killing (Is 1:21; Hos 6:9; Job 24:14; Prov 22:13; Ps 94:6); cf. Childs, *Exodus*, 421.

[18] "You shall not steal (תִּגְנֹב)" (Ex 20:15; Deut 5:19). As Alt ("Das Verbot des Diebstahls im Dekalog," *KSchr*, 1:333-40) observes, based on the position of this commandment within the Decalogue, the verb גנב designates kidnapping rather than stealing of an object (cf. Ex 21:16; Lev 9:11).

[19] "You shall not commit adultery (תִּנְאָף)" (Ex 20:14; Deut 5:18); cf. Lev 20:10; Hos 2:4/2; 3:1; 4:13; 7:4.

[20] As Macintosh (*Hosea*, 130-31) notices, the fact that the order of the commandments in Hosea differs from that found in the Decalogue does not mean that the Decalogue was not fixed at that time (contra Wellhausen); a similar order of commandments is found in Jer 7:9.

[21] The verb פרץ is used intransitively to describe the wine "bursting out" of its vats (Prov 3:10) or children "bursting forth" from the womb (Gen 38:29). Here the five absolute infinitives represent the collective subject of this verb. Theodoret of Cyrus (PG 81, 1569 C) observes that "your entire land will be filled with such stains (μιασμάτων)."

[22] PG 126, 632 C.

[23] PG 66, 148 A.

[24] Cf. Garrett, *Hosea, Joel*, 112; contra Jacob ("Osée," 40), who suggests that all Israel's crimes lead to bloodshed; see the commentary on 1:4.

[25] PL 21, 982 C.

[26] PG 71, 116 A.

[27] PG 126, 632 D. Theodore of Mopsuestia (PG 66, 148 B) explains that "subsequent bloodshed always mixes with the previous ones."

[28] Note the use of עַל־כֵּן "therefore" in the aetiological

stories of Genesis (2:24; 11:9); cf. Macintosh, *Hosea*, 133.

[29] PG 71, 116 C-D; cf. Theophylact of Bulgaria, PG 126, 633 B-D; according to Theodoret of Cyrus (PG 81, 1569 D), beasts, reptiles, and birds designate the mighty men while fish indicate the powerless ones; cf. Theodore of Mopsuestia, PG 66, 148 B.

[30] PL 25, 847.

[31] On the meaning of this verb, see the textual note on 4:3.

[32] The verb אמל "to be weak, feeble, languish" (Pu'lal) indicates loss of fertility (1 Sam 2:5; Jer 15:9).

[33] The Niph'al of the verb אסף "to be gathered" is construed with עם "people" (Gen 25:8; 35:29) and אבות "fathers" (Judg 2:10) meaning "to die" ("to be gathered to one's people/fathers"); hence, our translation of יֵאָסֵפוּ "they [fish] shall disappear." How could the fish of the sea be affected by a drought? According to Garrett (*Hosea, Joel*, 112), the shortage of food will cause overfishing and eventually a decline of this natural resource. That Hosea himself was puzzled by this fact may be seen in the use of "and even," only with "the fish of the sea."

[34] PL 21, 983 A.

[35] PL 25, 847.

[36] See Jacob, "Osée," 40.

[37] Cf. J. Limburg, *Hosea-Micah* (Interpretation; Atlanta: John Knox, 1988), 17.

[38] MT: וְעַמְּךָ כִּמְרִיבֵי כֹהֵן; LXX: ὁ δὲ λαός μου ὡς ἀντιλεγόμενος ἱερεύς "but my people are as a disputed priest"; S: wʿmk ʾyk khnʾ mthrʾ "your people are as a contentious priest"; V: *populus enim tuus sicut hii qui contradicunt sacerdoti* "for your people are as those who contend with a priest"; Tg: ועמך נצן עם מלפיהון "and your people argue with their teachers." The emended sentence ועמך ריבי כהן "My dispute is with you, O priest!" (so Oort, Guthe, Budde, Wolff) makes more sense in this context, and is supported

by the fact that in the following verses the priest is the addressee of this message; cf. Mays, *Hosea*, 67.

³⁹ MT: הַיּוֹם; LXX: ἡμέρας "by day" or "(certain) days"; S: *bᵉymmᵓ* "by day(light)"; but V: *hodie;* α': σήμερον "today."

⁴⁰ MT: לָיְלָה "at night"; LXX omits this word; but note that Theodore of Mopsuestia (PG 66, 148 C-D) uses a ms. of LXX which has νυκτός "at night."

⁴¹ MT וְדָמִיתִי אִמֶּךָ "I will make your mother perish"; but LXX (νυκτὶ ὡμοίωσα τὴν μητέρα σου "I have compared your mother to night") presupposes וְדִמִּיתִי (Piel), root I דמה "to be like"; V (*nocte tacere feci matrem tuam* "in the night I silenced your mother") and S (*wstqt* "and she [your mother] was silent") read perhaps דמם "to be silent." Note the T's interpretation of "mother," i.e., כנישה "assembly, synagogue."

⁴² MT: נִדְמוּ; LXX: ὡμοιώθη "(my people) are like"; V: *conticuit;* S: *štq.* As in v. 5, LXX presupposes I דמה "to be like," while V and S read דמם "to be silent."

⁴³ MT: Kethib: וְאֶמְאָסְאךָ; Qere: וְאֶמְאָסְךָ; the א is interpreted by the marginal Masora as superfluous; some mss. (e.g., Rossi) do not have it; LXX: κἀγὼ ἀπώσομαι σέ "I will reject you." Most modern scholars consider the final א in the Hebrew form a copyist's error, but it could also be, as Wolff (*Hosea*, 71; but first, van Gelderen) remarks, reminiscent of a voluntative form with suffix; yet the presence of a similar form without א in 1 Sam 15:23 refutes such a view; cf. Macintosh, *Hosea*, 138.

⁴⁴ MT: אָמִיר "I will exchange"; cf. LXX: τὴν δόξαν αὐτῶν εἰς ἀτιμίαν θήσομαι; V: *gloriam eorum in ignominiam commutabo*; the plural form (הֵמִירוּ "they changed"), proposed by Wolff (*Hosea*, 71) as a Masora's *tiqqun sopherim,* and supported by S (*ḥlpw*) and Tg (חליפו), should be discounted since, as Macintosh (*Hosea*, 143) points out, the MT reading is satisfactory, and there is no clear evidence of a *tiqqunim* tradition for the plural form. We follow MT reading since it

fits well in the context and, in addition, is supported by two important versions (LXX, V).

⁴⁵ MT: חַטַּאת "sin"; but LXX: ἁμαρτίας; V: *peccata*, both versions presuppose the plural.

⁴⁶ MT: נַפְשׁוֹ (but some mss., נַפְשָׁם); LXX: τὰς ψυχὰς αὐτῶν; V: *animas eorum*; S: *npshwn*; Tg: נפשהון; based on these textual observations, the plural suffix is preferable to the singular "his."

⁴⁷ MT: מַעֲלָלָיו "his deeds"; cf. S: *ʿbdyhwn*; Tg: עובדיהון מקלקליא "their perverted deeds"; but LXX: τὰ διαβούλια αὐτοῦ "his counsels"; cf. V: *cogitationes eius*.

⁴⁸ MT: וְלֹא יִפְרֹצוּ "but they will not multiply"; cf. S: *wlʾ sgyw* "and they did not multiply"; and the interpretative translation of the Tg: ולא יילדון בנין "and they will not beget sons"; but LXX: καὶ οὐ μὴ κατευθύνωσιν "and they shall by no means prosper"; note V: *et non cessaverunt* "(they played the whore) continually [lit.: and they have not ceased]."

⁴⁹ MT: לִשְׁמֹר זְנוּת וְיָיִן; we follow here LXX (τοῦ φυλάξαι πορνείαν. καὶ οἶνον …) and S (*wrḥmw znywt*) readings, which consider זְנוּת an object of לִשְׁמֹר. MT reading is supported by V (*in non custodiendo, fornicatio*) and Tg (ולא נטרו "they have not guarded").

⁵⁰ MT: יִקַּח־לֵב; here we follow the LXX reading (ἐδέξατο καρδία λαοῦ μου), taking עַמִּי "my people" along with v. 11.

⁵¹ MT: עֵצוֹ "his wood/tree"; LXX: ἐν συμβόλοις "signs"; S: *btrʿyth* "his mind"; Tg paraphrases: דבצלים אעיה "its wooden images."

⁵² MT: מַקְלוֹ "his staff"; LXX: ῥάβδοις αὐτοῦ "his staves"; S: *wḥwṭrh* "his staff"; cf. V: *baculus eius*.

⁵³ MT: הִתְעָה; LXX: ἐπλανήθησαν "they were led astray"; but V, S, Tg, all presuppose a 3rd masc. plural suffix ("them").

⁵⁴ MT: יְפָרֵדוּ; cf. αʹ: ἐχωρίζοντο "they separated with";

but LXX: συνεφύροντο; S: ḥlyṭn "they mingled with."

⁵⁵ MT: הַקְּדֵשׁוֹת "sacred (temple) prostitutes"; LXX: τετελεσμένων "inititates, consecrated"; V: *effeminatis* "transvestites"; S: *npqt šwq'* "street women."

⁵⁶ MT: יְלֵבוּ; LXX: συνεπλέκετο μετὰ πόρνης "it [the people] entangled itself with a prostitute"; cf. S: *'pq znyt'* "it embraced a prostitute"; but V (*vapulabit*) and α' (δαρήσεται "it will be flayed, trashed") seem to be closer to MT reading.

⁵⁷ MT: אַל־יֶאְשָׁם; but LXX (μὴ ἀγνόει "be not ignorant") presupposes the second person תֶאְשַׁם, required by the context; V: *non delinquat;* S: *l' tḥyb lyhwd'* "do not make Judah guilty."

⁵⁸ MT: בֵּית אָוֶן; LXX: εἰς τὸν οἶκον Ὢν; α', σ': ἀνωφελοῦς "vanities"; θ': ἀδικίας "wrongdoings"; V: *Bethaven;* Tg: בית אל "Bethel."

⁵⁹ Tg inserts an interpretative לשקר "(swear) falsely," since, according to the Law (cf. Deut 10:20), taking an oath was not a sin in itself.

⁶⁰ MT: הַנַּח־לוֹ; cf. V: *dimitte eum;* S: *šbwqw lh;* but LXX: ἔθηκεν ἑαυτῷ σκάνδαλα "he laid stumbling-blocks for himself"; Tg paraphrases: שבקו להון ית פולחני "they have abandoned my worship to them [idols]."

⁶¹ MT: סָר סָבְאָם; LXX: ᾑρέτισεν χαναναίους "he has chosen the Canaanites"; J. Zolli ("Hosea 4:17-18," *ZAW* 56 [1938]: 175) points out that LXX identified the "drunkards" (סֹבְאִים) with the Canaanites; (already for Philo of Alexandria, *De sobrietate* 10, χαναάν signifies σάλος "a tossing motion"); cf. Barthélemy, *Critique textuelle,* 513; S omits the whole phrase; V: *separatum est convivium eorum* "their feast is to be distinguished (from that of Judah)"; Tg: אסניאו שיריאן אונים שלטוניהון "their rulers have multiplied their banquets by oppression"; Houtsma proposed a conjecture, today followed by many scholars, בְּסֹד סֹבְאִים "in the company of the carousers"; another emendation was

offered by Torczyner, סָבָא סָבָאוּ "they carouse"; see Wolff, *Hosea*, 73.

[62] MT (אָהֲבוּ הֵבוּ) perhaps is a misreading of אָהֹב אָהֲבוּ (so Wolff); cf. σ′: ἠγάπησαν ἀγάπην; LXX: ἠγάπησαν; S: *wrḥmw*; but V (*dilexerunt adferre [ignominiam]* "they love to bring [disgrace]") considers הבו an infinitive of יהב "to give, provide"; cf. Macintosh, *Hosea*, 172.

[63] MT: מָגִנֶּיהָ "covering"; the translation "canopy" (cf. MT) was proposed by S. Morag, לשאלת ייחוד לשונו של הושע, *Tarbiz* 53 (1984): 489-511 (cf. מגינת לב in Lam 3:65 designates the hard covering around the heart; from the root גנן "to cover," noun מגן "shield"), hence a "canopy of disgrace"; Morag's rendition seems attractive in the context of sexual practices alluded in 4:13; on the other hand, G. R. Driver ("Linguistic and Textual Problems. Minor Prophets I," *JTS* 39 [1938]: 154-186) suggests a connection between the Hebrew word and the Arabic adjective *māʿin* "insolent," hence his translation "her impudent ones love shame" (cf. Wolff: "the dishonor <of the> shameless"); yet, as Macintosh (*Hosea*, 171) observes, this meaning is tautologous within the sentence. Some scholars (Wellhausen, Zolli, Houtsma), following LXX reading (ἐκ φρυάγματος αὐτῆς/αὐτῶν "from her/their arrogance") suggest an emendation to the Hebrew text, i.e., מִגְאֹנָהּ or מִגְאֹנָם "(they love dishonor) more than their pride." This emendation fits well in the context where Hosea speaks of the Israelites who abandoned "their pride" (Yahweh) for "dishonor" (idolatry); as Wellhausen points out, כָּבוֹד "glory," rather than גָּאוֹן "pride," might have been more appropriate as antonym of קָלוֹן "dishonor"; on the other hand, the Qumran text (4Qc: גניה[...]) is too short to be considered evidence in support of MT reading; as for V (*protectores eius* "his protectors") and Tg (רברביהון "their lords") these are ancient interpretations of the MT reading; S freely explains *wdḥltʾ* "and the idol"; see Barthélemy, *Critique textuelle*, 515.

⁶⁴ MT: צָרַר רוּחַ אוֹתָהּ "a wind wrapped her"; cf. V: *ligavit spiritus eam in alis suis*; LXX: συστροφὴ πνεύματος σὺ εἶ "you are a blast of wind"; S: *tṣrr* "will be bound"; Tg: "(the deeds of their lords are not good) just as it is impossible to gather wind in the fold of a garment"; although אוֹתָהּ "her" refers to people, the emendation אוֹתָם "them" (Weiser, Oort, BHS) fits better in the context.

⁶⁵ MT: מִזְבְּחוֹתָם; cf. V: *a sacrificiis suis*; but LXX: ἐκ τῶν θυσιαστηρίων αὐτῶν "because of their altars"; cf. S: *mn mdbḥyhwn*; Tg: מאוגרי טעותהון "from the altars of their idols." As Wolff (*Hosea*, 73) notices, the feminine plural of זֶבַח does not appear elsewhere in the Old Testament, and the MT reading may be the result of haplography מִמִּזְבְּחוֹתָם (so Wellhausen); this emendation is supported by LXX, S, Tg, and the other three occurrences of this word in the book (10:2, 8; 12:12); according to Barthélemy (*Critique textuelle*, 517), the very presence of the masculine plural of זֶבַח in 8:13 and 9:4 represents a strong argument against those who see in MT fem. pl. noun a dialectal feature of Hosea's language.

⁶⁶ When appearing at the beginning of a speech, the adverb אַךְ has an asseverative force, "surely, no doubt" (cf. Gen 26:9; 29:14; Judg 3:24; 20:39; 1 Sam 16:6). In other instances (cf. Gen 9:4; Ex 21:21; Lev 21:23; Num 18:15, 17), as in Os 4:4a, it may have a restrictive force, "however, yet," in contrast with the preceding assessment. Here, the adverb אַךְ indicates the beginning of a new unit; cf. Andersen and Freedman, *Hosea*, 345. Note that LXX uses here a final conjunction, ὅπως "that, in order that"; the main idea is that, given Israel's wickedness and God's subsequent punishment, both people and priests are equally guilty, and no one should plead or reprove the other.

⁶⁷ The verb יכח (Hiph'il) "to decide, prove, convict" (LXX uses a form of the verb ἐλέγχω "to put to shame; to prove") may indicate a conviction (Job 19:5; 32:12; Ps 50:21;

Prov 30:6) as well as a more general reproof (Gen 21:25; Lev 19:17; Is 29:21; Ezek 3:26; Am 5:10; Job 6:25; Prov 24:25).

⁶⁸ The noun כֹּהֵן "priest" is in vocative, though without an article. As Wolff (*Hosea*, 77) notices, the mention of the priest's "mother" (v. 5) and "sons" (v. 6) is a strong argument against collective meaning (so Macintosh, *Hosea*, 135: the priesthood as a group; Jacob, "Osée," 40f.; Garrett, *Hosea, Joel*, 116); note that the singular is secured by LXX, ἱερεύς "a priest"; Lohfink ("Zu Text und Form von Os 4,4-6," *Bibl* 42 [1961]: 305) remarks that כֹּהֵן in vocative never has a collective meaning.

⁶⁹ Mays, *Hosea*, 67.

⁷⁰ *Essence du prophétisme* (Paris, 1955), 295; cf. Macintosh, *Hosea*, 139; note that in the Chronicler and Deuteronomistic history, only the Jerusalem priesthood was considered legitimate.

⁷¹ PL 21, 983 B-C.

⁷² PG 71, 120 A-C; cf. Theophylact of Bulgaria, PG 126, 636 B-D.

⁷³ PG 66, 148 C.

⁷⁴ As Mays (*Hosea*, 68) notices, there is no mention of cultic prophets in the North, as it was true in the South (cf. Is 28:7; Mic 3:11; Jer 2:8; 5:31; 8:10). Thus it is unsurprising that Amos knows of no cultic prophet opposing his mission; cf. Wolff, *ThLZ* 81 (1956): 83-90. Wolff (*Hosea*, 77f.) considers the mention of "prophet" besides the "priest" a Judaean gloss.

⁷⁵ PG 81, 1572 A; Jerome (PL 25, 847-848) distinguishes between these "pseudo-prophets," on the one hand, and "Elijah, the prophet, Elisha, and other sons of the prophets, who prophesied in Samaria," on the other hand. Julian of Eclanum (PL 21, 983 C) calls them in a pejorative way "soothsayers" (*ariolis*).

⁷⁶ PG 66, 148 D.

⁷⁷ The verb כָּשַׁל "to stumble, stagger" may have a fig-

urative meaning, "to fail" of strength (Ps 31:11; Neh 4:4); perhaps LXX (ἀσθενήσεις "he will be feeble") picked this peculiar nuance of the verb.

[78] Cf. Wolff, *Hosea*, 77.

[79] Cf. Garrett, *Hosea, Joel*, 117.

[80] PG 66, 148 D.

[81] PG 71, 120 C; cf. Theophylact of Bulgaria, PG 126, 636 D.

[82] PL 25, 847.

[83] Cf. Mays, *Hosea*, 68; McComiskey, *The Minor Prophets*, 60: a reference to captivity, when all Israel's institutions will collapse; in Garrett's view (*Hosea, Joel*, 117), stumbling is caused by drunkenness (v. 7; cf. Jer 25:15-28). As Wolff (*Hosea*, 77) notices, the perfect consecutive has a future, resultative force, pointing to sin's consequences (cf. Is 8:15; 31:3; Jer 6:21); LXX (ἀσθενήσεις "he will be feeble") supports this interpretation.

[84] PG 81, 1572 A.

[85] PL 25, 847.

[86] Cf. Am 7:17: wife and children; Jer 22:26: king's mother.

[87] PL 21, 983 D.

[88] PL 25, 848.

[89] PG 126, 637 A; cf. Cyril of Alexandria, PG 71, 120 D: "Therefore, the synagogue of the Judaeans is rightly compared to gloom and darkness"; Theodoret of Cyrus, PG 81, 1572 A-B.

[90] The verb דמה "to destroy," here in Niph'al, ties this verse to v. 5 (וְדָמִיתִי); cf. Garrett, *Hosea, Joel*, 117.

[91] "The knowledge" (הַדַּעַת) is an abbreviated variant of the expression "knowledge of God" (דַּעַת אֱלֹהִים) in 4:1; see the commentary on 4:1.

[92] Cf. Mays, *Hosea*, 68.

[93] The verb מאס, meaning "to reject, scorn," requires a concrete object (9:17; Am 5:21; Is 5:24; Jer 6:19); cf. Wolff, *Ho-*

sea, 79; thus the "instruction" or "the knowledge" may refer here to the content rather than the act of transmission.

[94] PL 25, 848.

[95] PG 71, 120 D-121 A.

[96] See the commentary on 4:2; see also U. Cassuto (*Biblical and Oriental Studies* [translated by Abrahams; Jerusalem: Magnes, 1973], 1:79-100) who lists all the Hosean references to the Pentateuch.

[97] The verb כהן in Pi'el means "to act as a priest" (cf. Ex 28:1; Lev 7:35; Num 3:3).

[98] The mention of "sons" (cf. 1 Sam 2:27ff.; Hos 4:8; Am 7:17) points probably to the hereditary principle of the Israelite priesthood.

[99] According to Wolff (*Hosea*, 79), though the repetition of both verbs is reminiscent of the *lex talionis* formulas (Ex 21:23-25; Lev 24:18-20; Deut 19:21), Hosea's style is much closer to that found in curses (Ps 137:5; Josh 7:25; 1 Sam 15:33).

[100] PG 66, 148 D-149 A.

[101] PG 71, 121 A.

[102] PL 25, 848.

[103] In Wolff's view (*Hosea*, 80), a "traditionist" added this saying to the Hosean corpus. Yet, as Macintosh (*Hosea*, 141) notices, Wolff's hypothesis, besides being an excessive use of form criticism, ignores the similarity in theme (guilt of the priests followed by judgment) between vv. 4-6 and vv. 7-10. In addition, such shifts in person are a common feature of prophetic literature.

[104] The form רֻבָּם is a verbal noun of the root רבב "to become numerous." The translation proposed by Andersen and Freedman (*Hosea*, 342-45: "As they grew proud, so they sinned against me") alters the ironic parallel between the growth in number and the increase of the sin; cf. Garrett, *Hosea, Joel*, 119, n. 43.

[105] The verb חטא "to sin" basically means "to miss (a

target or way)"; cf. Gen 40:1; Ex 5:16; Judg 11:27; 1 Sam 26:21; 2 Sam 19:21; 1 Kgs 18:9; Prov 8:36; Is 65:20.

[106] Mays (*Hosea*, 70) explains this connection as follows: "Add another priest, and you add another sinner—the very opposite of what should have happened."

[107] PL 25, 849.

[108] PG 66, 149 B.

[109] The verb מוּר in Hiph'il means "to replace" an object with another (the second object has a prefixed בּ); cf. Lev 27:10; Ps 106:20; Jer 2:11.

[110] According to Jacob ("Osée," 41), the priest's "glory" is to stand before Yahweh as his servant (cf. Deut 10:8). This is probably the meaning of כֹּהֵן "priest" which commonly is connected to the root כּוּן "to stand upright" (so Gesenius and Buhl, *Hebräisches und aramäisches Handwörterbuch zum AT* [Leipzig, 1915], 332).

[111] The word קָלוֹן derives from the root קלל "to be light," hence the idea of lightness, disgrace, ignominy spelled out by the noun (cf. Is 22:18) in contrast with כָּבוֹד "glory" (root כבד "to be heavy"), as in this verse (cf. Prov 3:35; 6:33; Job 10:25).

[112] PG 71, 121 C.

[113] PG 126, 640 C.

[114] The word עָוֹן "iniquity, guilt; punishment of iniquity" derives from the root עוה "to twist, bend," hence the idea of perverting something which originally was straight or right. This term has a stronger connotation than its parallel, חטא "to miss a target or way." Other Hosean texts where these two terms occur in parallel are: 8:13; 9:9; 13:12.

[115] The term נֶפֶשׁ "soul" has here its original meaning, "throat" (cf. Prov 27:7); note its relation to Akkadian *napištu* "throat, life, soul."

[116] According to Mays (*Hosea*, 70), the sacrifices offered by Israel on many altars are sin in the eyes of Yahweh (Am 4:4f.). Thus when these priests encourage the people to limit

the true worship to animal sacrifices, one can say that they feed on the sin of the people. A similar interpretation is found in Macintosh, *Hosea*, 145; cf. Garrett, *Hosea, Joel*, 119f.

[117] PG 71, 124 B, D; cf. Theophylact of Bulgaria, PG 126, 640 D.

[118] PG 81, 1572 C; cf. Theodore of Mopsuestia, PG 66, 149 B.

[119] PL 25, 849.

[120] According to Mays (*Hosea*, 70), the occurrence of the singular "priest" in vv. 4 and 6, may be due to the proverbial character of v. 9 mentioning a "priest" (כֹּהֵן).

[121] PL 25, 849.
[122] PG 126, 641 A.
[123] PG 66, 149 C; cf. Julian of Eclanum, PL 21, 985 B.
[124] PG 71, 125 C.
[125] PG 126, 641 B.
[126] PG 25, 849.
[127] PG 71, 125 C.
[128] PL 21, 985 C.

[129] The verb פרץ "to increase, break out" (cf. 4:2) refers here to fertility, i.e., "to multiply" (cf. Ex 1:12; Is 54:3).

[130] The Hiph'il הִזְנוּ "they have played the whore" (cf. 4:18; 5:3) indicates Israel's participation in idolatrous acts of worship; outside Hosea's book, the Hiph'il of the root זנה is rendered "to cause to commit fornication" (cf. Ex 34:16; Lev 19:29); the intransitive meaning of the Hiph'il in Hosea may be a northern dialectal feature; cf. Macintosh, *Hosea*, 147.

[131] Wolff (*Hosea*, 82) notices that for the first time in the prophetic literature, the notion of "apostasy" is defined by the root "to forsake" (עזב). Hosea uses this verb only in v. 10. Jeremiah, his spiritual disciple, resorts to עזב more than a dozen times (1:16; 2:13; 5:7, etc.).

[132] PG 71, 125 D–128 A.
[133] PG 126, 641 C.
[134] PL 25, 850.

¹³⁵ The verb שָׁמַר usually means "to keep, observe, guard," and in the area of religion it is construed with objects such as "instruction" and "commandments." Here it should be translated "to devote oneself to," or "to love." The latter meaning is supported by the Syriac version (S), *wrḥmw znywt* "but they loved fornication."

¹³⁶ Some scholars (e.g., Harper, Mays, Wolff) consider the word זְנוּת "fornication" (cf. 6:10; Jer 3:2, 9) a technical term for "sacral marriage" between priests and cult prostitutes. Yet, as Macintosh (*Hosea*, 150) notices, vv. 10-11 concern not only the members of the hierarchy, but the entire population. Thus "fornication" has nothing to do with the ancient oriental practice of *hieros gamos*. People and priests embrace the same promiscuity (cf. vv. 13f., 15).

¹³⁷ The etymology of the word תִּירוֹשׁ "new wine, must" is still debatable. The derivation from יָרַשׁ "to take possession," suggested already by *ibn Janāḥ* (tenth-eleventh centuries) and, more recently, Rudolph, would anticipate the idea of alcohol intoxication spelled out by the phrase "to take one's heart" found in the same verse; see Macintosh, *Hosea*, 149; see also the commentary on 2:10/8.

¹³⁸ "Heart" (לֵב) in Hosea is the place of thoughts and emotions, the very center of life (cf. 7:2; 13:6, 8). "To take away the people's understanding" means to deprive them of rational, emotional, and volitional capacities.

¹³⁹ PG 71, 128 C-D.

¹⁴⁰ PL 25, 850; cf. Julian of Eclanum, PL 21, 986 A.

¹⁴¹ PG 71, 129 C.

¹⁴² PG 81, 1573 A.

¹⁴³ PL 25, 850.

¹⁴⁴ PG 81, 1573 B; cf. Theophylact of Bulgaria: "'Spirit' means here zeal (προθυμίαν)."

¹⁴⁵ PG 71, 132 A; cf. Julian of Eclanum (PL 21, 986 A) who identifies this "spirit" with "various demons."

¹⁴⁶ *Hosea*, 74.

¹⁴⁷ It remains unknown whether or not the verbs זנה "to play the whore" and נאף "to commit adultery" in the present context should be taken literally as an allusion to cultic practices (first mentioned by Herodotus, as a Babylonian custom) during which young women sacrificed their virginity with strangers at the sanctuaries. For details on this topic, see Rudolph, "Präparierte Jungfrauen?," *ZAW* 75 (1963): 65-73; L. Rost, "Erwägungen zu Hosea 4.13f.," *Festschrift Alfred Bertholet* (eds. W. Baumgartner, O. Eissfeldt, K. Elliger, L. Rost; Tübingen, 1950), 451-60; Wolff, *Hosea*, 86-87.

¹⁴⁸ Probably the verb זבח "to slaughter for sacrifice" refers to both offering sacrifices and the meals held thereafter under the trees' refreshing shade; cf. Mays, *Hosea*, 74. The Pi'el of this verb (the Qal is found in 8:13) may refer to either the intensity or the repetition of the act of offering; cf. Macintosh, *Hosea*, 153.

¹⁴⁹ The Pi'el of the root קטר (cf. 2:15/13, Hiph'il תַּקְטִיר) designates here the cultic act of burning incense; contra Macintosh, *Hosea*, 154: "they raise the smoke of their offerings." Except for 1 Sam 2:16 where Yahweh is worshipped, everywhere else the Pi'el is used in connection with other gods (cf. 11:2; 2 Kgs 17:11; 12:4; Is 65:3; Hab 1:16).

¹⁵⁰ Note the various uses of the attribute "good" (טוֹב) in Hosea's book: defining the primeval relationship between Yahweh (the "first husband") and Israel (2:9/7), or the divine spark within the human person, which represents the starting point of God's redemptive work (14:2/1), or the hedonistic aspect of the idolatrous cult frequented by Israel (4:13); see the commentary on 2:9/7.

¹⁵¹ PL 25, 851.

¹⁵² PG 66, 152 A-B.

¹⁵³ PG 71, 132 A-B; cf. Theophylact of Bulgaria, PG 126, 645 A-C.

¹⁵⁴ "Mountains" and "hills" may refer to the "high places" (בָּמוֹת), as places of worship, first on hills, mountains (2 Kgs

16:4), then on artificial platforms (cf. 1 Kgs 11:7; 14:23; 2 Kgs 17:9; Jer 19:5); the structure of these "high places" was very simple: a few trees, an altar for sacrifices, and "pillars" (מַצֵּבוֹת) and "Asheroth" as symbols of male/female deities. For a detailed description, see R. de Vaux, *Ancient Israel: Its Life and Institutions* (trans. by J. McHugh; New York: McGraw-Hill, 1961), 284ff.

[155] PL 25, 851.

[156] The verb פרד (Niph'al) means "to divide, separate" (Gen 2:10; Judg 4:11). In Pi'el, it appears only here in reference to the Israelites' separation from Yahweh's worship and their association with the hierodules.

[157] Sacred prostitution, male and female, was widely practiced in ancient Near East. For Mesopotamia (Akkadian *qadištu*), see "Code of Hammurabi," § 178-82; cf. *ANET*, 174. In Ugarit, the hierodules (*qdšm*) stand beside the priests; cf. Wolff, *Hosea*, 88. Hierodules made their way even in the Jerusalem temple (2 Kgs 23:7), though this Cannanite practice was prohibited by the law (Deut 23:18-19). The traditional interpretation that Hebrew קְדֵשׁוֹת and its Near Eastern correspondents would designate "sacred prostitutes" was recently challenged (so Gruber). For a detailed discussion, see Macintosh, *Hosea*, 157ff. Note that in 4:14 "whores" and "hierodules" are synonyms as in Gen 38, where Tamar is described as both זוֹנָה and קְדֵשָׁה; cf. Jacob, "Osée," 43.

[158] PG 126, 648 A.

[159] PG 81, 1573 C.

[160] PG 71, 132 C-D.

[161] "An unknowing people" (Wolff) is Yahweh's people whose understanding was taken away (vv. 11-12), now dying for lack of "knowledge" (v. 6).

[162] The root לבט appears only in Niph'al, and outside 4:14, it is found only in Prov 10:8, 10; the Hebrew root is probably related to Arabic *labaṭa* "to strike the ground" with a person, hence "to throw one down" (cf. BDB, 526).

163 Cf. Mays, *Hosea*, 75-76.
164 PL 25, 853; cf. Julian of Eclanum, PL 21, 986 C-D.
165 PG 71, 136 A.
166 PL 21, 987 A.
167 Cf. Mays, *Hosea*, 77.
168 PG 66, 152 D.
169 PG 126, 649 A.
170 PG 71, 137 A.
171 PL 25, 854.
172 PG 81, 1573 D.

173 Jacob ("Osée," 43) notices that the mention of Beer-sheba in Amos (5:5; 8:14), and Gilgal and Bethel in Hosea (4:15) may be considered an argument for reciprocal pilgrimages of Judah and Israel to their respective sanctuaries.

174 Cf. Mays, *Hosea*, 78. A Ugaritic text reads: "That powerful Baal had died, that the Prince, Lord of Earth, had perished. And behold, alive is powerful Baal! And behold existent the Prince, Lord of Earth!"; cf. Ginsberg, *ANET*, 140.

175 PG 71, 136 D.
176 PL 25, 854.
177 PL 21, 987 D.

178 According to Macintosh (*Hosea*, 166), the similarity between V ("like a frisky [*lasciviens*] cow") and LXX (ὡς δάμαλις παροιστρῶσα "like a mad heifer") is probably due to the influence of the popular Greek legend of Io, where Io is turned into a cow and stung by a gad-fly; cf. Theodoret of Cyrus, PG 81, 1576 C.

179 PG 66, 152 D-153 A.
180 PG 71, 137 C.
181 PL 25, 855.
182 PG 66, 153 A.

183 Garrett (*Hosea, Joel*, 138) compares the Hosean text with Ps 58:6/5 where חוֹבֵר "enchanter" can paralyze a cobra under complete hypnosis; thus "Let him alone!" means that Ephraim is in a trance and none can wake him.

[184] The word עֲצַבִּים "idols," always in plural (except Jer 22:28, singular!), derives from the root עצב "to fashion, shape." In Hosea, "idols" designates the "calf" (8:4f.; 13:2; 14:9), and perhaps the "teraphim" (3:4).

[185] PG 66, 153 A.

[186] Cf. Jacob, "Osée," 44; a similar use of הַנַּח לְ is found in Ex 32:10 where Yahweh addresses Moses. According to Wolff (*Hosea*, 91), Hosea urges his disciples not to bother with the stubborn Ephraim.

[187] PL 25, 855; cf. Cyril of Alexandria, PG 71, 139 A.

[188] The word סֹבְא "drink, liquor" (root סבא "to imbibe, drink largely") may indicate both wine and beer.

[189] On the root סור "to turn aside," meaning "to come to an end" (cf. Am 6:7; Is 11:13), see BDB, 694.

[190] An infinitive absolute followed by a finite form of the same root usually connotes intensity; cf. Macintosh, *Hosea*, 169f.: "they fornicate wildly." Here, the Hiph'il (הִזְנָה) is an intensive or internal Hiph'il, identical in meaning with the Qal; cf. GK § 53f.

[191] PG 66, 153 B.

[192] The verb צרר means "to bind, tie up, wrap," for instance, in a piece of garment (Ex 12:34; Prov 30:4; Job 26:8). Hosea's choice for this verb may be explained as a wordplay with סרר "stubborn" (v. 16) and סר "gone" (v. 18); cf. Garrett, *Hosea, Joel*, 139.

[193] PG 71, 140 C-D.

[194] PL 25, 856.

[195] PG 66, 153 B.

[196] MT: כִּי לָכֶם הַמִּשְׁפָּט; cf. LXX: διότι πρὸς ὑμᾶς ἐστι τὸ κρίμα "for the judgment is toward you"; the context requires that the "judgment" pertain to the wicked leaders (so Mays, Rudolph, Ward), rather than being their responsibility (so already the Tg: הלא לכון למידע דינא "Is it not your responsibility to know judgment?"; Macintosh, Weiser, Wolff).

¹⁹⁷ MT: לְמִצְפָּה "at Mizpah"; LXX translates τῇ σκοπιᾷ "in the watchtower"; cf. V: *speculationi;* S: *dwq'* "watchman, watchtower"; σ': τῇ πλατείᾳ "broad place"; Tg interprets למלפיכון "to your teachers," as the ones who "watch" (צפה) over their students; the occurrence of "Tabor" in the same verse refutes any translation/interpretation of the toponym "Mizpah."

¹⁹⁸ MT: תָּבוֹר "Tabor"; cf. α': Θαβώρ; S: *tbwr;* LXX: τὸ Ἰταβύριον; Tg: טור רם "high mountain"; interestingly enough, Matthew (17:1; cf. Mk 9:2) describes the place of Transfiguration as a "high mountain" (ὄρος ὑψηλὸν), and the Christian tradition (Cyril of Jerusalem in 348, followed by Epiphanius and Jerome) identified this "high mountain" with Mt. Tabor.

¹⁹⁹ MT: וְשַׁחֲטָה שֵׂטִים הֶעְמִיקוּ; LXX: οἱ ἀγρεύοντες τὴν θήραν κατέπηξαν "(the net which) those who hunt the wild animal have fixed"; cf. S: *wṣyd' dṣydyn ṭmrw pḥ'* "and the hunters who hunt hide traps"; V: *et victimas declinastis in profundum* "and you lowered the victims into the depth"; Tg: ודבחין לטעון מסגן "and they sacrifice to idols frequently"; as Macintosh (*Hosea,* 182) notices, all these versions are interpretative and should not be regarded as reflecting a *Vorlage* different from that of MT. We read here שַׁחַת "pit" (root שׁוּחַ "to sink down") instead of שַׁחֲטָה (a doubtful word < root שָׁחַט "to slaughter"?); this emendation fits well with the following verb הֶעְמִיקוּ "they dug deep."

²⁰⁰ MT: מוּסָר "chastisement"; LXX: παιδευτής "corrector"; V: *eruditor;* S: *'n' dyn 'rd'* "I will chastise"; following LXX and V, Wolff (*Hosea,* 94) proposes a different reading, מְיַסֵּר "I am chastising."

²⁰¹ MT: לְכֻלָּם "to all of them"; we follow here LXX reading (ὑμῶν) which presupposes לכם or לכלכם "to (all of) you."

²⁰² MT: הִזְנֵיתָ "you played the whore"; but LXX: ἐξεπόρνευσεν; V: *fornicatus est;* S: *zny;* all these read הִזְנָה

"he played the whore"; Tg interprets: טעו "they have gone astray."

²⁰³ MT: לֹא יִתְּנוּ מַעַלְלֵיהֶם; LXX: οὐκ ἔδωκαν τὰ διαβούλια αὐτῶν τοῦ ἐπιστρέψαι "they have not given their counsels to return"; cf. V: *non dabunt cogitationes suas ut reverantur*; but S: *lʾ šbqn lhwn ṣnʿthwn dntpnwn* "their deeds do not let them return"; cf. Tg: עובדיהון למתב לא שבקין. Some scholars (Wolff, Mays, Otteli) suggest that the MT reading is the result of a haplography, the original form being יתנום.

²⁰⁴ MT: גְּאוֹן; LXX, σ': ὕβρις "insolence"; θ', α': ὑπερηφανία "arrogance"; V: *arrogantia*; S: *ʾyqrh* "her glory"; Tg: יקר "glory."

²⁰⁵ MT: וְעָנָה; LXX: καὶ ταπεινωθήσεται "and it [the pride] will be brought low"; cf. S: *wntmkk*; V: *respondebit* "will answer"; as Macintosh (*Hosea*, 185) observes, the occurrence of בפניו "in his face" requires the Hebrew root ענה (I) "to answer, testify" (so V), rather than ענה (III) "to become low" (so LXX, S, Tg).

²⁰⁶ MT: יִמְצָאוּ; based on LXX (αὐτόν "him") and S (*nškḥwnh*), we supplied our translation with "him."

²⁰⁷ MT: בָּגָדוּ; cf. V: *praevaricati sunt* "they dealt falsely"; S: *dglw* "they acted treacherously"; Tg: במימרא דיוי שקרו "they have dealt faithlessly with the *Memra* [Word] of the Lord"; but note LXX: τὸν Κύριον ἐγκατέλιπον "they have forsaken the Lord."

²⁰⁸ MT: חֹדֶשׁ "new moon, month"; LXX: ἡ ἐρυσίβη "red blight," which is the Greek rendition of the Hebrew חָסִיל "locust" (1 Kgs 8:37; Joel 1:4), observation made already by Jerome, PL 25, 860; hence Wolff's translation: "Now the locust shall devour their fields"; we consider the MT reading satisfactory and well supported by α': νεομηνία "new moon"; cf. σ', θ'; V: *mensis* "month"; S omits the second half of v. 7.

²⁰⁹ Contra Jacob ("Osée," 46f.), who thinks that Hosea deals here primarily with political evils such as alliances

and fratricide wars.

[210] According to Andersen and Freedman (*Hosea*, 383), the phrase "house of Israel" designates both the religious and political leadership. But, since the other two phrases point to Israel's leaders, we consider Garrett's interpretation (*Hosea, Joel*, 141) more plausible: the "landed middle and upper classes"; a similar explanation is found in Wolff (*Hosea*, 97), who considers "house of Israel" an abbreviated form of the phrase "elders of the house of Israel" (זקני בית ישראל) (cf. Mic 3:1, 9; 1 Sam 11:3; 1 Kgs 21:8), landowners who were distinct from "princes" and "prophets."

[211] "House of the king" (king and princes) points to Samaria as the place where this oracle was first delivered; cf. Mays, *Hosea*, 79.

[212] PG 71, 141 B.

[213] PL 25, 856.

[214] Probably *Tell en-Naṣbeh*, 9 miles north of Jerusalem (1 Sam 7); figurines of Ashtarte, goddess of fertility, dating from the eighth century B.C., have been found here; cf. Garrett, *Hosea, Joel*, 143.

[215] Known today as *Jebel el-Tor*, Tabor is a mountain farther in the north, southwest of the Sea of Galilee, not far from the Jezreel Valley. Texts such as Deut 33:19 and Judg 4:6 allude to the "holiness" of this mountain. According to Eissfeldt ("Der Gott des Tabor und seine Verbreitung," *ARW* 31 [1934]: 14ff.), a god "Zeus Itaburios" was worshiped on Tabor in Hellenistic times; Mt. Tabor belongs geographically to three tribes, Zebulon, Naphtali, and Issachar.

[216] Today *Tell el-Hamman*, on the eastern side of the Jordan River; Shittim is first mentioned in the days of the conquest (Josh 2:1). Wolff (*Hosea*, 98) notices that the mention of Shittim would have evoked the apostasy of Baal-Peor (Num 25:1ff.); cf. 9:10.

[217] PG 126, 657 A.

[218] PL 25, 857.

[219] Garrett (*Hosea, Joel,* 143f.) reads "But I am fetters for all of them," vocalizing מוֹסֵר "fetters" (cf. Job 12:18) instead of מוּסָר "discipline" (MT): Yahweh would become fetters for those leaders who were traps for his people.

[220] PL 25, 857.

[221] PG 71, 141 D.

[222] PG 126, 657 B.

[223] Cf. Mays, *Hosea,* 81.

[224] "Ephraim" is used here as another name for the Northern Kingdom; cf. Cyril of Alexandria, PG 71, 144 C; but Theodoret of Cyrus (PG 81, 1577 B): "Ephraim and Israel, that is, the whole people."

[225] According to Garrett (*Hosea, Joel,* 144), the Hiph'il הִזְנָיתָ perhaps denotes causality (versus 4:10, 18 where the Hiph'il has the same meaning as the Qal), i.e., Ephraim causes the entire people to fornicate; cf. Wolff, *Hosea,* 94, 99 ("you, Ephraim, taught whoredom"); contra Andersen and Freedman (*Hosea,* 391), who argue for an intransitive meaning "you have been promiscuous."

[226] The verb טמא (here in Niph'al) indicates the idea of cultic defilement (cf. 6:10; Hithpa'el: 9:4).

[227] PG 71, 144 B.

[228] PG 66, 156 A.

[229] PG 126, 657 B-C.

[230] PL 25, 857-858.

[231] The word מַעֲלָלִים "deeds" is used by Hosea to designate the evil works of Israel (4:9; 7:2; 9:15; 12:3).

[232] For נתן ("to give") meaning "to permit," cf. Gen 20:6; Ex 3:19; Num 21:23.

[233] Here קֶרֶב does not refer to the inner side (for this notion Hosea uses לֵב "heart"; cf. 4:11), but the "midst" of the people (cf. Gen 24:3; 1 Sam 16:13).

[234] Mays (*Hosea,* 84) compares v. 4 to Rom 6:15ff. where Paul speaks of sin's enslaving power.

[235] PL 25, 858.

[236] PG 126, 657 C.

[237] PL 21, 990 A.

[238] Hosea probably chose גָּאוֹן "pride" for its assonance with עָוֹן "iniquity"; cf. Jacob, "Osée," 48.

[239] A common interpretation of "pride" points to Israel's trust in her syncretistic worship (so Targum, Rashi, and recently Danell); cf. Macintosh, *Hosea*, 186. Another interpretation underlines Israel's belief that there is no need for repentance; cf. Andersen and Freedman, *Hosea*, 392; similarly, Wolff, *Hosea*, 100 ("pride is the evidence of the audience's inability to repent").

[240] PG 126, 660 A.

[241] PL 21, 990 B.

[242] PL 25, 858.

[243] Cf. Macintosh, *Hosea*, 185.

[244] The verbal form כָּשַׁל is a "prophetic perfect" and thus rendered by present (GK § 106n).

[245] PL 25, 858; cf. Theodore of Mopsuestia, PG 66, 156 A-B.

[246] PG 81, 1577 B.

[247] "To seek (בקשׁ) God" means to communicate with him by cultic means (sacrifice, pilgrimage); cf. 2:9; 3:4; 4:15; 7:10.

[248] PG 71, 145 B.

[249] Wolff (*Hosea*, 100) considers the expression "seeking and (not) finding" a motif from the Baal myth of searching for the absent divinity in the underworld. According to Wolff, Hosea frequently makes polemic use of the language of Canaanite mythology (cf. 2:4-17); cf. Jacob, "Osée," 48.

[250] PG 126, 660 D-661 A.

[251] Only here חלץ has an intransitive meaning, "to withdraw, depart," which can be considered a dialectal feature (Rudolph); otherwise, this verb means "to remove," said of clothes (Deut 25:9f; Is 20:2).

[252] PL 21, 990 C.

253 PL 25, 860.
254 PG 126, 661 A.
255 PL 25, 859.
256 PG 66, 156 B.
257 Cf. Macintosh, *Hosea*, 191. According to Wolff (*Hosea*, 101), the "bastard sons" are the children conceived by the Israelite women during the sexual rites with the strangers.
258 Cf. Theodoret of Cyrus, PG 81, 1577 D-1580 A; Theodore of Mopsuestia, PG 66, 156 C; Julian of Eclanum, PL 21, 990 D.
259 PG 71, 145 C; cf. Theophylact of Bulgaria, PG 126, 661 B.
260 PL 25, 859.
261 Cf. Garrett, *Hosea, Joel*, 147.
262 PL 25, 860. Similarly, A. Caquot ("Remarques sur la fête de la néoménie dans l'ancien Israël," *RHR* 158 [1961]: 16), more recently, considers חדשׁ a complement of time rather than a subject; he also suggests that this word might designate the New Year's Day: "He [i.e., Yahweh] will devour their fields on New Year's Day."
263 Cf. Macintosh, *Hosea*, 192.
264 Andersen and Freedman, *Hosea*, 397.
265 Cf. Wolff, *Hosea*, 95.
266 PG 81, 1580 A; cf. Theodore of Mopsuestia, PG 66, 156 C; Theophylact of Bulgaria, PG 126, 661 C.
267 PG 71, 145 D.
268 MT: בַּגִּבְעָה; LXX translates again the place-name (cf. Mizpah, 5:1) ἐπὶ τοὺς βουνούς "upon the hills"; the S reading (*brmtʾ*—twice) may be the result of a dittography.
269 MT: בָּרָמָה; LXX translates: ἐπὶ τῶν ὑψηλῶν "upon the heights."
270 MT: בֵּית אָוֶן; LXX translates the toponym "Beth-Aven": ἐν τῷ οἴκῳ Ὢν "in the house of On."
271 MT: אַחֲרֶיךָ בִּנְיָמִין "after you, Benjamin"; cf. α', σ', θ': ὀπίσω σου; S: *btrk*; V: *post tergum tuum* "behind you"; but

LXX (ἐξέστη Βενιαμείν "Benjamin is astonished/terrified") presupposes the Hebrew root חרד "to be terrified," הַחֲרִידוּ "Terrify (Benjamin)!" (Wellhausen, Wolff) or אַחֲרִיד (an Aramaic *Aphel* form) "one terrifies (Benjamin)" (Rudolph); probably LXX reading is more an interpretation than a translation; cf. Macintosh, *Hosea*, 199.

272 MT: רָצוּץ ... עָשׁוּק; LXX: κατεδυνάστευσεν Ἐφραὶμ τὸν ἀντίδικον αὐτοῦ κατεπάτησεν τὸ κρίμα "Ephraim prevailed against his adversary, he trampled upon judgment"; note that LXX has active verbs, perhaps under the influence of Am 4:1 where both verbs are active; in addition, the LXX adds a direct object for the first verb: τὸν ἀντίδικον; V: *fractus iudicio*; S: *wʾlyṣ bdynʾ* "crushed by judgment."

273 MT: הוֹאִיל; LXX: ἤρξατο; V: *coepitt* "he began"; but note the assyndesis הוֹאִיל הָלַךְ "he willingly went"; cf. 9:9; GK § 120g.

274 MT: אַחֲרֵי־צָו "after commandment"; LXX: ὀπίσω τῶν ματαίων "after vanities"; V: *post sordem* "after dirt"; S: *btr sryqʾ* "after vanities (= idols?)"; Wolff (*Hosea*, 104), based on the LXX reading, considers צַו a synonym of שָׁוְא "vanity," though Macintosh (*Hosea*, 204f.) connects the former word (which appears also in Is 28:10, 13) with Arabic *ṣww* "empty." Andersen and Freedman (*Hosea*, 409f.) suggest "filth" from צוֹא (cf. Is 28:10, 13) in reference to a "detestable god."

275 MT: כָעָשׁ "like pus"; cf. α': βρωστήρ; V: *tinea*; Tg: כעשא "like moth"; but LXX: ὡς ταραχή "like a confusion"; cf. S: *ʾyk dlwḥy* "like trouble."

276 MT: כָרָקָב "like rottenness"; cf. V: *putredo*; α': σῆψις "decay"; LXX: ὡς κέντρον "like a sting (goad)"; S: *ʾrʾ* "leprosy."

277 MT: מֶלֶךְ יָרֵב; the MT reading is supported by LXX: βασιλέα Ἰαρείμ (Ἰαρείβ) "king I (a proper name)"; probably יָרֵב (*yārēb*) was considered the personal name of an Assyrian king, even though the position of the indefinite מֶלֶךְ before the proper name is quite odd; but the MT could also

be the result of a misdivision of an original phrase מלכי רב "the great king" (the final Yod on the first word is an *yod-compaginis* which ties the two words in one phrase); cf. *mlk rb* on an Aramaic (Sefire I) inscription, a calque on the Akkadian *šarru rabû*; cf. Andersen and Freedman, *Hosea*, 413f.; S: *mlkʾ dyrb* "king of Y (a place-name)"; V: *ultorem* "avenger"; perhaps V (cf. α', σ', θ') considered ירב as deriving from root ריב "to contend"; cf. Macintosh, *Hosea*, 212.

[278] MT: מָזוֹר "wound"; LXX: ὀδύνη "pain"; cf. S: *kʾbwhy*; Tg: מכאוביה; but V: *vinculum* "bond."

[279] MT: יֶאְשְׁמוּ; cf. α': πλημμελήσωσι "they will err"; S: *nḥwbwn*, all presuppose אשם "to be guilty"; but LXX (ἀφανισθῶσι "they are brought to naught") and V (*deficiatis* "you fail") imply שמם "to be desolated"; we follow here the MT reading; based on the parallelism with v. 15b, the meaning of the verb אשם should be something connoting "to bear/suffer punishment"; thus the main idea of this saying is that the Israelites will "seek" the Lord when they will be under divine "punishment" or in the midst of "distress."

[280] MT: יְשַׁחֲרֻנְנִי "they will seek me early"; cf. LXX: ὀρθριοῦσι πρὸς με; V: *mane consurgunt ad me*; S: *nqdmwn;* LXX adds λέγοντες "saying" (= Hebrew לֵאמֹר) connecting v. 15 with 6:1; cf. S: *wnʾmrwn;* Tg: יימרון.

[281] See Alt, "Hosea 5:8-6:6, ein Krieg und seine Folgen in prophetisher Beleuchtung," in *KSchr*, 2:163-87.

[282] On this period see "Introduction. Historical Background: The Assyrian Expansion and the Last Years of Israel."

[283] PL 25, 861-862.

[284] PG 81, 1580 B; cf., more recently, Good ("Hosea 5:8-6:6: An Alternative to Alt," *JBL* 85 [1966]: 273-86), who still thinks that the setting of this pericope is cultic.

[285] PG 71, 149 A-B.

[286] PG 126, 664 C; cf. Cyril of Alexandria, PG 71, 149 A-B.

287 *Hosea*, 197f.

288 To indicate the idea of alarm, Hosea uses two verbs: (a) תקע "to blow" the "horn" (שׁוֹפָר), used in both worship and battle (Jer 6:17; Joel 2:1), or the "trumpet" (חֲצֹצְרָה) (Num 10:9; 31:6); and (b) רוע (Hiph'il) "to shout"; the meaning of the latter verb, "to raise an alarm," is given by the parallel with the former verb.

289 Gibeah, today *Jebaʻ*, one mile west of *Er-Rām*, and one mile south of *Mukhmās* (*Michmash*); cf. Macintosh, *Hosea*, 194; contra the traditional view that identifies Gibeah with *Tell el-Fūl*, three miles north of Jerusalem.

290 Ramah, today *er-Rām*, five miles north of Jerusalem.

291 Beth-aven (בֵּית אָוֶן), elsewhere a nickname for Bethel, the "house of wickedness" (cf. 4:15; 10:5), should be taken here as a place name; Beth-aven, a Benjamite city, is identified with *Khirbet Tell el-ʻAskar*, north of *Mukhmās*; Jerome (PL 25, 861) interprets Beth-aven as "Bethel in the tribe of Ephraim."

292 PL 21, 991 A.

293 PG 66, 156 D.

294 The form נֶאֱמָנָה "what is sure; established; reliable" is a Niph'al participle fem. sing. from the root אמן "to confirm."

295 The word תּוֹכֵחָה "chastisement" (cf. 2 Kgs 19:3; Is 37:3; Ps 149:7) derives from the root יכח "to chastise, correct, instruct" (cf. 4:4), but in this context its meaning draws closer to "judgment" or "punishment." According to Wolff (*Hosea*, 113), Hosea uses this word to underscore the positive dimension of Israel's "correction."

296 PG 71, 149 D.

297 PG 66, 157 A.

298 PG 126, 665 A.

299 PG 25, 862.

300 Cf. Mays, *Hosea*, 89.

301 Cf. Macintosh, *Hosea*, 202.

302 The word עֶבְרָה means "overflow, arrogance, fury" and is commonly found in parallel with אַף "anger" (13:11; Am 1:11; Is 9:18; Ps 90:9, 11).

303 Cf. Andersen and Freedman, *Hosea*, 408.

304 PG 71, 152 C.

305 PG 126, 665 D.

306 PL 21, 991 B.

307 PL 25, 862.

308 The verbs עשׁק "to oppress, extort" (Deut 24:14; Am 4:1; Jer 7:6; Ezek 22:29) and רצץ "to crush" (Deut 28:33; 1 Sam 12:3; Am 4:1; Is 58:6) are derived from the legal field. As Wolff (*Hosea*, 114) notices, a characteristic of Hosea's book is to speak of war using terms from Israel's legislation (cf. 5:10).

309 PG 71, 153 D.

310 PG 81, 1580 C.

311 PG 66, 157 C.

312 PG 126, 668 A.

313 PL 25, 863.

314 The noun עָשׁ should be translated "pus" (so Wolff, Rudolph, Mays) rather than "moth" (cf. BDB, 799, based on the comparison with Arabic *ʻθθ;* Andersen and Freedman: "larvae") because the latter attacks garments (Is 50:9) and not humans. The meaning "pus" was first proposed by G. R. Driver who connected the Hebrew word to the Arabic root *ġθθ* "became lean, meagre," and the noun *ġθyθt* "purulent matter"; cf. Rowley, *Bulletin of the John Rylands Library* 39 (1956): 200f.; Macintosh (*Hosea*, 207) renders "an emaciating disease," relating this word to the Arabic verb *ʻšš* "became emaciated."

315 The word רָקָב means "rottenness, decay" (Job 13:28); "decay of bones, caries" (Hab 3:16; Prov 12:4; 14:30).

316 The independent pronoun אֲנִי "I" underscores the idea that Yahweh is the one who administers the punishments to Ephraim and Judah.

317 PG 71, 156 A-B; cf. Theodoret of Cyrus, PG 81, 1580 D; Theodore of Mopsuestia, PG 66, 157 C-D.

318 PL 21, 992 A-B.

319 PL 25, 864.

320 The word מָזוֹר "wound" (cf. Jer 30:13) derives from the verb זוּר "to press down and out"; note Arabic *zyr* "to draw forcibly together; to press"; but Dahood: "to flow"; cf. KBL, 267. Thus, the image painted here is that of an open wound (Andersen and Freedman: "oozing infection"; Macintosh: "lesions" of a disease) whose matter needs to be pressed out.

321 Andersen and Freedman (*Hosea*, 413) suggest that, given the parallelism between Ephraim ("they went to Assyria") and Judah, the subject of וַיִּשְׁלַח "and he sent" is the Southern Kingdom; cf. Mays, *Hosea*, 91.

322 Hosea uses the independent pronoun הוּא "he" for the Assyrian king to underscore his weakness in contrast to Yahweh (cf. אֲנִי, אָנֹכִי "I" in vv. 12, 14) who is always at work against the sinful nations.

323 The form יִגְהֶה is a *hapax legomenon*; the translation "(he cannot) cure" relies on the parallelism with the verb רפא "to heal"; note the Aramaic cognate *gh'* "to be freed" (in Aph'el "to set free"); cf. BDB, 155.

324 PL 25, 864-865.

325 The verb שלח "to send" has no object here, but based on LXX (ἀπέστειλε πρέσβεις "he sent elders") we may supply "elders" or "messengers."

326 Cf. Oppenheim, *ANET*, 284a

327 PG 71, 157 A-B; cf. Jerome (PL 25, 864) who mentions LXX (*Iarib*), σ' (*ultorem* = ἐκδικητήν?), α', and θ' (*iudicem*) versions.

328 PG 81, 1581 A; cf. Theodore of Mopsuestia, PG 66, 160 A; Theophylact of Bulgaria, PG 126, 669 A.

329 The participle מַצִּיל "rescuer" derives from the verb נצל (Hiph'il) "to take away" (property: Gen 31:9; prey from

the mouth of animals: 1 Sam 17:35; Am 3:12; Ezek 34:10). Note that in Hos 2:12/10 the same verb is followed by the common phrase "from my hand" (cf. Is 43:13).

³³⁰ The word כְּפִיר is conventionally rendered "young lion"; the BDB (498) distinguishes between the "young lion" able to hunt (Jer 25:38; Is 11:6; Ps 104:21), and גּוּר the "whelp" (Ezek 19:2, 3).

³³¹ Cf. Mays, *Hosea*, 92.

³³² PG 126, 669 C.

³³³ PG 81, 1581 B-C; cf. Theodore of Mopsuestia, PG 66, 160 A.

³³⁴ Cf. Andersen and Freedman, *Hosea*, 416.

³³⁵ PG 71, 160 B.

³³⁶ PL 25, 866.

³³⁷ PG 71, 161 A.

³³⁸ The denominative verb שָׁחַר (Pi'el) "to seek early or eagerly," from שַׁחַר "dawn," is found in the Wisdom literature (God: Job 8:5; wisdom: Prov 1:28) and the Psalms (God: 63:2; 78:34).

³³⁹ PG 71, 161 B-C.

³⁴⁰ LXX inserts τὸν θεὸν ἡμῶν "our God."

³⁴¹ MT: יָךְ; LXX: πατάξει; V: *percutiet*; S: *wtbrn* "and he bruised us"; some scholars (Wellhausen, Mays, Wolff, Jeremias, *BHS*) suggest that the abbreviated form of MT is due to haplography, reconstructing a consecutive imperfect (jussive + *waw*), וַיַּךְ "and he struck"; yet, as Macintosh (*Hosea*, 216, 220) notices, the Syriac version which exhibits the conjugation should not be considered strong evidence for such an emendation, since neither LXX nor V has a conjunction. We translated יָךְ by a past tense because the jussive (the short form *yaqtul-*) alone has a perfective meaning; moreover, the parallelism with טָרָף (perfect) "he has torn" requires a past action in the second member.

³⁴² MT: יְחַיֵּנוּ "he will revive us"; cf. V: *vivificabit*; S: *wnḥyn*; note that LXX (ὑγιάσει "he will heal [us]") and σ' (ἐπιδήσει

"he will bind [us]") continue the striking-healing imagery of v. 1.

³⁴³ MT: מִיֹּמָיִם "after two days"; cf. LXX: μετὰ δύο ἡμέρας; V: *post duos dies*; S: *ywmt'* "in days"; Tg: "in the days of consolations to come in the future."

³⁴⁴ MT: בַּיּוֹם הַשְּׁלִישִׁי "on the third day"; cf. LXX: ἐν τῇ ἡμέρᾳ τῇ τρίτῃ; Tg: ביום אחיות מיתיא "on the day of the resurrection of the dead."

³⁴⁵ MT: יְקִמֵנוּ "he will raise us up"; cf. V: *suscitabit nos*; S: *nqymn*; Tg: יקימיננא; but LXX: ἀναστησόμεθα "we shall be raised," perhaps harmonizing this form with the subject of the following verb; cf. Macintosh, *Hosea*, 224.

³⁴⁶ MT: מוֹצָאוֹ "his going forth"; cf. Quinta: ὡς ὄρθρον βέβαια ἡ ἐπιφάνεια αὐτοῦ "as sure as the dawn is his appearance"; V: *egressus eius*; S: *mpqh*; Tg: paraphrases במפקיה "in its going forth" (about the light of the morning); but LXX (εὑρήσομεν αὐτόν "we shall find him") probably is a misreading of נִמְצָאֵנוּ; see Wolff, *Hosea*, 105.

³⁴⁷ MT: יוֹרֶה; LXX: καὶ ὄψιμος (τῇ γῇ) "and latter rain (to the earth); cf. V: *et serotinus terrae*; but S: *dmrw' l'r'*; cf. Tg: דמרוי ערעא "that saturates the earth"; as Macintosh (*Hosea*, 226, 228) notices, there are two interpretations of the MT reading: either a noun ("early rain") or a Hiph'il of ירה related to רוה "to fill, water"; the first alternative, though supported by LXX and V, can not explain the construction with the word "earth"; the second interpretation, supported by S, Tg, and the occurrence of a similar phrase in one of the Qumran hymns (1 QH iv 6), seems more plausible in this context; the verbal form can be explained as a dialectal feature of Hosea's language.

³⁴⁸ MT: חָצַבְתִּי בַּנְּבִיאִים "I have hewn them in pieces by the prophets"; LXX: ἀπεθέρισα τοὺς προφήτας ὑμῶν "I have mown down your prophets"; V: *dolavi in prophetis* "I have hewn into prophets"; S: *psqt nby'* "I have hewn the prophets"; Tg: אזהרתנון בשליחות נביי "I warned them

through the mission of my prophets"; LXX and S have "the prophets" as a direct object of the verb, though MT and Tg see in these prophets an instrument of God's intervention.

[349] MT: וּמִשְׁפָּטֶיךָ אוֹר "and your judgments, a light which goes forth"; cf. V: *et iudicia tua quasi lux* "and your judgments like light"; note that a few V mss., e.g., ms. of Fleury, have *mea* instead of *tua*; cf. Barthélemy, *Critique textuelle*, 526-27; but LXX (καὶ τὸ κρίμα μου ὡς φῶς), S (*wdyny ʾyk nhwrʾ*), and Tg (ודיני כניהור), all presuppose וּמִשְׁפָּטִי כָאוֹר "and my judgment like light"; we follow here the LXX reading, supported by S and, surprisingly, by Tg whose textual history is independent from that of LXX.

[350] MT: חֶסֶד; LXX: ἔλεος "mercy"; Mt 9:13 is a direct quotation from the Septuagint; V: *misericordiam* "mercy"; S: *tybwtʾ* "goodness"; Tg: עבדי חסדא "acts of kindness."

[351] MT: וְלֹא "and not"; cf. V: *et non*; S: *wlʾ*; but LXX: ἤ "rather than"; Tg: מדדבח "than he that sacrifices."

[352] For a detailed discussion on this topic, see Macintosh, *Hosea*, 216ff.

[353] The ideal repentance is outlined by Jesus in the parable of the "Prodigal Son," where the penitent turns the good intention into action, going back to his father (cf. Lk 15:18-20).

[354] PG 126, 673 B.

[355] PG 66, 160 C.

[356] PG 71, 161 D-164 A.

[357] Macintosh (*Hosea*, 219) interprets the return in 5:15 and 6:1 as a regression of both parties to a "place" from which a new beginning is possible.

[358] Cf. Andersen and Freedman, *Hosea*, 419f. The verb טרף indicates the eating of the victim after killing it; note the parallelism between this verb and אכל "to eat" in Gen 37:33. The basic meaning of טרף is "to tear (to pieces)," and this verb is commonly associated with large beasts, "lion" and "wolf," sometimes "panther." The verb נכה (Hiph'il)

refers to a murderous strike (in parallel with הרג "to kill"; cf. Ex 2:12-14).

³⁵⁹ The verb קוּם (Hiph'il) "to raise" may have as a direct object either a sick person (Ps 41:11: here the sick is near death; his enemies hope he will never rise [קוּם Qal] again) or a dead person (Is 26:19; cf. Qal: Ps 88:11; 2 Kgs 13:21); thus this verb's rendition depends on the context in which it occurs.

³⁶⁰ Cf. Andersen and Freedman, *Hosea*, 420f. The primary meaning of חיה (Pi'el) is causative, "to make alive, to revive," rather than permissive, "to let live" (Ex 1:22; Num 31:15).

³⁶¹ According to Wolff (*Hosea*, 118f.), the sequence "after two days, on the third day" sounds like a proverb whose genuine significance is unknown to us. In any event, it does not allude to the ancient beliefs in the resurrection of a fertility god (Adonis, Tammuz; so Baudissin, *Adonis und Esmun* [Leipzig, 1911], 411ff.) because the text concerns a people rather than a deity; cf. Mays, *Hosea*, 95. For Macintosh (*Hosea*, 221f.), this phrase is a "rhetorical device" to describe a short period of time.

³⁶² Cf. Andersen and Freedman, *Hosea*, 422.

³⁶³ *Adversus Marcionem* IV 43; *Adversus Iudaeos* XIII, 23; cf. McCarland, "The Scripture Basis of 'On the Third Day,'" *JBL* 48 (1929): 124-37.

³⁶⁴ PG 81, 1581 C-D.

³⁶⁵ PG 71, 164 A-B.

³⁶⁶ PG 126, 673 C-D.

³⁶⁷ PL 25, 867.

³⁶⁸ PG 66, 160 C.

³⁶⁹ Cf. Garrett, *Hosea, Joel*, 158f.

³⁷⁰ PG 81, 1584 A.

³⁷¹ PG 66, 160 D.

³⁷² The word מוֹצָא "going forth" derives from the root יצא "to go out" and it refers to the sunrise (Ps 19:7).

³⁷³ As Macintosh (*Hosea*, 225) notices, a connection be-

tween שַׁחַר "dawn" and the Ugaritic deity *Šḥr* (*Šaḥru*) (so May) should be rejected for the simple reason that Yahweh cannot be compared with a pagan god.

[374] PL 25, 868.
[375] PL 21, 993 B-C.
[376] PG 81, 1584 A.
[377] PG 71, 164 C.
[378] PG 126, 676 B-C.
[379] Cf. Wolff, *Hosea*, 119.
[380] See Mays, *Hosea*, 96. But Macintosh (*Hosea*, 227) argues that here, as in chapter 2, Hosea polemically attributes to Yahweh the functions of Baal and his sphere of influence.
[381] See the introductory section to 6:1-3.
[382] On the meanings of this word, see the commentary on 2:21/19 and on 4:1.
[383] PG 81, 1584 B.
[384] PG 71, 165 A-B.
[385] PG 126, 677 B.
[386] The verb חצב "to hew in pieces" designates the work on stone, i.e., hewing out a sepulchre (Is 22:16), a vine-press (Is 5:2), or a cistern (Deut 6:11; 2 Chr 26:10); or simply cutting off, presumably, wood (Is 10:15); the same verb is chosen by Isaiah (51:9) to depict Yahweh's victory over the primeval monster Rahab. Attested in Akkadian (*ḥaṣābu*), the root *ḥṣb* is also found in Ugaritic, Phoenician, Aramaic, and Arabic. In the preexilic prophets, this verb describes Yahweh who uses Assyria as an ax to bring judgment upon his people (Is 10:15; cf. Jer 2:13: the pagan gods are compared with a hewn-out cistern); cf. Schunck, "חָצַב *ḥāṣab*," *TDOT*, 5:125ff. Rudolph (*Hosea*, 132f., 139) proposes the meaning "to incise," interpreting this line as an allusion to Moses, the prophet, who carved the Ten Commandments on stone. Yet the parallel with הרג "to kill" does not support such an interpretation. Note that Ugaritic *ḥṣb* means "to fight, slay" (in parallel with *mḫṣ*); cf. C. H. Gordon, *UT* 404a no. 997.

387 In 12:14 Hosea probably refers to Moses; the son of Beeri seems familiar with the prophetic traditions related to Elijah and Elisha (1:4); see the commentary on 1:4 and 12:14.

388 McComiskey (*The Minor Prophets*, 92) sees in these prophets the heralds and witnesses of Israel's destruction. The idea conveyed here is that Israel's demise, far from being the result of some political factors, is according to God's will.

389 PL 21, 993 D.

390 The word אוֹר "light" may refer to the light of the sun (cf. Judg 5:31; Hab 3:4).

391 Andersen and Freedman (*Hosea*, 429) suggest that this line echoes a well rooted tradition (cf. Ps 56:14; Eph 5:14) concerning the connection between the light of the rising sun and the dawn of resurrection.

392 PG 71, 168 A-B.

393 The verb חפץ "to desire" may refer to a husband's desire for his wife (Deut 21:14), or Yahweh's delight in his people (Num 14:8). Interestingly enough, this verb never refers to a secular object; cf. Botterweck, "חָפֵץ *ḥāpēṣ*; חֵפֶץ *ḥēpeṣ*," *TDOT*, 5:92ff. Because of its superior moral qualifications, the verb was used here with Yahweh as its subject.

394 PG 81, 1584 C.

395 PG 71, 168 B, D.

396 PG 126, 680 B.

397 PG 66, 161 C.

398 PL 25, 869.

399 MT: כְּאָדָם "like Adam/man"; LXX: ὡς ἄνθρωπος "like a man"; cf. S: ʾyk br nšʾ; V: *sicut Adam* "like Adam"; Tg: כדריא קדמאי "like previous generations."

400 MT: עֲקֻבָּה מִדָּם "tracked with blood"; cf. θ': ἡ πτέρνα αὐτῆς ἀφ' αἵματος "her footstep is from blood"; α': περικαμπὴς ἀπὸ αἵματος "bent round through blood"; but LXX: ταράσσουσα ὕδωρ "which troubles the water."

⁴⁰¹ MT: וּכְחַכֵּי אִישׁ גְּדוּדִים "as robbers wait in ambush"; LXX: καὶ ἡ ἰσχύς σου ἀνδρὸς πειρατοῦ "your strength (is that) of a pirate"; cf. S: ʿwšnky ʾyk dgbrʾ gysʾ; Quinta: ὡς λόχος πολυχειρίας λῃστρικῆς "like the ambush of a piratical multitude of hands"; V: et quasi fauces virorum latronum "like the throat of the robbers."

⁴⁰² MT: חֶבֶר "a gang"; V: pariceps "a partner"; S: ʾštwtpw "they are partners"; Tg: אתחברו "they are united"; all these versions read חבר as a verb, "to unite"; but LXX: ἔκρυψαν "they hid."

⁴⁰³ MT: שַׁעֲרִירִיָּה; Qere: שַׁעֲרוּרִיָּה; LXX: φρικώδη "horrible thing"; V: horrendum; S: tmhʾ "amazement"; Tg: שנו "strangeness."

⁴⁰⁴ MT: שָׁת; LXX: ἄρχου τρυγᾶν σεαυτῷ "begin to gather the harvest for yourself"; V: pone messem tibi "put the harvest for yourself"; S: ʿbd lk qṭpʾ "make a harvest for yourself."

⁴⁰⁵ MT: רָעוֹת "wicked deeds"; but LXX, V, S have singular nouns.

⁴⁰⁶ MT: יָבוֹא; LXX: πρὸς αὐτὸν εἰσελεύσεται "(a thief) shall come in to him [i.e., Ephraim]"; V: ingressus est; S: ʿl.

⁴⁰⁷ MT: בַּחוּץ "outside"; cf. V: foris; S: bšwqʾ "in the streets"; LXX: ἐν τῇ ὁδῷ αὐτοῦ "in his way."

⁴⁰⁸ MT: וּבַל־יֹאמְרוּ; compare S: wlʾ ʾmryn blbhwn; Tg לא מחשבין בלבהון "they do not say to their hearts"; but LXX: ὅπως συνᾴδωσιν ὡς συνᾴδοντες τῇ καρδίᾳ αὐτῶν "that they may concert together as those singing in accord with their heart."

⁴⁰⁹ Cf. Andersen and Freedman, *Hosea*, 433.

⁴¹⁰ Cf. Macintosh, *Hosea*, 238.

⁴¹¹ PG 81, 1584 D.

⁴¹² PG 71, 169 A-B.

⁴¹³ PL 25, 869-70; cf. Julian of Eclanum, PL 21, 994 A-C.

⁴¹⁴ For more details concerning these various interpretations, see Macintosh, *Hosea*, 236f.; Andersen and Freedman, *Hosea*, 438f.

⁴¹⁵ Cf. Barthélemy, *Critique textuelle*, 527-31.

⁴¹⁶ Garrett (*Joel, Hosea,* 162f.) suggests that *ʾādām*, the personal name of the first man, is used by Hosea as a pun for the city "Adam" to which the adverb "there" in v. 7b might refer.

⁴¹⁷ This phrase, designating the enemies of those who put their trust in God (cf. Is 31:2; Ps 28:3; Prov 6:12), consists of the verb פעל "to do, make," attested in Phoenician, and corresponding semantically to classical Hebrew עשה. The second element of the phrase, אָוֶן "wickedness," is found in the metaphorical name "Beth-aven" for "Bethel" (4:15; 10:5), pointing to idolatry; yet in v. 8 the context requires a more general meaning, i.e., "evil" (but note LXX: ἐργαζομένη μάταια; V: *operantium idolum;* and the ancient interpreters, such as Jerome, Cyril of Alexandria, Theodore of Mopsuestia).

⁴¹⁸ The form עֲקֻבָּה, a *hapax legomenon,* is a passive participle fem. sing., absolute state, related to עקב "to follow at the heel; to assail insidiously (figurative)," a denominative verb from the noun עָקֵב "heel." In 12:3-4 "Jacob," whose name is related to the verb עקב "to grasp one's heel" (cf. Gen 25:25), is followed by the same verb but with its figurative meaning ("to assail insidiously").

⁴¹⁹ Cf. Noth, "Beiträge zur Geschichte des Ostjordanlandes I," *PJ* 37 (1941): 59ff.

⁴²⁰ Cf. Mays, *Hosea,* 101; Macintosh, *Hosea,* 241.

⁴²¹ The noun חֶבֶר is an Aramaic loan-word used in Prophets and Deuteronomy in a pejorative sense, "group, gang"; the wandering bands of *ʿpr* (Ugaritic, Egyptian), associated with the root *ḫbr* "to unite," appear in Akkadian as *ḫabiru;* cf. the Amorite (Mari) noun *ḫibrum* (same root *ḫbr* to which Hebrew חבר "to unite" is related) "clan"; cf. Cazelles, "חָבַר *chābhar;* חָבֵר *chābhēr,*" *TDOT,* 4:193ff.

⁴²² The form חַכֵּי is an infinitive construct, Pi'el, of the root חכה "to wait (in ambush)"; the final "Yod" points to

this root's original third radical, "Yod"; this form can be a dialectal feature or just an orthographic variant of the form with final "He"; GK § 75aa.

[423] The word זִמָּה "plan" derives from the geminate verb זמם "to devise, plan"; except for Job 17:11 where this word has a neutral connotation, it always has a negative meaning, "evil plan" (Is 32:7; Ps 119:150; Prov 10:23; 21:27); cf. S. Steingrimsson, "זמם zmm," TDOT, 4:89.

[424] Note the freedom Hosea takes in using well-established grammatical constructions of Hebrew. Thus, in דֶּרֶךְ יְרַצְּחוּ־שֶׁכְמָה, the verb יְרַצְּחוּ "they commit murder" by its medial position breaks off the construct chain "(on) the way to Shechem" which is against the Hebrew grammar rules. This "broken syntactic chain" is a syntactic peculiarity well attested in Hosea's book (7:5; 8:2; 14:3); cf. Barthélemy, *Critique textuelle*, 532. The vocalization of the locative שֶׁכְמָה "to Shechem" is quite odd if one takes into account the regular pattern found in שְׁכֶמָה (Gen 37:14).

[425] The city of Shechem (today *Tell Balātah* near Nablus) has a long history. For instance, the inhabitants of Shechem were annihilated by Levi and Simeon for the rape of their sister Dinah (Gen 34). In this ancient Levitical city used for refuge (cf. Josh 20:7; 21:21; 1 Chr 6:52), Rehoboam was anointed king (1 Kgs 12:1). It is unlikely that Hosea alludes here to such remote events as those narrated in Gen 37; cf. Garrett, *Hosea, Joel*, 164.

[426] Cf. Mays, *Hosea*, 101; Jacob, "Osée," 56.

[427] PL 25, 871; cf. Julian of Eclanum, PL 21, 995 A.

[428] PG 71, 176 C.

[429] LXX: ἔκρυψαν ἱερεῖς ὁδὸν "the priests hid the way"; but MT: "As robbers wait in ambush, so does a gang of priests."

[430] PG 66, 164 A-B. According to Gen 34, Shechem seduces Dinah, Jacob's daughter by Leah, and then asks for her hand in marriage. Hamor, Shechem's father, proposes an alliance

[431] Cf. Macintosh, *Hosea*, 243f. According to Wolff ("Heimat," 94, n. 70), this was an attack against the Levitic and prophetic opposition with its center in Shechem. In support of his view, Wolff mentions Hosea's positive attitude toward Shechem vis-à-vis his polemic against other places of worship (e.g., Bethel, Gilgal, Mizpah, Tabor, Samaria).

[432] Some scholars (Wellhausen, Weiser, Harper, Wolff) saw in "the house of Israel" an allusion to Bethel (cf. 10:15, where LXX renders "Bethel" [MT] with "house of Israel").

[433] So, e.g., Mays, *Hosea*, 102; cf. other places where Judah occurs: 1:7; 3:5; 4:15; 5:5.

[434] Andersen and Freedman, *Hosea*, 443.

[435] The form שַׁעֲרִירִיָּה "horrible thing" is a *hapax legomenon*; the Masoretes suggested a Qere form שַׁעֲרוּרִיָּה based on its occurrences in Jeremiah's book (Jer 5:30; 23:14); cf. שַׁעֲרֻרִת (Jer 18:13); the noun is construed after a pattern with the third radical doubled (cf. נַאֲפוּפִים "adultery" in 2:4), from an unattested root שער. Note that in Jer 5:30 שַׁעֲרוּרִיָּה is paralleled by שַׁמָּה "horror," and Jer 29:17 has a similar phrase הַתְּאֵנִים הַשֹּׁעָרִים "rotten figs." According to Jacob ("Osée," 56), the Hosean form sounds almost like שַׁעַר יהוה "the gate of Yahweh" which makes one think of שַׁעַר הַשָּׁמַיִם "the gate of heaven," a name given to Bethel (Gen 28:17).

[436] On the parallel טמא // זנה, see 5:3 and the commentary.

[437] The word קָצִיר "harvest" has a neutral connotation (positive: 10:12; negative: 10:13); here the context (the particle גַּם "also" links Judah to Israel in terms of similar fate) requires a negative sense, a harvest of judgment (cf. Is 18:5; Jer 51:33); cf. Andersen and Freedman, *Hosea*, 443f.

[438] Literal: "he (i.e., Yahweh) set/prepared ..."; the form שָׁת has a passive connotation as in Job 38:11 where the third person sg. of the same verb may be translated by a passive; cf. McComiskey, *The Minor Prophets*, 97.

[439] PL 25, 871-72.

[440] PG 71, 177 B.

[441] PG 66, 164 B.

[442] The image of Yahweh as Israel's "healer" is well attested in Hosea's book (5:13; 6:1; 9:3; 14:5/4). But in Hosea, the verb רפא has a wider semantic area than "to heal" a plague, for it may also designate God's forgiveness (14:5/4); cf. Jacob, "Osée," 56.

[443] The phrase שׁוּב שְׁבוּת stands in parallel with רפא "to heal" indicating the restoration of Israel's fortunes; the word שְׁבוּת is derived from שׁוּב "to return"; cf. Dietrich, "שׁוּב שְׁבוּת." *Die Endzeitliche Wiederherstellung bei den Propheten*, BZAW 40 (Giessen, 1925).

[444] According to Andersen and Freedman (*Hosea*, 444), the fem. pl. רעות "wicked deeds" may allude to the "heifers" (עגלות) of Beth-aven (10:5) which match the "calf" (עגל) of Samaria (8:5, 6).

[445] Cf. the more common phrase עשׂה שׁקר (2 Sam 18:13). Note Hosea's predilection for the verb פעל "to do, make" (cf. 6:8), used in the Old Testament especially when idolatry is concerned; see the commentary on 6:8.

[446] Cf. Wolff, *Hosea*, 123f.

[447] PG 126, 685 B.

[448] See the commentary on 4:2; the root גנב "to steal" compared with the verbs designating the act of "robbery" has an element of secrecy; cf. V. Hamp, "גָּנַב *gānabh*," *TDOT*, 3:41f.; perhaps that is why in 7:1 the "thief" is described as going inside to steal while the robbers raid "outside" (בַּחוּץ).

[449] The verb פשׁט "to strip off, make a raid" is especially used of marauding (Judg 9:33; 1 Sam 23:27; 1 Chr 14:9).

[450] PG 71, 180 D.

451 PL 25, 873.
452 PG 81, 1588 A.
453 PG 71, 181 B.
454 PL 21, 996 C; cf. Theodore of Mopsuestia, PG 66, 165 A.
455 PG 81, 1588 B.
456 MT: בֹּעֵרָה מֵאֹפֶה "(an oven) burning from a baker" (lit.); LXX: καιόμενος εἰς πέψιν κατακαύματος "glowing with flame for hot-baking"; S: *dyqd lm'pyt'*; LXX and S follow the Hebrew text in terms of syntax (the *atnach* accent under the second word requires that these two forms be read together); but these two versions vocalize differently the second form, מַאֲפֶה "thing baked," found only in Lev 2:4. Note V: *succensus a coquente* "fired by the baker"; Tg: דאזי ליה נחתומא "which the baker heated for himself." Since תַּנּוּר "oven" is a masc. noun, the final ה on בֹּעֵרָה may be a paragogic "He" used in poetry (GK § 90f); cf. Macintosh, *Hosea*, 257. According to Wolff (*Hosea*, 107), the final ה might have originally been a part of the pronoun הֵם "they" whose final ם was lost (haplography) to the following word מֵאֹפֶה which starts with the same consonant (i.e., "they burn like an oven"; cf. Tg, Wellhausen).
457 MT: הֶחֱלוּ "they make sick"; but LXX: ἤρξαντο; S: *šrwy*; V: *coeperunt*; Tg: שריאו; all presuppose הֵחֵלּוּ "they began."
458 MT: יוֹם מַלְכֵּנוּ "the day of our king"; cf. V: *dies regis nostri*; but LXX: ἡμέραι τῶν βασιλέων ὑμῶν "days of our kings."
459 MT: חֵמָת "heat"; but LXX (θυμοῦσθαι "to be inflamed") presupposes an infinitive, חֲמֹת; cf. Wolff, *Hosea*, 107.
460 MT: לֹצְצִים "scoffers" (Po'lel of ליץ); cf. V: *inlusoribus*; but LXX: λοιμῶν "pestilent fellows"; cf. S: *byš'* "evil men."
461 MT: קֵרְבוּ "they brought near"; cf. V: *applicuerunt* "they applied (their heart)"; but LXX: ἀνεκαύθησαν "(their hearts) are inflamed"; cf. S: *ḥm*. Based on LXX and S, Sellin, Wolff, and Mays proposed קָדְחוּ "they are kindled" as the

Vorlage; cf. Barthélemy, *Critique textuelle*, 539.

⁴⁶² MT: אֹפֵהֶם "their baker"; α': ὁ πεσών "the baker"; V: *coquens eos* "(the heart) which bakes them"; but S: *rwgzhwn*; Tg: רגזהון "their anger"; LXX: Ἐφραίμ "Ephraim." As Wolff (*Hosea*, 107) observes, the following verse supports S and Tg, hence the proposed reading אַפָּהֶם "their anger/passion."

⁴⁶³ Cf. Noth, *The Old Testament World* (translated by V. Gruhn; Philadelphia, 1966), 159f.

⁴⁶⁴ PL 25, 874; cf. Julian of Eclanum, PL 21, 997 B; Cyril of Alexandria, PG 71, 181 D.

⁴⁶⁵ PG 66, 165 B; cf. Theophylact of Bulgaria, PG 126, 688 D.

⁴⁶⁶ PG 81, 1588 B-C.

⁴⁶⁷ PG 71, 184 A; cf. Theophylact of Bulgaria, PG 126, 689 A.

⁴⁶⁸ Note that the Christian writers (among others, Theophylact of Bulgaria, PG 126, 689 B) explain "adultery" as another term for idolatry. More recently, Andersen and Freedman (*Hosea*, 455) equate the "adulterous" with the priests.

⁴⁶⁹ PG 71, 185 B.

⁴⁷⁰ PL 25, 874.

⁴⁷¹ PL 25, 875.

⁴⁷² According to Macintosh (*Hosea*, 260f.), "to stretch out the hand" means to give a signal; thus, when the opportunity comes Pekah gives a signal to his co-conspirators.

⁴⁷³ For Wolff (*Hosea*, 125), the "scoffers" are the prophet's enemies, those who have ridiculed him. But the context in which this term appears makes one think of political conspirators; note LXX rendition, λοιμῶν "pestilent fellows"; cf. S: *byš'* "evil men."

⁴⁷⁴ PG 81, 1588 D-1589 A.

⁴⁷⁵ PG 126, 692 B-C.

⁴⁷⁶ PL 21, 997 C.

⁴⁷⁷ PG 126, 693 A.

478 The term "heart" (לֵב) in Hebrew includes all the aspects of a person: vital, emotional, voluntative, and noetic; in this particular case, the "heart" represents the voluntative center (conceiving/planning); cf. Fabry, "לֵב *lēḇ*; לֵבָב *lēḇāḇ*," TDOT, 7:399-437.

479 PG 71, 188 B; cf. Theodore of Mopsuestia, PG 66, 168 A.

480 MT: זָרְקָה "sprinkled upon"; LXX: ἐξήνθησαν "came upon"; cf. S: *npq* "came out."

481 MT: בְּכָל־זֹאת; cf. LXX: ἐν πᾶσι τούτοις; this phrase is missing in S.

482 MT (אִיסְּרֵם "I will chastise") should be read as a Pi'el, אֲיַסְּרֵם; cf. Wolff, Hosea, 107; LXX: παιδεύσω.

483 MT: לְעֵדָתָם "to their assembly"; cf. α': τῆς συναγωγῆς αὐτῶν; V: *coetus eorum*; LXX: τῆς θλίψεως "of their affliction"; S: *dshdwthwn* "of their witness"; Tg: לעיצתהון "of their counsels." Based on LXX, one may propose לְרָעָתָם.

484 MT: יִתְגּוֹרָרוּ; LXX: κατετέμνοντο "they cut themselves"; V: *ruminabant* "they ruminated"; S: *mtktšyn* "they struggled"; Tg: הוו כנשין "they were gathering"; LXX represents probably the original reading, יִתְגּוֹדָדוּ.

485 MT: יָסוּרוּ; cf. σ': ἐξέκλιναν ἀπ' ἐμοῦ "they turned away from me"; cf. V: *recesserunt a me*; LXX: ἐπαιδεύθησαν ἐν ἐμοί "they were instructed by me"; but S (*mrdw*) and Tg (מרדו) presuppose the root סרר "to rebel" which is also supported by the preposition בּ "against."

486 MT: יִסַּרְתִּי; LXX omits the first verb, reading only κατίσχυσα "I strengthened"

487 MT: לֹא עָל "not [to] what is above"; LXX: εἰς οὐθέν "to nothing"; cf. S: *'l l' mdm*; but σ' (εἰς τὸ μὴ ἔχειν ζυγόν) and V (*ut essent absque iugo*) presuppose עֹל "yoke." Based on LXX, one may assume an original with a reversed word order, עַל לֹא "to [what is] not."

488 The verb בלל "to mix, mingle" (the Hithpolel form in Hos 7:8 is a *hapax legomenon*) is used in liturgical contexts

as referring to the mixture of flour (cakes) and oil (Ex 29:40; Lev 2:5; Num 7:19).

⁴⁸⁹ According to Andersen and Freedman (*Hosea*, 466), the Hithpolel may have either a middle or a reflexive meaning. The reflexive option would point to Ephraim's adopting foreign manners and thus losing his national identity. The middle meaning emphasizes Ephraim's continuous confusion ("he is completely mixed").

⁴⁹⁰ The perfect of היה "has become" underlines the completeness or certainty of Ephraim's new status; cf. McComiskey, *The Minor Prophets*, 108.

⁴⁹¹ The noun עֻגָה (Gen 18:6; 1 Kgs 17:13; 19:6) derives from a root ʿ-w-g not found in biblical Hebrew but attested in Arabic (*ʿawija* "to be curved") and it refers perhaps to the (oval/round?) shape of this bread.

⁴⁹² PG 71, 188 D; cf. Theophylact of Bulgaria, PG 126, 693 C.

⁴⁹³ PL 21, 998 B.

⁴⁹⁴ PL 25, 877.

⁴⁹⁵ PG 81, 1589 B; cf. Theodore of Mopsuestia, PG 66, 168 B.

⁴⁹⁶ Andersen and Freedman (*Hosea*, 467) suggest, based on the parallel with 5:7 (בָּנִים זָרִים "bastard sons"), that these "foreigners" might refer to Ephraim's own bastard children. But in the context of 7:9 "foreigners" is likely another term for Assyria and Egypt (cf. "peoples," v. 8).

⁴⁹⁷ The word כֹּחַ may refer to physical strength (Lev 26:20; Judg 16:5; Is 44:12), but also to power of a people or king (Josh 17:17; Is 49:4; Dan 8:22).

⁴⁹⁸ See the "Introduction I. Historical Background: The Assyrian Expansion and the Last Years of Israel."

⁴⁹⁹ PG 71, 189 A.

⁵⁰⁰ The verb זרק "to sprinkle" is commonly used with blood in a sacrificial setting (Ex 24:6; Lev 17:6; Num 18:17; 2 Kgs 16:13).

[501] PL 25, 877; cf. Julian of Eclanum, PL 21, 998 C.
[502] PG 71, 189 B.
[503] The "pride" (גְּאוֹן) refers here to Israel's self-confidence or arrogance (cf. Am 6:8); see the commentary on 5:5.
[504] PL 25, 877.
[505] PG 71, 189 C.
[506] On the meaning of בקשׁ, see the commentary on 5:6.
[507] On the meaning of פתה, see the commentary on 2:16/14.
[508] PG 81, 1589 D.
[509] PL 21, 998 D.
[510] PL 25, 878.
[511] Wolff (*Hosea*, 127) draws attention to the motif of a fluttering bird (cf. 11:11) found also in Tiglath-pileser III's Annals for the year 733 B.C.; cf. Macintosh, *Hosea*, 274.
[512] PL 25, 879.
[513] PG 66, 168 C.
[514] PL 21, 999 B.
[515] PG 71, 192 C.
[516] PG 126, 697 A.
[517] PL 25, 879.
[518] According to Wolff (*Hosea*, 127), this cry of woe (cf. 9:12) marks the climax of the collection of sayings.
[519] Cf. 9:17 (about Israel wandering among the nations). Hosea uses in 4:12 a different root, תעה (Hiph'il) to render the idea of going astray, far away from God, through divination and idolatry; see the commentary on 4:12.
[520] PG 81, 1592 A.
[521] The root פשׁע may denote rebellion in a political (1 Kgs 12:19; 2 Kgs 1:1; 3:5; 2 Chr 10:19) or a religious sense (Is 1:28; 46:8; 53:12; Am 4:4; Dan 8:23).
[522] Cf. Is 13:6; 22:4; 51:19; Jer 48:3; Am 5:9.
[523] The pronoun אָנֹכִי "I" underlines the idea that Yahweh himself wants to redeem Israel.
[524] The word כְּזָבִים "lies" (cf. 12:2) implies willful per-

version of God's image; cf. Andersen and Freedman, *Hosea*, 473.

525 The same root, פדה, is used in Deuteronomy (9:26; 13:6; 21:8) to describe the deliverance from Egypt.

526 PL 25, 880.

527 The root ילל commonly translated "to wail" designates an inarticulate scream as in funerary laments or witnessing a catastrophe; cf. Baumann, "ילל *yll*; יְלֵל *yᵉlēl*; יְלָלָה *yᵉlālâ*," *TDOT*, 6:82-87.

528 Macintosh (*Hosea*, 280) suggests that מִשְׁכְּבוֹת "beds, couches" may denote here sexual intercourse as in Lev 18:22; Judg 21:11f.; Is 57:8.

529 Cf. יִתְגּוֹדָדוּ "they gash themselves" — emended text based on LXX reading: κατετέμνοντο "they cut themselves."

530 PG 71, 193 B-C.

531 PG 126, 697 C.

532 PL 21, 999 C.

533 PG 66, 169 B; cf. Theodoret of Cyrus, PG 81, 1592 C; Theophylact of Bulgaria, PG 126, 697 D.

534 The root סרר is used in 4:16 to depict Israel's stubbornness; see the commentary on 4:16.

535 Cf. Mays, *Hosea*, 112.

536 Note that the root יסר has the basic idea of discipline or chastisement; see the commentary on 7:12.

537 PG 66, 169 C.

538 PL 21, 999 D-1000 A.

539 PG 81, 1592 C.

540 PL 25, 881.

541 PG 126, 700 C.

542 The emended text עַל לֹא is based on LXX reading; see the textual note on 7:16 above.

543 PL 25, 882.

544 PL 25, 881.

545 PG 71, 197 A-B.

⁵⁴⁶ Cf. Macintosh, *Hosea*, 288.

⁵⁴⁷ MT: אֶל־חִכְּךָ "to your palate" (lit.); cf. V: *in gutture tuo sit tuba* ; LXX: εἰς κόλπον αὐτῶν ὡς γῆ "on their lap, like a land"; S: *pwmk ʾyk qrnʾ* "your mouth like a horn."

⁵⁴⁸ MT: אֱלֹהָי "my God"; cf. V: *deus meus* ; LXX: ὁ θεός "O God"; S: *ʾlhn* "our God."

⁵⁴⁹ MT: יִשְׂרָאֵל; LXX and S omit this word; in Wolff's (*Hosea*, 131) view, these two versions may represent the original reading.

⁵⁵⁰ MT: אוֹיֵב יִרְדְּפוֹ lit.: "An enemy shall pursue him" (cf. S, V, Tg); but LXX (ἐχθρὸν κατεδίωξαν "they pursued the enemy") considered the pronominal suffix as the affix 3mpl, and, by consequence, the subject "enemy" became the object of the verb; cf. Wolff, *Hosea*, 131.

⁵⁵¹ MT: הֵשִׂירוּ "they set up officials" (Hiph'il of שׂרר) but LXX: ἦρξαν "they ruled"; cf. S: *wʾštltw*; V: *principes extiterunt*.

⁵⁵² MT: יִכָּרֵת; but LXX (ἐξολεθρευθῶσιν "they will be destroyed") shows a plural verb — in reference to "idols"; cf. S, Tg.

⁵⁵³ MT: זָנַח "he rejected"; but LXX (ἀπότριψαι "cast off!") presupposes זְנָחִי; cf. α', θ'; V: *proiectus est* "it was rejected."

⁵⁵⁴ MT: כִּי מִיִּשְׂרָאֵל "for from Israel"; LXX: ἕως τίνος οὐ μὴ δύνωνται καθαρισθῆναι ἐν τῷ Ἰσραήλ "How long will they be unable to purge themselves in Israel?"; V: *quia ex Israel et ipse est*; S: *mṭl dmn ʾysrʾl hw*.

⁵⁵⁵ MT: יִהְיֶה; but 4QpHosᵇ: היה; cf. Macintosh, *Hosea*, 311. The perfect (Qumran) is supported by LXX: ἦν "was"; cf. S.

⁵⁵⁶ MT: שְׁבָבִים "pieces"; cf. 4QHosᵇ: [ם]בבי[שו; cf. Macintosh, *Hosea*, ad loc.; Tg: נסרי לוחין "bits of boards"; LXX: πλανῶν "(your calf was) a deceiver"; cf. S: *lṭʿywtʾ* "as an error."

⁵⁵⁷ MT: אֵין־חֵפֶץ בּוֹ; LXX: ἄχρηστον "worthless"; cf. S; but V: *immundum* "unclean."

⁵⁵⁸ MT: יִתְּנוּ; but LXX: παραδοθήσονται "they shall be

delivered (to the nations)" and S: *nštlmwn* presuppose a passive, יִתְּנוּ.

⁵⁵⁹ MT: וַיָּחֵלּוּ "they began" (<חלל); but LXX (καὶ κοπάσουσι "they will cease") presupposes the root חדל "to cease"; V: *et quiescent* "and they will have rest"; cf. S: *wnttnyḥwn*. We read here וַיָּחִילוּ a form of the verb חיל "to be in labor, writhe" (cf. Rudolph, Wolff, Andersen and Freedman).

⁵⁶⁰ MT: מִמַּשָּׂא; cf. S: *mn šqlʾ*; V: *ab onere* "from the burden"; but LXX (τοῦ χρίειν "[they shall cease a little] to anoint [a king]") presupposes מִמְּשֹׁחַ.

⁵⁶¹ MT: לַחֲטֹא; cf. S: *lḥṭyʾ* "to sin"; LXX: εἰς ἁμαρτίας ἐγένοντο αὐτῷ θυσιαστήρια ἠγαπημένα "[his] beloved altars became sins to him"; V: *ad pecandum* "for sinning."

⁵⁶² MT: זִבְחֵי הַבְהָבַי; but LXX (θυσιαστήρια τὰ ἠγαπημένα "beloved altars") presupposes the root אהב "to love"; note that V (*hostias adfer adfer*) divided the second form into הב הב (imperative of יהב "to give").

⁵⁶³ MT: מִצְרַיִם יָשׁוּבוּ; LXX adds καὶ ἐν Ἀσσυρίοις ἀκάθαρτα φάγονται "and they shall eat unclean things among the Assyrians."

⁵⁶⁴ The MT reads: "set the horn to your palate (חִכְּךָ)." The parallel between חֵךְ "palate" and שָׂפָה "lip" in Prov 5:3 makes one consider Hosea's choice a dialectal variant for lips.

⁵⁶⁵ According to Wolff (*Hosea*, 137), "House of Yahweh" is a prophetic replica to the political expression *bît humria*, found in Tiglath-pileser III's Annals (cf. Heb. בֵּית עָמְרִי), "House (Land) of Omri." Phrases like "Beth ("house") + proper name" were also used as place names (e.g., Beth-Haran, Beth-Dagon).

⁵⁶⁶ PL 21, 1000 C.

⁵⁶⁷ PG 126, 701 B-C.

⁵⁶⁸ PG 81, 1593 A.

⁵⁶⁹ The image of נֶשֶׁר "vulture" is frequently used to de-

scribe an enemy (Deut 28:49; Jer 4:13; 48:40; Lam 4:19; Ezek 17:3).

[570] PG 81, 1593 A.

[571] PG 71, 197 C-D.

[572] PL 25, 883.

[573] Cf. McComiskey, *The Minor Prophets*, 119; on elliptical sentences, see GK § 147.

[574] Cf. Macintosh, *Hosea*, 292.

[575] PG 66, 172 A.

[576] On the meaning of בְּרִית, see the commentary on 2:20.

[577] Cf. Jacob, "Osée," 61.

[578] Cf. Andersen and Freedman, *Hosea*, 489.

[579] See the textual note on 8:2 above.

[580] PL 25, 883.

[581] PG 81, 1593 B.

[582] PG 66, 172 B.

[583] PL 21, 1000 D.

[584] In the Hebrew Bible טוֹב "good" is used as a personal name for God (cf. Am 5:14f.; Mic 6:8).

[585] PL 21, 1001 A.

[586] PG 71, 200 C.

[587] Andersen and Freedman (*Hosea*, 491) suggest that Hosea chose אוֹיֵב "enemy" as a parody for אֹהֵב "lover" (2:9).

[588] PL 25, 883.

[589] PL 25, 883-84.

[590] PG 66, 172 C.

[591] PG 81, 1593 B-C.

[592] According to Wolff (*Hosea*, 139), the root עצב I "to form," from which the word עֲצַבִּים "idols" derives, points contemptuously to a homophonous root עצב II "to hurt, pain."

[593] For Andersen and Freedman (*Hosea*, 492-93), the destruction of the idols represents a portent of the national catastrophe.

594 Cf. Garrett, *Hosea, Joel*, 183, n. 12.

595 Cf. Mays, *Hosea*, 118; Macintosh, *Hosea*, 304.

596 The imperative "Reject!" is supported by LXX reading; see the textual note on 8:5 above.

597 PL 25, 884.

598 PG 71, 201 C.

599 The word נִקָּיוֹן "purity" derives from the root נקה "to be empty." The verb (Niph'al) is found in Num 5:31 with the meaning "to be empty/free of guilt" (innocent); hence נִקָּיוֹן, which appears three times with כַּפַּי "my palms" (cf. Gen 20:5; Ps 26:6; 73:13), may denote innocence.

600 PG 66, 172 D.

601 *Hosea*, 141.

602 The *hapax legomenon* שְׁבָבִים may be connected to the Arabic verb *sabba* "to cut" or the Middle Hebrew שָׁבַב "to hew"; for a detailed discussion on the meaning of this word, see Macintosh, *Hosea*, 308-310.

603 PG 81, 1593 D.

604 Cf. Andersen and Freedman, *Hosea*, 497. On pseudosorites, see O'Connor, "The Pseudosorites: A Type of Paradox in Hebrew Verse," JSOTSup 40 (1987): 161-72.

605 PG 71, 204 B.

606 PG 66, 173 A.

607 PG 81, 1596 A.

608 PG 126, 708 C.

609 Cf. Wolff, *Hosea*, 142.

610 PL PG 66, 173 B.

611 PL 25, 886.

612 PG 81, 1596 B.

613 PG 71, 205 A.

614 PG 126, 709 B.

615 Cf. Mays, *Hosea*, 121.

616 PL 25, 887.

617 PL 21, 1003 A.

618 On the relationship between תנה "to pay a prostitute"

and אֶתְנָה "wages, pay," see the commentary on 2:14/12.

[619] Cf. Oppenheim, *ANET*, 284; Wolff (*Hosea*, 143) notices that, in political documents of the eighth century B.C., the breach of a treaty was labeled "whoredom."

[620] PG 81, 1596 B.

[621] Cf. McComiskey, *The Minor Prophets*, 129.

[622] PG 126, 712 A.

[623] Cf. emended text; see the textual note on 8:10 above.

[624] PL 25, 887.

[625] PG 66, 173 C.

[626] PG 71, 208 A-B.

[627] As Jacob ("Osée," 64) notices, Hosea plays on the double meaning of the root חטא "to sin" and "to make a sin-offering; to purify from sin."

[628] According to Andersen and Freedman (*Hosea*, 508), Ephraim's altars are condemned because they are employed for alien sacrifices mentioned in v. 13.

[629] PL 25, 888-89.

[630] PG 81, 1596 C.

[631] PG 126, 713 A.

[632] PG 71, 208 C.

[633] For the latter interpretation's arguments, see Macintosh, *Hosea*, 326; the phrase אֵל זָר "strange (illicit) god" appears in Ps 44:21; 81:10; cf. Is 17:10; 43:12; and in pl. in Deut 32:16.

[634] This written Torah contained the Decalogue to which 4:2 alludes; see the commentary on 4:2.

[635] PL 25, 888.

[636] PL 21, 1004 A-B.

[637] PG 66, 173 D. A similar interpretation is found in Theodoret of Cyrus, PG 81, 1596 C-D; and Theophylact of Bulgaria, PG 126, 713 A.

[638] On זֶבַח as the most common sacrifice in the preexilic times, see Rost, "Erwägungen zum israelitischen Brandopfer," BZAW 77 (1958): 177-83.

⁶³⁹ PG 81, 1597 A. A similar interpretation is found in Theophylact of Bulgaria, PG 126, 716 A-B.

⁶⁴⁰ PG 66, 173 D–176 A.

⁶⁴¹ PL 25, 888.

⁶⁴² PG 71, 209 C.

⁶⁴³ The verbal sequence זכר "to remember," פקד "to punish" has a strong legal connotation (9:9; cf. 7:2 זכר where appears alone); see Childs, *Memory and Tradition in Israel* (London, 1962), 32.

⁶⁴⁴ On "iniquity"—"sin," see the commentary on 4:8.

⁶⁴⁵ PG 66, 176 A.

⁶⁴⁶ In Hosea "forgetting" equates with "faithlessness" (2:13/11; 4:6; 13:6); cf. Mays, *Hosea*, 124.

⁶⁴⁷ PG 71, 213 A.

⁶⁴⁸ PL 25, 889-890.

⁶⁴⁹ PG 81, 1597 C. A similar interpretation is found in Theodore of Mopsuestia, PG 66, 176 B.

⁶⁵⁰ MT: אֶל־גִּיל "toward exultation"; but LXX (μηδὲ εὐφραίνου "neither make merry"; cf. V, S) presupposes אַל תָּגֵל.

⁶⁵¹ MT: דָּגָן "grain"; S omits this word; according to Macintosh (*Hosea*, 339), this is not a real omission because Syriac ʾdr means both "corn" and "threshing floor."

⁶⁵² MT: לֹא יִרְעֵם (verb רעה II "to feed"); cf. V: *non pascet eos* "(it) will not feed them"; S: lʾ nsbʿwn "they will not be filled (by the threshing floor)"; but LXX (οὐκ ἔγνω αὐτούς "[the threshing floor] did not know them") presupposes יְדָעָם or יֵדָעֵם from the root ידע "to know."

⁶⁵³ MT: בָּהּ "her"; but LXX, V, S, Tg, all read בָּם "them," which fits better in the context.

⁶⁵⁴ MT: וְיָשֻׁב "shall return"; but LXX (κατῴκησεν) reads יָשַׁב "dwelt" probably because of v. 3a (MT: יֵשְׁבוּ; LXX: κατῴκησαν).

⁶⁵⁵ MT: זִבְחֵיהֶם "their sacrifices"; LXX, V, all read "sacrifices" together with the following words, and consider

יין "wine" the subject of יַעֲרְבוּ "please (him)"; but note S (lʾ nbsmwn lh dbḥyhwn "their sacrifices will not please him") which takes into account the parallelism of the members.

[656] MT: מִשֹּׁד "from destruction"; LXX (πορεύονται ἐκ ταλαιπωρίας Αἰγύπτου "they go forth from the trouble of Egypt") considers "Memphis" the subject of "gather," and מַחְמַד, read as a place name, Μαχμάς, the subject of "bury"; note S: bbzʾ "through plunder."

[657] MT: קִמּוֹשׂ "nettles"; cf. V: urtica "stinging-nettle"; LXX: ὄλεθρος "destruction"; S: nwkryʾ "foreigners."

[658] MT: יֵדְעוּ; cf. V: scitote; S: ndʿ; Tg: יִדְעוּן; αʹ, σʹ: καὶ ἔγνω; based on LXX reading (κακωθήσεται "shall be afflicted"), van Hoonacker (cf. Wolff, Hosea, 150) proposes יָרִיעַ "(Israel) will shout" introducing a direct speech. But as Rudolph (Hosea, ad loc.) suggested, the verb may be taken with what precedes. Thus, Israel "will know (experience)" the imminent punishment predicted by the prophet.

[659] MT: מַשְׂטֵמָה "hostility"; but LXX: μανία "madness"; cf. V: amentiae; S: šryḥwtk "your intemperance."

[660] MT: צֹפֶה; LXX: σκοπὸς Εφραιμ "the watchman of Ephraim (is with God)"; cf. V: speculor Ephraim; S: dwqʾ ʾprym "Ephraim is a watchman."

[661] MT: אֱלֹהָי; LXX: μετὰ θεοῦ "with God"; according to Wolff (Hosea, 151), the MT reading is secondary and does not fit with אֱלֹהָיו "his God" (LXX: θεοῦ) in v. 8b.

[662] MT: הֶעְמִיקוּ; cf. V: profunde peccaverunt "they profoundly sinned"; LXX takes this verb with what precedes (μανίαν ... κατέπηξαν "they established ... madness").

[663] MT: הַגִּבְעָה "Gibeah"; but LXX translates, τοῦ βουνοῦ "of the hill."

[664] The pair שמח—גיל is found in Joel 2:21; Zeph 3:14; Ps 16:9, etc.

[665] PL 21, 1005 A.
[666] PL 25, 890.
[667] PG 81, 1597 C.

[668] PG 66, 176 B-C.
[669] Cf. Wolff, *Hosea*, 153.
[670] PG 126, 717 B.
[671] PG 66, 176 C.
[672] PG 71, 213 D-216 A.
[673] See Mays, *Hosea*, 126.
[674] PL 21, 1005 B.
[675] PG 81, 1597 D.
[676] PG 66, 176 C.
[677] PG 126, 717 B.
[678] PG 71, 216 A.
[679] PL 25, 891.
[680] PG 81, 1600 A.
[681] PL 25, 892.
[682] PG 176 D.
[683] The verb ערב "to be sweet, pleasing" is a technical term used in the cultic sphere (Ezek 16:37; Jer 6:20; Mal 3:4; Ps 104:34).
[684] Cf. Andersen and Freedman, *Hosea*, 528. On the contrary, Jerome (PL 25, 892) indicates that the people's offerings will not enter the house of the Lord (i.e., the temple in Jerusalem) because this was destroyed with fire by the Babylonians.
[685] PG 81, 1600 B.
[686] PL 21, 1005 D-1006 A.
[687] PG 71, 216 B-C.
[688] The word חג "feast" refers primarily to the three annual festivals: Unleavened Bread, Weeks, and Tabernacles.
[689] PL 21, 1006 B.
[690] PG 126, 720 D-721 A.
[691] PG 71, 217 B.
[692] According to Wolff (*Hosea*, 156), the "tents" refer to those inhabited by the pilgrims during the festival.
[693] PG 81, 1600 C.
[694] PG 71, 220 B.

Commentary: Hosea 4-11

[695] PL 25, 892.

[696] PG 66, 177 D.

[697] PG 126, 721 A-B. A similar interpretation is found in Julian of Eclanum, PL 21, 1006 B.

[698] The word שִׁלּוּם "retribution" appears in two other texts (Is 34:8: paralleled by נָקָם "vengeance"; and Mic 7:3).

[699] The word אֱוִיל "fool" has also a moral connotation, i.e., evil person (Prov 1:7; 15:5; cf. Jer 4:22; Is 19:11; Ps 107:17).

[700] The phrase "man of spirit" is probably a variant for "man of God" (אִישׁ הָאֱלֹהִים), a prophetic title found in the Old Testament (1 Sam 9:6; 1 Kgs 12:22; 2 Kgs 5:8).

[701] The substantivized participle Pu'al מְשֻׁגָּע "mad" derives from the root שׁגע connected probably to Arabic śajaʿa "to coo" (of male pigeon); hence about a bubbling person (2 Kgs 9:11; Jer 29:26).

[702] PL 25, 894.

[703] PG 71, 220 D.

[704] The word "hostility" (מַשְׂטֵמָה) found only in Hos 9:7, 8 derives from the root שׂטם "to bear a grudge, cherish animosity" (Gen 27:41; 49:23; Ps 55:4; Job 16:9). The word משטמה appears in the Qumran writings (e.g., "War Scroll" 13:11: "You created Belial for the pit, angel of hostility; his [dom]ain is in darkness, his counsel is for evil and wickedness"). In the book of Jubilees (10.7; 11.5; 17:16) this word is a name of Satan.

[705] PL 21, 1007 A.

[706] PG 66, 180 A.

[707] PG 81, 1600 D.

[708] PG 71, 221 D.

[709] PL 21, 1007 B.

[710] PG 66, 180 B.

[711] PL 25, 895.

[712] PG 81, 1601 A.

[713] Cf. Jacob, "Osée," 69.

[714] PL 21, 1008 A.

715 PG 66, 180 B-C.

716 PG 126, 725 C.

717 PL 25, 895.

718 MT: כְּבִכּוּרָה; LXX: ὡς σκοπὸν "as a watchman."

719 MT: בְּרֵאשִׁיתָהּ; LXX: πρώϊμον "early"; V: *in cacumine eius* "in its top."

720 MT: אֲבוֹתֵיכֶם; LXX, V, S, all presuppose אֲבוֹתֵיהֶם "their fathers"; other versions in Hexapla have ὑμῶν "your."

721 MT: כְּאָהֳבָם "like their loving" (infinitive construct + suffix); LXX: ὡς οἱ ἠγαπημένοι "as the loved ones"; in Wolff's view (*Hosea*, 160), a better alternative would be to read this form either as a noun, אֹהֲבָם (cf. 3:1) or as an active participle (Pi'el), מְאַהֵב (cf. 2:7/5-15/13); V: *sicut ea quae dilexerunt*; cf. S: ʾyk drḥmw.

722 MT: בְּשׁוּרִי מֵהֶם (root שׁוּר II "to go away"); cf. α': ἐκκλίναντός μου ἀπ' αὐτῶν "when I turn away from them"; V: *cum recessero ab eis*; Tg: בסלקותי שכינתי מנהון "when I remove my presence from them"; but LXX (σάρξ μου ἐξ αὐτῶν "my flesh is from them") misreads בְּשָׂרִי.

723 MT: לָצוּר שְׁתוּלָה; LXX: εἰς θήραν παρέστησαν τὰ τέκνα αὐτῶν "they exposed their children as a prey"; θ': εἰς πέτραν πεφυτευμένοι οἱ υἱοὶ αὐτοῦ "his sons are planted in rock." According to Wolff (*Hosea*, 160-161), MT represents the most recent phase, θ' occupies a middle position, and LXX indicates probably the oldest phase. Note also V: *Tyrus erat fundata in pulchritudine* "(Ephraim) was Tyre established in beauty"; cf. Tg: דמיא לצור באצלחותה בשליותה "she [i.e., Israel] is like Tyre in her prosperity and ease."

724 MT: אֶל־הֹרֵג "to the slayer"; LXX: εἰς ἀποκέντησιν "for slaughter."

725 MT: אֱלֹהָי "my God"; LXX: ὁ Θεὸς "God."

726 Wolff, *Hosea*, 163.

727 Jacob, "Osée," 70.

728 Bach (*Die Erwählung Israels in der Wüste* [dissertation; Bonn, 1952]) names this tradition "discovery tradition."

[729] PG 71, 229 B.
[730] PL 25, 896.
[731] PL 21, 1008 B.
[732] PG 81, 1601 B-C.
[733] PG 66, 180 C.
[734] Idols are to be detested (Deut 7:26). In the second century B.C. the statue of Zeus set up by Antiochus IV Epiphanes in the Temple in Jerusalem was called שִׁקּוּץ מְשׁוֹמֵם "the abomination of desolation" (Dan 11:31; 12:11); cf. Andersen and Freedman, *Hosea*, 541.
[735] The city, where the sanctuary בית פעור "house of Peor" (Deut 3:29) has been located, is commonly identified with *Khirbet ʿAjūn Mūsa*, 3 miles west of Shittim; cf. Wolff, *Hosea*, 165.
[736] PL 25, 896.
[737] PG 81, 1601 C.
[738] The word "glory" in the context of v. 11 could mean a large offspring. In Judg 18:21, the noun כְּבוּדָה is found near טַף "children" and מִקְנֶה "cattle," and it refers to a multitude of children (cf. Prov 23:5; Is 21:16); see Weinfeld, כָּבוֹד *kābôd*, *TDOT*, 7:25. This interpretation is also found in Jerome, PL 25, 897.
[739] Hos 9:11 is the only example of the verb עוּף "to fly" in Hithpoʿel which here may have an iterative meaning; cf. Andersen and Freedman, *Hosea*, 542.
[740] According to Mays (*Hosea*, 133-34), the sequence "birth, pregnancy, conception" found in v. 11 points to the reversal of bearing children, the cessation of fertility.
[741] PG 126, 729 A.
[742] PG 81, 1601 C-D.
[743] PL 21, 1009 A.
[744] PG 66, 181 A.
[745] PL 25, 898.
[746] PG 81, 1604 A-B.
[747] PG 66, 181 B.

[748] So Wolff, *Hosea*, 166.
[749] PG 81, 1604 B-C.
[750] PG 126, 732 A-B.
[751] Cf. Macintosh, *Hosea*, 374.
[752] PG 81, 1604 C.
[753] PG 66, 181 C.
[754] PG 71, 233 D.
[755] PL 25, 899.
[756] *Hosea*, 136.
[757] On the location of Gilgal, see the commentary on 4:15.
[758] Cf. Jacob, "Osée," 71.
[759] PL 21, 1010 A.
[760] PG 81, 1604 C.
[761] PG 66, 181 C.
[762] The verb גרשׁ "to drive out, banish" is used with respect to Adam and Eve driven out of Paradise, away from the presence of God (Gen 3:24). In legal passages (Lev 21:7, 14; Num 30:10; cf. Ezek 44:22), the same verb refers to a divorced woman; see Ringgren, "גָּרַשׁ *gārash*," *TDOT*, 3:68-69.
[763] PG 126, 733 B.
[764] PG 71, 236 C.
[765] PG 81, 1604 D.
[766] PG 66, 181 D.
[767] PL 25, 900.
[768] According to Andersen and Freedman (*Hosea*, 546), the masculine plural suffix on "womb" shows that God's punishment is not directed exclusively at the women but it concerns all the people.
[769] PG 126, 736 B.
[770] Cf. Macintosh, *Hosea*, 378.
[771] Jacob ("Osée," 72) notices that Saul's rejection is described by the same terms (1 Sam 15:23, 26).
[772] The verb נדד "to flee, wander" is found mostly in ex-

ilic and postexilic texts, in pieces of elevated prose replacing the more common roots ברח and נוס; it refers to restless and panicky wandering (Is 16:3; 21:14; Jer 49:5) see Gross, "נָדַד *nādad,*" *TDOT,* 9:227-31. The verb נדד appears in the story of Cain (Gen 4:12). Braun ("Der Fahrende," *ZThK* 48 [1951]: 32ff.) connects LXX term πλανήτης "wanderer" (a *hapax legomenon*) with Sophocle's expression πλανήτης Οἰδίπους, suggesting that Hosea might be considered the spiritual father of the "eternal Jew" motif.

773 PL 21, 1010 C.
774 PG 66, 181 C-184 A.
775 PG 71, 240 A.
776 MT: בּוֹקֵק; LXX: εὐκληματοῦσα "with many branches"; V: *frondosa* "with many leaves/ leafy"; Tg: בזיזא "ravaged." The form בוקק should be connected to Arab *baqqa* "to branch off"; cf. Wolff, *Hosea,* 170.
777 MT: יְשַׁוֶּה; LXX: εὐθηνῶν "abundant"; V: *adaequatus est* "became equal"; S: *dᶜbdt* "which yielded." The basic meaning of שוה is "to place" but when preceded by "fruit" it could be rendered "to yield fruit."
778 MT: חָלַק לִבָּם "he divided their heart"; LXX: ἐμέρισαν καρδίας αὐτῶν "they have divided their hearts"; α', σ': ἐμερίσθη καρδία "the heart is divided"; cf. V: *divisum est cor eorum*; S: *ʾtplg lbhwn*; the context requires a passive form, חָלַק "divided" from the root חלק I "to divide."
779 MT: יֶאְשָׁמוּ; cf. S: *nthybwn* "they shall be guilty"; but LXX (ἀφανισθήσονται "they shall be destroyed") and V (*interibunt*) assume שמם "to be desolated, appalled."
780 MT: דִּבְּרוּ "they spoke"; cf. S: *mllw*; LXX: λαλῶν "speaking"; V: *loquimini* "you speak."
781 MT: כְּרֹאשׁ; LXX: ὡς ἄγρωστις "like a weed"; V: *quasi amaritudo* "like bitterness"; Tg: כריש חוין בישין "like the poison of venomous serpents."
782 MT: שֹׁכֵן (sg.); but LXX: κατοικοῦντες "inhabitants" (plural); cf. V: *habitatores.*

783 MT: יָגוּרוּ; LXX: παροικήσουσιν "they shall dwell near" (cf. גור I "to dwell"); but α': ἐσεβάσθησαν; V: *coluerunt* "they worship"; Tg: פלחו "they shall fear"; all presuppose גור III "to be afraid."

784 MT: לְעֶגְלוֹת (pl.); cf. V: *vaccas*; Tg: לעגליא; but LXX (τῷ μόσχῳ) and S (*lʿglʾ*) presuppose a singular (לעגל).

785 MT: וּכְמָרָיו; LXX: καθὼς παρεπίκραναν αὐτόν "as they provoked him"; but α': τεμενίτης "consecrated"; S: *ʿmh wkwmrwhy* "its people and priests"

786 MT: יָגִילוּ; LXX: ἐπιχαροῦνται "they shall rejoice"; cf. V: *exultaverunt*.

787 On מלך ירב, see note on 5:13.

788 MT: מֵעֲצָתוֹ; LXX: ἐν τῇ βουλῇ αὐτοῦ "in his counsel"; V: *in voluntate sua*. Wellhausen suggested the reading מֵעַצְבּוֹ "of its idol"; cf. Macintosh, *Hosea*, 405.

789 MT: נִדְמָה "(Samaria) was reduced to silence"; but LXX: ἀπέρριψε Σαμάρεια βασιλέα αὐτῆς "Samaria has cast off her king"; cf. V: *transire fecit Samaria regem suum*.

790 *Hosea*, 172-73.

791 The translation "luxuriant vine" fitting the context well, is based on LXX reading (εὐκληματοῦσα "with many branches") and on an Arabic cognate verb *baqqa* "to grow profusely"; see the textual note above; see also Andersen and Freedman, *Hosea*, 549-50. The Hebrew word בּוֹקֵק derives from the verb בקק "to lay waste" (Qal: Is 24:1; Jer 19:7; Pi'el: Jer 51:2).

792 This is the only place in the Old Testament where גֶּפֶן "vine" is construed as a masculine noun, which can be explained as either a dialectal variant or an indication that the "vine" is Israel; cf. McComiskey, *The Minor Prophets*, 159.

793 PL 25, 902.
794 PL 21, 1011 A.
795 PG 81, 1605 A.
796 PG 71, 240 C.
797 Cf. Garrett, *Hosea, Joel*, 207.

⁷⁹⁸ On מַצֵּבוֹת "pillars," see the commentary on 3:4.
⁷⁹⁹ See Mays, *Hosea*, 139.
⁸⁰⁰ PG 66, 184 B.
⁸⁰¹ PG 71, 240 D.
⁸⁰² Cf. Jacob, "Osée," 73-74.
⁸⁰³ Cf. Macintosh, *Hosea*, 390-91.
⁸⁰⁴ See the textual note above.
⁸⁰⁵ PL 21, 1011 B.
⁸⁰⁶ PL 25, 903.
⁸⁰⁷ PG 66, 184 B; cf. Theodoret of Cyrus, PG 81, 1605 B.
⁸⁰⁸ By replacing "Yahweh" (יהוה) with "he" (הוּא), Hosea meant to underscore that Yahweh is "He Who Is." A similar use of the 3rd ms pronoun is attested in the Qumran texts. For instance, 1QS 8.13 (cf. Martínez, *The Dead Sea Scrolls Translated. The Qumran Texts in English* [2nd edition; Leiden: Brill & Grand Rapids: Eerdmans, 1996], 12) reads: "to walk to the desert in order to open there His (הואה) path"; cf. Jacob, "Osée," 74, n. 1.
⁸⁰⁹ The verb ערף "to break the neck (of an animal)" (Ex 13:13; 34:20; Deut 21:6; Is 66:3) is a denominative from עֹרֶף "back of neck, neck." In Hos 10:2 this verb is used figuratively of breaking down altars.
⁸¹⁰ See the commentary on 7:13 and 9:6.
⁸¹¹ PG 71, 241 A.
⁸¹² "Fear of God" in the language of the Old Testament describes a profound religious experience rather than a psychological reality; see Fuhs, "יָרֵא *yārēʾ*; יָרֵא *yārēʾ*; יִרְאָה *yirʾâ*; מוֹרָא *môrāʾ*," *TODT*, 6: 290ff.
⁸¹³ Cf. Macintosh, *Hosea*, 393.
⁸¹⁴ PL 25, 903.
⁸¹⁵ PG 81, 1605 B-C.
⁸¹⁶ PG 71, 241 B-C.
⁸¹⁷ PG 66, 184 C.
⁸¹⁸ Cf. Mays, *Hosea*, 140; Wolff, *Hosea*, 175; contra Macintosh (*Hosea*, 397), who interprets this phrase as a reference

to Israel's alliances with great powers.

[819] The word שָׂדַי "field" is an archaic form for שָׂדֶה.

[820] Cf. Andersen and Freedman, *Hosea*, 554.

[821] PL 25, 903.

[822] PL 21, 1012 B.

[823] PG 81, 1605 C; cf. Theodore of Mopsuestia, PG 66, 184 D.

[824] PG 71, 244 A-B.

[825] The MT has sg. שְׁכַן (< st. abs. שָׁכֵן) "inhabitant," while LXX reads plural οἱ κατοικοῦντες. According to Wolff (*Hosea*, 171), the Hebrew word could be an old collective noun.

[826] Thus, for instance, Julian of Eclanum, PL 21, 1012 C.

[827] The root גור III "to tremble" appears sometimes in cultic settings (Ps 22:24; 33:8). Garrett (*Hosea, Joel*, 209, n. 89) suggests that phrase גּוּר בָּעַל (2 Chr 26:7) should be rendered "the dread of Baal" rather than "sojourner of Baal" (< גור I "to dwell").

[828] On "Beth-aven," see the commentary on 4:15.

[829] See the commentary on 8:5-6.

[830] We read the singular "calf" based on LXX (cf. S) reading; see the textual note above. According to Rudolph, the MT plural עֶגְלוֹת "heifers" should be understood as an abstract plural meaning "calfery" > "the calf cult"; see the discussion in Macintosh, *Hosea*, 399-400. Andersen and Freedman (*Hosea*, 555) take this plural noun as an example of *plurale majestatis* designating the name of a deity (a goddess?).

[831] The verb אבל means "to mourn" for the deceased. Note an interesting parallel in Ezek 8:14 where the women of Jerusalem "mourn" for god Tammuz (the Mesopotamian variant of Baal).

[832] Israel is depicted as a calf's people rather than Yahweh's; cf. Hosea's prophecy on Lo-Ammi "No-My-People," 1:9.

[833] Hosea is the first Old Testament author to use the term כֹּמֶר "idol-priest" (cf. 2 Kgs 23:5; Zeph 1:4; with respect to Baal's worship), instead of the more common כֹּהֵן "priest,"

to designate the idolatrous priests. W. Mowinckel (",כֹּמֶר כמר," ZAW, 36 [1916]: 238f.) connects כֹּמֶר to the root *kmr* "to be excited" (the Mari texts describe *kumrum* as an ecstatic); see Ringgren, "כֹּהֵן *kōhēn*," *TDOT* 7, 65. A form *kb-ma-ri* (cf. var. *ku-ma-ri*) "priests" associated with Ninurta's worship (in a sacrificial context) appears in Late Bronze texts from Emar (northern Syria); cf. Pentiuc, "West Semitic Terms in Akkadian Texts from Emar," *JNES* 58 (1999): 91-93.

[834] Cf. Mays, *Hosea*, 141.

[835] PG 81, 1605 D.

[836] PG 71, 244 D.

[837] The verb גִיל commonly means "to rejoice, exult," but Macintosh (*Hosea*, 400) suggests that it may also have the meaning "to show distress" (cf. Saadya on Ps 2:11). Yet the regular connotation "to exult" is firmly supported by the ancient versions (e.g., LXX: ἐπιχαροῦνται "they shall rejoice"); see the textual note above.

[838] In the case of the "calf," כָּבוֹד "glory" refers to the external aspect of the idol (e.g., golden ornamentation).

[839] The verb גָּלָה "to depart, remove" may also mean "to go into exile" (Judg 18:30; 2 Kgs 17:23; 25:21; Is 5:13). The perfect used here designates completed action, though the captivity has not yet started; cf. McComiskey, *The Minor Prophets*, 166-67. Note that 1 Sam 4:22 uses the same language with respect to the ark of covenant captured by the Philistines: "The glory (כָּבוֹד) has departed (גָּלָה) from Israel."

[840] Cf. Macintosh, *Hosea*, 401.

[841] *Hosea*, 557.

[842] PL 25, 905.

[843] The verb יבל "to bring, carry" is used when one speaks of a tribute (Ps 68:30; Is 18:7).

[844] According to Andersen and Freedman (*Hosea*, 557), the use of מִנְחָה "gift, tribute" suggests the idol will be carried to Assyria by Israel rather than taken as booty by the

great power.

⁸⁴⁵ On the phrase "great king," see the commentary on 5:13.

⁸⁴⁶ Cf. Macintosh, *Hosea*, 403f.; Rashi observes that 1 Kgs 12:28 uses the cognate verb יָעַץ "to make plans" when speaking of Jeroboam I's cultic strategy. On the contrary, Wolff (*Hosea*, 176) suggests that עֵצָה means "political plan" (cf. Is 30:1). Yet the former interpretation fits better in the context.

⁸⁴⁷ PG 81, 1605 D-1608 A; cf. Theodore of Mopsuestia, PG 66, 185 B.

⁸⁴⁸ PG 71, 245 C.

⁸⁴⁹ See the commentary on 4:5.

⁸⁵⁰ Mays (*Hosea*, 142) interprets "king" as a title for the calf-idol of vv. 5f.

⁸⁵¹ The word קֶצֶף is a *hapax legomenon* commonly related to the root קצף "to be angry," hence in this text the word designates the "agitation" or "boiling" of water; cf. Macintosh, *Hosea*, 406.

⁸⁵² PL 25, 906-907.

⁸⁵³ PL 21, 1012 D.

⁸⁵⁴ PG 66, 185 C.

⁸⁵⁵ PG 126, 744 C-D.

⁸⁵⁶ PG 71, 248 B.

⁸⁵⁷ On בָּמוֹת "high places," see the commentary on 4:11-13.

⁸⁵⁸ According to Andersen and Freedman (*Hosea*, 559), the verb שׁמד "to be destroyed" (Niph'al) designates usually the extermination of persons, not of things; thus "Israel's Sin" may be the name of an idol.

⁸⁵⁹ PL 25, 907.

⁸⁶⁰ PG 66, 185 C.

⁸⁶¹ PG 71, 248 C-D; cf. Theophylact of Bulgaria, PG 126, 745 B-C.

⁸⁶² MT: חָטָאתָ (second person sg.), but LXX: ἥμαρτεν; cf.

V: *peccavit* (third person sg.).

[863] MT: עֲלָוָה; LXX: ἀδικίας "iniquity"; cf. V: *iniquitatis*; S: *dʿwlʾ*; MT is due perhaps to the metathesis of עַוְלָה (Wolff).

[864] MT: בָּאתִי; LXX: ἦλθεν "he came"; according to Ziegler (*Duodecim prophetae*), ἦλθεν is a an inner corruption of ἦλθον; V: *iuxta desiderium meum* "according to my wish."

[865] MT: וְאֶסְרֵם should be read וַאֲיַסְּרֵם (7:13); cf. Wolff, *Hosea*, 178; LXX: παιδεῦσαι αὐτούς; V: *corripiam eos*; but Tg: אאסרם "I will bind them."

[866] MT: בְּאָסְרָם; LXX: ἐν τῷ παιδεύεσθαι αὐτούς; V: *cum corripientur* suppose the root יסר "to chastize" rather than אסר "to bind" (so Tg: כמיסר "as one who ties [a yoke]").

[867] MT: עֵינֹתָם (= Ketib) "before both their eyes"; but עוֹנֹ־תָם (= Qere) "both their iniquities" is supported by LXX (ἐν ταῖς δυοῖν ἀδικίαις αὐτῶν), V, and S.

[868] MT: אַרְכִּיב; LXX: ἐπιβιβῶ "I will mount Ephraim"; V: *ascendam*.

[869] MT: יַחֲרוֹשׁ; cf. V: *arabit*; but LXX: παρασιωπήσομαι "I will pass (over Judah) in silence."

[870] MT: יְשַׂדֶּד; cf. V: *confringet* "he will harrow"; LXX: ἐνισχύσει "he will prevail."

[871] MT: לְפִי־חֶסֶד; cf. V: *in ore misericordiae* "in the mouth of mercy"; LXX: εἰς καρπὸν ζωῆς "for the fruit of life."

[872] MT: נִירוּ לָכֶם נִיר; LXX: φωτίσατε ἑαυτοῖς φῶς γνώσεως "light for yourselves the light of knowledge"; V: *innovate vobis novale* "restore the fallow land." As Wolff (*Hosea*, 180) notices, the LXX reading (γνώσεως) makes more sense in the context than MT וְעֵת "it is the time." The MT reading is due perhaps to a misreading of ד as ו. Note V: *quoniam est tempus* "for there is time."

[873] MT: לִדְרוֹשׁ (infinitive); LXX: ἐκζητήσατε "Seek!" (imperative).

[874] MT: עַד־יָבוֹא וְיֹרֶה "until he comes and teaches"; note that ירה II Hiphʿil "to cause to rain" is not attested in the

Old Testament; V: *cum venerit qui docebit* "when he comes who will teach"; LXX: ἕως τοῦ ἐλθεῖν γενήματα "until the fruits (of righteousness) come (to you)."

⁸⁷⁵ MT: בִּדְרָכֶךָ; cf. V: *in viis tuis*; LXX: ἐν τοῖς ἁμαρτήμασί σου "in your sins"; perhaps the LXX is a corruption or correction of an original reading, ἅρμασι "chariots"; cf. Macintosh, *Hosea*, 427.

⁸⁷⁶ MT: וְקָאם; according to Wolff (*Hosea*, 181), א in קאם is a secondary linear vocalization (cf. GK § 72p).

⁸⁷⁷ MT: שַׁלְמַן; LXX: Σαλαμάν; V: *Salman* ; S: *šlmʾ*.

⁸⁷⁸ MT: בֵּית אַרְבֵּאל; cf. σ': ἐν τῷ οἴκῳ τοῦ ἀρβεήλ; but LXX: ἐκ τοῦ οἴκου Ἱεροβοάμ "of the house of Jeroboam"; V: *a domo eius qui indicavit Baal* "from his house that indicated Baal."

⁸⁷⁹ MT: עָשֹׂה; cf. V; but LXX (ποιήσω "I will do") presupposes אֶעֱשֶׂה.

⁸⁸⁰ MT: בֵּית־אֵל; LXX: οἶκος τοῦ Ἰσραήλ "house of Israel."

⁸⁸¹ MT: מִפְּנֵי רָעַת רָעַתְכֶם "because of the wickedness of your wickedness" (lit.); cf. V; but LXX: ἀπὸ προσώπου κακιῶν ὑμῶν.

⁸⁸² Cf. Andersen and Freedman, *Hosea*, 561.
⁸⁸³ Cf. Jacob, "Osée," 75.
⁸⁸⁴ Cf. Wolff, *Hosea*, 183.
⁸⁸⁵ See the commentary on 9:9.
⁸⁸⁶ PL 21, 1013 A.
⁸⁸⁷ PG 81, 1608 B.
⁸⁸⁸ PG 71, 249 B.
⁸⁸⁹ Cf. Wolff, *Hosea*, 184.
⁸⁹⁰ PL 25, 908.
⁸⁹¹ PG 66, 185 D.
⁸⁹² PG 71, 252 A.
⁸⁹³ See the textual note above.
⁸⁹⁴ Cf. Macintosh, *Hosea*, 413.
⁸⁹⁵ Cf. Wolff, "Das Geschichtsverständnis der alttesta-

mentlichen Prophetie," *EvTh* 20 (1960): 218-35.

[896] Andersen and Freedman (*Hosea*, 566) suggest that "iniquity" in Hosea could designate an idol, like "Sin" and "Shame."

[897] PL 25, 908.

[898] PG 126, 748 A; a similar interpretation on the dual transgression of Israel (i.e., idolatry and apostasy) is found in other ancient Christian writers: Cyril of Alexandria, PG 71, 252 B; Julian of Eclanum, PG 21, 1013 C-D; Theodoret of Cyrus, PG 81, 1608 B-C; Theodore of Mopsuestia, PG 66, 188 A.

[899] Cf. "stubborn heifer" (פָּרָה סוֹרֵרָה), another metaphor for Israel, in 4:16; see the commentary ad loc.

[900] Cf. Wolff, *Hosea*, 185.

[901] PL 25, 909.

[902] PG 81, 1608 C.

[903] PG 66, 188 A.

[904] PL 21, 1014 B.

[905] Cf. Macintosh, *Hosea*, 420; ibn Ezra: the yoke of commandments.

[906] On "righteousness" (צְדָקָה) and "mercy" (חֶסֶד), as covenantal terms, see the commentary on 2:21/19.

[907] PG 126, 749 C.

[908] PL 25, 910.

[909] Cf. LXX reading (φῶς γνώσεως); see the textual note above.

[910] PG 66, 188 C.

[911] PG 81, 1609 B.

[912] PG 71, 257 B.

[913] The basic meaning of the root בטח is "to feel secure, be unconcerned"; cf. A. Jepsen, "בָּטַח *bāṭach*," *TDOT*, 2:89.

[914] See the textual note above.

[915] The word גִּבּוֹר means "hero"; here, it refers to professional soldiers (cf. 2 Sam 20:7).

[916] Oppenheim, *ANET*, 278-79.

917 Oppenheim, *ANET*, 284-85.
918 PL 25, 912.
919 PL 25, 912.
920 The verb רטשׁ in Pi'el illustrates the mass murder of children by dashing them in pieces upon the rocks (cf. 2 Kgs 8:12; Is 13:16; Ps 137:9).
921 Thus, for instance, Cyril of Alexandria, PG 71, 260 A-B; Theodoret of Cyrus, PG 81, 1609 C; Julian of Eclanum, PL 21, 1015 B.
922 Oppenheim, *ANET*, 282.
923 Cf. Mays, *Hosea*, 149.
924 Cf. LXX interpretation "house of Israel"; see the textual note above.
925 PL 25, 913.
926 PL 21, 1015 C.
927 PG 81, 1609 D; cf. Theodore of Mopsuestia, PG 66, 189 B.
928 PG 71, 261 A-B.
929 PG 126, 756 C.
930 PL 25, 914.
931 MT: כִּי; most scholars take כִּי here in a temporal sense, "when"; but the ancient versions, LXX (ὅτι "because"), V (*quia*), Tg, S, suppose a causal sense.
932 MT: וּמִמִּצְרַיִם "And out of Egypt"; as Macintosh (*Hosea*, 439) notices, Tg offers a temporal interpretation: "And from the time of Egypt, I called them sons (בנין)."
933 MT: לִבְנִי "my son"; cf. V: *filium meum* ; S: *bry*; α' and θ': τὸν υἱόν μου; but LXX: τὰ τέκνα αὐτοῦ "his children"; according to Wolff (*Hosea*, 190), the LXX ("his children") harmonizes "Israel" in v. 1a with "them" in v. 2; as for the Tg reading, בנין "sons," this tries to avoid a Christological interpretation; cf. Macintosh, *Hosea*, 439.
934 MT: קָרָאוּ; cf. V; but LXX: καθὼς μετεκάλεσα "as I called (them)."
935 MT: מִפְּנֵיהֶם "from them" reflects a wrong division

of the consonants (cf. V: *a facie eorum*); LXX (ἐκ προσώπου μου. αὐτοί "from my face; they ...") supposes מִפָּנַי הֵם.

[936] MT: תִרְגַּלְתִּי; LXX: συνεπόδισα "I bound their feet"; σ′: ἐπαιδαγώγουν "I taught"; S: *dbrt* "I led"; V: *quasi nutritius*; as for the Hebrew form, this is a Tiph'el verb; cf. GK § 55h.

[937] MT: קָחָם; but LXX: ἀνέλαβον αὐτόν "I took him up"; V: *portabam eos* "I carried them"; S: *wqblt 'nwn* "I received them"; all suppose the first person singular, וָאֶקָּחֵם.

[938] MT: זְרוֹעֹתָיו "his arms"; but LXX: τὸν βραχίονά μου "my arm" (cf. S, V).

[939] MT: בְּחַבְלֵי אָדָם; LXX: ἐν διαφθορᾷ ἀνθρώπων "when men were destroyed"; V: *in funiculis Adam* "with the ropes of Adam."

[940] MT: כִּמְרִימֵי; LXX: ὡς ῥαπίζων ἄνθρωπος "like a man smiting (*another* on his cheek)"; V: *quasi exaltans* ; S: *'yk hw dmrym* "like one who lifts."

[941] MT: עֹל "yoke"; cf. V, S; it is not found in LXX; the imagery (father-son) in chapter 11 requires a different vocalization of the MT form, עוּל "infant."

[942] MT: וְאַט אֵלָיו אוֹכִיל "and I bent down [Hiph'il imperfect of נטה] to him that I might feed him"; LXX: καὶ ἐπιβλέψομαι πρὸς αὐτόν, δυνήσομαι αὐτῷ "and I will look well at him, I will prevail over him"; V: *et declinavi ad eum ut vesceretur* "I lower [food] to him so that he may eat."

[943] MT: לֹא "not" at the beginning of v. 5 is perhaps a hearing mistake for לוֹ "to him" (Wolff); LXX: reads αὐτῷ "to him" and takes it with v. 4.

[944] MT: יָשׁוּב "he returns"; cf. V; but LXX: κατῴκησεν "he dwelt" (יָשַׁב; cf. 9:3).

[945] MT: אֶל־אֶרֶץ; LXX: Ἐφραίμ "Ephraim (dwelt in Egypt)."

[946] MT: וְחָלָה "(the sword) whirls" (= Qal of חוּל); cf. Tg: ותחול; LXX: ἠσθένησεν "(the sword) became weak"; cf. S; V: *coepit* "began" (= Hiph'il of חלל).

[947] MT: בַּדָּיו "his bars" (cf. בַּד II); LXX: ἐν ταῖς χερσὶν

αὐτοῦ "(the sword became weak) in his hands"; cf. S; V: *electos eius* "his elected"; Tg: גיברוהי "his warriors."

[948] MT: וְאָכָלָה "it devours"; but LXX: φάγονται "they devour"; cf. S.

[949] MT: תְּלוּאִים "they are hung"; LXX: ἐπικρεμάμενος "hang over"; cf. V: *pendebit*.

[950] MT: לִמְשׁוּבָתִי "on apostasy from me"; LXX: ἐκ τῆς κατοικίας αὐτοῦ "from his dwelling-place"; V: *ad reditum meum* "to my returning"; S: *lmtb lwty* "to return to me."

[951] MT: וְאֶל־עַל; LXX: καὶ ὁ θεὸς ἐπί "and God with (his precious things shall be angry)"; V: *iugum autem* "but the yoke" (= עֹל); cf. α': καὶ πρὸς ζυγόν; S: *wlʾlh* "to God." We read here בַּעַל "Baal" following Sellin's suggestion, supported by the parallel with v. 7a (cf. Wolff, *Hosea*, 192).

[952] MT: יִקְרָאֻהוּ; LXX: τὰ τίμια αὐτοῦ "his precious things" (= יְקָר); α': καλέσει αὐτόν "he will call him"; V: *imponetur ei* "it is set upon him." Perhaps, the MT reading is due to a scribal mistake, i.e., combining two words (הוּא "he" and יִקְרָאוּ "they call") into one word (cf. Sellin).

[953] MT: לֹא יְרוֹמֵם; LXX: οὐ μὴ ὑψώσῃ αὐτόν "and he shall not at all exalt him"; V: *simul quod non auferetur* "at once, which will not be removed."

[954] MT: יַחַד in a negative context may be translated with "not at all."

[955] MT: אֲמַגֶּנְךָ "(how) can I surrender you" (= מגן I "to deliver up" [only in Pi'el]; cf. Gen 14:20); LXX: ὑπερασπιῶ σου "shall I protect you?"; cf. V, S.

[956] MT: נִחוּמָי "remorse"; LXX: ἡ μεταμέλειά μου "my repentance"; cf. V; α', σ': παράκλησις "consolation"; θ': τὰ σπλάγχνα τοῦ ἐλέους μου "the inwards of my compassion" (= רַחֲמָי).

[957] MT: יַחַד "totally" (lit.); LXX: ἐν τῷ αὐτῷ "at once"; cf. V.

[958] MT: וְלֹא אָבוֹא בְּעִיר; cf. LXX: καὶ οὐκ εἰσελεύσομαι εἰς πόλιν "and I will not enter into the city"; V, S. The MT

reading may be considered an example of dittography, i.e., וְלֹא אֲבַעֵר "I will not exterminate"; cf. Wolff, *Hosea*, 193.

⁹⁵⁹ MT: בָּנִים מִיָּם "sons from the sea" (lit.); cf. V: *filii maris*; LXX: τέκνα ὑδάτων "children of waters"; Tg: גלותא ממערבא "the captives from the west."

⁹⁶⁰ MT: וְהוֹשַׁבְתִּים "I shall settle them" (Hiph'il of יָשַׁב); but the presence of the preposition עַל and LXX reading (ἀποκαταστήσω αὐτούς "and I will restore them [to their houses])" suppose וַהֲשִׁיבוֹתָם "I shall return them" (Hiph'il of שׁוּב).

⁹⁶¹ Cf. Jacob, "Osée," 80.

⁹⁶² Cf. Mays, *Hosea*, 152.

⁹⁶³ Cf. Wolff, *Hosea*, 196.

⁹⁶⁴ According to Macintosh (*Hosea*, 437), the term נַעַר "boy, lad" was chosen to underscore Israel's status in Egypt, since this term means also "servant."

⁹⁶⁵ PG 71, 264 A-B.

⁹⁶⁶ PG 66, 189 B.

⁹⁶⁷ PG 81, 1609 D-1612 A; cf. Theophylact of Bulgaria, PG 126, 757 A.

⁹⁶⁸ Cf. Mays, *Hosea*, 153.

⁹⁶⁹ PL 25, 915-916.

⁹⁷⁰ Cf. Garrett, *Hosea, Joel*, 221.

⁹⁷¹ PG 126, 757 B.

⁹⁷² Cf. Mays, *Hosea*, 154.

⁹⁷³ On "burning incense," see the commentary on 2:15/13; on "sacrifices," see the commentary on 8:13.

⁹⁷⁴ On "Baals," see the commentary on 2:15/13.

⁹⁷⁵ PL 21, 1017 A.

⁹⁷⁶ PL 25, 914.

⁹⁷⁷ PG 71, 265 A.

⁹⁷⁸ PG 126, 757 D.

⁹⁷⁹ The same root רפא "to heal, care" appears in one of the Exodus narratives, the story of the bitter water of Marah (Ex 15:22-26). God promises the Israelites that if they will

observe his commandments he won't bring any disease on them, for he is Yahweh, their "healer."

[980] PG 71, 265 B.
[981] PG 66, 189, C.
[982] PG 126, 760 A.
[983] Garrett (*Hosea, Joel*, 224) suggests that "human" may be an allusion to Moses as an intermediary between God and his people during the wilderness' years.
[984] PL 25, 917.
[985] PG 126, 760 C.
[986] According to Macintosh (*Hosea*, 451), the mention of Assyria as Israel's "king" may be an indication that king Hoshea was already arrested and brought into captivity.
[987] PG 71, 268 D, 269 A-B.
[988] Mays (*Hosea*, 155-56; cf. KBL, 109), suggests בַּד; V has "oracle-priests" (Is 44:25; Jer 50:36) but this meaning does not fit well in the context.
[989] PG 66, 192 B.
[990] Admah and Zeboim are mentioned together with Sodom and Gomorrah in Gen 10:19; 14:2, 8; the text of Deut 29:23 adds that Admah and Zeboim were destroyed with the other two cities (cf. Gen 19:24-25). Why Admah and Zeboiim instead of better known Sodom and Gomorrah? Perhaps these two cities reflect a northern tradition; cf. Macintosh, *Hosea*, 462-63.
[991] PL 25, 920.
[992] PG 81, 1612 C-D.
[993] PG 71, 273 A.
[994] Cf. Jacob, "Osée," 82-83.
[995] Cf. Wolff, *Hosea*, 202.
[996] PL 25, 920.
[997] PL 21, 1019 B.
[998] PG 71, 276 A-B.
[999] PG 81, 1613 A; cf. Theodore of Mopsuestia, PG 66, 192 D; Theophylact of Bulgaria, PG 126, 768 A.

[1000] One may add that Jer 31:20 is probably the oldest commentary on Hos 11:8-9.
[1001] See Jacob, "Osée," 83.
[1002] PL 25, 921.
[1003] PG 66, 193 A.
[1004] PG 81, 1613 B.
[1005] PL 21, 1020 B.
[1006] PL 25, 921.
[1007] Mays, *Hosea*, 159.
[1008] PG 81, 1613 C; cf. Julian of Eclanum, PL 21, 1020 B.
[1009] PG 71, 277 A; cf. Theophylact of Bulgaria, PG 126, 768 C.

III. THE LAST SAYINGS (12-14)

1. Ephraim and Jacob (12:1/11:12-12:15/14)[1]

11:12/12:1. Ephraim has surrounded me with deceit and the house of Israel with treachery. But Judah still walks[2] with God, and is faithful to the Holy One.[3] 2/1. Ephraim herds[4] the wind, and pursues the east wind all day long; they multiply falsehood and violence;[5] they make a treaty with Assyria, and oil is carried[6] to Egypt. 3/2. Yahweh has a dispute with Judah, and he will punish Jacob according to his ways, and repay him according to his deeds. 4/3. In the womb he deceived his brother, and in his manhood[7] he wrestled with God. 5/4. He wrestled[8] against an angel and he prevailed; he wept and pleaded with him. At Bethel[9] he found him, and there he spoke with him.[10] 6/5. Yahweh, God of Hosts; Yahweh is his name. 7/6. As for you, return to your God, observe mercy and justice, and wait continually for your God. 8/7. Canaan[11] — false balances in his hand! He loves to oppress.[12] 9/8. Ephraim said, "Indeed, I am rich; I have found a fortune[13] to myself. All my[14] gains do not amount to an offense which is sin.[15] 10/9. But I am Yahweh your God[16] from the land of Egypt. Once more I will make you dwell in the tents as in the days of the appointed festival. 11/10. I spoke through[17] prophets, and I myself multiplied the visions, and by means of the prophets I spoke in parables.[18] 12/11. If Gilead was evil, surely they have become worthless. In Gilgal they sacrifice bullocks.[19] Thus their altars will be like stone-heaps on the furrows of the field. 13/12. Jacob fled to the

345

land of Aram, Israel served for a wife, for a wife he kept sheep. 14/13. But by a prophet Yahweh brought up Israel from Egypt; by a prophet he was kept. 15/14. Ephraim has bitterly grieved [him]. He will leave his bloodshed on him; his Lord will bring back his reproach on him.

Chapter 11 with its emphasis on Yahweh's saving love toward Israel represents the conclusion of a long section, chapters 4-11. With chapter 12 begins a new complex made of the last sayings of prophet Hosea.

The main theme of this pericope, looking to the past, is the accusation (vv. 1, 2, 4, 8, 12, 13, 15) of Israel whose history was from the onset marked by "deceit" (כַּחַשׁ) (v. 1), "falsehood" (כָּזָב) (v. 2) and "treachery" (מִרְמָה) (vv. 1a, 8) in her relationship with God. Ephraim's behavior (vv. 1, 9) is almost identical to that of his ancestor, patriarch Jacob/Israel (vv. 4-5, 12). Among the "masters of deception" the prophet lists Ephraim (vv. 2, 8), Jacob (vv. 4, 13), and the inhabitants of Gilgal (v. 12). Judah's attitude contrasts sharply with that of Ephraim (v. 1) at least for a time since in v. 3 one is told that Yahweh has a "dispute" (רִיב) even with Judah. A threat (v. 3) and an exhortation to repentance (v. 7) are followed by the proclamation of God's judgment (vv. 10, 12). Verse 15 repeats in a modified form the threat of v. 3.

The unity of this chapter is secured by Hosea's typical way of connecting verses with various terms and motifs. For instance, the term "treachery" (מִרְמָה) (v. 1a) is echoed in "bitterness" (תַּמְרוּרִים) (v. 15a) and the motif of "observance" (שׁמר) goes through vv. 7, 13, 14.[20]

The relationship between the Jacob traditions used by Hosea in chapter 12 and those found in the book of Genesis is still debated. Some aspects reported in Genesis are underscored, while others are completely passed by in silence. Is this the mark of ignorance? In any event, there is no clear conclusion from Hosea on the character of Jacob. The patriarch is portrayed with both his mistakes and virtues and no critical appraisal is offered.

The sayings found in this literary unit were probably delivered in Bethel (v. 5) and Gilgal (v. 12) in the first years of Shalmaneser V (727-722 B.C.), when what remained from the Northern Kingdom was oscillating between Egypt and Assyria.[21]

Verse 1 introduces a sharp contrast between the two Israelite kingdoms "Ephraim" / "house of Israel"[22] and "Judah." The pronominal suffix first person singular refers to God and not to the prophet.[23] Thus, in relationship with God, Ephraim acts with "deceit" (כַּחַשׁ) and "treachery" (מִרְמָה),[24] as an apostate nation, while Judah is "faithful" (נֶאֱמָן) to the "Holy One" (קְדוֹשִׁים).[25] Judah's conduct is also described as a "walking" (רוּד) with "God" (אֵל; cf. 11:9). But if one assumes with Nyberg,[26] that אֵל refers to the Canaanite god "El," and קְדוֹשִׁים the "holy ones" represent his heavenly court, Judah is as idolatrous as Ephraim. One of the weak points of this view is that Hosea never uses אֵל for the Canaanite deity but rather for the God of Israel (cf. 11:9). When referring to the Canaanite pantheon, Hosea uses בַּעַל "Baal" (2:15/13, 1816; 11:2; 13:1).[27] According to Jerome,[28] "saints" designate the "angels or patriarchs and prophets and others who were submissive to God's authority." Julian of Eclanum[29] writes: "'Judah,' thus far somewhat different from her brother, 'descended as a witness with God, and faithful with the holy.' That is to say, having followed the pious king Hezekiah, Judah was zealous to display the majesty of the divine protection and the faith of the promise, and she placed the confidence of her salvation in her strength, among the utmost sufferings." Theodore of Mopsuestia[30] explains: "Since earlier they turned toward the untruth and worship of idols and they lived all together in ungodliness, having no respect for me, I ensnared them by necessity with those evils." Cyril of Alexandria[31] notices: "But he designates the games of idolatry as a lie (ψεῦδος), and the veneration of the vain things (ματαίων); perhaps he designates the prideful rebellion (ὕβριν) against God as impiety (ἀσέβειαν)."

In v. 2 Ephraim's "deceit" / "treachery" is explained in political-military terms. The Ephraimites multiply "falsehood" (כָּזָב), vacillating between Assyria and Egypt (cf. 2 Kgs 17:3-4), and thus they prepare a way for "violence" (שֹׁד) which will befall the nation (cf. 7:13). "Oil" (שֶׁמֶן)[32] parallels "covenant" (בְּרִית) and both refer to Israel's alliances with the two great powers. Cyril of Alexandria[33] observes: "The land of the Samaritans used to produce oil, and this commodity was in esteem in Egypt whose land had no oil." Julian of Eclanum[34] explains: "Obviously having abandoned God's defense, which was to have been gained by deserts, not by prayer, they bought assistance at one time from the Assyrians, at another time from the Egyptians, assigning money to the Assyrians, and to the Egyptians oil, namely, the fertile gifts of the soil; obviously by the means of a single image, he designated many things." Theodoret of Cyrus[35] writes: "For 'oil' indicates trade with oil. He does not accuse the trade in itself, but he hints at one of these two possibilities: either they offered oil as a gift to the king of the Egyptians, or that offering gold, they asked compassion from him, asking that he may be their protector." The change of subject ("they" concerning the alliance with Assyria, and "the oil is carried") reflects different fractions within the "house of Israel"; some were pro-Egyptian others pro-Assyrian.[36] Yet, warns the prophet, these political maneuvers are as vain and destructive as "herding" (רעה) / "pursuing" (רדף) the wind (cf. 8:7; Is 44:20), especially the "east wind" (קָדִים), the scorching "sirocco" (in Arabic ḥamsīn) (cf. 13:15; Ezek 17:10). Theodore of Mopsuestia[37] interprets: "For she [Israel] continuously accomplished such things, which, like a burning heat (καύσωνος), which destroys the fruits, were able themselves to bring decay on them." Cyril of Alexandria[38] explains: "For although it was possible to live under my shade, he went away as a fugitive to the burning heat. But the burning heat signifies the kindling from afflictions, and the burning calamity."

Verse 3 announces that Yahweh has a "dispute" (רִיב)[39] with Judah and that he will repay Jacob according to his deeds (see similar phraseology in 4:9). "Jacob" refers here to the Northern Kingdom (cf. Is 9:7; Mic 1:5). Its choice instead of the more common "Israel" was dictated by the historical allusions to patriarch Jacob in vv. 4-5. Hosea's message is that the present conduct of Israel is better understood in the light of the life of her eponymous ancestor Jacob.

Israel's "deceit" / "treachery" (v. 1) has its root in Jacob's early beginnings (v. 4). For even in the womb of his mother Jacob "deceived" (עקב) his brother. Hosea combines here two traditions found in Genesis. First, he refers to the tradition recorded in Gen 25:21-26, where Jacob "grasped the heel" (vb. עקב denominative of עָקֵב "heel") of his twin-brother. Second, he makes use of the tradition preserved in Gen 27:36 where Esau notices the correspondence between Jacob's character and his name's meaning, i.e., "Jacob" (יַעְקֹב) is the one who "supplanted (עקב) me twice."[40] Cyril of Alexandria[41] interprets: "That Jacob was clever from the swaddling-clothes, or more precisely even prior to his mother's labor, he tries to show in his catching his brother by the heel (πτερνίσαι) inside the maternal womb. For though the action was the work of the divine power (not because we say that in the womb the baby caught Esau by his heel [πτερνίσαι] on his own power), nevertheless, God, according to [his] foreknowledge (πρόγνωσιν) accomplished the work as for one who would become good." Theodoret of Cyrus[42] writes: "At the time of the labor pains, that one [Jacob] seizing his brother's heel came forth into the light, foretelling who he would be and that he would gain by good fraud the blessing of the first-born."

In the second half of the verse, Jacob is presented in his prime / maturity ("manhood" אוֹן). The word אוֹן has been perhaps chosen for its similarity with אָוֶן "wickedness."[43] "He wrestled with God" (שָׂרָה אֶת אֱלֹהִים) alludes to the patriarch's new name יִשְׂרָאֵל "Israel" received at the Jabbok ford after the fight with God (Gen 32:24-32; the name יִשְׂרָאֵל is explained as consisting of two words שׂרה "to wrestle" and אֵל "God"). Theodoret of Cyrus[44] writes: "When he grew as an adult, he excelled so much in virtuous deeds, that he could persuade the divine zeal (προμήθειαν), and at one time he feared the arrival of Esau and entreated God, he did not just enjoy assistance from God, but also he seemed to wrestle by night with the one who appeared and to pluck the victory, in order to reject fear from his mind, considering that the one who prevails over the glory of God will not be inferior to men." Cyril of Alexandria[45] explains: "For an angel in the form (ἐν εἴδει) of God wrestled with him; then his thigh grew numb. However, the divine Jacob confessed such a great grace in the wrestling. For he says: 'For I saw God face to face, and my soul was saved' [Gen 32:30]. Therefore, the mystery about Christ was predicted through the wrestling with the angel. The descendants of Jacob continued to oppose Christ, whom the prophets called 'angel of great counsel' [Is 9:6; cf. LXX]. For instance, some do not accept the numbness (νάρκησιν), that is his redemption (λύτρωσιν). Others do not want to confess that they saw in him face to face the one who is, in nature, and truly God. For in himself

Emmanuel showed us the Father, saying: 'Whoever has seen me, has seen the Father' [Jn 14:9]. Thus, the means of the contest (ἀθλήσεως) prefigured the mystery. God records the incident as a success (κατόρθωμα) for Jacob." Theophylact of Bulgaria[46] writes: "The prophet calls the same person in that place 'God' and 'angel,' as Moses, in order to prefigure (προτυπώσωσι) Christ, who is also the 'angel of great counsel' of the Father, and mighty God."

Verse 5 may be divided into two parts. The first part is a continuation of v. 4 where a few details are added: Jacob wrestled with an "angel" (מַלְאָךְ) rather than with a "man" (אִישׁ) as in Gen 32:25. In Hosea's interpretation, an example of "inner biblical exegesis,"[47] the angel "prevails" (יכל)[48] while in the Genesis narrative the mysterious wrestler seeing that "he did not prevail (יכל) against Jacob" (v. 25) smites his hip and asks Jacob to let him go before the dawn breaks (v. 26). Moreover, he recognizes that Jacob "fought" (שָׂרִיתָ) with God and men and "prevailed" (וַתּוּכָל) (v. 29). Julian of Eclanum[49] writes: "An angel with a man's appearance opposed him, and condescended to wrestle with a fearful man, in such a way, however, that he did not disparage him with revealed majesty, but fought like an equal or inferior with a rival."

Hosea presents Jacob in a quite different posture from that found in Genesis: a vanquished Jacob "weeps" (בכה) and "pleads" (Hithpa'el חנן) with the angel. But the prophet is silent on the goal of such a tearful entreaty[50] on Jacob's side. Perhaps Hosea meant to say that Jacob, the ancestor of the present self-confident Israel, was overcome and brought to submission by God. This could be read as a warning to treacherous Israel which cannot prevail against God; the only choice Israel has is to entreat God for mercy.[51]

The second part of v. 5 makes use of another Jacob tradition linked to the royal sanctuary in Bethel (cf. Am 7:13). Both Gen 28:10ff. and 35:1ff. mention Jacob at Bethel. The first text refers to Jacob's dream on his journey to Mesopotamia, while the second narrative ties Jacob to Bethel after his return from exile. Hosea remarks that Jacob "found" (מצא) the angel-champion at Bethel and had a conversation with him, which most likely implies Jacob's second visit at Bethel when God blessed him and explained his new name, "Israel." The same verb "to speak" (Pi'el דבר) is used both in Hosea (12:5) and Genesis (35:13, 15). Theodore of Mopsuestia[52] interprets: "For they were occupied with the worship of idols, honoring in my name those who have nothing in common with it. They honor me as if I were present there, though I was absent. That is why one reads 'In the house of On they found me,' for 'They found me as if I were present there'; as they should have honored me as God, but in this way they offered to the idol the name and honor of God." Cyril of Alexandria[53] explains: "For Jacob went up to Bethel, and God appeared before him, and there the promise of the blessing was spoken to him, as we have just indicated, but you do not seek God in his house, but rather and very zealously you run into the sacred precincts of Baal, and you ask words not from God but rather oracles from the demons. And while the divine Jacob going up to Bethel, namely, 'to the house of God,' denounced the idols, you, on the contrary, set up a carved image (γλυπτόν) in the house of God." By identifying "Jacob" with Judah, Jerome[54] interprets the patriarch's "wrestling" with the angel as a victory for the former: "And he [Jacob] grew strong against the angel; and he was comforted by the blessing of the one whom he overcame. And he wept, and asked him, that is, the angel, saying: 'I will not let you go unless you bless me' [Gen 32:26]. When, at his father's and mother's advice, he fled to Mesopotamia, he met the same angel at Bethel, who spoke to him; he spoke with us, namely, in the father he spoke also to the sons, and in Jacob he also loved Judah; from that time up to the present, the memory of his name had persevered and because it was imposed on him by the angel and by God. Since these things are so, you too, O Judah, imitate your ancestor, implore and beg the Lord of the Hosts, and return to him."

Verse 6 reproduces a liturgical formula, "Yahweh, God of Hosts" (יהוה אֱלֹהֵי הַצְּבָאוֹת) which is not found in Genesis but appears in Hosea's contemporary, the prophet Amos (4:13; 9:5).[55] The emphasis falls on God's absolute might: Yahweh is God of the heavenly hosts.[56] Julian of Eclanum[57] explains: "In such a way you should remember your God so that always you do acknowledge him as champion (*propugnatorem*) and lord." Cyril of Alexandria[58] notices: "For whoever is saved in God's memory (μνήμη), has ever-green glory. For God honors those who love him." Probably "hosts" refer to the angelic beings Jacob saw in his dream at Bethel (Gen 28:12).[59] This majestic name contrasts with the short generic name used by the Israelites (i.e., אֵל "God"; cf. 11:9; 12:1).[60] The last word of v. 6, זִכְר "remembrance, name" (from the root זכר "to remember, mention") shows that "Yahweh" is God's personal name which is to be remembered or invoked. One may add that the terms זִכְר "remembrance" and שֵׁם "name" (cf. Exod 15:3) appear sometimes in parallel (cf. Exod 3:15; Ps 135:15).

Verse 7 contains an exhortation addressed to the present Israel ("as for you"; cf. 11:8 where Israel appears in the second person) in three points: (a) "return" (שׁוּב)[61] to God; (b) "observance" (שׁמר) of "mercy" (חֶסֶד)[62] and "justice" (מִשְׁפָּט)[63]; and (c) "wait" (Pi'el קוה)[64] "continually" (תָּמִיד) for God. One can notice that moral-social values occupy a central position being flanked by two religious acts, return from apostasy and waiting for God. The latter act means a continuous hope for God and his saving intervention (cf. Ps 25:5; 37:34) in contrast with a self-confident attitude like that shown by Jacob. Thus mercy and social justice can be attained only in a continuous relationship with God marked by repentance and hope. Jerome[65] writes: "Do not say that this [i.e., penitence] is enough, but rather observe God's precepts, have compassion toward others, so that you may also acquire compassion. Pronounce true judgment, so that in whatever you have judged, it may be judged about you. And trust in your God always, or continually approach your God, so that all the time advancing in virtue, you get closer to your God." Cyril of Alexandria[66] interprets: "Therefore 'mercy' signifies love. 'Love is the fulfillment of law' [Rom 13:10]. For close to this: 'It does not work evil' [1 Cor 13:5], as the blessed Paul says. 'Judgment' is righteous dealing or righteousness, and observance of the divine law and will. For 'judgment' is called 'law' by the Divine Scripture. But 'to approach God forever' may signify the mind's genuine desire and inclination toward him, and to have aversion for those who are not gods, who are perhaps from creation or from wood and stone."

A new theme begins in v. 8 and continues in vv. 9-10. These verses raise the question whether there is any connection between moral and social realms. Social injustice and oppression is the basic characteristic of "Canaan" (כְּנַעַן)[67] (cf. Prov 31:24; Job 40:30; Zech 14:21: כְּנַעֲנִי "merchant") using "false balances" (מֹאזְנֵי מִרְמָה; defined as an abomination to Yahweh; cf. Prov 11:1; forbidden by the Law; cf. Deut 25:13; in contrast with "honest balances" [מֹאזְנֵי צֶדֶק] in Lev 19:36; Ezek 45:10). One may notice that Ephraim did not follow the divine exhortation (v. 7) since instead of observing mercy and justice, he "loves" (אָהֵב) to "oppress" (עָשַׁק).[68] Theodore of Mopsuestia[69] interprets: "After he has invited them by those words to conversion, then again he imputed evil to them. 'For you,' he says, 'demonstrated yourselves to be no less than the Canaanites, whom God, after he cast them out because of their impiety and wickedness, substituted with you.'" Cyril of Alexandria[70] explains: "For 'balance of injustice are found in his hands,' namely, inequality and greediness. For, like the Gentiles who do not know God, he honored the accursed oppression. But he did not want to think that he went wrong in doing this."

A rich Ephraim, identified here with Canaan, sees neither "wrongdoing" (אָוֹן) nor "sin" (חֵטְא) in the fact that he is "rich" (עשר) (v. 9). He rather considers his wealth a sign of divine blessing. Yet boasting over one's fortune or "gains" (יְגִיעַ: also "toils, labors") is a sin condemned in Deut 8:17. Instead of boasting, the faithful should thank God for his gifts which include wealth. Theodore of Mopsuestia[71] explains: "Therefore gathering goods from injustice, he enjoyed his riches, may further he even consider the enjoyment he derives from them as sweet.... One should consider that everything he collected by unjust works will be destroyed because of the injustice with which he collected them: whenever God wants to inflict penalties for the transgressions for which they continue to be scrutinized." Verse 8 explains the meaning of the word מִרְמָה "treachery" in v. 1 as a reference to the social injustice and economic fraud. In Hosea's view, the economic prosperity of Jeroboam II's reign had as a reverse Ephraim's moral decay.[72] Note the word-play on אוֹן "fortune" (also "strength, maturity"; cf. v. 4) and אָוֶן "wrongdoing, offense." Moreover, remarks Hosea, Ephraim "found" (מצא) fortune instead of finding / meeting the God of Bethel (cf. v. 5).

Verse 10 reproduces the old credo "I am Yahweh your God from the land of Egypt" (cf. 11:1; Exod 20:2) which in this context alludes to a new exodus. Yahweh is not Baal thought to be the source of Israel's prosperity (2:10/8), but God of the election and covenant, the Lord of history.[73] Cyril of Alexandria[74] writes: "When he says 'I led up' [ἀνήγαγον] he brings us the memory of the things which happened to them, up to their entrance into the land promised to the holy fathers."

In the second part of v. 10, God promises that he will make Israel dwell "again" (עֹד) in the "tents" (אֹהָלִים)[75] as in the days of the "appointed festival" (מוֹעֵד). This line may refer to Israel's journey through the wilderness which followed the Exodus-event, interpretation supported by the plural "as in the days of" (כִּימֵי) which hardly refers to a specific festival (e.g., the Feast of Booths / Tabernacles [Lev 23:39-43; Deut 16:9-12]).[76] Thus Israel's return from exile (the new Exodus) will be succeeded by a simple life similar to that of the wilderness (cf. 2:16-17: "the days of her [Israel] youth"), a hint at the period of abstinence following the return of the adulterous wife to Hosea (cf. 3:1-4). Jerome[77] interprets: "For I am the Lord your God who brought you out of the land of Egypt, when you were serving the Pharaoh and were building cities from clay and straw, I still assign for you a place of penitence, and I urge by many promises that you return to me; still I will make you live in tents as in the days of festivity. He calls the day of festivity 'scenopegia,' in the seventh month, the fifteenth day of the month, after the children of Israel went out of Egypt. Just as, he says, in that time I liberated you from Egypt, and you dwelled in the tents in the holy land, hurrying to go to the place of the temple; so I will now take you out of tribulation, distress and imminent captivity, if you will do what I instructed."

Verse 11 seems to be an isolated saying with no clear connection to its context. Or perhaps Hosea meant to say that the new Exodus and the subsequent period will be marked by prophecy.[78] Yahweh underscores the role of the "prophets" (נְבִיאִים) through whom he revealed himself to the people. Three are the ways of divine revelation: "speech" (דבר עַל), "visions" (חָזוֹן), "parable, analogy" (דמה). This line alludes to the past prophets starting with Moses, the prophet of the Exodus (cf. 12:14). Yet the shift from perfect verbs in v. 11a to imperfect in v. 11b shows that the prophets were still active in Hosea's time.[79] Note 6:5 where the prophets are depicted as Yahweh's instruments of Israel's chastisement. Except for 4:5 Hosea has a good opinion about the prophets' important role in the history of salvation. Jerome[80] writes: "For I am he who, through all the prophets and various types of visions, became similar to men, and I summoned you to repentance. Is it not of human resemblance when Moses prays lifting up his hands that Jesus [i.e., Joshua] may conquer Amalek, and in him the mysteries of the cross may be revealed? Or is not God compared in the hands of the prophets, when Jonah is three days and nights in the depths, so that he may represent the Lord rising from Hades on the third day?" Julian of Eclanum[81] observes: "Never did I give up my healing care, but through my prophets as much by speaking as by acting I stood firm, so that they might understand and confess my providence...." Theodoret of Cyrus[82] explains: "Indeed you justly endure this punishment, because you did not fear though you received the predictions of this punishment through the prophets, nor did you desire to change your opinion; and you did these things though the prediction occurred not only by words but also by deeds. For this was what happened with the divine Hosea, who, according to the divine commandment, married a woman at one time a prostitute (πόρνην), at another time adulteress (μοιχεύτριαν), who became an image of God of all, and accused the people's transgression of law. That is why he teaches, that, 'I used various revelations, not revealing my own nature (for this is invisible), but forming the image for your use.'"

In v. 12 Hosea deals with events which occurred in Gilead (cf. 6:8)[83] and Gilgal (cf. 9:15).[84] In 6:8 Gilead (today *Khirbet Jalʿad*, 6 miles south of Jabbok) is described as a city of "evil doers," due to those fifty Gileadites who helped Pekah to overthrow king Pekahiah in 736 B.C. (cf. 2 Kgs 15:25). This time, the city is labeled simply "evil" (אָוֶן), probably because of a present wrongdoing known to the audience,[85] and its inhabitants are designated "worthless" (שָׁוְא) as they head for the Assyrian exile.[86]

Gilgal (today *Khirbet el-Mefjer*), an important Israelite sanctuary located in the Jordan Valley (Josh 4:19), is considered in 9:15 the source of Ephraim's "wickedness" (רָעָה). In light of 4:15 (cf. Am 4:4; 5:5), the "wickedness" refers to some fertility rites performed in this sanctuary. In 12:12, sacrificing "bullocks" (שְׁוָרִים) (probably in a non-Yahwistic setting, since the offering itself is not rejectable) attracts God's punishment which turns the idolatrous altars into "stone-heaps (גַּלִּים) on the furrows of the field." Jerome[87] writes: "Whatever idols they worship, they do not sacrifice bullocks to the gods, but they offer sacrifices to the bullocks [cf. V: *bobus immolantes*], imitating the error of Samaria." Note the word-play "Gilead" / "Gilgal" / *gallîm*, based on the common element גַּל "stone-heap."

Verses 13-15 resume the Jacob tradition. The patriarch is depicted as fleeing to the land of Aram (cf. Paddan-Aram in Gen 25:20) where he "served" (עבד; the same root is used in Gen 29:25 to designate Jacob's work for Rachel) as a shepherd for a wife (i.e., Rachel) (v. 13). This line refers to the same tradition recorded in Gen 27:43; 29:18; 30:31. The reason of Jacob's "flight" (ברח) may be his treachery against Esau (12:3). Hosea paints the patriarch as a vulnerable character, ready to become a servant in order to get a wife.[88] The root "to keep" (שמר; cf. Gen

30:31) links the Jacob tradition to that of the Exodus: as Jacob kept the sheep for a wife (v. 13), the same way Israel was preserved by a prophet, i.e., Moses (v. 14). The mention of "Israel" (rather than Jacob) in relation to the wife in v. 13b underscores the continuity between the patriarch and his descendants (the contemporary Israel).[89]

In v. 14 the "prophet" (נָבִיא) stands in contrast with the "woman" (אִשָּׁה) mentioned in v. 13. The wife symbolizes the natural life of a man (loving, working, raising children), while the prophet points to a more spiritual destiny (marked by submission to God).[90] Through a prophet,[91] Moses (cf. the Great Prophet: Deut 18:15-18; 34:10), Israel was brought out of Egypt and then kept (by the proclamation of the Law) during the 40-year journey through the wilderness. Jerome[92] explains: "Since once he had mentioned Jacob and Israel, he connected father and sons, and recollects the following story when, in the prophet Moses, the Lord led Israel out of Egypt, and the twelve tribes which constituted Israel, were guarded by the prophet who brought them out." If Jacob represents and explains the wrong conduct of Israel in history, the prophet (Moses, Hosea himself) indicates Yahweh's leadership with respect to Israel.[93] Cyril of Alexandria[94] writes: "For God saved Israel and brought her out of the house of slavery by the mediation of Moses who has been a prophet and the first-fruits [ἀπαρχή] among the prophets. And he not only brought [her] out of Egypt, but he also guarded [her]. For she continued to worship truly the God who is one in essence." In the view of Theodoret of Cyrus,[95] God's "guarding" Israel refers to the journey through the wilderness when Moses also played an important role. Theophylact of Bulgaria[96] sees in this line a reference to Moses and Joshua. If they were liberated through Moses, "they were guarded by Joshua of Nun who calls himself a prophet; and that is a type of

Christ."

Verse 15 shows that Ephraim (i.e., Jacob's descendants) "bitterly" (תַּמְרוּרִים) "grieved" (כעס)[97] Yahweh. The sin of Ephraim seems to be his involvement in Canaanite worship.[98] According to Cyril of Alexandria,[99] this line alludes to the decision of king Jeroboam I to set up two golden calves at Bethel and Dan. Therefore the "Lord" (אֲדֹנָי is found only here in Hosea) will repay him according to his deeds: he will leave the "bloodshed" (דָּמִים) on Ephraim (a cultic legal formula for the capital sentence; cf. Lev 20:9, 11, 12), and let the "reproach" (חֶרְפָּה) against God return to the guilty people. Hosea underscores the idea that Yahweh as the Lord of history is the one who will execute the sentence.[100]

2. The Destruction (13:1-14:1/13:16)

1. When Ephraim used to speak, all trembled;[101] he was exalted[102] in Israel; but he incurred guilt through Baal and died. 2. And now they keep on sinning and make for themselves cast images from their silver, according to the model of idols,[103] the work of craftsmen, all of it! They say to themselves: "Those who sacrifice men[104] kiss calves." 3. Therefore they shall be like morning mist, like dew that vanishes early, like chaff [blown][105] from the threshing floor, like smoke from the window. 4. But I am Yahweh your God[106] from the land of Egypt. You know no God but me, there is no Savior except me. 5. I pastured[107] you in the wilderness, in the land of drought.[108] 6. When I pastured them, they were filled; once satisfied, their hearts grew proud, and thus they forgot me. 7. So I will be[109] like a lion to them, like a panther I lurk[110] on the way. 8. I will attack them like a she-bear bereft [of her cubs], and I will tear open the enclosure of their heart. Then the

dogs shall devour them,[111] wild beasts shall tear them. 9. I[112] will destroy you, O Israel! Who is your helper[113] except me? 10. Where[114] now is your king that he may save you in all your cities, and your rulers, of whom you said, "Give me king and officials." 11. I gave you a king in my anger, and I took [him] away in my fury. 12. Ephraim's iniquity is bound up, his sin is stored away. 13. When the pangs of birth come for him, he is an unwise[115] son. His time is due, but he does not stand at the womb's opening. 14. Shall I ransom them from the power of Sheol? Shall I redeem them from Death? O Death, where are your plagues?[116] O Sheol, where are your sting?[117] Compassion is hidden from my eyes! 15. Though he may flourish[118] among the reeds,[119] the east wind of Yahweh will come, rising from the wilderness. His fountain shall go dry,[120] his spring shall be parched. It shall strip the treasury[121] of every desirable thing. 14:1/13:16. Samaria shall bear her guilt,[122] for she has rebelled against her God. By the sword they shall fall; their babes shall be dashed in pieces, and their pregnant women split open.

This pericope contains the following literary units: vv. 1-3; 4-8; 9-11; 12-13; 13:14-14:1. The first unit is a judgment speech against the past and present Ephraim: his basic sin—idolatry (vv. 1-3). Verse 4 begins a new unit (vv. 4-8) with the addressee unnamed. The focus falls here on the past where the roots of Israel's wickedness are to be found. As in the present times, in the past, the economic prosperity has its reverse in the moral collapse of the people. The third unit, vv. 9-11, has Israel as addressee, though thematically close to the previous unit. The threats are against the leadership: king and high officials. Verses 12-13 represent a new unit whose addressee is again "Ephraim." His guilt is "stored up" even though he is not aware of it. The last unit (13:14-14:1) contains a series of divine sentences culminating with the fall of Samaria.

The sayings of this pericope reflect a period of relative prosperity for Israel following the death of Tiglath-pileser III (727 B.C.). This period was marked by Israel's oscillation between Assyria and Egypt. Verses 8-9 are better understood if the last king Hoshea ben Ellah was already taken captive by Shalmaneser V. Moreover, the picture painted in 14:1 presupposes the siege of Samaria. Thus the most likely date of this pericope is 724 B.C.

Verses 1-3 outline the past and present religious history of Israel dominated by apostasy. In the past, Ephraim used to produce "terror" (רתת) all around as often as he was speaking.[123] For this reason, he was "exalted" (נשׂא), esteemed as a leading tribe in Israel. This line presupposes the tradition of Ephraim's superiority with respect to Manasseh his brother found in Jacob's blessing (Gen 48); or it alludes to two of the most representative men of this tribe, Joshua (Josh 24:30) and Jeroboam I (1 Kgs 11:26; 12:20).[124] Jerome[125] interprets: "When Ephraim, i.e., Jeroboam, Nabath's son from the tribe of Ephraim, spoke, terror fell upon Israel, i.e., the ten tribes. In place of terror, which in Hebrew is called 'rathath,' which Symmachus and Teodotion translated as 'tremor,' the Septuagint translated δικαιώματα 'justifications.' Such terror fell upon Israel, that she sinned against and offended God in Baal, and she died losing the one who says: 'I am life' [Jn 14:6]. For 'A soul which has sinned will itself die' [Deut 24;16]." Similarly, Julian of Eclanum[126] writes: "Inusmuch as in this place Ephraim designates Jeroboam the prince of the division who decreed that the people worship the images of heifers." Cyril of Alexandria[127] offers a different interpretation: "He accuses not only the ten tribes individually but all Israel, and says, that since the ordinances were given to them by Moses, through which they were educated how to worship God and in what manner to bring sacrifices, they consecrated such things as these to Baal, that is, to the idols. For sometimes a part signifies the whole. For they did not offer sacrifices to God at all but rather they consecrated festivals to the works of their hands and offered worship, first-fruits (sacrifices), adoration, gifts and thank-offerings; and robbing God of his glory, they attributed it to the carved images." Despite his terrifying political aura, Ephraim has become "guilty" (אָשֵׁם) through Baalism and "died" (וַיָּמֹת). Although in consecutive imperfect, this verb designates a process, i.e., "dying" rather than a clearcut moment in time "he died." Theophylact of Bulgaria[128] explains: "'And he died'; spiritually, in so far as he has become a slave of the idols, physically, in so far as he was delivered to the enemies." Thus the tragedy of 721 B.C. was only the climax of a long decomposing process which began a long time in Israel's past with the territorial amputation effected by Tiglath-pileser III in 733 B.C. (cf. 7:9: "Israel is swallowed up"; 2 Kgs 15:29).

Despite of Ephraim's approaching end, Hosea's contemporaries are "now" (עַתָּה) following their ancestors' footsteps manufacturing "cast images" (מַסֵּכָה)[129] and encouraging both human sacrifices and idolatry. This line should be read along with the Deuteronomist's commentary on the collapse of Samaria (2 Kgs 17). In the Deuteronomist's view, the Israelites where brought into exile for they "rejected all the commandments of Yahweh their God and made for themselves cast images (the same collective singular מַסֵּכָה) of two calves" (v. 16). Thus, unlike Jeroboam I who set up two calves in Dan and Bethel, Hosea's contemporaries contributed to the proliferation of idolatry by manufacturing cast images, copies after the original extant at Bethel.[130] The phrase "according to the model of idols (עֲצַבִּים)" precludes any positive interpretation of the two calves as a pedestal of the invisible Yahweh. On the contrary, the calves were considered idols, representing Baal, the god of fertility. "They kiss calves (עֲגָלִים)"[131] underscores the irony of the situation: the Israelites sacrifice human beings and kiss lifeless idols, the mere work of the craftsmen (v. 2). The word "men" (collective אָדָם) refers probably to the firstborn sacrificed during the fertility rites.[132] Jerome[133] interprets: "When there are no animal sacrifices, they desire that human beings be sacrificed on their account, not only in whose perishing but also in whose bloodshed they take pleasure." Cyril of Alexandria[134] writes: "He says, this is not my word, nor would I even speak in such a way. But they themselves, i.e., the worshippers of the idols say that it is necessary to sacrifice men to them. And so, he laughs at the thought and ridicules the attempt, when he adds saying: 'For they did not have calves' in all likelihood. That is why, they honored the human sacrifice."

According to the divine verdict (introduced by לָכֵן "therefore"), they will become as transitory as the object of their worship. The similes used here, "morning mist" (עֲנַן בֹּקֶר), "dew" (טַל),[135] "chaff" (מֹץ) (cf. Is 17:13; Ps 1:4) and "smoke" (עָשָׁן) (cf. Is 51:6), point to the Assyrian exile when the Israelites will be carried away from their own land as quickly as the passing of these ephemeral phenomena (v. 3). A similar interpretation is found in Theodoret of Cyrus:[136] "In the same way the cloud of the enemies will destroy you, and the land in which you are now living will be deserted."

Verse 4 begins a new unit focusing on the wondrous acts Yahweh has performed during the Exodus-event and Israel's journey through the wilderness (vv. 4-5). God's remark concerning Israel's pride and apostasy (v. 6) is followed by the divine verdict on the people's wrongdoings (vv. 7-8).

In v. 4 Yahweh identifies himself with the God of Israel since her stay in Egypt, a reference to the Exodus (cf. 11:1). Verse 1a is a self-presentation formula similar to that found in the opening of the Decalogue (Exod 20:2; Deut 5:6), whereas v. 1b is the narrative version of the first commandment.[137] The proclamation of pure monotheism ("no God but me") with emphasis on Yahweh's saving activity (note the title מוֹשִׁיעַ "Savior") anticipates Deutero-Isaiah (Is 43:11; 45:5). Cyril of Alexandria[138] notices the sharp contrast between this clear proclamation of monotheism and two episodes in Israel's past history: the golden calf worshipped after the Exodus (Deut 32:32), and the two golden calves set up by king Jeroboam I at Bethel and Dan (1 Kgs 12:28). "To know" (ידע)[139] God means personal relationship with him through untainted worship and observance of moral precepts.

Verse 5 points to Yahweh's fatherly care for Israel during her 40-year wandering through the "wilderness" (מִדְבָּר). Yahweh, like a good shepherd (cf. Jn 10:9), tended his flock through a "land of drought" (אֶרֶץ תַּלְאֻבוֹת), with no water or food (cf. 11:3; 12:10). Theodoret of Cyrus[140] interprets: "In other words, I supplied the necessary things fitting you, 'manna' from heaven, quails from the sea, and water from the rock."

In v. 6 the focus shifts from the wilderness to the fertile land of Canaan. Yahweh's shepherding and abundant pasturage echo the period following the conquest of the promised land. Prompted by prosperity, pride and forgetfulness (cf. 2:15/13) was Israel's answer to God's tender love (cf. Deut 6:12ff.; 11:15f.; 31:20; Jer 2:5ff.). Jerome[141] writes: "And now they ate, and were full and they raised their heart, and they forgot the one whose kindness they ought to have been mindful of. Nor could Israel, in forty years, reach the land over Jordan, through such vastness of the desert where not only fruit and trees and vines, but not even any grass grows, if the Lord had not provided everything.... And he gave them the angels' bread, manna from heaven, which they never ate in Egypt, and the waters from the rock that followed them. However, according to the apostle [i.e., Paul; 1 Cor 10:4], the rock is Christ." Theodore of Mopsuestia[142] interprets: "For after they had entered the promised land and enjoyed such goods exceeding any human hope, and after they became great before the inhabitants of the world, because of my work for them, they no longer remembered that I gave them the abundance of such goods."

Verses 7-8 represent Yahweh's verdict on Israel's apostasy. In order better to convey his message, Yahweh resorts to therimorphism as he compares himself with several animals of prey. One may add that the curse of ravaging beasts (lion, panther, bear) appears in ancient Near Eastern treaties as a stipulation for those who break the treaty.[143] The God of Exodus, the loving father (11:1ff.), the "Savior" (v. 4b), the good shepherd (13:5), suddenly becomes the ravaging beast and the nation's terminator. He himself, not a human or animal agent (cf. Lev 26:22), behaves like a "lion" (שַׁחַל) (cf. Hos 5:14), "panther" (נָמֵר), and a ferocious "she-bear" (דֹב) deprived of her cubs (cf. Prov 17:12; Lam 3:10),[144] lurking and attacking her prey. Then the remains of the mutilated Israel will be completely devoured and torn by the dogs and the "wild beasts" (חַיַּת הַשָּׂדֶה). This gruesome picture brings forward the saying of Amos on the "day of Yahweh" (Am 5:18f.). One of the more graphic descriptions is found in v. 8a where Yahweh promises that he "will tear open the enclosure (סְגוֹר "chest") of their heart," depriving Israel of life. The same idea of a complete, quick and traceless annihilation reappears in v. 3. This time Hosea underscores the violent and inexorable character of God's judgment on Ephraim.

Perhaps Hosea used the verbal form אָשׁוּר [*ʾāšûr*] "I lurk (gaze) [on the way]" (v. 7b) as a homophonous hint at the Assyrians (אַשּׁוּר [*ʾaššûr*]) who will put an end to the Northern Kingdom bringing its citizens into captivity (721 B.C.).[145] This is also Cyril of Alexandria's[146] interpretation: "Therefore, I will come upon them as a panther and leopard. For they will be deported to Assyria. I will encounter them as a she-bear in want (ἀπορουμένη), that is, either hungry perhaps, or extremely distraught because her cubs had been taken away.... For the untamed peoples of Assyria are compared to bear cubs living in woods because they are very inclined towards savage life." Similarly, Theodoret of Cyrus[147] writes: "For I will make beast-like enemies rise against him which will treat him in the way of a panther or leopard."

Verse 9 begins another unit which runs as a divine oracle with Israel in the second person. The verdict of vv. 7-8 continues throughout vv. 9-11 in a more rhetorical style. The Hebrew perfect שִׁחֵתִיךָ "I will destroy you" underscores the definitive character of the judgment initiated in the past (after 733 B.C.), still on the way in the present, and to be completed in the future. In v. 9b Yahweh reiterates the statement made in v. 4b that there is no "Savior" (מוֹשִׁיעַ) besides him; this time the term used is עֹזֵר "helper" (cf. Deut 33:26-27; Ps 146:5). As in vv. 7-8 where Yahweh, the "Savior," becomes "wild beast," in v. 9 the "helper" of Israel turns into her "destroyer." Following Cyril of Alexandria's[148] reading, τῇ διασπορᾷ σου "in your dispersion," rather than the LXX, τῇ διαφθορᾷ σου "in your ruin," Theophylact of Bulgaria[149] interprets this line as a reference to the captivity: "Who will help you 'in your dispersion (διασπορᾷ),' in which you were scattered, sent into captivity by the Assyrians and Egyptians?" And further, Theophylact notices: "Some of the copies [i.e., of the Septuagint] have 'in the ruin' (τῇ διαφθορᾷ), and this then makes sense for he calls 'ruin' the complete desolation (ἐρήμωσιν), which the captives have experienced."

Verse 10a echoes the common view that the "king" (מֶלֶךְ) should "save" (יֹשַׁע)¹⁵⁰ his people from any foreign invasion.¹⁵¹ The mention "in all your cities" may be read as a reference to the Assyrian sieges of Samaria and other north-Israelite cities.¹⁵² The term שֹׁפְטִים designates the "rulers" rather than "judges," in a narrow, technical sense. This interpretation is supported by the presence of the additional word שָׂרִים "officials" in v. 10b. If Yahweh is no longer Israel's helper, the king and officials have no saving power. These lines allude to the imprisonment of the last king Hoshea along with other officials by Shalmaneser V, around 724 B.C. (2 Kgs 17:4). Theodore of Mopsuestia¹⁵³ explains: "For neither care from the king nor care from the general will bring any profit; for he will be helpless, when I act in opposition. And further it seems to me that you put aside entirely the leader Samuel, a righteous and virtuous man, who worked hard as priest and leader of the people, saying that you need to have a king as other nations, who will assist you in battles against foreigners. But the time came when you realized your thoughtlessness; for those who in your opinion reigned over you will be of no use for you, since all your cities will fall into the same ruin."

In Hosea's view, the inauguration of the monarchic regime was tolerated rather than wanted by Yahweh (v. 11). This negative view of monarchy, as an institution requested by the Israelites under the political influence of their neighbors, may be also found in 1 Sam 8:4-9 (cf. Judg 9). King and high officials constitute the main target of this speech. The end of the monarchy marked by Yahweh's "fury" (עֶבְרָה) corresponds to its beginning dominated by God's "anger" (אַף). The imperfect verbs allude to the entire line of kings from Saul to Hoshea ben Elah.[154] According to Jerome,[155] some consider Saul the king given in anger and Zedekiah the monarch taken in fury; others take this line as referring to Jeroboam I and Zedekiah. Similarly, Julian of Eclanum[156] writes: "Some took Jeroboam who was the author of the division of the tribes as the king given in fury, and understood the king taken in indignation as being Hoshea under whom Israel became captive." For Theodoret of Cyrus,[157] the "given and taken" king is Saul eventually replaced by David. According to Theodore of Mopsuestia,[158] Hosea alludes here to the beginning and the end of the Israelite monarchy.

Verses 13:12-14:1 form the last unit of this pericope focusing on divine judgment and Ephraim's destruction.

Verse 12 announces that Ephraim's "iniquity" (עָוֹן) is "bound up" (צָרַר) (cf. Is 8:16; Job 14:17), whereas his "sin" (חַטָּאת)[159] is "stored" (צָפַן) (cf. Ps 27:5; Ezek 7:22). The image created here is that of an archive where written documents having been bound up are stored away for future times. Likewise, the sins of Ephraim (apostasy, idolatry, trust in human means) are preserved intact for a future retribution (cf. 8:13; 9:9). In spite of all tribulations befalling the Northern Kingdom since 733 B.C. a final payment still awaited Israel. Julian of Eclanum[160] notices that Israel's crimes (*scelera*) "as if they were guarded under some seal, remained in the judge's memory." Theodoret of Cyrus[161] explains: "'Hidden is his sin' means his wickedness is deeply rooted. But I will enwrap him in so many evils in order that he be tortured like a woman in labor." According to Cyril of Alexandria,[162] this line refers to Jeroboam I who, "just as he received in his soul the covered foundation (καταβολήν) of an evil seed," set up two golden calves to detour the Israelites from going up to Jerusalem.

The new metaphor, "mother's birth pangs," found in v. 13 continues the idea in v. 12. If in Jer 6 and 22 this metaphor refers to the mother, in Hosea the emphasis falls rather on the child. Ephraim is not a teachable son. He did not learn from his past that sin attracts punishment. Instead of returning in repentance to Yahweh he still lingers in the midst of his sinful life. Endurance in suffering leads to a new life (cf. Is 66:7ff.) but Ephraim is an "unwise" (לֹא חָכָם) son. According to Eccl 8:5, the "wise" knows the right time for every activity. Ephraim is reluctant to get out of his mother's womb in order to start a new life. The Hebrew word for חֶבְלֵי "birth pangs" alludes to חַבְלֵי אָדָם "human cords" (11:4) with which God taught his son to walk. Now he is going to punish the nation (the mother) with "birth pangs."[163] Jerome[164] explains: "When the day of travail and captivity comes, he will be unable either to stand firm or endure." For Cyril of Alexandria,[165] the son is the last king of Israel, Hoshea ben Elah: "For when your sons are crushed, he says, none will survive. For he [i.e., king Hoshea] will be taken as slave and captive, and along with others he will go to Assyria. Thus, wise is the one who sings: 'The Lord is my strength and my praise' [Ps 117:14]. For all power and salvation are from him, and besides him there is no savior."

Verse 14 indicates that due to Ephraim's persistence in wrongdoing, the mother's womb turned into a grave.[166] "Death" (מָוֶת) and "Sheol" (שְׁאוֹל) though personalized have no mythical elements in them (i.e., "Death" in Hosea is not to be identified with Mot ["death"], the Canaanite god of the underworld). "Ransom" (פדה) (cf. 7:13)[167] and "redeem" (גאל)[168] may refer to assisting a helpless person, in the present context, to the deliverance of Israel from death. In v. 14 Yahweh is confronted with a dilemma similar to that found in 11:8-9: Ephraim's iniquity is recorded and thus must be punished. Yet Yahweh is a good and loving God; he is also the Almighty whose power extends over Death and Sheol. Unlike 11:8-9 where God's last word is forgiveness, this time he decides to punish the nation: "compassion" (נֹחַם) is "hidden" (סָתַר) from his eyes. By underscoring God's supremacy over death and underworld, the prophet introduces a type for the resurrection, both national (Israel's restoration) and personal.[169] In St. Paul's interpretation (1 Cor 15:55), relying on the Septuagint reading, Christ's resurrection represents the final victory over death. Death and Sheol have no more terrifying power over Christ's disciples. Jerome[170] writes: "Moreover the Lord liberated everyone, and redeemed them through the suffering of the cross and the shedding of his blood, when his soul descended into Hades, and he did not experience corruption to his flesh; and he speaks of the death itself as well as the Hades: 'I will be your death, O Death!' For that reason I have died so that you may die through my death. 'I will be your sting, O Hades' for you devoured all with your gullet." Cyril of Alexandria[171] explains: "Obviously they became subjected to it [i.e., death] because of the sins committed against the Creator and because of Adam's transgression in the beginning.... He redeemed us from the hands of the Hades, namely, from the tyranny of death, and Christ's death represents the means of redemption. For he willingly endured death on cross for us and he triumphed over principalities and powers by nailing on the cross the written record against us [cf. Col 2:14-15; 1 Cor 15:55]." Theodoret of Cyrus[172] writes: "These [lines] typically (τυπικῶς) refer to the return of the Judaeans. For he figuratively (τροπικῶς) calls life in captivity Hades and death. But it received complete (ἐντελὲς) and true (ἀληθὲς) fulfillment after our Savior's resurrection (ἀνάστασιν). For after our first fruit (ἀπαρχῆς) had risen, we all received the hope of resurrection." Theodore of Mopsuestia[173] interprets: "For after all these things I instructed them by punishment (τιμωρίᾳ), and within a little I will release you all from the death itself beyond any human hope." And he shows that all these refer to the Assyrians and the punishment brought against Israel through them. Similarly, Julian of Eclanum[174] suggests that Hosea refers to the Assyrian army, but in the conclusion of his commentary, Julian underlines the fact that 13:14 does not concern exclusively Sennacherib's military intervention, but as Paul remarks in 1 Cor 15, the Hosean passage alludes to "the resurrection which is to come." Theophylact of Bulgaria[175] writes: "All these which happened to the Israelites were types of the divine dispensation (εἰκονομίας) for all. He liberated the souls from the hand of Hades. For these are in Hades not in death; for they are immortal. The bodies are in death; for they are mortal. Everyone who sins is in Hades, in so far as his soul becomes without form (ἀειδής)."

Verse 15 depicts Ephraim as briefly flourishing among the "reeds" (emended text: אָחוּ). The last term alludes to the pro-Egyptian policy adopted by Hoshea ben Elah after the death of Tiglath-pileser III (727 B.C.). But given the preserved iniquity of Ephraim as well as Yahweh's "hidden" compassion, this policy proves of no avail. The "east wind" (קָדִים), "sirocco," will rise from the wilderness, an allusion to the Assyrian troops (cf. 12:2), and will make Ephraim's fountains dry up. It will "strip" (שָׁסָה; cf. 2 Kgs 17:20; Is 17:14; Jer 30:16) the treasury of its precious things. Assyria is called the "east wind of Yahweh" for she is only an agent or instrument of judgment under God's authority. Jerome[176] offers a rather allegorical interpretation of the wilderness: "Or if by wilderness we understand the virginal womb of Holy Mary, for from human seed she brought forth no fruit; but the simple and most pure sprout fruitful by a union gave birth to him, the flower who says in the Song of Songs: 'I am the flower of the field, the lily of valleys' [Song 2:1]." Julian of Eclanum[177] connects this line with Sennacherib's failed cam-paign against Jerusalem (cf. 2 Kgs 18-19): "The burning wind from the desert refers to the angel, who destroyed the Assyrian army in a single night. Not that they believe that the angels, about whom the Gospel [Mt 18] teaches that daily they behold the Father's face, dwell in the desert, but because of the swiftness of vengeance, since one hundred eighty-five thousand [troops] were slain in one single night [2 Kgs 19:35]." Theodoret of Cyrus[178] explains: "By these he signifies Cyrus the Persian who marched against and destroyed the empire of the Assyrians or Babylonians, who annihilated the whole royal family, and who took away resources of absolute power. For he figuratively (τροπικῶς) calls these 'founts' (πηγὰς) and 'water-courses' (φλέβας)." Theodore of Mopsuestia[179] sees in the destroying wind from the desert an allusion to the king of Babylonians who "comes like a burning wind and destroys all Israel altogether." Cyril of Alexandria[180] offers a rather figurative interpre-tation: "Therefore the prophetic word says to us that Christ offered himself to death like a dry wind which dries up his springs and water-courses. When the burning wind blows the entire region of death becomes dry."

The last verse of this unit, 14:1, belongs thematically to chapter 13 rather than chapter 14.[181] With a sharp realism as that of a gifted reporter, Hosea describes the last days of the capital of Samaria[182] besieged by the Assyrian troops between 724-721 B.C. (cf. 2 Kgs 17:5). Jerome[183] explains: "It must be believed that these things befell him in the time of captivity and distress, when they lost their native land, and those who escaped the sword were brought into eternal servitude." The reason for which Samaria is punished is that she "rebelled" (מרה) (cf. Deut 21:20; Ps 78:8) against God (a reference to the bloody revolutions and the worship of idols). This is the interpretation of Theodoret of Cyrus[184] which sees in Samaria's destruction a consequence of her attitude against God's will. Therefore its inhabitants will die by the sword (cf. 7:16), babes will be dashed in pieces (cf. 10:14) and pregnant women will be split open (cf. 2 Kgs 15:16).

3. Love's Triumph (14:2/1-9/8)[185]

2/1. Return, O Israel, to Yahweh your God, for you have stumbled in your iniquity. 3/2. Take words with you and return to Yahweh. Say to him: "Take away[186] all iniquity and accept what is good. We will offer the fruit of our lips.[187] 4/3. Assyria shall not save us; we will not ride upon horses; we will say no more, 'Our God,' to the work of our hands, since in you the orphan finds mercy." 5/4. "I will heal their apostasy;[188] I will love them generously.[189] For my anger has turned away from him. 6/5. I will be like the dew to Israel; she shall blossom like the lily. She shall strike root like the Lebanon. 7/6. Her shoots shall spread out. Her beauty shall be like the olive tree, her fragrance like Lebanon. 8/7. They shall once again dwell[190] in my shadow. They shall grow grain.[191] They shall flourish like the vine, his fame like the wine of Lebanon. 9/8. What has Ephraim to do with idols any more? I, I will answer[192] and watch over him.[193] I am like an evergreen cypress; your fruit is found in me."

The pericope 14:2/1-9/8 consists of two distinct sections: A prophetic appeal to Israel's repentance (vv. 2-4) and a divine speech proclaiming its salvation (vv. 5-9). In the latter section Israel appears in the third person except for v. 9b where she is mentioned in the second person. Verse

5 announcing the healing love of Yahweh represents the central point of this pericope.

Although chapters 11 and 14 are close each other thematically (cf. the key-terms used in either pericope: מְשׁוּבָה "apostasy"; v. 5; cf. 11:7; שׁוּב "return" vv. 2, 8; cf. 11:5; רפא "to heal" v. 5; cf. 11:3), chapter 11 has a legal setting, while the "Sitz im Leben" of chapter 14 is rather cultic (cf. the phrase יהוה אֱלֹהֶיךָ "Yahweh your God" found only in 12:10; 13:4 and 14:2). Moreover, the audience of chapter 11 is much larger than that of chapter 14 where Hosea addresses the narrow circle of his disciple. Thus chapter 14 is closer to chapters 12-13 than to chapter 11.[194]

With respect to the date, one may assume that the sayings included in this pericope belong to the last phase of Hosea's activity, probably after the beginning of the siege of Samaria by Shalmaneser V (ca. 724 B.C.). Ephraim (i.e., what was left from the Northern Kingdom after the intervention of Tiglath-pileser III in 733 B.C.) is approaching the end; neither idolatry (v. 9a) nor alliances with Assyria (v. 4) could save the wayward people from ruin.

Verses 2-4 represent the prophetic appeal to Israel's repentance. The people "stumbled" (כשׁל)[195] in their own "iniquity" (עָוֹן) (cf. 5:5), namely, God brings a corresponding punishment over Israel for her wrongdoings. Hosea's language oscillates between judgment and salvation. The prophet mentions God in the third person to underscore the great distance between him and his faithless people, but at the same time he calls the latter Israel (a reference to Yahweh's initial love; cf. 11:1) and not Ephraim which is a rather political, administrative name for the Northern Kingdom after 733 B.C.[196] In light of what follows, the basic idea of this verse is that there is no way to re-enter personal communion with Yahweh but through genuine repentance. The covenantal phrase "Yahweh your God" (12:10; 13:4; cf. Exod 6:7; 8:28; 10:8, 17; 15:26; 16:12; 20:2) directs Israel's return to the Exodus-event and the wilderness period as a time of ideal relationship between Yahweh and his people. The basis of such a call to repentance is God's goodwill to heal Israel (v. 5).[197] Theodore of Mopsuestia[198] writes: "Now, however, incline towards God, considering his thoughts. You acted impiously in regard to them and you plunged yourself into such a great weakness. And receiving by hope the deliverance of the evils which befell you, make haste to take care of your own duties."

In v. 3 the Israelites are urged to take with them "words" (דְּבָרִים) as they are returning to Yahweh. The term "words" refers to the people's confession before Yahweh. Jerome[199] interprets: "'Take, he says, with you words,' that is, prayers and confession of trespasses, and return to the Lord as much with words as with deeds." This confession consists of two brief supplications by which Israel acknowledges her state of sinfulness alongside the persistence of a grain of "good": (a) "to forgive" (נשׂא) Israel's iniquity (cf. Exod 34:7; Num 14:18); (b) to accept what is still "good" (טוֹב) in her life; "good" describing the proper attitude of man toward God is the latter's gift (cf. 3:5);[200] and Israel's promise: "to offer" (Pi'el שׁלם)[201] the "fruit of our lips" (cf. Prov 13:2), a reference to prayer as a means to get in touch with God. According to Ps 51:17, "the sacrifice acceptable to God is a broken spirit, a broken and contrite heart." Note in this context Hosea's negative view on purely external sacrifices (4:8; 5:6; 6:6; 8:13). Jerome[202] relates Israel's "good" to Yahweh's willingness to forgive: "For unless you remove our wrongdoings, we can not have whatever good we might offer to you." The "fruit of our lips," in the view of same writer designates the "praises to the

Lord and the action of thankfulness." According to Julian of Eclanum,[203] the semantic area of "good" in this line is determined by the final phrase "bulls of our lips" (cf. MT) which designates the offering of praise given to God (cf. Ps 51:19). Theodoret of Cyrus[204] explains: "For since you offer such a supplication to him, you do not receive the wages of injustice but rather you will live in the enjoyment of all sorts of goods." For Theodore of Mopsuestia,[205] the "words" represent a bridge in restoring the relationship between God and his people. Cyril of Alexandria:[206] "[Be]come rich in supplies of goods, promise to bring to him the gifts of the lips, the thank-offering songs (ᾠδὰς) and confession (ἐξομολόγησιν). For such things as these are the fruits of the tongue." Theophylact of Bulgaria[207] explains: "Supplicate him and by that you may not receive the fruits of injustice, namely, the captivity and its evils, but rather you may receive the good things."

Verse 4 continues Israel's confession in v. 3 by adding one more observation: Assyria (5:13; 8:9) is unable to save Israel; and two new promises: (a) "we will not ride upon horses," i.e., not trust in the military arsenal (cf. 8:14; 10:13); and (b) we will renounce idolatry (8:6; 13:2). The confession ends up with a general remark on God's "compassion" (רחם; cf. 1:6; 2:25) for the least fortunate, the "orphan" (יָתוֹם) (Exod 22:22f.; Deut 10:18; Ps 10:14; 68:6). Israel as helpless as an orphan (Lam 5:3) can appeal to Yahweh's compassion.[208] Jerome[209] explains: "He [Israel] is called orphan because he lost God, his father." Theodoret of Cyrus[210] writes: "He will deem you worthy of all care, as if you were neglected and uncared for like an orphan. And I will bestow healing on you, releasing you from oppressing evils." Cyril of Alexandria[211] interprets: "If someone would like to call Israel 'orphan' (for he properly departed from God the Father, although he clearly said: 'Israel is my first-born son' [Exod 4:22]), I would say that it is rightly understood."

Verses 5-9 reproduce Yahweh's speech with Israel in the third person plural, except for v. 9b where the people show up in the second person singular. Verse 5 is the climax of this pericope centered on the theme of salvation. Yahweh solemnly proclaims that he will "heal" (רפא; cf. 5:13; 6:1; 7:1; 11:3) Israel's "apostasy" (מְשׁוּבָה; cf. 11:7); he knows that his people are unable to get rid of this malady (5:4; 7:2; 11:5) and "to return" (שׁוּב) to him. Thus Yahweh after his own inner "conversion" (הפך) (cf. 11:8-9), decides to take this step in place of his helpless people. God promises that he "will love (אהב; cf. 3:1; 11:1) them generously (נְדָבָה)."[212] This is a unconditional, free-willing, merciful, and forgiving love; the love of a father who loves his children generously, and spontaneously and expects nothing in return; this is God's long-suffering love for Israel. Jerome[213] explains: "For I formerly was angry at them for the sins they had committed, but now I will show compassion (*miserebor*) because of my clemency (*clementiam*)." That Yahweh's love is the last word during the passionate dialogue with Israel can be noticed from the last part of v. 5 where the divine partner announces that "anger" (אף) has "turned away" (שׁוּב) from his people. Israel's return in Hos 14:5/4 may be compared with the repentance of the prodigal son (Lk 15:11ff.). God responds generously to repentance in either case. In the parable of the prodigal son he sees the repentant child and "ran to meet him"; in Israel's case God begins the healing as soon as Israel shows the first signs of repentance.[214] If love unconditionally flows from Yahweh upon Israel it means that love is the foremost attribute of the divine person. In this case, Hosea may be considered the spiritual forerunner of John the Evangelist who gave one of the most beautiful definitions of God when he wrote "God is love" (1 Jn 4:8). Theodoret of Cyrus[215] explains: "I will surround you affectionately (γνησίως) and I will cease all chastisement inflicted on you. I will bestow upon you my gifts like a dew, so that you may blossom like a lily." Theodore of Mopsuestia[216] writes: "He will show one and the same love to all, just as he will remove all wrath from you." Cyril of Alexandria[217] notices that God loves Israel "confessedly (ὁμολόγως), namely, confessedly (ὁμολογουμένως) and unhiddenly (ἀκρύπτως)." Theophylact of Bulgaria[218] explains ὁμολόγως "confessedly" found in the LXX reading as ἀναμφιλόγως "indisputably."

Beginning with v. 6, Hosea uses several metaphors to depict God's generous love for Israel. The motifs in metaphors are found in the love songs in the Song of Songs. The plant imagery functions as a polemic against the Canaanite fertility rites. Nevertheless, it is the people who blossom and not the plants since Yahweh is the Lord of history working with the people rather than with the vegetation.[219] In v. 6, Yahweh compares himself with the "dew" (טַל) (described as a mystery: Job 38:2; a heavenly gift: Ps 110:3)[220] which makes Israel blossom like the "lily" (שׁוֹשַׁנָּה)[221] and strike her roots (cf. 9:16) like the trees of Lebanon (לְבָנוֹן).[222] Theodore of Mopsuestia[223] explains: "She (i.e., Israel) will increase in great number like one who is crowded together among the cedar-trees." These blessings are due to God's release of love (v. 5). "I will be" (אֶהְיֶה) (in contrast with "I will not be" [לֹא אֶהְיֶה]; cf. 1:9) points to the very name of Yahweh (cf. Exod 3:14b) as the author of Israel's new life (cf. Is 26:19 where dew and resurrection appear together).[224] Although invisible, God's action, as that of the dew whose drops cannot be seen, is quite efficient.[225] Under the divine providence, Israel's new life is marked by beauty and surprise ("lily"), firmness and durability ("Lebanon"). Cyril of Alexandria[226] writes: "It is altogether as enriching and watering the mind of those who have been called to repentance by the consolation from above. It is clear that it is by consolation of the Spirit, for the dew comes from above. 'It will blossom as a lily.' He will give up its fragrance in Christ, and the odor of a undefiled life, and the elect will be a flower in the future." Theodoret of Cyrus[227] explains: "The soul set free from the filth of sin and adorned with the most brilliant garment of Baptism is compared to this [i.e., lily]." Theophylact of Bulgaria[228] writes "I will bestow my bounties upon them as a dew, and they will blossom as a lily."

Verse 7 speaks of Israel whose "shoots" (יֹנְקוֹת) (Ps 80:12) spread out; whose "beauty" (הוֹד "glory") is comparable to the olive tree (Jer 11:16; Ps 52:10); and whose "fragrance" (רֵיחַ) (cf. Song 4:11, in an erotic context) matches the perfume of the forest of Lebanon replete with fragrant flowers and herbs. Israel's new life is not only strong and wonderful (cf. v. 6) but also pleasant and fragrant. Cyril of Alexandria[229] notices: "Thus the fruit of those who have been called will be fragrant, and acceptable as a sacrifice by God who loves the virtue." This life is also abundant, if one considers the "shoots" an allusion to Israel's offspring (in contrast with 9:12).[230] Theophylact of Bulgaria[231] interprets this line allegorically as an allusion to the apostles: "The shoots of Israel, which is well-pleasing to God, are the apostles, who went out and taught all the nations."

In v. 8 a triple promise is followed by a comparison. The Israelites will dwell in Yahweh's "shadow" (צֵל) (i.e., under God's protection; cf. Ps 17:8; 36:7; 91:1; or in the delightful company of a lover; cf. Song 2:3); they will grow "grain" (דָּגָן) (in contrast with 8:7; but note 2:23/21-24/22) and flourish themselves like the "vine" (גֶפֶן) (cf. 10:1). Israel's "fame" (lit. "mention [of a name]" זִכְרוֹ) will be as the "wine" (יַיִן) of Lebanon. Julian of Eclanum[232] explains:

"[T]he ardor (*flagrantia*) of your glory will be as great as that of the wine, the best one being produced on the mount of Lebanon." For Theodoret of Cyrus,[233] the fragrant wine of Lebanon alludes to the "sweet-smelling scent of the virtue." Theodore of Mopsuestia[234] writes: "Having returned, they will enjoy their own goods, and persevere, having the abundant supply of fruits through my providence." For Cyril of Alexandria,[235] the phrase "they will be satisfied with corn" (cf. LXX: μεθυσθήσονται σίτῳ) means that they will be "partners in the eternal life and in the overabundance of the spiritual power." Read in their historical context, these lines refer to Israel's return from exile. After a purifying journey through the wilderness (cf. 9:3; 12:10), the Israelites will dwell again in the fertile land of their ancestors (cf. 2:17/15, 20/18b; 11:1).

Verse 9 opens with a rhetorical question: What has Ephraim to do with the "idols" (עֲצַבִּים) (cf. 4:17; 8:4; 13:3) in his new existence? The mention of "Ephraim," the name of the Northern Kingdom in the midst of God's promises concerning Israel's new life, is quite surprising. Perhaps Hosea intended to warn his contemporaries about the danger, extant even in the new life, of a "return" to idolatry. Yahweh will "answer" (ענה) and "watch" (שׁור) (cf. 13:7)[236] over his people. The root ענה "to answer" reflects here as in 2:16/14ff. a harmonious relationship between God and his people marking the times of restoration. Yahweh is carefully "watching" or "looking after" (cf. Job 7:8) Israel to answer her prayers.

Yahweh is like an "evergreen cypress" (בְּרוֹשׁ רַעֲנָן), the source of Israel fruitfulness (פְּרִי "fruit"; a wordplay with "Ephraim"); in contrast with 9:16: "they shall yield no fruit." This is the only place in the entire Old Testament where Yahweh is likened to a tree. The point of such unusual comparison is that Yahweh, and not the sacred tree of the fertility cult (cf. 4:12), is the living tree (perhaps a type of the tree of life in Gen 3:22).[237] Since normally the cypress tree does not bear fruit, one may conclude that in Yahweh alone Israel may find life and fruitfulness.[238] Salvation is the gift of God rather than man's endeavor. The paradox in v. 9b (the fruit is described as belonging to Israel yet it is found in Yahweh) points to a sort of mystical union where the two partners though united are still distinct.[239] Jerome[240] interprets: "From ἀρκεύθοις, i.e., juniper-trees, also according to the seventy interpreters [i.e., the Septuagint], Solomon is said to have made the doors of the temple, because Christ through whom we approach the Father has this nature that he always flourishes, always brings forth new fruits, and never loses his verdue." Julian of Eclanum[241] explains: "For I am the one who listens to those who pray, who is able and accustomed to heal those who are worn out, to correct those who are wrong, to make those who are sterile fertile, to find the lost, to raise the dead, and to lift those whom I have invigorated to such a height that they seem to advance from the palm-trees or bushes to fir-trees and cypresses." Theodore of Mopsuestia[242] writes: "Since this tree is ever-green, he says, that just as that tree has forever the foliage from the leaves, so they also will continually have an abundance of goods, and they will enjoy them through my providence." Cyril of Alexandria[243] explains: "That the whole fertility of those who obey God is fully assured only in Christ and through Christ, he himself will fully assure in the inspired Gospels: 'Without me you can do nothing' [Jn 15:5]." Theophylact of Bulgaria[244] remarks: "For the fruit of the virtues is from Christ, the Logos."

4. Epilogue (14:10/9)

10/9. Who is wise will consider these [words]. He who is prudent will take note of them. Indeed, the ways of Yahweh are straight. Righteous ones walk in them. But rebels stumble in them.

The epilogue (v. 10) was written by Hosea himself in the Wisdom style and vocabulary (Eccl 8:1; Ps 107:43).[245] One may add that there are scholars who suggest that v. 10 was compiled by one of the spiritual disciples of Hosea during the exile or in the post-exilic period. As an argument, they adduce the personal appeal for wise understanding; the reader is no longer able to get to the core of the book's message, so the reader lived at a certain distance in time from Hosea.[246] Or, as Wolff noticed,[247] the vocabulary of the epilogue is Hosean (e.g., Hosea uses פֹּשְׁעִים for "rebels," while the Wisdom literature prefers רְשָׁעִים).

In v. 10a, emphasis falls on the difficulty of the book. The "prudent" (נָבוֹן) and "wise" (חָכָם) (cf. 13:13) are called to grasp the meaning of "these" [words] (אֵלֶּה). In v. 10b, a distinction is made between the "righteous" (צַדִּקִים) and the "rebels" (פֹּשְׁעִים) (cf. 7:13; 8:1). If the former shape their lives according to Yahweh's straight "ways" (דְּרָכִים; i.e., "commandments"; cf. Deut 8:6; 10:12; 11:22) shown in the book, the latter "stumble" (כשל) (cf. 4:5; 5:5; 14:2/1) in them, namely, they receive God's punishment for their repeated wrongdoings (cf. Ps 1; Prov 10:29). According to Jerome,[248] the "obscurity of the volume and difficulty of the explanation" underscored by the epilogue could be overcome only by a personal relationship between Christ and the reader. Christ as the great teacher may illumine and guide the reader's mind in search for types and motives of this rather intricate writing of the Old Testament.

One of the more interesting points of this epilogue is that it contains a principle of interpretation. In order to understand Hosea's words the exegete has to be one of the righteous people. A similar idea is found in Jesus' words: "Anyone who resolves to do the will of God will understand."[249] Thus moral life, besides knowledge, plays a key role in the intricate process of exegesis. The reader is urged to use his knowledge and to lead his life according to God's commandments so that he may be able to cast a few glimpses into the mysterious depth of God's person. Cyril of Alexandria[250] explains: "For the apprehension (κατάληψις) of the divine words does not fall away from those who certainly want to understand. But no one could grasp the parable and the obscure word, the sayings of the sages, and the riddles, except through the illumination (δᾳδουχίας) from above."

Notes

[1] The English versions add 12:1 to chapter 11 as 11:12. This explains our numbering for the verses of chapter 12. Thus, 11:12 in an English translation corresponds to 12:1 in MT (= LXX). In the commentary we use the MT numbering only.

[2] MT: עֹד רָד עִם־אֵל; cf. V: *autem testis descendid cum Deo* "but (Judah) descended with God as a witness"; but LXX: νῦν ἔγνω αὐτοὺς ὁ θεός "now God knew them" (= יְדָעָם).

[3] MT: וְעִם־קְדוֹשִׁים נֶאֱמָן; LXX: καὶ λαὸς ἅγιος κεκλήσεται θεοῦ "and they shall be called God's holy people"; V: *et cum sanctis fidelis* "and faithful with the holy ones." Due to the parallel with אֵל "God," we suggest taking קְדוֹשִׁים as a plural of majesty designating the "Holy One" (= God).

[4] MT: רֹעֶה רוּחַ; LXX: πονηρὸν πνεῦμα "(Ephraim is) an evil spirit." The verb רדף "to pursue" in the following member points to רעה I "to tend, herd"; this meaning is

supported by the versions: V: *pascit ventum* "(Ephraim) herds the wind"; α': ποιμαίνει ἄνεμον; S: *rʿ rwḥ*.

⁵ MT: וָשֹׁד; V: *vastitatem*; S: *wbztʾ*; but LXX (καὶ μάταια "and vain things") supposes וְשָׁוְא "deceit" (Wellhausen).

⁶ MT: יוּבָל "is carried"; LXX: ἐνεπορεύετο; V: *ferebat* ; S: Œwblw "they carry."

⁷ MT: וּבְאוֹנוֹ; cf. V: *et in fortitudine sua* "in his strength"; S; α', σ', θ'; all these read אוֹן "strength," hence the rendition "manhood"; but LXX: καὶ ἐν κόποις αὐτοῦ "and in his labors."

⁸ MT: וַיָּשַׂר; V: *et invaluit*; σ': κατεδυνάστευσε; all suppose שׂרר "to be/act as a prince" (denominative); but LXX (καὶ ἐνίσχυσεν "and he prevailed") and α' (καὶ κατώρθωσε) point to שׂרה "to persevere, exert oneself"; as Macintosh (*Hosea*, 483ff.) notices, many interpreters assume here שׂור a by-form of שׂרה.

⁹ MT: בֵּית־אֵל; LXX: ἐν τῷ οἴκῳ Ὤν "in the house of On" (cf. 4:15; 5:8; 10:5, 8).

¹⁰ MT: עִמָּנוּ; cf. V: *nobiscum* "with us"; but LXX: πρὸς αὐτόν "to him"; S: ʿmh; and the context require "with him."

¹¹ MT: כְּנַעַן; cf. LXX: Χαναάν; but α': μετάβολος "merchant"; cf. Tg: תגרין.

¹² MT: לַעֲשֹׁק; LXX: καταδυναστεύειν "to oppress"; S: wlmṭlm "to defraud"; many scholars suggest לְעַקֵּשׁ "to defraud"; cf. Wolff, *Hosea*, 207.

¹³ MT: אוֹן לִי; LXX: ἀναψυχὴν ἐμαυτῷ "refreshment to myself"; but V (*idolum mihi* "[I found] an idol for myself") and S (*ly kʾbʾ* "a trouble for me") misread אָוֶן.

¹⁴ MT: כָּל־יְגִיעַי; LXX: πάντες οἱ πόνοι αὐτοῦ "all his labors."

¹⁵ MT: אֲשֶׁר־חֵטְא "which is sin"; LXX: ἃς ἥμαρτεν "which he sinned."

¹⁶ MT: אֱלֹהֶיךָ; LXX adds ἀνήγαγόν σε "who brought you up (out of the land of Egypt)."

¹⁷ MT: עַל; cf. V: *super*; LXX: πρὸς "to"; S: ʿm "with"; Wolff

(*Hosea*, 207) suggests that עַל "over" points to the superiority of the divine partner.

[18] MT: אֲדַמֶּה "I spoke in parables" (Pi'el of דמה I); but LXX: ὡμοιώθην "I was represented"; cf. V: *adsimilatus sum* (= אֶדַּמֶּה, Hithpa'el of דמה I; cf. Is 14:14).

[19] MT: שְׁוָרִים; cf. V: *bubus* ; LXX: ἄρχοντες "leaders" (= שָׂרִים).

[20] Cf. Andersen and Freedman, *Hosea*, 595-96.

[21] Cf. Wolff, *Hosea*, 209.

[22] The phrase בֵּית יִשְׂרָאֵל "house of Israel" refers to both political and religious leadership; see the commentary on 5:1.

[23] Cf. Mays, *Hosea*, 160; contra Wolff, *Hosea*, 208.

[24] The same word מִרְמָה "treachery" is used of Jacob in Gen 27:35; on כַּחַשׁ "deceit," see the commentary on 4:2.

[25] The form קְדוֹשִׁים is perhaps a "plural of majesty"; cf. Prov 9:10; 30:3; and GK §124h; but note the singular קָדוֹשׁ "Holy One" in Hos 11:9. Wolff (*Hosea*, 210) suggests taking this word as a designation for pious people (cf. Ps 34:10), e.g., prophets and Levites in Hosea's circle.

[26] Cf. Nyberg, *Studien zum Hoseabuche*, 93; Pope, *El in the Ugaritic Texts*, VTSup 2 (Leiden, 1955), 13. The Old Testament speaks of God and his court of "holy ones" (cf. Deut 33:3; Zech 14:5; Ps 89:8; Job 5:1).

[27] Cf. Wolff, *Hosea*, 210.

[28] PL 25, 922.

[29] PL 21, 1021 B-C.

[30] PG 66, 193 B.

[31] PG 71, 277 C; cf. Theophylact of Bulgaria, PG 126, 769 C.

[32] Oil used to be sent as a gift by a vassal in order to make official the alliance with the suzerain power; cf. Mc.Carthy, "Hosea XII 2: Covenant by Oil," *VT* 14 (1964): 219.

[33] PG 71, 280 D.

[34] PL 21, 1021 C.

[35] PG 81, 1616 A-B.

[36] Cf. Macintosh, *Hosea*, 478.
[37] PG 66, 193 C.
[38] PG 71, 280 B.
[39] On רִיב "dispute," see the commentary on 4:1.
[40] As Wolff (*Hosea*, 211) noted, the real meaning of the Mesopotamian—West Semitic name *Yaḥqub-ilu* (Jacob) "May god protect" was unknown by both Hosea and Genesis traditions.
[41] PG 71, 281 C.
[42] PG 81, 1616 C.
[43] Cf. Macintosh, *Hosea*, 482.
[44] PG 81, 1616 C-D.
[45] PG 71, 284 A-B; cf. Theophylact of Bulgaria, PG 126, 774 B.
[46] PG 126, 774 B.
[47] Cf. Eslinger, "Hosea 12:5a and Genesis 32:29: A Study in Inner Biblical Exegesis," *JSOT* 18 (1980): 91-99.
[48] By juxtaposing "wrestling" with "prevailing," Hosea offers an interpretation of the name "Israel" different from that found in Genesis. Hosea's view is close to recent hypotheses regarding the meaning of "Israel": "May El persist, prove himself ruler" (KBL, 442; BDB, 975); cf. Macintosh, *Hosea*, 485.
[49] PL 21, 1022 B-C.
[50] Based on Esth 8:3, one may consider this line an example of hendiadys: weeping and imploring constitutes a single act, i.e., entreating with tears; cf. Andersen and Freedman, *Hosea*, 613-14.
[51] Cf. Mays, *Hosea*, 164.
[52] PG 66, 196 B.
[53] PG 71, 285 C-D.
[54] PL 25, 925.
[55] Cf. Jacob, "Osée," 88.
[56] Cf. Eissfeldt, "Jahwe Zebaoth," *Miscellanea Academica Berolinensia* II/2 (1950), 128-50.

[57] PL 21, 1023 A.

[58] PG 71, 288 A.

[59] Cf. McComiskey, *The Minor Prophets*, 202.

[60] Cf. Garrett, *Hosea, Joel*, 241.

[61] Jacob ("Osée," 88) detects in the unusual construction שׁוּב "to return" + בְּ "in" instead of אֶל "to" an almost mystical note. Wolff (*Hosea*, 214) considers בּ a *Beth instrumenti* underscoring the idea that Israel's return is possible only by God's assistance.

[62] On חֶסֶד "mercy," see the commentary on 4:1.

[63] On מִשְׁפָּט "justice," see the commentary on 5:1.

[64] The connection between קוה "to wait" (Pi'el) and קָו "stretched line, rope" suggests the idea of tension, i.e., a tense expectancy"; cf. Macintosh, *Hosea*, 493.

[65] PL 25, 926.

[66] PG 71, 288 D.

[67] The meaning of כְּנַעַן is "the land of the red purple"; cf. Noth, *The Old Testament World*, 52.

[68] On עשׁק "to oppress," see the commentary on 5:11.

[69] PG 66, 196 D.

[70] PG 71, 289 B; cf. Theophylact of Bulgaria, PG 126, 780 C.

[71] PG 66, 196 D-197 A.

[72] Cf. Macintosh, *Hosea*, 497.

[73] Cf. Mays, *Hosea*, 167.

[74] PG 71, 292 B.

[75] On the "tents" and the Feast of Booths (Tabernacles), see the commentary on 9:5.

[76] Andersen and Freedman (*Hosea*, 618) see in מוֹעֵד "assembly" an abbreviation of the phrase אֹהֶל מוֹעֵד "the tent of meeting" rather than the designation of an "appointed festival."

[77] PL 25, 927.

[78] Cf. Jacob, "Osée," 89.

[79] Cf. Wolff, *Hosea*, 215.

[80] PL 25, 928.

[81] PL 21, 1024 C.

[82] PG 81, 1620 C.

[83] See the commentary on 6:8.

[84] See the commentary on 9:15.

[85] Cf. Andersen and Freedman, *Hosea*, 619.

[86] Cf. Macintosh, *Hosea*, 505. According to Wolff (*Hosea*, 215), שָׁוְא refers here to the futility of the pagan worship (Ps 24:4; 31:7).

[87] PL 25, 929.

[88] Cf. Mays, *Hosea*, 170.

[89] Cf. Macintosh, *Hosea*, 509.

[90] Cf. Jacob, "Osée," 89.

[91] According to Andersen and Freedman (*Hosea*, 620ff.), the repetition of נָבִיא "prophet" alludes to two prophets, i.e., Moses and another prophet (e.g., Elijah, Samuel). But this interpretation is unlikely since the parallelism of the members, the most common device in Hebrew poetry, relies on repetition.

[92] PL 25, 930.

[93] Cf. Wolff, *Hosea*, 216.

[94] PG 71, 297 A.

[95] PG 81, 1621 B; cf. Theodore of Mopsuestia, PG 66, 200 B.

[96] PG 126, 785 B.

[97] Most of the occurrences of כעס (Hiph'il) "to grieve" are in the Deuteronomistic history (Deut 4:25; 9:18; 1 Kgs 14:9, 15; 2 Kgs 17:11; 21:6) and Jeremiah (7:18; 8:19; 11:17).

[98] Cf. Mays, *Hosea*, 171.

[99] PG 71, 297 C.

[100] Cf. Jacob, "Osée," 90.

[101] MT: רְתֵת "trembling" (*hapax legomenon*) is attested in 4QH 4, 33; cf. Wolff, *Hosea*, 219; V: *horror*; α': φρίκην; σ': τρόμον; but LXX: δικαιώματα "ordinances" (= תּוֹרוֹת).

[102] MT: נָשָׂא הוּא "he was exalted"; S: *whw' rb'* "and he was

great"; LXX: αὐτὸς ἔλαβεν "he himself took"

[103] MT: כְּתְבוּנָם; LXX: κατ' εἰκόνα "according to the model (of idols)"; V: *quasi similitudinem*.

[104] MT: זֹבְחֵי אָדָם "those who sacrifice men"; LXX: θύσατε ἀνθρώπους "Sacrifice men!"; cf. V: *immolate homines* (= זִבְחוּ).

[105] MT: יְסֹעֵר; LXX: ἀποφυσώμενος "blown away"; V: *raptus*; Wolff (*Hosea*, 219) proposes the reading יְסֹעַר "it is blown" (Pu'al), required by מֹץ "chaff" as subject, instead of יְסֹעֵר "he blows" (Po'el) found in MT.

[106] MT: אֱלֹהֶיךָ "your God"; LXX adds: "who establishes the heaven, and creates the earth, whose hands have framed the whole host of heaven: but I showed them not to you that you should go after them: and I brought you up."

[107] MT: יְדַעְתִּיךָ "I knew you"; but LXX: ἐποίμαινόν σε "I pastured you"; cf. V, S, Tg (= רעה I).

[108] MT: תַּלְאֻבוֹת "drought" (a *hapax legomenon* < * l-ʾ-b "to be thirsty," attested in Arabic); LXX: ἐν γῇ ἀνοικήτῳ "in an uninhabited land"; V: *solitudinis* "wilderness."

[109] MT: וָאֱהִי "I was"; but LXX: καὶ ἔσομαι; V: *et ego ero* (= וְאֶהְיֶה "I will be").

[110] MT: אָשׁוּר "I will lurk" (= שׁוּר II); cf. Tg: דכמין "lurking"; but LXX (Ἀσσυρίων) and V (*Assyriorum*) presuppose אַשּׁוּר.

[111] MT: וְאֹכְלֵם שָׁם כְּלָבִיא "And I will devour them there like a lion"; cf. V; but LXX (καὶ καταφάγονται αὐτοὺς ἐκεῖ σκύμνοι δρυμοῦ "the (lion) cubs of the forest will devour them there") supposes a plural יֹאכְלוּם שָׁם כְּלָבִים "the dogs will devour them there"; as Wolff (*Hosea*, 220) notices, Hosea never uses לָבִיא for a lion; thus the subject might be כְּלָבִים "dogs."

[112] MT: שִׁחֶתְךָ "he destroyed you"; LXX: τῇ διαφθορᾷ σου "in your ruin"; V: *perditio tua*; S *ḥbltk* "I destroyed you"; we propose the following emendation (cf. S and context): שִׁחַתִּיךָ "I will destroy you."

¹¹³ MT: כִּי־בִי בְעֶזְרֶךָ "for in me, in your help"; LXX: τίς βοηθήσει "who will help [you]?"; Wolff (*Hosea*, 221) explains MT as a case of dittography starting with בִּי עֶזְרֶךָ "in me [is] your help."

¹¹⁴ MT: אֱהִי; LXX: ποῦ "where?"; cf. V; Tg; all presuppose אַיֵּה.

¹¹⁵ MT: הוּא־בֵן לֹא חָכָם "he is an unwise son"; cf. LXX: οὗτος ὁ υἱός οὐ φρόνιμος; but LXX copies used by the Greek Patristic interpreters (Theodoret of Cyrus, Theodore of Mopsuestia, Cyril of Alexandria, Theophylact of Bulgaria) have: οὗτος ὁ υἱός σου ὁ φρόνιμος "he is your wise son." Jerome (PL 25, 936) explains the latter reading: "Instead of 'unwise son,' LXX reads: "'That wise son,' namely, the one you consider wise but on the contrary should be understood 'unwise.'"

¹¹⁶ MT: דְּבָרֶיךָ "plagues" (= דֶּבֶר); cf. σ′: πληγή σου "your plague"; LXX: δίκη "penalty," and νίκη "victory" (in some mss. of the LXX; cf. 1 Cor 15:54); cf. S: *zkwtk* "your victory"; V: *mors tua* "your death."

¹¹⁷ MT: קָטָבְךָ; LXX: τὸ κέντρον σου "your sting" (cf. 1 Cor 15:55); cf. V: *morsus tuus*.

¹¹⁸ MT: יַפְרִיא "he flourishes"; LXX: διαστελεῖ "he divides"; cf. V: *dividet* (= יַפְרִיד).

¹¹⁹ MT: בֵּן אַחִים; LXX: ἀνὰ μέσον ἀδελφῶν "among brothers"; cf. V: *inter frates*; Wolff (*Hosea*, 222) suggests reading the rare word אָחוּ "reeds" (Gen 41:2); cf. Ugaritic *'aḥ* "meadow"; hence בֵּין אָחוּ "among the reeds."

¹²⁰ MT: וְיֵבוֹשׁ "and he will be ashamed of himself" (= בּוֹשׁ); but LXX: ἀναξηρανεῖ "it shall dry up" (= יבשׁ) is supported by the parallel verb חרב, and V, S, 4QXII (cf. M. Testuz, "Deux fragments inédits des manuscrits de la Mer Morte," *Sem* 5 [1955]: 38).

¹²¹ MT: אוֹצָר; LXX: τὴν γῆν αὐτοῦ "his land."

¹²² MT: תֶּאְשָׁם; LXX: ἀφανισθήσεται "will be destroyed"; cf. V: *pereat* (= שׁמם).

[123] Andersen and Freedman (*Hosea*, 629) suggest that it was a decree of God delivered through Ephraim that produced terror in the midst of the people. For Macintosh (*Hosea*, 520), this speech connotes the decision of the ten tribes to separate from the united Israel and to set up the two calves in Dan and Bethel (1 Kgs 12:16ff.).

[124] According to Wolff (*Hosea*, 225), "Ephraim" does not refer to the tribe but rather to the contemporary leaders from the royal residence of Samaria located in the region of Mt. Ephraim.

[125] PL 25, 931.

[126] PL 21, 1026 C.

[127] PG 71, 300 A-B; cf. Theodore of Mopsuestia, PG 66, 200 D.

[128] PG 126, 788 B.

[129] In Ex 32:4 the term מַסֵּכָה "cast image" designates the "golden calf." Manufacturing and worshipping "idols" (פֶּסֶל) was forbidden by the Decalogue (Ex 20:4-5). On the calf of Bethel, see the commentary on 8:5.

[130] Cf. Macintosh, *Hosea*, 524.

[131] According to 1 Kgs 19:18, the worshippers of Baal used to prostrate before and kiss the deity's cultic representation.

[132] Cf. Wolff, *Hosea*, 225.

[133] PL 25, 931; cf. Theodoret of Cyrus, PG 81, 1621 D.

[134] PG 71, 301 B.

[135] On "morning mist" and "dew," see the commentary on 6:4.

[136] PG 81, 1624 A.

[137] Cf. Mays, *Hosea*, 174.

[138] PG 71, 304 C.

[139] On the concept of "knowledge of God," see the commentary on 4:2.

[140] PG 81, 1624 C; cf. Theodore of Mopsuestia, PG 66, 201 C; Cyril of Alexandria, PG 71, 304 D.

[141] PL 25, 934.
[142] PG 66, 201 C.
[143] Cf. Mays, *Hosea*, 176.
[144] Yahweh is compared with a she-bear bereft of her cubs for he himself was deprived of the common Israelites through the guile of the royal and priestly leaders who turned the people into children of Baal; cf. Garrett, *Hosea, Joel*, 259.
[145] Cf. Macintosh, *Hosea*, 532-33.
[146] PG 71, 308 B, C; cf. Theodore of Mopsuestia, PG 66, 201 D.
[147] PG 81, 1624 D.
[148] PG 71, 308 D; see the textual note on v. 9 above.
[149] PG 126, 796 A-B.
[150] The root יָשַׁע *yāšaʿ* "to save" may allude to the last king's name "Hoshea"; cf. Macintosh, *Hosea*, 538.
[151] Note the other Hosean texts concerning Israel's monarchy: 7:3-7; 8:4-10; 10:3f., 7, 15.
[152] Cf. Garrett, *Hosea, Joel*, 261.
[153] PG 66, 204 A-B.
[154] Cf. Wolff, *Hosea*, 227.
[155] PL 25, 936.
[156] PL 21, 1029 A.
[157] PG 81, 1625 B.
[158] PG 66, 204 C.
[159] "Iniquity" and "sin" appear in parallel in 4:8; 8:13; 9:9; 12:9.
[160] PL 21, 1029 B.
[161] PG 81, 1625 C; cf. Theophylact of Bulgaria, PG 126, 797 A.
[162] PG 71, 309 C.
[163] Cf. Macintosh, *Hosea*, 545.
[164] PL 25, 936.
[165] PG 71, 312 B.
[166] Cf. Wolff, *Hosea*, 228.
[167] The root פָּדָה designates the transfer of property from

a owner to another (Lev 27:27; Deut 9:26).

[168] The root גאל indicates the act of redemption performed by a person in behalf of relative (Lev 25:25; Ruth 3:13).

[169] Garrett, *Hosea, Joel*, 265.

[170] PL 25, 937.

[171] PG 71, 312 C, D.

[172] PG 81, 1628 A.

[173] PG 66, 205 A.

[174] PL 21, 1030 A.

[175] PG 126, 800 B-C.

[176] PL 25, 939.

[177] PL 21, 1030 D-1031 A.

[178] PG 81, 1628 C; cf. Theophylact of Bulgaria, PG 126, 804 A.

[179] PG 66, 205 D.

[180] PG 71, 316 A.

[181] Macintosh (*Hosea*, 556) notices that in the Testuz's fragment from the Dead Sea Scrolls a dividing space appears between 14:1 and 14:2.

[182] Note other references to Samaria: 7:1; 8:5, 6; 10:5, 7.

[183] PL 25, 941.

[184] PG 81, 1628 D.

[185] The English versions add 14:1 to chapter 13 as 13:16. This explains our numbering for the verses of chapter 14. Thus 14:1 in an English translation corresponds to 14:2 in MT (= LXX). In the commentary we use the MT numbering only.

[186] MT: כָּל־תִּשָּׂא; cf. V: *omnem aufer iniquitatem* "take away all iniquity"; but LXX: ὅπως μὴ λάβητε "so that you may not receive (our iniquity)."

[187] MT: פָּרִים שְׂפָתֵינוּ "the bulls of our lips"; LXX: καρπὸν χειλέων ἡμῶν "the fruit of our lips"; if one considers the final ם on פָּרִים an old Canaanite case ending (cf. Wolff, *Hosea*, 231), then LXX ("fruit") represents the original reading.

[188] MT: מְשׁוּבָתָם "their apostasy" (= שׁוּב); LXX: τὰς κατοικίας αὐτῶν "their dwellings" (= ישׁב).

[189] MT: נְדָבָה; LXX: ὁμολόγως "manifestly"; V: *spontanee*; Tg: בנדבא "freely."

[190] MT: יֹשְׁבֵי בְצִלּוֹ "the inhabitants of his shadows" (a *status constructus* broken by a preposition; cf. Is 9:1); LXX: καθιοῦνται "they will dwell"; cf. S: *wntbwn*.

[191] MT: יְחַיּוּ דָגָן; LXX: ζήσονται καὶ μεθυσθήσονται σίτῳ "they shall live and be satisfied with corn."

[192] MT: עִנִּיתִי; LXX: ἐγὼ ἐταπείνωσα αὐτόν "I humbled him"; V: *exaudiam* "I will listen."

[193] MT: וַאֲשׁוּרֶנּוּ "I will watch over him" (= שׁוּר II); LXX: καὶ ἐγὼ κατισχύσω αὐτόν "I will strengthen him"; V: *dirigam eum* "I will arrange him."

[194] Cf. Wolff, *Hosea*, 234.

[195] On כשׁל "to stumble," see the commentary on 5:5.

[196] Cf. Macintosh, *Hosea*, 560.

[197] Cf. Mays, *Hosea*, 186.

[198] PG 66, 208 B-C.

[199] PL 25, 942.

[200] Jacob ("Osée," 96) takes טוֹב "good" as a synonym for "word" (cf. Song 7:10; Job 34:3; Ps 39:3) on basis of Aramaic טיבא "report."

[201] The basic meaning of the root שׁלם is "to repay"; thus Israel must repay with prayers and praises Yahweh's forgiving love; cf. McComiskey, *The Minor Prophets*, 229f.

[202] PL 25, 942.

[203] PL 21, 1031 D-1032 A.

[204] PG 81, 1629 A.

[205] PG 66, 208 C.

[206] PG 71, 317 D.

[207] PG 126, 808 A.

[208] Cf. Mays, *Hosea*, 187. Israel became an orphan when the nation, along with its religious and political institutions, was destroyed; cf. Garrett, *Hosea, Joel*, 272.

[209] PL 25, 942.

[210] PG 81, 1629 A.

[211] PG 71, 320 C.

[212] The form נְדָבָה "free motivation" (in Hos 14:5: an adverbial accusative; cf. GK § 118k) or "voluntary offering" (given spontaneously) derives from the root נדב (Hithpa'el) "to make a voluntary decision/contribution" (Judg 5:2, 9; 1 Chr 29:5, 6); cf. KBL, 671f.

[213] PL 25, 943.

[214] Cf. Macintosh, *Hosea*, 568-69.

[215] PG 81, 1629 A-B.

[216] PG 66, 209 A.

[217] PG 71, 320 D.

[218] PG 126, 809 C.

[219] Cf. Mays, *Hosea*, 188.

[220] During the rainless summer the dew is the only means to water the ground and keep such cultures as grapes and melons alive; cf. Dalman, *Arbeit und Sitte in Palästina*, I (Gütersloh, 1928), 514ff. Note that in 6:4; 13:3 the dew is a symbol of the transitory character of the people.

[221] Lilies wonderfully blossom in the deserted areas and among thorn bushes (cf. Song 2:1f; 4:5; 5:13; 6:2; "lilies of the field"; cf. Mt 6:28f.).

[222] The forest of Lebanon was seen in the ancient Israel as the forest-model (cf. Is 2:13; Ps 29:5; 104:16; Song 4:12).

[223] PG 66, 209 A.

[224] Cf. Macintosh, *Hosea*, 571.

[225] Cf. Wolff, *Hosea*, 236.

[226] PG 71, 321 A.

[227] PG 81, 1629 C.

[228] PG 126, 809 D.

[229] PG 71, 321 C.

[230] Cf. Macintosh, *Hosea*, 572.

[231] PG 126, 812 C.

[232] PL 21, 1033 A.

[233] PG 81, 1632 A.

[234] PG 66, 209 B.

[235] PG 71, 324 A.
[236] On the meaning of שׁוּר, see the commentary on 13:7.
[237] Cf. Wolff, *Hosea*, 237.
[238] Cf. Mays, *Hosea*, 189-90.
[239] Cf. Jacob, "Osée," 97.
[240] PL 25, 945.
[241] PL 21, 1033 B.
[242] PG 66, 209 B-C.
[243] PG 71, 325 C.
[244] PG 126, 816 B.
[245] So, among others, Garrett, *Hosea, Joel*, 281f.
[246] Cf. Macintosh, *Hosea*, 583.
[247] *Hosea*, 239.
[248] PL 25, 946.
[249] Cf. Jacob, "Osée," 98.
[250] PG 71, 325 D.

SELECTED BIBLIOGRAPHY

Albright, W. F. "The Son of Tabeel (Isaiah 7:6)." *BASOR* 140 (1955) 34-35.

_____. *Archaeology and the Religion of Israel.* Baltimore, 1956.

Alt, A. "Das System der assyrischen Provinzen auf dem Boden der Reiches Israel." *KSchr,* 2:188-205; 209-212.

_____. "Das Verbot des Diebstahls im Dekalog." *Kschr,* 1:333-40.

_____. "Der Stadtstaat Samaria." *Kschr,* 3:258-302.

_____. "Hosea 5:8-6:6, ein Krieg und seine Folgen in prophetisher Beleuchtung." *Kschr,* 2:163-87.

_____. "Tiglathpilesers III erster Feldzug nach Palästina." *Kschr,* 2:150-62.

Andersen, F. I. and D. N., Freedmnan. *Hosea. A New Translation with Introduction and Commentary.* AB 24. New York: Doubleday, 1980.

Bach, R. "Die Erwählung Israels in der Wüste." Ph.D. dissertation. University of Bonn, 1952.

Barthélemy, D. *La critique textuelle de l'Ancien Testament. 3. Ezéchiel, Daniel et les 12 Prophètes.* Göttingen: Vandenhoeck & Ruprecht, 1992.

_____. *Les devanciers d'Aquila. Première publication intégrale du texte des fragments du Dodekaprophéton.* VTSup 10 (1963).

_____. "Redécouverte d'un chaînon manquant de l'histoire de la Septante." *RB* 60 (1953) 18-29.

Batten, L. W. "Hosea's Message and Marriage." *JBL* 48 (1929) 257-73.

Baudissin, W. W. *Adonis und Esmun.* Leipzig, 1911.

Baumann, A. "ילל *yll;* יְלֵל *y^elēl;* יְלָלָה *y^elālâ.*" *TDOT,* 6:82-87.

Begg, C. *The Nonmention of Amos, Hosea and Micah in the Deuteronomistic History.* BN 32 (1986).
Bitter, S. *Die Ehe des Propheten Hosea. Eine auslegungsgeschichtliche Untersuchung.* Göttinger Theologische Arbeiten 3. Göttingen: Vandenhoeck & Ruprecht, 1975.
Blankenbaker, G. "Tradition and Creativity: Hermeneutical Use of Language in Hosea 1-3." *Seminar Papers Series* 21 (1982) 15-29.
Blenkinsopp, J. *A History of Prophecy in Israel.* Revised and Enlarged. Louisville, Kentucky: Westminster JKP, 1996.
Botterweck, G. J. "חָפֵץ ḥāpēṣ; חֵפֶץ ḥēpeṣ." *TDOT,* 5:92-107.
Braun, H. "Der Fahrende." *ZThK* 48 (1951) 32-38.
Bright, J. *A History of Israel.* 3rd edition; 3rd impression. London: SCM Press, 1984.
Brown, F., S. R. Driver, C. A. Briggs. *A Hebrew and English Lexicon of the Old Testament.* Oxford: Clarendon, 1907.
Brueggemann, W. *Theology of the Old Testament. Testimony, Dispute, Advocacy.* Minneapolis: Fortress, 1997.
Buber, M. *The Prophetic Faith.* Translated by C. Witton-Davies. New York, 1949.
Budde, K. "Der Abschnitt Hosea 1-3 und seine grundlegende-religionsgeschichtliche Bedeutung." *ThStKr* 96 (1925) 1-89.
_____. "Hosea 1 und 3." *Theologische Blaätter* 13 (1934) 337-42.
Buss, M. J. *The Prophetic Word of Hosea, a Morphological Study.* BZAW 111. Berlin, 1969.
Caquot, A. "Remarques sur la fête de la néoménie dans l'ancien Israël." *RHR* 158 (1961) 1-18.
Cassuto, U. *Biblical and Oriental Studies.* Translated by I. Abrahams. Jerusalem: Magnes, 1973.
Cazelles, H. *Introduction critique à l'Ancien Testament. Introduction à la Bible* 2. Edited by H. Cazelles. Paris: Cerf, 1973.

_____. "חָבַר *chābhar;* חָבֵר *chābhēr."* *TDOT,* 4:193-97.
Childs, B. S. *Introduction to the Old Testament as Scripture.* 5th ed. Philadelphia: Fortress, 1979.
_____. *Memory and Tradition in Israel.* London, 1962.
_____. *The Book of Exodus. A Critical, Theological Commentary.* OTL. 3rd printing. Louisville: Westminster, 1974.
Clements, R. E. "Understanding the Book of Hosea." *Review and Expositor* 72 (1975) 405-423.
Coppens, J. "L'Histoire matrimoniale d'Osée. Un nouvel essai d'interprétation. Festschrift Nötscher." BBB 1 (1950) 38-45.
Dalman, G. *Arbeit und Sitte in Palästina* I-II. Gütersloh, 1928, 1932.
Day, E. "Is the Book of Hosea Exilic?" *AJSL* 26 (1909) 105-132.
Dietrich, E. L. שוב שבות. *Die Endzeitliche Wiederherstellung bei den Propheten.* BZAW 40. Giessen, 1925.
Driver, G. R. "Linguistic and Textual Problems. Minor Prophets I." *JTS* 39 (1938) 154-86.
Eichrodt, W. *Theologie des Alten Testaments.* 5th ed. 2 vols. Stuttgart, 1957.
Eissfeldt, O. "Der Gott des Tabor und seine Verbreitung." *ARW* 31 (1934) 14-41.
_____. *Einleitung in das Alte Testament.* 3rd ed. Tübingen, 1964.
_____. "Jahwe Zebaoth." *Miscellanea Academica Berolinensia* II/2 (1950) 128-50.
Elliger, K. and W. Rudolph, eds. *Biblia Hebraica Stuttgartensia.* Suttgart, 1977.
Eslinger, L. M. "Hosea 12:5a and Genesis 32:29: A Study in Inner Biblical Exegesis." *JSOT* 18 (1980) 91-99.
Fabry, H. -J. "לֵב *lēḇ;* לֵבָב *lēḇāḇ."* *TDOT,* 7:399-437.
Fahlgren, K. H. *Sᵉdaka.* Uppsala, 1932.
Fohrer, G. "Tradition und Interpretation im Alten Testament." *ZAW* 73 (1961) 24-30.

Freedman, D. N. "Pottery, Poetry, and Prophecy." *JBL* 96 (1977) 5-26.

Fuhs, H. F. "יָרֵא *yārē'*; יָרֵא *yārē'*; יִרְאָה *yir'â*; מוֹרָא *môrā'*." *TODT*, 6:290-315.

Garrett, D. A. *Hosea, Joel.* The American Commentary 19A. Broadman & Holman, 1997.

Gelston, A., ed. *The Old Testament in Syriac According to the Peshitta Version.* Leiden: Brill, 1980.

Gelston, A. "The Peshitta of the Twelve Prophets." Pages 267-69, 290-92 in *The Peshitta: its early text and history.* Edited by P. B. Dirksen and M. J. Mulder. Leiden, New York, Copenhagen, Cologne, 1988.

Gesenius' Hebrew Grammar. Edited by E. Kautzsch; translated and revised by A. E. Cowley. 2nd ed. Oxford, 1910.

Gesenius, W., F. Buhl. *Hebräisches und aramäisches Handwörterbuch zum AT.* Leipzig, 1915.

Good, E. M. "Hosea 5:8-6:6: An Alternative to Alt." *JBL* 85 (1966) 273-86.

_____. "The Composition of Hosea." *SEÅ* 31 (1966) 21-63.

Gordis, C. H. "Hosea's Marriage and Message: A New Approach." *HUCA* 27 (1954) 9-35.

Gordon, C. H. *Ugaritic Textbook.* Analecta Orientalia 38. Rome: Pontificium Institutum Biblicum, 1965.

Gressmann, H. *Die älteste Geschichtsschreibung und Prophetie Israels. Von Samuel bis Amos und Hosea.* SAT 2.1. 2nd ed. Göttingen, 1921.

Gross, W. "נָדַד *nādad*." *TDOT*, 9:227-231.

Gunneweg, A. H. J. *Mündliche und schriftliche Tradition der vorexilischen Prophetenbücher als Problem der neueren Prophetenforshung.* FRLANT 73. Göttingen, 1959.

Hamp, V. "גָּנַב *gānabh*." *TDOT*, 3:39-45.

Harper, W. R. *Amos and Hosea.* ICC. Edinburgh: T & T Clark, 1905.

Harvey, J. "Le 'rîb-Pattern,' réquisitoire prophétique sur

la rupture de l'alliance." *Bibl* 43 (1962) 172-96.

Haupt, P. "Hosea's Erring Spouse." *JBL* 34 (1915) 41-53.

Hayes, J. H., ed. *Old Testament Form Criticism*. Trinity University Monograph Series in Religion 2. San Antonio: Trinity University Press, 1974.

Herrmann, S. *A History of Israel in Old Testament 's Times*. Translated by J. Browden. Philadelphia, 1975.

Huehnergard, J. "Biblical Notes on Some New Akkadian Texts from Emar (Syria)." *CBQ* 47 (1985) 428-34.

Humbert, P. "Les trois premiers chapitres d'Osée." *RHR* 77 (1918) 157-71.

_____. "Osée le prophète bédouin." *RHPhR* 1 (1921) 97-118.

Jacob, E. "Osée." Pages 7-98 in E. Jacob, C.-A. Keller, S. Amsler, *Osée, Joël, Abdias, Amos*. Commentaire de l'Ancien Testament 11a; Neuchatel: Delachaux et Niestlé, 1965.

Jaspers, K. *The Axial Age of Human History. Identity and Anxiety: Survival in Mass Society*. Glencoe, 1960.

Jastrow, M. *Dictionary of the Targumim, the Talmud Babli and Yerushalmi, and the Midrashic Literature*. New York: The Judaica Press, 1992.

Jenni, E. "Das Wort ʿōlam im Alten Testament." *ZAW* 64 (1952) 235-39.

Jepsen, A. "בָּטַח *bāṭach*." *TDOT*, 2:88-94.

_____. *Untersuchungen zur israelitisch-jüdischen Chronologie*. BZAW 88. Berlin, 1964.

Jerome. *In Osee prophetam*. PL 25, 815-946.

Julian of Eclanum (Pseudo-Rufinus of Aquileia). *Commentarius in Oseam*. PL 21, 961-1034.

Kapelrud, A. S. *The Prophets in the Shelter of Elyon — G. W. Ahlström*. JSOTSup 31 (1984) 175-83.

Kittel, R. *Geschichte des Volkes Israel*. 2nd ed. Stuttgart, 1925.

Koehler, L. and W. Baumgartner. *The Hebrew and Aramaic Lexicon of the Old Testament*. Translated and edited by M. E. J. Richardson. Leiden: Brill, 1994-2000.

Kuhrt, A. *The Ancient Near East*. Routledge History of the Ancient World. 2 vols. London & New York: Routledge, 1995.

Kutal, B. *Liber Prophetae Hoseae. E textu originali latine et metrice versus, explanatus, notis criticis et philologicis illustratus*. Commentarii in Prophetas Minores 1. Olomucii, 1929.

Kyl, Y. ספר הושע. Jerusalem: Mosad Harav Kook, 1973.

Limburg, J. *Hosea-Micah*. Interpretation. Atlanta: John Knox, 1988.

Lindblom, J. *Hosea literarische untersucht*. Acta Academiae Aboensis. Humaniora 5. Âbo: Âbo Akademie, 1927.

_____. *Prophecy in Ancient Israel*. 2nd ed. Philadelphia: Fortress, 1963.

Lods, A. *Histoire de la littérature hebraïque et juive, depuis des origines jusqu'à la ruine de l'état juif (135 après J. Chr.)*. Paris: Payot, 1950.

Lohfink, N. "Zu Text und Form von Os 4,4-6." *Bibl* 42 (1961) 303-332.

Macintosh, A. A. *A Critical and Exegetical Commentary on Hosea*. The International Critical Commentary. Edinburgh: T & T Clark, 1997.

Martínez, F. G. *The Dead Sea Scrolls Translated. The Qumran Texts in English*. 2nd ed. Leiden: Brill & Grand Rapids: Eerdmans, 1996.

Mauchline, J. *The Book of Hosea. Introduction and Exegesis*. The Interpreter's Bible, vol. 6. Edited by G. A. Buttrick et al. Nashville: Abingdon, 1956.

Mays, J. L. *Hosea*. OTL. Philadelphia: Westminster, 1969.

McCarland, S. V. "The Scripture Basis of 'On the Third Day.'" *JBL* 48 (1929) 124-37.

McCarthy, D. J. "Hosea XII 2: Covenant by Oil." *VT* 14 (1964) 215-21.

McComiskey, T. E. *The Minor Prophets*. Grand Rapids: Baker, 1992.

Morag, S. "ייחוד לשונו של הושע לשאלת׳." *Tarbiz* 53 (1984) 489-511.

Mowinckel, W. "כֹּמֶר, כמר." *ZAW* 36 (1916) 238-39.
Nebe, G. -W. "Eine neue Hosea-Handschrift aus Höhle 4 von Qumran." *ZAW* 91 (1979) 292-94.
Neef, H.-D. "Der Septuaginta-Text und der Massoreten-Text des Hoseabuches im Vergleich." *Bibl* 67 (1986) 195-220.
Neher, A. *L'essence du prophétisme*. Paris, 1955.
Nestle, E. "Miszellen. 9. Gomer bath diblaim." *ZAW* 29 (1909) 233-34.
North, F. S. "Hosea's Introduction to his Book." *VT* 8 (1958) 429-32.
Noth, M. *Die israelitischen Personennamen im Rahmen der gemeinsemitischen Namengebung*. BWANT 3.10. Stuttgart, 1928.
_____. "Beiträge zur Geschichte des Ostjordanlandes I," *PJ* 37 (1941) 59ff.
_____. "Beiträge zur Geschichte des Ostjordanlandes III: Die Nachbaren der israelitischen Stämme im Ostjordanlande." *ZDPV* 68 (1951) 1-50.
_____. *The Old Testament World*. Translated by V. Gruhn. Philadelphia, 1966.
Nyberg, H. S. "Das textkritische Problem des Alten Testaments am Hoseabuch demonstriert." *ZAW* 52 (1934) 241-54.
_____. *Studien zum Hoseabuche. Zugleich ein Beitrag zur Klärung des Problems der alttestamentlichen Textkritik*. Uppsala Universitets Årsskrift. Uppsala: Almqvist & Wiksells, 1935.
O'Connor, M. "The Pseudosorites: A Type of Paradox in Hebrew Verse." JSOTSup 40 (1987) 161-72.
Patterson, G. H. *The Septuagint Text of Hosea compared with the Massoretic Text*. New Haven: Tuttle, Morehouse & Taylor, 1891.
Pentiuc, E. "West Semitic Terms in Akkadian Texts from Emar." *JNES* 58 (1999) 81-96.
Pezron, P. *Essay d'un commentaire literal et historique sur les*

prophètes. Paris, 1693.

Pidoux, G. "Le Dieu qui vient. Esperence d'Israël." *Cahiers Théologiques* 17 (1947) 12ff.

Pope, M. H. *El in the Ugaritic Texts.* VTSup 2. Leiden, 1955.

Pritchard, J. B., ed. *Ancient Near Eastern Texts Relating to the Old Testament.* 3rd ed. Princeton: Princeton University Press, 1969.

Rabenau, K. von. "Beeroth." Pages 210f. *Biblisch-historisches Handwörterbuch* 1. Edited by B. Reiche and L. Rost; Göttingen, 1964-66.

Renaud, B. "Osée 1-3: analyse diachronique et lecture synchronique. Problèmes de méthode." *RevSR* 57 (1983) 249-60.

Rendtorff, R. "Erwägungen zur Frühgeschichte des Prophetentums in Israel." *ZThK* 59 (1962) 145-67.

Ringgren, H. "גָּרַשׁ *gārash.*" *TDOT*, 3:68-69.

_____. "כֹּהֵן *kōhēn.*" *TDOT*, 7:60-65.

Robinson, H. W. *The Hebrew Prophets. Studies in Hosea and Ezekiel.* London, 1948.

Rost, L. "Erwägungen zu Hosea 4.13f." Pages 451-60 in *Festschrift Alfred Bertholet.* Edited by W. Baumgartner, O. Eissfeldt, K. Elliger, L. Rost. Tübingen, 1950.

_____. "Erwägungen zum israelitischen Brandopfer." BZAW 77 (1958) 177-83.

Rowley, H. H. "The Marriage of Hosea." *Bulletin of the John Rylands Library* 39 (1956) 200-233.

Rudolph, W. *Hosea.* KAT 13.1. Gütersloh: Gerd Mohn, 1966.

_____. "Eigentümlichkeiten der Sprache Hoseas." Pages 313-17 in *Studia biblica et semitica - Th. C. Vriezen.* Wageningen: H. Veenman, 1966.

_____. "Präparierte Jungfrauen?" *ZAW* 75 (1963) 65-73.

Schmidt, H. "Die Ehe des Hosea." *ZAW* 42 (1924) 245-72.

Scholz, A. *Commentar zum Buche des Propheten Hoseas.* Würzburg, 1882.

Schunck, K. D. "חָצַב ḥāṣaḇ." *TDOT*, 5:125-27.
Sellin, E. *Das Zwöfprophetenbuch. Hosea.* 3rd ed. 2 vols. KAT 12. Leipzig 1930.
Soggin, J. A. "Der prophetische Gedanke über den heiligen Krieg, als Gericht über Israel." *VT* 10 (1960) 79-83.
Sperber, A., ed. *The Bible in Aramaic Based on Old Manuscripts and Printed Texts.* Vol. 3. *The Latter Prophets According to Targum Jonathan.* 2nd. impression. Leiden: Brill, 1992.
Steingrimsson, S. "זמם zmm." *TDOT*, 4:87-90.
Szabø, A. "Textual Problems in Amos and Hosea." *VT* 25 (1975) 500-524.
Testuz, M. "Deux fragments inédits des manuscrits de la Mer Morte." *Sem* 5 (1955) 38-39.
The Amarna Letters. Edited and translated by W.L. Moran. Baltimore & London: The Johns Hopkins University Press, 1992.
The Babylonian Talmud translated into English. Edited by I. Epstein. London: Soncino, 1938-1961.
Theodore of Mopsuestia. *Commentarius in Oseam prophetam.* PG 66, 124-209.
Theophylact of Bulgaria. *Expositio in prophetam Oseam.* PG 126, 563-820.
The Works of Josephus: New Updated Edition. Translated by W. Whiston. 12th printing. Peabody, MA: Hendrickson, 1996.
The Works of Philo: New Updated Edition. Translated by C. D. Yonge. 4th printing. Peabody, MA: Hendrickson, 1997.
Toy, C. H. "Note on Hosea 1-3." *JBL* 32 (1913) 75-79.
Treitel, L. *Die alexandrinischen Uebersetzung des Buches Hosea.* Karlsruhe, 1887.
Tur-Sinai, N. H. הלשון והספר. vols. 3. Jerusalem, 1948-55.
Tushingham, A. D. "A Reconsideration of Hosea, Chapters 1-3." *JNES* 12 (1953) 150-59.
Van Dam, C. *The Urim and Thummim. A Means of Revelation in Ancient Israel.* Winona Lake: Eisenbrauns, 1997.

Vaux, R. de. *Ancient Israel: Its Life and Institutions*. Translated by J. McHugh. New York: McGraw-Hill, 1961.

Vellas, B. M. ΩΣΗΕ. ΕΙΣΑΓΩΓΗ-ΜΕΤΑΦΡΑΣΙΣ ΕΚ ΤΟΥ ΕΒΡΑΙΚΟΥ-ΚΕΙΜΕΝΟΝ ΤΩΝ Ο'-ΣΧΟΛΙΑ. 5 vols. ΕΡΜΗΝΕΙΑ ΠΑΛΛΙΑΣ ΔΙΑΘΗΚΗΣ. Athens, 1947-1950.

Vogels, W. "'Osée-Gomer' car et comme 'Yahweh-Israël.' Os 1-3." *NRTh* 103 (1981) 711-27.

_____. "Diachronic and Synchronic Studies of Hosea 1-3." *BZ* 28 (1984), 94-98.

Watson, W. G. E. *Classical Hebrew Poetry. A Guide to its Techniques*. 2nd. ed. JSOT 26. Sheffield, 1995.

Weber, R. et al., eds. *Biblia Sacra iuxta Vulgatam Versionem*. Vol. 2. 2nd ed. Stuttgart, 1975.

Weinfeld, M. "כָּבוֹד *kāḇôḏ*." *TDOT* 7, 22-38.

Weiser, A. and K. Elliger. *Das Buch der Zwölf Kleinen Propheten*. 2 vols. ATD 24-25. Göttingen, 1967.

Wellhausen, J. *Prolegomena zur Geschichte Israels*. Berlin, 1883.

Wolff, H. W. "Das Geschichtsverständnis der alttestamentlichen Prophetie." *EvTh* 20 (1960) 218-35.

_____. "Die Ebene Achor." *ZDPV* 70 (1954) 76-81.

_____. "Erkenntnis Gottes im Alten Testament." *EvTh* 15 (1955) 426-31.

_____. *Hosea. A Commentary on the Book of the Prophet Hosea*. Translated by G. Stansell. Edited by P. D. Hanson. Hermenia. Philadelphia: Fortress, 1989.

_____. "Hoseas geistige Heimat." *ThLZ* 81 (1956) 83-94.

_____. "'Wissen um Gott' bei Hosea als Urform der Theologie." *EvTh* 12 (1952-53) 533-54.

Ziegler, J., ed. *Duodecim prophetae*. Septuaginta. Vetus Testamentum Graecum 13. Göttingen, 1963.

Zolli, J. "Hosea 4:17-18." *ZAW* 56 [1938] 175.

www.ingramcontent.com/pod-product-compliance
Lightning Source LLC
Chambersburg PA
CBHW021847230426
43671CB00006B/295